OPERATIONS RESEARCH

Operations research

OPERATIONS RESEARCH

An Introduction to Modern Applications

William C. House, *Editor*

princeton
philadelphia
new york
london

Published simultaneously in Canada by Book Center, Inc.

Library of Congress Catalog Card Number: 72-124625
International Standard Book Number: 0-87769-052-9

First Printing

Printed in the United States of America

to Dr. Frank May and Professor Judson Neff

Acknowledgment

I would like to thank Phil Balsmeier who has really done yeoman service in helping to prepare this book.

Contents

Part 1 | Introduction to Operations Research 1

1 | Operations Research—The Basics
by E. Leonard Arnoff and M. J. Netzorg 4

2 | Operations Research as a Tool for Decision Making
by Hans J. Laue 20

3 | Decision Models, Part 1
by James C. Emery 45

4 | Decision Models, Part 2
by James C. Emery 55

5 | New Directions in Operations Research
by John Dearden and John Lastavica 67

Discussion Questions 81

Bibliography 84

Part 2 | Mathematical Programming: Graphic, Simplex, Parametric, and Integer Programming Methods 87

6 | Sales-Production Coordination through Mathematical Programming
by Norbert Lloyd Enrick 89

7 | Linear Programming: Solution, Interpretation, and Sensitivity Analysis
by Floyd W. Windal 104

8 | Linear Programming: Some Implications for Management Accounting
by Ronald V. Hartley 115
9 | Production and Market Planning with Parametric Programming
by James T. Godfrey, W. Allen Spivey, and George B. Stillwagon 125
10 | Integer Linear Programming
by Clifford C. Petersen 141
11 | Linear and Integer Programming Applied to Capital Budgeting
by Phillip W. Balsmeier 163

Discussion Questions 175

Bibliography 177

Part 3 | **Mathematical Programming: Transportation and Assignment Methods** 181

12 | The Transportation Problem—A Special Case of Linear Programming
by T. A. B. Szandtner 184
13 | An Example of the Transportation Problem Solved by Vogel's Approximation Method
by Henry Malcolm Steiner 193
14 | A Production-Scheduling Decision Model for Demand Exceeding Normal Manufacturing Capacity
by Raphael Perry 202
15 | Procurement Scheduling: A Transportation Formulation
by Marvin Tummins and R. Frank Page 217
16 | Job-Assignment Method
by Richard L. Carter and E. Noah Gould 230
17 | Dynamic Programming: An Introduction
by Floyd W. Windal 239

Discussion Questions 247

Bibliography 249

Part 4 | **Applications of Mathematical Programming to Marketing, Production, and Financial Problems** 251

18 | A Linear Model for Sales Planning: A Case Study of a Jewelry Firm
by M. Golden and E. Sanford 253
19 | A Goal Programming Model for Sales Effort Allocation
by Sang M. Lee and Monroe M. Bird, Jr. 266
20 | Allocating Advertising Dollars by Linear Programming
by James F. Engel and Martin R. Warshaw 274
21 | On-Line Blending for Production Profit
by F. A. Tillman and E. S. Lee 287

22 | Introduction to Linear Programming for Production
by J. Frank Sharp 293

23 | Plant Sizing for a Seasonal Product Demand Using a Linear Programming Model
by Lawrence D. Vitt 307

24 | Application of Linear Programming to Short-Term Financing Decision
by James C.T. Mao 321

25 | Capital Budgeting: A Pragmatic Approach
by Alexander A. Robichek, Donald G. Ogilvie, and John D.C. Roach 340

Discussion Questions 357

Bibliography 360

OPERATIONS RESEARCH

PART I Introduction to Operations Research

Operations research can be defined as the systematic application of mathematical and statistical techniques to the solution of governmental, business, and educational problems. Such problems are often complex and comprehensive, requiring solution on an integrated, total basis rather than in piecemeal form. Techniques drawn from diverse fields such as physics, psychology, economics, engineering, and mathematics can be coupled to fast, flexible, and large-capacity electronic computers to permit study and solution of complex problems too time-consuming and unmanageable to be tackled by manual methods.

Arnoff and Netzorg point out that operations research techniques are particularly useful in balancing conflicting objectives where there are many alternative courses of action, departmental conflicts of interests, and a large number of complex, interacting variables. The operations research approach includes analysis of the system studied, construction and testing of a mathematical or statistical model, developing problem solutions, determining conditions under which a model solution is valid, and implementing results. Operations research has been used to solve many functional problems in a variety of industries and can assist managers in improving managerial decisions and basic business operations.

Operations research should be used in conjunction with integrated, decision-oriented management information systems, as Arnoff indicates. The design of such systems requires determining basic organization objectives, the decisions to be made (i.e., which ones, how, and by whom), what information is needed to make these decisions (i.e., when needed, in what amounts, and what data must be collected and/or generated). A joint interdisciplinary effort will be needed to develop the most satisfactory decision-oriented management information system.

According to Laue, operations research is characterized by a total system orientation, commitment to the scientific method, and use of specialized mathematical and statistical techniques. Particular emphasis is placed on the development of models that can be manipulated more easily than the actual systems they represent and the formulation of valid measures of performance. Inventory, allocation, dynamic programming, waiting line, sequencing, replacement, competitive, and simulation models can be used to solve problems involving such activities as financial, purchasing, physical distribution, production, marketing, project management, research and development, and personnel endeavors.

Emery points out that analytical decision models permit a problem to be expressed in mathematical form, include a measure of effectiveness to be optimized, and can be used in conjunction with computers to develop optimum decisions from a wide range of alternatives. The most useful decision models are those which are reasonably realistic, relatively simple, and are keyed to computationally feasible procedures. Models can be simplified by using single parameter values, uncomplicated mathematical relationships, aggregate rather than individual variables, and submodels for problem segments within an aggregate, overall model.

Simulation and heuristic models are useful in measuring and predicting the consequences of policies to be followed in the operation of production, inventory, queuing systems, etc., particularly for problems too complex to be handled by analytic techniques. Sensitivity studies indicate the impact of changes in the model on problem solutions. The transaction processing system can provide data for decision models more automatically, accurately, and economically in many cases than a separate collection and processing activity. Man-machine decision systems permit effective utilization of man and machine capabilities in coping with problems too ill defined and complex for either to handle alone. As decision processes are shifted from man to machine, however, the role of the model builder becomes more important and it is essential that the decision maker thoroughly understand the decision system.

Dearden and Lastavica assert that operations research requires a team approach, team members drawn from diverse fields, a mathematical model, and interaction and involvement with the decision makers. Optimizing techniques such as linear programming have proved useful in solving limited kinds of operating problems but have not been widely used to tackle higher level management problems. The availability of time-sharing services has permitted the use of nonoptimizing techniques (e.g., simulation) to solve a wider range of problems than would be possible with analytic models. Logistics, long-range planning, marketing, and information systems are the most fruitful areas of operations research specialization. Better communications between researchers and managers is the key to more effective use of available information technology and problem-solving techniques.

1 | Operations Research—The Basics

by E. Leonard Arnoff and M. J. Netzorg

It is a cliché that the problems confronting business decision makers today are more complex in nature and more far-reaching in scope than ever before. Fortunately, new methods, techniques, and tools are also making decision making easier—for the executive who is able and willing to use them.

One of the most important of these new techniques is operations research. For orientation of businessmen and consultants who have not yet had personal experience with its use, this article describes operations research—what it is, where it originated, how it is used in problem solving, and where it has been applied in industry.

What Operations Research Is

Operations research (commonly referred to as OR) is the systematic, method-oriented study of the basic structure, characteristics, functions, and relationships of an organization. Such study is intended to provide the executive with a sound, scientific, and quantitative basis for decision making.

Operations research is based on the fact that in economic systems, just as in the physical world, there is a great deal of orderliness, even where this is not readily apparent. Thus, OR is concerned with determining (1) how a system behaves under a wide range of conditions, (2) the relationships

---

EDITOR'S NOTE: "Operations Research—The Basics," by E. Leonard Arnoff and M. J. Netzorg. Reprinted by permission of *Management Services*, January-February. Copyright 1965 by the American Institute of Certified Public Accountants, Inc.

which explain why the system behaves in this manner and, finally, (3) the manner and timing through which this behavior should be changed so as to best achieve the organization's goals.

Operations research is concerned with the relationships of the activity under study to all other *pertinent* elements of the system. It is also concerned with evaluation of the host of possible alternative courses of action open to the decision maker.

The roots of operations research are as old as science and the management function. OR uses techniques adapted from many fields, such as physics, psychology, industrial engineering, and—most particularly—symbolic logic, mathematics, probability, and statistics. In addition, new methods, techniques, and tools have been developed or adapted specifically for OR-type problems. Many of these developments are of recent origin—within the past five to ten years—so that one can now solve scientifically a host of important problems that were heretofore handled on a judgmental basis.

The capabilities, flexibility, speed, and scope of usefulness of electronic computers have aided in the growth of operations research. They have made possible the study and solution of problems of a complexity that was previously beyond the time limits that confront any feasible number of individuals, no matter how competent. Some operations research techniques require the use of computers, but in a number of areas highly effective work can be accomplished with little or no use of computer time. Under no circumstances is the computer a substitute for intelligence, thought, business imagination, and acumen.

The results of successful operations research, for the decision maker, are these:

1. Assistance in substantially improving the operations under his control and better achieving the goals of the organization
2. Increased knowledge and insight into the basic facts, characteristics, and relationships of the business
3. More effective, more responsive, and broader control
4. Better, more timely, and more quantitative information
5. A reduction of the time and effort required for routine decisions ("management by exception")
6. More time for planning and managing.

OR-type Problems

Operations research has become increasingly useful to management, especially for solving those problems which affect more than one functional unit (division, department, section, etc.) within a firm. Such problems involve conflicts of interests, where a policy most favorable to one unit is rarely most favorable to the others. These conflicts of interest must be resolved to determine those policies and decisions that will maximize the effectiveness of the organization as a whole.

These problems have been called "executive-type" problems. They have arisen as a direct consequence of the functional division of labor in business enterprises—brought about by the rapid growth, diversification, and decentralization of industry. With the increased segmentation of the management function came increased attention of applied scientists to problems generated in the various functional units. From their efforts emerged a number of branches of applied science—including chemical, industrial, and mechanical engineering; industrial psychology; statistical quality control; industrial economics; and others. As each functional unit developed and better achieved its own objectives, executive-type problems increased in frequency and importance.

The solution of executive-type problems demands a highly refined balance of departmental objectives and over-all corporate objectives. *Operations research is devoted to the solution of executive-type problems—to provide management with a scientific basis for solving problems involving the interaction of functional units of the organization in terms of the best interest of the total organization.*

To illustrate an executive-type problem, consider briefly some of the objectives and conflicts involved in the inventory decisions of a firm:

Manufacturing seeks to minimize the unit costs of production (including set-up costs); hence, it favors long, uninterrupted production runs. This would result in large inventories composed of relatively few products.

Personnel is also interested in inventories. It wishes to stabilize labor and minimize the costs of hiring and layoff as well as employee discontent. This can be achieved by producing to finished inventory during times of slack customer demand.

Sales seeks to give outstanding service to customers and, hence, wishes to maintain a large inventory of a wide variety of products readily accessible in many locations. Further, it wishes manufacturing to be flexible and able to fill special orders on short notice.

Finance generally seeks to minimize the capital tied up in inventory and, hence, wishes a high rate of inventory turnover, that is, low inventory levels.

Other departments are also seriously affected by the production and inventory plan that is selected.

These objectives are, of course, in conflict with each other. The problem here is to determine the inventory policy which is best for the organization as a whole. Almost every managerial position is affected by the operating plan that is chosen and how well it is executed. However, because of the diverse objectives, and especially because of the conflicts among the objectives, choosing a plan is a controversial executive problem. Where the decision is made through negotiation and depends on the relative powers of persuasiveness of the individual departmental or divisional executives concerned, the outcome can easily be a plan of action that is far afield from what would best serve the company's over-all interest.

It is under such circumstances that operations research is of highest value. It is a highly useful means by which to clarify and simplify decision making in the face of business uncertainties and risks, such as incomplete knowledge of future sales volumes and of the plans of competitors; in the face of a multiplicity of alternative courses of action; and in the face of conflicts of interest within the company.

Another type of situation where operations research is highly useful is under conditions where conflict of interest may be secondary in importance but where there are a great number of factors to be considered, highly complex interactions, and a sheer bulk of data.

Since operations research is a relatively new discipline, let us discuss its origin and development and how it works—and give a brief description of a few of the hundreds of decision areas in which it has been successfully applied.

Origin of Operations Research

Operations research's development began in the United Kingdom in 1939 when a group of scientists was assigned to the Operational Staff in Britain's military organization. This group of scientists included physicists, psychologists, engineers, mathematicians, and others. The group was divided into teams to study large-scale military problems. The inclusion of several disciplines on a team was found to lead to gratifying results in that the interplay among the scientists often yielded new and successful approaches to complicated problems. Outstanding contributions to the war effort included the effective use of radar, the allocation of British Air Force planes to missions, and the determination of the best patterns to be used in searching for submarines.

The dramatic success of these first efforts led to the formation of more such groups in the British armed services and in all branches of the United States military organization. Today, a substantial number of operations researchers are engaged in military operations research.

Immediately after World War II the methods and techniques so successfully applied by the military were adapted to business and industry. Further developments, many of them along new lines, have also been successful. It is this rapidly increasing body of knowledge—methodology, techniques, and special analytic approaches—that gives strength to operations research as it exists today.

How OR Works

Operations research, like all scientific research, is based on scientific methodology, which proceeds along the following lines:

1. Analysis of the system—to determine the objectives of the study and the specifications, form, and characteristics of the solution to the problem. Before this can be done, there must be a good, unbiased working knowledge of the existing system. (This is materially assisted through flow charting the relevant parts of the business under study.) Basic to this stage is identification of decision points, plus determination of relevant factors and the extent to which they are subject to control. The eventual solution, accordingly, is conditioned by restrictions as to what must be done and what must not be done, as well as by consideration of limiting values and expressions of management policies.

It is at this stage that the general approach is established and the problem is formulated and often partitioned into interconnected subproblems. It is at this stage that broad appraisal is made as to both the cost and the pay-off value of a successful study and estimates are made of the required time and effort. This, combined with an appraisal of the difficulty of the study and the probability of its success, determines whether it is worthwhile (feasible) to undertake an operations research study—and, if so, in what scope and depth.

This first stage, as described above, is commonly referred to as an *orientation-feasibility study*. An important product of the orientation-feasibility study is a detailed research plan which sets forth the one or more phases of the study in such a manner that, phase by phase, results can be implemented and benefits achieved without awaiting the completion of the full study.

2. Construction of a representation of the system—a "model"—that has sufficient likeness to the real situation so that the model, rather than the system, can be manipulated meaningfully. The formal model is usually a mathematical representation of the system under study, designed in such a way as to facilitate the most effective evaluation of the influence of the various factors that affect the decisions.

3. Testing the model. The model must reflect those (and only those) real world conditions that are pertinent to problem solution. Collection and analysis of pertinent data then lead to appropriate modification and refinement of the model.

4. Solving the model. The model is then solved; that is, for any given set of conditions within stated policies and restrictions, the model is used to establish recommended courses of action. The analyst also calculates the effect of relaxing or tightening restrictions or of changing one or more policies.

5. Controlling the model and solution. At this point, controls must be established to indicate the limits within which the model and its solution can be considered as sufficiently reliable and to indicate under what future conditions and in what manner either the model or solution will have to be modified.

6. Implementing results. Finally, when the research is at an appropriate stage of progress, steps must be taken to put its findings to work.

The use of a model is common place; for instance, every factory schedule is a model. The accounting system of a firm is also a model, and often a very complex one. The power of operations research model building is that it is able to encompass a multitude of factors and a multitude of yardsticks and, hence, to resolve highly complex problems. A schedule is a model whose primary yardstick is time, with money important but secondary. An accounting system turns all the variables to money values, so that all other variables play a secondary role. The operations research approach typically involves a delicate weighting and balancing along interlocking measurement scales.

The use of an operations research model is especially important and advantageous in that it permits experimentation "on paper," without manipulation of the actual system. In using the model, one can assess the *sensitivity* (response) of the system to a wide variety of conditions—without requiring either the time, expense, or risks associated with experimenting with the system itself (if such experimentation would, in fact, be possible and meaningful). The appropriate transition from one set of conditions to another set of conditions can also be determined. Hidden relationships can be brought to light and brought to bear upon decisions and control of activity. Accordingly, operations research is particularly advantageous in dynamic (changing) situations.

The operations research approach to a problem gives consideration to the practical solution, as contrasted to the purely mathematical, or theoretical, solution. Analyses are performed to determine when further research or refinement will be more costly than the potential savings. Alternative solutions, indicating the cost of deviations from the computed optimal solution, are also derived and presented to management, thus giving management a better basis for selecting from among a group of alternative courses of action

The use of operations research assures a sufficiently complete solution to a problem rather than a "patchwork" solution. The tendency in industry and business today is to be in a continual state of firefighting, treating the *symptoms* of problems rather than the true *causes.* Furthermore, the best solution for a particular component of a system when studied in isolation may be quite different from the solution when the overall system is studied. For example, the stockage policies at a group of warehouses will generally be different when each warehouse is considered individually than when the total warehousing system is considered.

Since operations research is frequently involved in research, as contrasted to the application of previously developed techniques, there always exists the possibility of not being able to arrive at a full solution. However, the methodology of operations research provides an approach to problem solution that maximizes the probability of success in accomplishing the research objectives.

In summary, operations research, when applied to suitable problems by competent practitioners, leads to proper solution of problems—problems that could not be so clearly and decisively understood, stated, or handled by any other means.

Operations research has been applied in virtually every kind of business and industry. Among others, it has been used extensively in the petroleum, paper, chemical, metal processing, aircraft, rubber, transport and distribution, mining, and textile industries. Operations research has been very successful in aiding executives in solving problems in such areas as these:

Production

Planning and scheduling
Purchasing—materials and supplies
Raw material and in-process inventory management
Make or buy decisions
Allocation of fixed facilities and manpower
Equipment and materials utilization
Maintenance and replacement of equipment and facilities
Waiting lines (bottlenecks)
Plant location

Marketing and Distribution

Allocation of sales effort
Salesmen's compensation plans
Allocation of advertising dollars
Evaluation of advertising effectiveness
Product mix
Finished goods inventory management
Pricing and bidding strategy
Forecasting (demand, supply, price)
Warehouse location
Centralization vs. decentralization
Transportation
Warranty
Customer service

Investment and Finance

Facilities planning
Selection of process and equipment
Replacement policy
Diversification and acquisition
Budgeting
Portfolio selection
Sampling in accounting
Financial planning and control
Financial forecasting
Organization structure
Centralization vs. decentralization
Communication
Long-range planning
Organization of problem-solving groups
Stockholder control

Others

Evaluation of problem-solving groups
Research and development expenditure
Design of experiments
Urban planning and area redevelopment
Various uses of sampling
Credit analysis (e.g., credit card accounts)
Benefit plans—executives and employees
Decision-oriented management information systems

The following brief descriptions give further indication of the immense range of problems and situations where operations research has been successfully applied. While reference is made to studies in specific industries, the problems involved often have basic underlying structures that conform to general types. So the solutions that were obtained could be paralleled in many industries, with those modifications required to take full account of the individuality that gives truth to the saying ... "but my business is different."

The design, development, and implementation of an optimal production and inventory management system—in a machine-tool company. This application covered the planning and control of the ordering; scheduling; sequencing; dispatching; machine loading; warehousing; assembly; and raw, in-process, and finished goods inventory functions. Included also were analyses and appropriate changes in data collection, generation, and processing (computers and *decision-oriented* management information systems) and in forecasting. Decision rules and procedures were developed for both day-to-day operation and long-range planning.

Production planning and labor stabilization—in the rubber industry. In an industry where demand is highly seasonal, factory production rates and manpower levels were determined so as to minimize the sum of the costs of (1) hiring and layoff of personnel, (2) carrying inventory, and (3) overtime.

Planning and scheduling of materials, processes, manpower, and facilities—in a refinery complex. A method was developed for determining the selection and use of resources so as to maximize profit. Price-volume relationships were analyzed, and optimum product mixes were established for market planning. (This is an extension of optimum blending procedures for gasolines, middle distillates, and heavy fuel oils.)

The selection and scheduling of research and development projects—in the pharmaceutical industry. The estimated pay-off, cost, effort, and likelihood of success were determined for each potential research project. Available funds, manpower, and skills were then allocated so as to determine an overall research program with greatest profit potential.

Maintenance and replacement program — in a trucking company. The study determined the optimum preventive maintenance and replacement program. The structure of the system was analyzed for a variety of basic alternative policies. Included in the analyses were the costs of maintenance and road failures.

Group replacement vs. individual replacement—of light bulbs in manufacturing companies and municipalities. For items that do not deteriorate with age or with use but which ultimately fail, the determination is made whether or not to replace in a group and, if so, when to do so. This problem arises since the cost per unit for group replacement (before failure) is less than the cost per unit for individual replacement (after failure).

The maintenance of mechanical equipment—for large, world-wide governmental agencies. These studies were concerned with the optimum number and location of maintenance shops, personnel requirements, stockage policies at depots and in the field, and the question of assembly vs. component part replacement.

The determination of optimum reserve generating capacity—in the electric utility industry. An analysis was made of shortage policies, maintenance programs, customer demand, and interconnections—to determine when to add generators and of what size. A major task here was the determination of the probabilities of equipment breakdown (forced outages) for the total system.

The determination of warehouse dock facilities—for a department store. Variations in the number and time of daily truck arrivals, the servicing times (loading and/or unloading), restrictions on the parking facilities, and customer and company truck waiting times were taken into account in determining the dock requirements for a warehouse which was to replace three existing warehouses.

The determination of facility requirements (cranes, docks, etc.) to accommodate the expected volumes and mixes of ores and coal received at a port. Factors considered included (1) the characteristics of ships arriving at the docks, (2) the effects of these characteristics on unloading rates and dock space, (3) limitations on the number of ships that can wait in the harbor, and (4) the cost associated with ships delayed in unloading due to insufficient facilities versus (5) the cost of idle unloading facilities.

Establishing, monitoring, and updating master plans for urban renewal and city planning. This requires integrated analyses of growth patterns (population and industry); the resulting effects on city income; and the sociological implications of various housing, recreational, office, and transportation systems.

The allocation of salesman effort—for a light-bulb manufacturer. This study involved determining the number of salesmen needed, sales territory boundaries, and the number of sales calls to make on each type of dealer so as to maximize the total profitability of the sales effort.

The establishment of an optimal distribution system—for a bulk-chemical producer. Optimum product mix, product reorder levels and order quantities, number and location of warehouses, the assignment of customers to warehouses, and the assignment of warehouse facilities to production plants were determined. Storage, transportation, and production costs, as well as customer service levels, were considered.

The selection of coal for coke plants. The objective of this study was to minimize the total cost of a given amount of coke. The costs of transportation, mining, and conversion (coal to coke) were included, along with consideration of the availability of coal at each mine and the capacity at each coke plant.

Planning for seasonal retail sales. Sales patterns for numerous products—sold by approximately 10,000 dealers with different geographical locations, types of stores, and sales volumes—had to be considered in developing a sampling plan for estimating end-user purchases. The results were then used to develop production, distribution, and marketing programs in a highly seasonal business.

The determination of an optimal warranty system—for a durable goods manufacturer. This study included the evaluation and change of settlement policies; where and by whom the claims should be settled; optimum product quality level; and how product problems can be quickly detected, evaluated, and corrected.

The development of bidding strategies for obtaining leases for oil exploration. Included in this study were the development of a predictor of future production for a given lease and an analysis of the relationship between the amount bid and the likelihood of obtaining the lease for that bid.

The OR Approach

Great care must be taken to assure that the right problem is being formulated and then solved—in its proper scope. As noted earlier, the use of an operations research model is especially advantageous here, inasmuch as it permits assessing the response, or sensitivity, of the system to a wide variety of conditions. In particular, it enables the analyst to determine the sensitivity of the solution to individual factors and, in turn, to determine the importance of such factors in obtaining still further improvements in the system.

A study conducted for an airline illustrates the operations research approach in assuring a complete, yet practical, solution:

A commercial airline sought to determine (1) how frequently it should conduct classes for the training of stewardesses, and (2) the size that these classes should be. This rather limited problem was formulated precisely, and a decision rule was obtained for administering the school so as to minimize the sum of the costs involved.

In the course of solving the problem, the operations research team discovered that the effectiveness with which the school was operated was very sensitive to the number of stewardesses required by the airline. Consequently, an investigation was undertaken as to how these requirements were determined at each base and, hence, for the total system.

This led, in turn, to the development of a procedure for minimizing the number of stewardesses (including reserve stewardesses) required at each base. This step required developing (1) new procedures for the preparation of individual flying assignments ("bids," prepared monthly) and (2) new provisions for "makeup" flying whenever flying assignments were missed (due to cancelled flights, etc.).

However, this investigation revealed that a base's requirements for staffing were sensitive to the assignment of flights to that base and that the total system's staffing requirements were sensitive to the number and location of bases and the assignment of flights to each of them.

A study was therefore undertaken to determine (1) how many bases there should be, (2) where the bases should be located, and (3) how the flights should be assigned to each base in order to yield the best possible performance of the total system.

However, since flights could not be assigned to bases without considering the male crews (the male crews and stewardesses flew the same monthly "bids"), the study was finally generalized to consider the total crew.

Once each of these aspects of the system's operations had been analyzed, the results of the several phases were synthesized and overall planning procedures for training and utilization of personnel were developed.

Further studies of utilization of aircraft, maintenance policies, etc., were also suggested by the study, because of relationships which were revealed. These studies were subsequently undertaken. In addition, the study and its corresponding model put the company on a better basis for conducting its negotiations with the flight personnel unions, inasmuch as the implications of new contract terms could be determined in advance.

In this example, the "symptoms" were not indicative of the true problem; it was the overall approach that eventually indicated the total problem that had to be solved. However, the intermediate steps were so conducted that the solution was optimized each time, subject to the constraints imposed by the rest of the system.

It is important to note that the benefits obtained from solving the overall problem were substantially greater than those that would have been obtained by solving the limited problem originally stated.

Organizing for an OR Study

For each specific project, an OR task force should be formed consisting of qualified operations researchers as well as personnel directly involved with the subject area under study. These latter personnel will supply necessary technical know-how and experience, will assist in collecting and generating data, and will also assist in working out the details of implementation.

The joint task force should, in turn, report to a steering committee consisting of the managers (or representatives) of those functions of the company most vitally connected with, and affected by, the study. The steering committee should usually consist of three to five members, although at times it is desirable to have additional representation. The task force should meet regularly with the steering committee, approximately two to four times per month, and with individual members of the committee even more frequently.

In turn, the task force and the steering committee should meet with a top management committee—typically every six to ten weeks. Ordinarily, the top management committee for the OR study is a regularly functioning committee already in existence. This committee is usually a fairly large one including representation from each and every major function of the company. In many instances, members of the steering committee are also regular members of the top management committee.

In some instances the nature and scope of the problem, as related to the company structure, are such that only a single management committee is needed, usually consisting of three to ten members.

The use of the operations research task force, a steering committee, and a top management committee yields many important benefits—so important, in fact, that it is safe to assert that *an operations research study will seldom be effective unless such committees are used.* With proper use of the committees, the benefits include the following:

1. These committees serve as filters for the research, help prevent errors of both commission and omission, provide additional know-how, and generally guide the team *during* the study, thereby increasing the chances of success. (In particular, interactions among functions are uncovered where they might otherwise be missed.)

2. Since the committees represent the areas affected by and involved in the study, the OR team is not put in the position of an outsider (e.g., staff) trying to tell others (e.g., operating personnel) what to do. Everyone has a sense of participation and contribution and also a much better opportunity for discussion and, hence, understanding, thereby increasing chances for acceptance and successful implementation. Furthermore, implementation can then be carried out more readily and quickly.

3. Several levels of management and operating personnel are thereby educated in the nature of operations research, making them more aware of its potentialities and its limitations.

The success of operations research in any company often depends as much on management as it does on the operations research staff. Hence, wherever possible, the informal discussions on operations research at the committee meetings should be supplemented by a series of formal sessions on OR—designed to develop a better understanding by management. Such sessions have been conducted—with great success—in a large number of companies.

4. Further OR projects will usually be suggested by these committees, thereby inducing a better acceptance of and environment for operations research at all levels of the company.

Words of Caution

Whenever operations research is mentioned, executives are likely to express some bewilderment over the fact that results have ranged all the way from limited success to the highest usefulness and profitability.

So far, this article has discussed the steps, the procedures, the attitudes, the probings, and the methodology—which are a minimal basis upon which to build toward success. In so doing, the positive side has been accentuated. However, there is also a need to point out the negative side. Certain common traps and pitfalls can easily be, and have been, the ruination of otherwise good work. Some of these pitfalls are fairly obvious, while others are so subtle and deeply hidden that unless careful heed is taken their presence is not even suspected.

At the very outset of problem solving—the problem selection and formulation phase—a number of pitfalls can and do arise. Here, the executive and the operations researcher have the joint task of selecting the right problem and of defining it completely and accurately. Is the right problem being solved? Is the problem being considered in its proper scope, or will the gains be localized and at the expense of other parts of the organization ("sub-optimization")? Will the solution pertain to the actual system under study and properly reflect the goals of the organization as well as the imposed restrictions? Are appropriate measures of performance being used? The problem formulation phase is probably the most important and most difficult part of the entire study. Deliberate and skillful planning is especially required here.

Data gathering can represent a very large part of the time and cost of an operations research study. Hence, an early analysis of the sensitivity of the solution to the input data should always be made, since it will save gathering unneeded data and will often indicate the areas in which measurement and control (and, hence, better data) are most important. Fortunately, a system reasonably close to optimum usually gives excellent results. Hence, rough, order-of-magnitude estimates will often give considerable insight into system behavior and results.

Solving the problem also contains some potential dangers. Not the least of these is over-concern with the elegance of the solution, which can lead to an elaborate and correct answer that may be too late or too complex to be used. It also can lead to "over-optimization," that is, attempting to obtain the last few percentage points of improvement by a detailed and expensive analysis. A less complicated model will often yield most of the potential gain, at considerably less cost and with much greater likelihood of success; in fact, the cost of any further gain may well exceed the gain itself.

Other pitfalls in problem solving include (1) taking a "cookbook" approach when a custom design is needed (as, for example, precipitous use of standard lot-size formulas, (2) warping the problem to fit an available model, technique, or tool (3) substituting high-speed, brute force computer groping for sound analysis, (4) failing to test the model and the solution adequately prior to implementation, and (5) failing to establish proper controls on the results.

Estimating benefits from system improvements requires a word of caution, in that theoretical benefits are usually not completely achieved and potentials must be discounted in order to give realistic, practical expectations of accomplishments. The disappointment of not fully achieving a potential gain can overshadow the benefits that are actually attained, even when such benefits are sizable.

A number of operations research studies have not realized great potential because the results were not fully accepted. Many of these studies were technically sound, but the operations researcher failed to communicate properly with management. It is the operations researcher's responsibility to translate his highly specialized and technical thoughts, concepts, and ideas into the realm of experience of the executive and into the language of the business and to translate complex solutions and formulas into tools and procedures that can be readily used. Further, it is essential that the operations researcher determine and develop the procedures necessary for smooth transition from the original system to the new system.

One further word of clarification is that, in fact, a truly optimum solution is never achieved. Rather, what is called an optimum solution is such only for the problem as specifically stated, the area covered, and the conditions that existed at that point in time. However, the fact that a solution may not be truly optimum does not mean that substantial gains cannot be achieved.

Finally, what may appear to be a pitfall is the fact that a good operations research study may raise more questions than it answers. However, this can lead to a more penetrating inquiry into the operation of the system and what it is intended to do—with the ultimate result of greater insight into the system and even more far-reaching benefits and improvements. This inquiring aspect of operations research is one of its strongest attributes.

Dos and Don'ts of Operations Research

In problem selection and formulation:

Do solve the right problem.
Do consider the problem in its proper scope.
Do use appropriate measures of performance.
Do develop a solution pertaining to the actual system under study.
Do develop a solution properly reflecting the organization's goals.

In solving the problem:

Don't be over-concerned with the elegance of the solution.
Don't over-optimize.
Don't settle for a standard approach if a custom design is needed.
Don't warp the problem to fit an available model, technique, or tool.
Don't substitute high-speed computer groping for sound analysis.
Don't fail to test the model and solution adequately before implementation.
Don't fail to establish proper controls.

Note

1. See E. Leonard Arnoff, "Operations Research and Decision-Oriented Management Information System," *Management Accounting*, June 1970, pp. 11-16 for a more complete discussion of this point.

2 Operations Research as a Tool for Decision Making

by Hans J. Laue

When you ask a professional in operations analysis, more often called operations research (OR), for an explanation of his science, you may hear a definition like the following:

> Operations research is the art of giving bad answers to problems to which worse answers would otherwise be given.

Defining OR in this way avoids the rigidity which makes most definitions of difficult activities ultimately useless. Another more usual definition of OR could be:

> Application of scientific method and analysis to management problems to provide executives with a sound quantitative basis for decision making in the face of complex relationships, of uncertainty and risks, of conflicts of interest, and of alternative courses of action.

This still does not tell the full story. What, then, is OR?

CHARACTERISTICS OF OPERATIONS RESEARCH

A statement on the characteristics of OR should include:

1. Total system orientation.
2. Commitment to scientific method.
3. Use of special mathematical techniques.

The first two characteristics, total system orientation and scientific method, portray a point of view or an attitude. According to some of the

Editor's Note: From *The Journal of Industrial Engineering*, September 1967, pp. 539-549. Reprinted by permission of the publisher, American Institute of Industrial Engineers, Inc., and author.

earlier practitioners of OR, it is this viewpoint that makes the difference. Advocates of the more recent emphasis on special mathematical techniques maintain that it is the skillful use of these techniques that makes the difference between OR and not OR.

Total system orientation means that the activity of any part of an organization has some effect on the activity of most other parts. Accordingly, to evaluate any decision or action in an organization, one needs to identify all significant interactions and to evaluate their combined impact on the performance of the organization as a whole. An opposite orientation would be to cut a problem down to size, possibly isolating it from its environment.

When we think of scientific research we usually think of the experimental method. This approach generally is not practical in OR work because of the nature of the problems investigated. However, this position is not unique in science: take the astronomer, for example, who cannot bring the universe into a lab to manipulate. The closest he can approach this ideal is to study a representation of the universe, which he calls a "model."

We may say that a model is a representation of reality. Models are typically used to gain insight, to observe and measure, to transform, to test, to discover significant variables, to investigate the relationship between variables, to determine an optimal value. Models can be analyzed and manipulated more easily than the real system. Proposed changes or hypotheses can be tested on the model, holding some properties constant while varying others.

Recent years have seen rapid growth in the number of specialized mathematical techniques that are used in constructing and optimizing models. OR practitioners build and use mathematical models when studying organized man-machine systems and, hence, carry out experiments in this symbolic way. Models may appear in any form, from the simplest to very complicated and difficult constructions, but their underlying principle is relatively simple. In symbolic expression, the basic form of all OR models is:

$$P = f(C_i, U_j)$$

where the system's overall performance, P, is a function of a set of controllable aspects of the system C_i, and a set of uncontrollable aspects, U_j.

The most difficult part of an OR study may be the development of an adequate measure of the system's performance, because this measure must reflect the relative importance of the many objectives involved in every management decision. These objectives are of two types:

1. Those which involve retaining things of value (minimize inputs, expenditures, and so forth).
2. Those which involve obtaining things of value (maximize outputs, income, and so forth).

The "things" may be resources (time, money, energy) or states of the system (market share, public acceptance). Once a model has been set up, a solution is sought which optimizes the measure of performance, P. To obtain such a solution, one seeks those values of the controllable variables that maximize (or minimize) the performance, P. The optimizing values of the controllable variables, C_k, are then expressed as functions of the uncontrollable variables:

$$C_k = f_k(U_j).$$

These relations are called the "decision rules."

The conditions which bear on organized systems are subject to change over time. Thus, there is no permanent solution to a management problem, and OR work must use procedures that can be adapted to changing conditions.

PROBLEM CONTENT

When a manager talks about decisions that he has to make, a frequent belief is that his problems are different from those confronting other executives. He is of course right in thinking that his problems are different, but they are not different in every respect. Problems can be viewed in two aspects: form and content. Two problems seldom have the same content, but almost all the problems that an executive faces will appear in one of only a few different forms. An understanding of the distinction between form and content is valuable for an appreciation of how OR can be of use to management.

Managers generally look at problems according to their content, that is, the area of business in which these problems arise. On the other hand, the form in which problems appear has to do with their underlying logical structure. We will come back to the form of problems further on. The following listing illustrates some major areas in which OR has been successfully applied in business, industry, and government.

Finance, Budgeting, and Investments

1. Cash flow analysis, long-range capital requirements, alternative investments and sources of capital, dividend policies, design and control of investment portfolios.
2. Credit policies, credit risks, and delinquent account procedures.
3. Developing of auditing procedures, automated data processing systems, and accounting systems.

4. Pilferage problems.
5. Claim and complaint procedures.

Purchasing, Procurement, Exploration

1. Development of rules for buying supplies with stable or significantly varying prices.
2. Determination of quantities, timing, source of purchases.
3. Prices, storage capacity and cost, deterioration and shrinkage, substitute suppliers, location of suppliers, and transportation costs.
4. Bidding policies and probabilities of winning bids.
5. Predictions of competitive behavior.
6. Strategies for exploration and exploitation of raw material sources like oil, ore, and coal deposits.
7. Purchase of assemblies versus in-house manufacture, repetitive purchasing of large items with spare parts stocking requirements, inventory and repair costs and maintainability considerations.
8. Type and size of major items of equipment, time and manner of replacement, rental rather than purchase, rebuilt versus new equipment.

Physical Distribution

1. Locations and sizes of warehouses, distribution centers, and retail outlets.
2. Distribution policy.
3. Internal space allocation for display and stock accessibility.
4. Decisions on company-owned outlets versus franchises.
5. Multilevel inventory control systems, transportation policies.
6. Worldwide logistics and supply systems for both military and industrial applications.

Facilities Planning

1. Number and location of factories, warehouses, service yards, hospitals and educational institutions; their sizes and interactions.
2. Harbors and docking facilities for ocean and inland water transportation.
3. Facilities for railroads, trucking, and air transportation.

Manufacturing

1. Allocation of production orders to plants on the basis of production and transportation costs.

2. Production planning and production scheduling, including decisions on product mixes, sequencing, overtime, additional shifts.

3. Stabilization of production and employment, the effects of instability, and the cost of hiring, training, lay-offs, and firing.

4. Planning and scheduling of job shop operations.

Replacement, Modernization

1. Equipment replacement, depreciation, obsolescence.

Construction, Maintenance, Project Scheduling

1. Evaluation and development of maintenance policies, both preventive and corrective.

2. Maintenance crew and repair facilities sizes, crew and equipment utilization, effects of maintenance policies and scheduling on smoothness of operation and labor utilization.

3. Project scheduling and control, including allocation of resources to projects, timing, analysis of activities that are likely to delay the project, monitoring of construction, development, and repair projects.

Marketing

1. Product selection, timing of new products, demand forecasting, competitive actions, size of sales budget and its allocation to direct selling, sales promotion and advertising, the relation of this budget to pricing.

2. Number of salesmen, size of sales territories, number of accounts to be handled per salesman, frequency of calling on accounts, proportion of time to be spent on prospective accounts.

3. Advertising strategies, selection of advertising media, distribution of budget to media, advertising message, and frequency of advertising.

4. Determination of whether service should be provided by manufacturer or franchised dealer, what kind and where service should be provided, guarantee policy and period.

Personnel

1. Selection of personnel, mixes of age and skills, factors influencing labor turnover, causes for absenteeism, accident prevention.

2. Recruiting policies, assignment to jobs, measurements of performance, incentive schemes, productivity.

3. Impact of automation and the feasibility of accelerating automation without undue hardship.

Research and Development

1. Budgets for research, allocation to basic or applied research, selection of individual projects, size of research and development facilities, staffing, effectiveness and organization of research activities.

2. Determination of areas for concentration of research and development.

3. Evaluation of alternative designs, the life expectancy and reliability that should be designed into a product.

4. Control of development projects, determination of time and cost requirements.

Transportation and Logistic Systems

1. Development of operational transportation and support concepts.

2. Analyses of logistical support systems.

3. Analyses of air, rail, highway, and waterway transportation systems. (These studies are closely linked to economic development planning for large regions and emerging countries.)

Urban Renewal and Development

1. Evaluation of concepts and alternatives in urban planning, land uses, development of integrated urban centers, community facilities, shifts in population, future demands on transportation facilities and road systems, traffic studies, smog control, and so forth.

FORM OF PROBLEMS AND SOLUTION TECHNIQUES

OR approaches have been used in many industries. The preceding applications seem quite varied, but since the same type of problem occurs in so many diverse industries, the problem-solving models that have been developed can be conveniently grouped into nine basic forms. Together with useful techniques from mathematics and statistics, these models constitute the basic repertoire of the OR analyst. They can be used, singly or in combination, to solve most problems that confront managers. A convenient grouping is as follows:

1. Mathematical techniques.
2. Statistical techniques.
3. Inventory models.
4. Allocation models.
5. Dynamic programming models.
6. Waiting line models.
7. Sequencing models.
8. Replacement models.
9. Competition models.
10. Simulation techniques.
11. Search and heuristic methods.

Each of these is discussed briefly here.

Mathematical Techniques

In principle, any mathematical method can become a useful tool for the OR analyst. The methods that have been most commonly applied are: differential equations, linear difference equations, integral equations, operator theory, symbolic logic, vector and matrix theory. Optimization methods include, for example, gradient methods, unconstrained and constrained optimization, and Lagrange multipliers. It is beyond the scope of this presentation to go beyond a mere mention of these theories. Any textbook on college calculus will contain a treatment of such material.

Statistical Techniques

Some of the most commonly applied techniques come from probability theory and statistics. They include discrete and continuous probability, combinatorial analysis, renewal theory, random walks, Markov processes, and general stochastic processes. Statistical techniques include inference, point and interval estimation, testing of hypotheses, control charts, linear and multiple regression, correlation, analysis of variance. All these methods are very useful for dealing with uncertainty, errors, sampling, estimation, and prediction. Again, this presentation will not attempt to go beyond a listing of the techniques. For some introductory textbooks, see References (11) and (12).

Inventory Models

Inventory models deal with idle resources like material, people, and money. The problem is how frequently and in what quantities to order or to produce in order to minimize total cost. Total cost is the sum of cost of managing, holding cost of inventory, and cost of shortages, if this latter cost can be quantified.

The following costs increase as inventory increases: investment in stock and facilities, obsolescence, handling taxes, insurance. These costs decrease as inventory increases: reviewing, ordering, transportation, quantity purchase price, cost of lost or delayed sales, expediting, redistribution according to emergency orders.

Shortage costs are difficult or impossible to measure. In such cases one may evaluate operating costs for various assumed levels of shortages (fraction of orders that cannot be filled). The result is a cost-effectiveness relationship that can be used by management to select an appropriate balance between cost and shortages. The typical inventory pattern for one item over time may be represented as in Fig. 2-1, where

a = trigger level of reordering,
b = order quantity,
c = time between orders,
d = time between placing and receiving orders, and
e = quantity of customer's back orders.

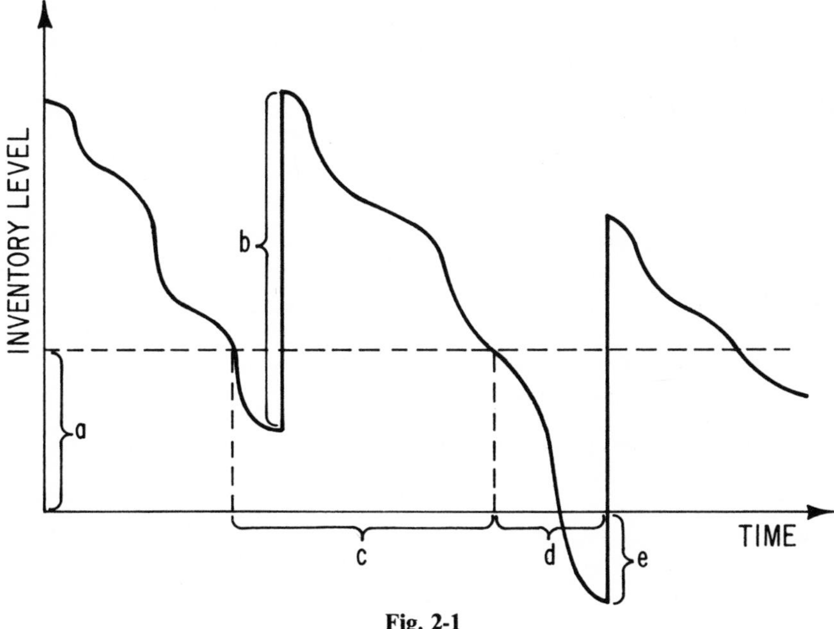

Fig. 2-1

These parameters may be fixed or variable, according to the situation or the operating policy in force.

Solution methods for inventory problems are well developed. Minimum-cost decision rules for ordering policies are obtained by calculus, probability theory, theory of stochastic processes, dynamic programming, and computer simulation. See also References (13) and (14).

Allocation Models

The simplest problem of this kind involves the assignment of a number of jobs to the same number of resources, perhaps men. There is a cost or profit associated with each possible combination, and the solution is the maximization of this profit (or minimization of the cost). Because of its characteristics, this type of problem is called the "assignment problem."

A complication is introduced in this kind of model if some jobs require more than one resource. Most distribution problems are of this type; therefore, this type of problem is called the "transportation problem."

When resources and demands are limited, a more refined model is used. In this case, the problem consists in determining the most profitable mix and level of activities to perform within the given constraints, and the optimal amount and distribution of the given resources must be determined. In general, this formulation is called the "mathematical programming problem"; when the constraints may be expressed as linear equations, the more specific name "linear programming problem" is given.

To give you an idea of what linear programming means, consider the following.

Example: Assume that you want to decide between alternate ways of spending an eight-hour day, that is, you want to allocate your resource time. Assume that you find it five times more fun to play ping-pong in the lounge than to work, but you also feel that you should work at least three times as many hours as you play ping-pong. Now the decision problem is how many hours to play and how many to work in order to maximize your objective: "fun."

Let

X number of hours spent working, and
Y number of hours spent playing.

You want to maximize your fun, F, where

$$F = X + 5Y. \qquad \text{Eq. 1}$$

Your total time per day is limited to eight hours:

$$X + Y \leqslant 8. \qquad \text{Eq. 2}$$

And, finally, you should work at least three times as long as you play:

$3Y \leqslant X.$ Eq. 3

Obviously, you cannot spend a negative number of hours, hence

$X \geqslant 0, \ Y \geqslant 0.$ Eq. 4

Now let us graph the "objective function," Equation 1, and the "restrictions," Equations 2, 3, 4, on a coordinate plane. The results appear in Fig. 2-2.

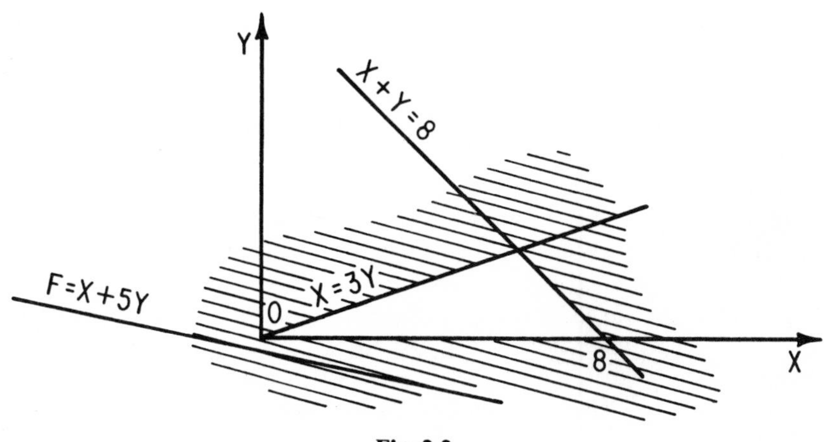

Fig. 2-2

The shaded area is the "infeasible region" that results from the restrictions, Equations 2 through 4. The question is to find the "best" solution to the problem:

Maximize $F = X + 5Y.$

For $X = Y = 0$, we have $F = 0$, which means that you neither play nor work, but do nothing. The solution $F = 0$ is shown graphically in Fig. 2-3.

Since you want to do some work, we now increase X, which finds its limit at 8 (Point A), namely, the total number of hours at your disposal. Hence, $F(A) = X + 5Y = 8 + 0$. (See Fig. 2-4.)

From Fig. 2-5 you see that raising the value of F from zero to eight corresponds to a parallel translation of the line F. You also see that we can shift F farther in the same direction, always passing through some point of the feasible area, up to Point B.

Now, B is the intersection of lines

$X + Y = 8$

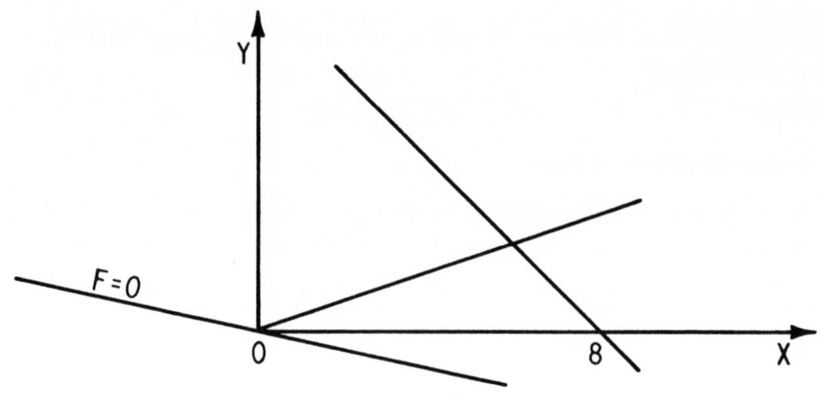

Fig. 2-3

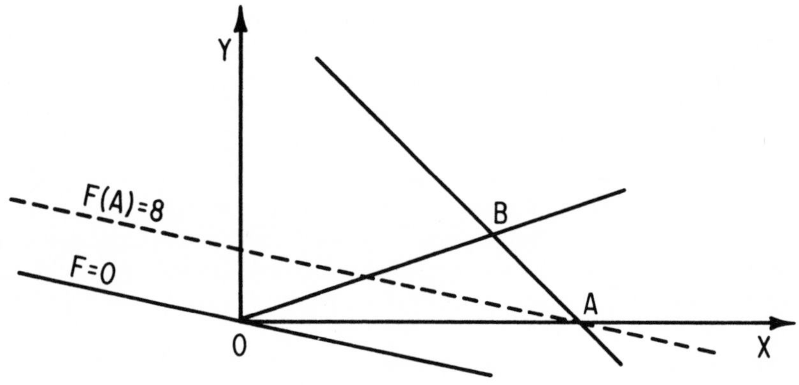

Fig. 2-4

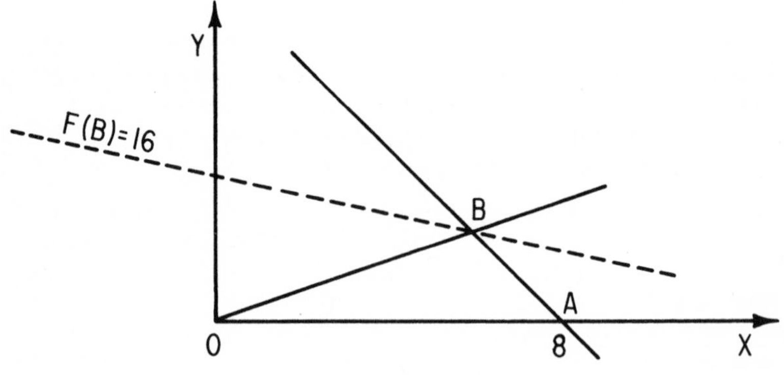

Fig. 2-5

and

$$-X+3Y=0.$$

That is,

$$B = \{X=6, Y=2\},$$

so that our objective has assumed its maximum value at B:

$$F(B) = 6 + 5 \times 2 = 16.$$

For further introduction to allocation problems, see References (15) and (16).

Dynamic Programming Models

Dynamic programming is a relatively recent approach to problems in which decisions have to be made sequentially over time or space. Instead of optimizing each decision as it occurs, dynamic programming takes account of the effects of current decisions on future periods and adjusts every decision to yield the best overall performance.

Dynamic programming models are especially suitable for processes that extend over a number of time periods. The method consists of a search for the optimal combination of decisions to be taken in all periods and requires the manipulation of a large amount of information. Hence, the use of an electronic computer is nearly always indispensable. An example will best illustrate the principles of dynamic programming.

Example: A family is moving from the East to the West Coast. They plan to drive across the country to combine the move with sightseeing. Their point of departure and their destination are fixed, but they have some choice of route segments in between. Each segment is more or less desirable from a sightseeing point of view, and they want to travel the sequence of route segments that will give them the "most" in sightseeing. The total trip will have to be done in four stages, as shown in Fig. 2-6. The arrows represent the available route segments.

Let the "sightseeing value" of going from Point i to Point j be s_{ij}. Then the problem is to maximize the sum

$$S_{19} = s_{1i} + s_{ij} + s_{jk} + s_{k9},$$

where

i may be 2 or 3,
j may be 4, 5, or 6, and
k may be 7 or 8.

The values of s_{ij} are given in Table 2-1.

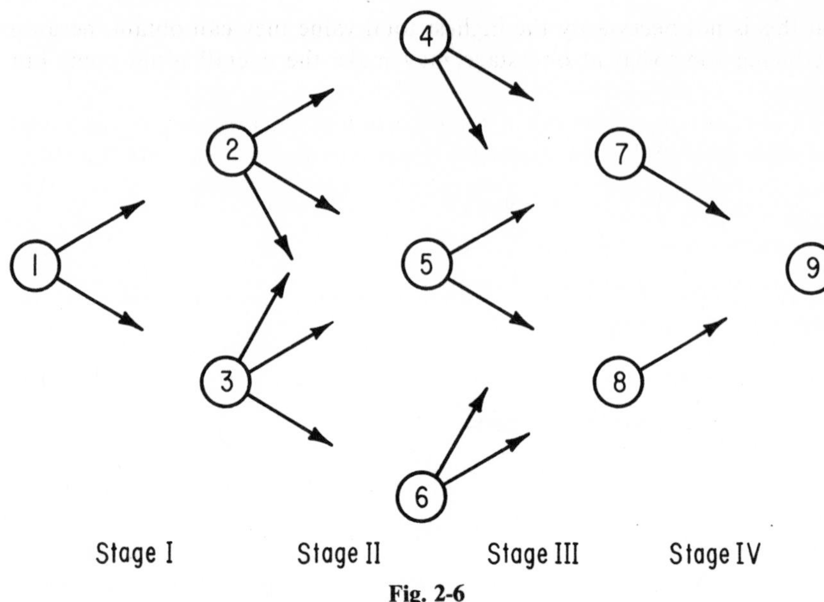

Fig. 2-6

Table 2-1

Stage I

	2	3
j =	2	3
i = 1	4	2

Stage II

j =	4	5	6
i = 2	6	1	5
3	3	4	2

Stage III

j =	7	8
i = 4	2	1
5	6	2
6	3	5

Stage IV

j =	9
i = 7	2
8	5

Now, if the family chooses the largest value stage after stage, they will, for example, have:

$$S_{19} = s_{12} + s_{24} + s_{47} + s_{79} = 4 + 6 + 2 + 2 = 14.$$

But this is not necessarily the highest total value they can obtain, because sacrificing somewhat at one stage may make the overall result come out higher.

In dynamic programming, a small portion of the problem is first solved and then more and more stages are taken into the solution until the entire span of stages is covered. Usually, the procedure starts from the end. Let us see how this works.

Stage IV: There are two possibilities for going to Destination 9, given that the family was at either 7 or 8:

$$S_{79} = 2, \quad \text{and} \quad S_{89} = 5.$$

For Stages III and IV, there are six possibilities:

$$S_{49} = \begin{cases} s_{47} + s_{79} = 2 + 2 = 4 \\ s_{48} + s_{89} = 1 + 5 = 6 = S^*_{489} \end{cases}$$

$$S_{59} = \begin{cases} s_{57} + s_{79} = 6 + 2 = 8 = S^*_{579} \\ s_{58} + s_{89} = 2 + 5 = 7 \end{cases}$$

$$S_{69} = \begin{cases} s_{67} + s_{79} = 3 + 2 = 5 \\ s_{68} + s_{89} = 5 + 5 = 10 = S^*_{689} \end{cases}$$

Thus, an "optimal" route selection results for going to the destination, given that the family is at either 4, 5, or 6. The optimal choices for the last two stages are denoted by stars. If this procedure is carried back to the starting point, it will give the overall optimal choice S^*_{19}. Note that, with any succeeding iteration, one need only take into account the starred (optimal) policies of the partial problems before.

Stages II, III, and IV:

$$S_{29} = \begin{cases} s_{24} + S^*_{489} = 6 + 6 = 12 \\ s_{25} + S^*_{579} = 1 + 8 = 9 \\ s_{26} + S^*_{689} = 5 + 10 = 15 = S^*_{2689} \end{cases}$$

$$S_{39} = \begin{cases} s_{34} + S^*_{489} = 3 + 6 = 9 \\ s_{35} + S^*_{579} = 4 + 8 = 12 = S^*_{3579} \\ s_{36} + S^*_{689} = 2 + 10 = 12 = S^*_{3689} \end{cases}$$

We see that at this iteration, the optimal route from 3 to 9 is not unique.

Stages I, II, III, and IV:

$$S_{19} = \begin{cases} s_{12} + S^*_{2689} = 4 + 15 = 19 = S^*_{12689} \\ s_{13} + S^*_{3579} = 2 + 12 = 14 \\ s_{13} + S^*_{3689} = 2 + 12 = 14 \end{cases}$$

This results in the optimal route: 1, 2, 6, 8, 9 with value 19. This is considerably different from choosing the "best" route at each stage successively, which gave a value of only 14. For a good discussion of dynamic programming, see Reference (17).

Waiting Line Models

Waiting line models are also called "queueing models" because they are applied to problems concerning the random arrival of customers to receive some service at a collection of service points. Such models are characteristic of toll booths, sales counters, docking facilities, the study of breakdown and repair of machinery, and other problems. The objective of this approach is to determine the optimal number of personnel or facilities to service customers who arrive randomly, balancing the cost of service with the cost of waiting or congestion.

The mathematical theory of queues is highly developed. Probability theory and differential and integral equations are used in it extensively. An example will illustrate the applications.

Example: In a large automobile repair shop, the foreman complains that his mechanics must wait too long at the spare parts counter before receiving service. The manager, however, wants to keep costs low by having the minimum number of parts servers at the counter. The problem, thus, involves balancing the cost of extra parts servers against the value of the time saved by reducing the waiting time of mechanics.

Suppose that it takes a parts man an average of two minutes to serve a mechanic and that the average time between arrivals of mechanics at the counter is three minutes. At first glance the solution appears to be to employ one parts server. However, because of the random pattern of arrival of mechanics, the waiting line varies considerably over time. By using queueing theory, it is possible to predict the average waiting time per mechanic for the cases of having one, two, three, or more parts servers at the counter. Under the described circumstances, the queueing model gives an average waiting time per mechanic of 240 seconds for the case of one

Table 2-2

Number of Parts Servers	Cost of Parts Servers	Cost of Waiting Time of Mechanics Before Being Served	Total Cost
1	$32	$80.00	$112.00
2	64	5.00	69.00
3	96	0.66	96.66

server, of 15 seconds for two servers, and of two seconds for three servers. During the eight-hour working day, there are a total of 160 visits by mechanics to the parts counter. Assuming that the cost of wages and overhead for parts servers is $4.00 per hour and for mechanics, $7.50 per hour, we obtain the costs per eight-hour day shown in Table 2-2. The results of the study indicate that two parts servers will provide the minimum cost solution. See also References (18) and (19).

Sequencing Models

This class of problems concerns determining the optimal sequence in which to service customers, or to perform a set of jobs, in order to minimize total processing time or another suitable measure of performance.

Only very simple problems of this kind can be solved explicitly. Generally, the number of alternatives to be considered is so high that they cannot all be examined. A typical class of such problems is machine scheduling.

If we had to schedule ten jobs over two machines, and the jobs had to be processed in the machines in the same order, there would be nearly four million possible combinations ($10! = 10 \cdot 9 \cdot 8 \cdot 7 \cdot 6 \cdot 5 \cdot 4 \cdot 3 \cdot 2 \cdot 1$). Just imagine the astronomic number of combinations that would result if more than two machines were involved and if the sequence of jobs over some machines could be different.

In view of this, most such problems are attacked by simulation or heuristic methods. Although many of these techniques result in only approximations of the true optimum, the solutions are generally better than those derived from experienced judgment alone.

For the class of problems in which some precedence relations are given, that is, certain jobs must be completed before others can be started, specialized techniques have been developed. These techniques are currently applied to many large projects like construction, maintenance, assembly, and testing. The two most prominent techniques are called PERT and CPM. See also Reference (20).

Replacement Models

A determination of whether and when to replace aging facilities is made in replacement models. In general, there are two classes of such facilities: items that deteriorate during use and items that suddenly fail.

The first case includes such items as vehicles, machine tools, and appliances. The model considers the cost of investment, amortized over time, plus operation and maintenance as well as salvage costs. Solutions are obtained quite easily by calculus and dynamic programming.

The second case includes items like light bulbs, tires, electronic components, or personnel. The model considers replacing items as they fail, replacing all items at specified intervals, or any combination of these; hence, the problem consists of finding a replacement policy that minimizes the sum of the costs of the items, the cost of group replacements, and the cost of individual replacements at failure. Statistical sampling and probability theory are the customary tools used in such models.

Competition Models

These models are used when two or more individuals make decisions in situations that involve a conflict of interest. The models can be grouped into three categories: decision making under certainty, under risk, and under uncertainty.

The first category applies when the competitor's reaction is known in advance with certainty. In the second case, the competitor's choice is not known with certainty but can be predicted subject to error. In the third case, nothing is known in advance about the competitor's reaction.

There are three major ways of dealing with such problems. Game theory, although a conceptual framework of great importance, provides solutions for only very simple such problems. A second way of dealing with competition models is to apply statistical decision theory, which can be used successfully in most situations. Finally, the technique of gaming (as distinct from game theory) can be brought to bear on problems that do not allow explicit formulation of all alternative actions or outcomes. Gaming is a type of simulation in which the context of the competition is simulated, but the competitors are people, called players. War-gaming has long been applied in military contexts, and the development of management-gaming for the training of executives has recently brought the benefits of this method to industry.

The following example, summarized from Reference (22), illustrates the selection of a strategy by means of a simple model of applied game theory.

Example: Suppose that a man and wife, Ray and Dotty, are planning a camping trip and that Ray likes high altitudes and Dotty likes low altitudes. The camping area is crisscrossed by a network of trails, four running in each direction. Ray and Dotty have agreed that they will camp at a trail junction and that Ray will choose the junction's east-west trail and Dotty will choose the north-south trail. The trail junctions have the altitudes (in thousands of feet) shown in Table 2-3. Ray is attracted to E-W Trail 1, because only this trail includes the highest spot at 7,000 feet. But since he knows that, in this case, Dotty may choose N-S Trail 4, this would result in his camping at 1,000 feet. So he looks for the trail that will not bring him too low: he chooses Trail 3, on which the lowest elevation that he can be forced to endure is 3,000 feet. Likewise, Dotty looks for the N-S Trail that cannot force her too high up, and she selects N-S Trail 2 on which the highest elevation is 3,000.

Table 2-3

		Dotty			
	N-S Trails	1	2	3	4
	E-W Trails				
	1	7	2	5	1
Ray	2	2	2	3	4
	3	5	3	4	4
	4	3	2	1	6

We now note that an interesting fact has occurred: Ray has made sure that he cannot be forced below 3,000 feet, and Dotty has made sure that she cannot be obliged to camp above 3,000 feet, and the result is that the intersection of trails (3, 2) is exactly 3,000 feet. In other words, either player can ensure a 3,000 feet campsite by his own efforts, in the face of a skillful opponent; and he will do better than this if his opponent is careless.

Both competitors use in this case the "minimax" strategy. Dotty minimizes the maximum elevation of the campsite, while Ray minimizes the maximum difference in elevation between the camp and the highest elevation. For a discussion of game theory, see References (21) and (22).

Simulation Techniques

Simulation techniques are used as an alternative to direct analysis of problems. The interrelationships of the model are usually programmed into a computer. For example, in the simulation of a distribution system, the computer is instructed to simulate events such as shipments, customer orders, and inventory receipts. Consequences such as costs, inventory levels, and stockouts are then tabulated.

Simulation is a very powerful tool. Once the simulation model has been designed, it takes little time to run a simulation on a computer. In a few minutes a large processor can evaluate a full year's operation of a 50-warehouse distribution system involving thousands of items.

There are two types of simulation techniques: Monte Carlo and retrospective. In the first technique, the computer generates factors like demand, delayed shipments, and so forth, by computing probabilities or by inspecting probability tables that have been provided in the program. In retrospective simulation, historical data are fed into the machine. The output then shows the results that would have been obtained if the decision criteria had been the ones then programmed into the computer. For further discussion on simulation, see References (23), (24), (25), and (26).

As an example of a simulation, consider the following situation. Assume that we want to know the chance that a hand of cards at bridge will contain all four aces and that we have neither the statistical knowledge to solve the problem analytically nor a pack of cards with which to experiment. One way of approaching the problem would be to place 48 white and four black balls in an urn and take out random samples of 13. Carrying out this experiment a great number of times, we could then take the proportion of times that we draw four black balls as an estimate of the proportion of bridge hands that would contain four aces. This example illustrates that simulation can be used to yield approximate experimental results provided that an adequate representation of the real situation is possible.

Search and Heuristic Methods

In the widest sense, search means an endeavor to find something. Some search is done at random, looking for the desired object here and there indiscriminately. Directed search, on the other hand, makes use of prior information or experience gained during the process to narrow the endeavor down to the areas that most likely contain the desired objective.

The dictionary defines the word heuristic as "serving to discover or to stimulate investigation." In the context of computer and OR work it has been used to denote self-adapting or learning systems, and many authors have applied it as a synonym for directed search.

A number of computational techniques used for example in allocation, dynamic programming, and sequencing models may be considered methods of directed search. There is a large group of problems for which, perhaps, computer capacity is exceeded, computation time is excessive, or no useful analytical techniques are known. In many of these cases directed search methods may be used to obtain solutions for which either the probability of having found the overall optimum may be calculated, or a measure of the difference between the approximate solution that was found and the truly optimal solution may be given.

Heuristic problem-solving routines seem to be very promising for future OR work. They can be used in automatic systems because they are formulated with the necessary exactness and may help to build a bridge between strictly analytical formulations and the kind of operating principles that managers have used habitually.

ORGANIZING AND IMPLEMENTING OR

One may approach the initiation of an OR activity in a company in three ways:

1. Hiring an external consulting group.
2. Training people from the organization or hiring experienced OR specialists.
3. A combination of consultants and company personnel.

Attempting to begin OR activities without at least one experienced person would be a mistake, but hiring a specialist may be difficult, since experience in this field is in great demand. Alternatively, one can begin an OR program by recruiting suitable persons from within the company. They should be competent scientists or engineers, have an interest in OR approaches, and be given some time in which to familiarize themselves thoroughly with new methods. Such a team should comprise at least two people to provide fruitful interaction. In addition to a scientific degree, the team members should have a good knowledge of mathematics and statistics, an interest in finding solutions to complex problems, and, finally, the ability to communicate effectively with persons at all levels of the company.

The most effective approach to initiating an OR activity seems to be to hire an outside group to work with the internal group, until the company team is sufficiently prepared to work under their own guidance—perhaps after two years. Even after this initial period, it is advantageous to continue the use of outside consultants to insure objectivity and breadth of scope.

Eventually, the company OR team might include personnel trained in applied mathematics (OR degrees fall in this category), statistics, a physical science, engineering, economics, sociology, and psychology. Courses for the OR team may be organized within the company with suitable participation and supervision by consultants. There are many textbooks available for this purpose. Also, courses are often available in this field at nearby universities or through university extensions.

The question of where to locate OR in the organizational structure of a company has received a good deal of attention. Obviously, there is no one preferred position for all companies; successful OR departments have reported to the President, the Vice President-Finance, the Controller, the Vice President-Production, and the Vice President-Research and Development, to quote some instances. An increasing number of companies include their OR staff in a management services group together with their computer operations and programming personnel.

As in most situations, experience is an excellent teacher. The second OR project always seems to go more smoothly than the first because the team builds knowledge from the lessons learned in previous tasks. Consequently, great care should be given to the selection and management of a company's initial OR endeavor. If properly chosen and soundly executed, the first effort will foster management confidence in undertaking additional applications of OR for problems of greater complexity. On the other hand, if the beginning project is too broad in scope and sluggish in results, disappointment with OR seems inevitable.

One effective way of selecting a task for a new OR program is to examine the company's major decision areas and to identify the few that would benefit most from an OR study. The first problem selected should be limited in scope and well defined so that the payoff can be easily identified.

There will, of course, be a temptation to use the OR team for emergency trouble-shooting. Although some work in this area will always be done, OR can contribute most significantly to long-range problems. A group preoccupied exclusively with present crises cannot effectively develop methods to prevent crises in the future.

PHASES OF AN OR STUDY

In the execution of an OR project, we may distinguish seven phases. Problem formulation is often the most important phase of a study. It comprises the definition of the main and subobjectives and a listing of the variables that significantly influence the main objective. A definition of uncontrollable variables reflecting the state of nature, the external business environment, competitive actions in the market, governmental regulations, and similar factors is important. Another aspect of this phase is determining the range of prediction in terms of long or short-range planning.

In the second phase, a model is developed. Mathematical, statistical, or logical symbolism is used to describe the restrictions and the objective in terms of the variables. Since a model can only approximate complex situations, great care must be exercised at this stage of the study.

Data collection constitutes the third phase. Selecting data and testing existing data for validity are essential, and sometimes it is necessary to initiate new ways of collecting data. Electronic data-processing equipment is often indispensable for data collection and preparation in larger studies.

Solving the model is the next step. In this phase either the original mathematical model is solved analytically before data have been inserted or the accumulated data are used to arrive at a solution in numerical terms.

Next comes testing the solution to prevent implementations that will not pay off as expected. The testing involves an analysis of the sensitivity of the solution to slight changes in assumptions, external and internal conditions, and level of operation.

Implementation is the following phase. This should be an integral part of any OR study because writing down recommendations without seeing to their application is a waste of time and money. When management has decided to put a new system into operation, line managers connected with the area of study and OR personnel alike must be responsible for the new procedures until they are firmly established.

Monitoring the new system in terms of both its correct use and possible changes in conditions follows after implementation. Of great benefit is a thorough evaluation of the results of operating the new system compared with the results of operating the system that was replaced. Such an evaluation determines the relative success of the study and the usefulness of OR activities. Finally, a one-shot application of OR techniques can hardly have the effect that a continuous monitoring of the system will have. Continuous monitoring guarantees modification of the system as external and internal conditions and demands change over time.

CONCLUSIONS

Small and large companies alike can benefit from the use of OR approaches; the difference is one of size, not of substance. The duration of OR studies in industry typically ranges from a few weeks to a year for single projects, and considerably longer for large integrated systems.

The task of of the OR specialist is, on the basis of his training and the findings of his research, to provide management with the background information necessary to informed decision making. The specialist must be prepared to discuss, defend, and modify his conclusions as new facts come to light, and he must take responsibility for the implementation of the program. Perhaps the single most important factor that in general determines success or failure of OR work is the acceptance and backing which it receives from management.

Management is gradually becoming an applied science. Modern executives are increasingly aware of the benefits that accrue from applying OR and other management services to policy and operating decisions. There is a growing need for an executive function with responsibility for coordinating management services, which have collectively become known as management sciences. An executive who acquires knowledge in this field may help his company to become as advanced in its management systems as in its technological systems.

Suggested Further Reading

General References

(1) Ackoff, Russell L., and Rivett, Patrick, *A Manager's Guide to Operations Research*, John Wiley & Sons, New York, 1963.
An excellent, easily-readable, 100-page book.

(2) Bursk, Edward C., and Chapman, John F., *New Decision-Making Tools for Managers,* Mentor (#MQ624), 1963.
A collection of 17 nonmathematical *Harvard Business Review* reprints, including applications to finance, marketing, product strategy, and production.

(3) Churchman, C. W., Ackoff, R. L., and Arnoff, E. L., *Introduction to Operations Research,* John Wiley & Sons, New York, 1957.
Discussion of a variety of operations research situations in the firm, with emphasis on implementation of studies.

(4) di Roccaferrera, Giuseppe M. Ferrero, *Operations Research Models for Business and Industry,* South-Western Publishing Company, 1964.
Basic treatment of statistical analysis, mathematical programming, queueing theory, and Monte Carlo. Contains much of the required math.

(5) Hillier, Frederick S., and Lieberman, Gerald J., *Introduction to the Techniques of Operations Research,* Holden-Day, San Francisco, August, 1967.
Quite full treatment of many operations research techniques. Requires basic college math.

(6) Manne, Alan S., *Economic Analysis for Business Decisions,* McGraw-Hill Book Company, New York, 1961.
A simplified treatment of several operations research techniques, through the use of descriptive examples.

(7) Miller, David W., and Starr, Martin K., *Executive Deicisions and Operations Research,* Prentice-Hall, Englewood Cliffs, New Jersey, 1964.
Comprehensive coverage of problems and techniques. Requires little knowledge of math.

(8) Saaty, Thomas L., *Mathematical Methods of Operations Research,* McGraw-Hill Book Company, New York, 1959.
A comprehensive summary of mathematical techniques used in operations research. Knowledge of calculus is assumed.

(9) Sasieni, Maurice, Yaspan, Arthur, and Friedman, Lawrence, *Operations Research—Methods and Problems,* John Wiley & Sons, New York, 1959.
A good basic text. May require a math refresher for some of the problems.

(10) Sisson, Roger L., and Sieber, Harry F., *Management Science Selections,* Data Processing Digest, 1965.
Brief, nonmathematical descriptions of several operations research topics.

Probability and Statistics

(11) Freund, John E., *Mathematical Statistics,* Prentice-Hall, Englewood Cliffs, New Jersey, 1962.
A good introduction to probability theory and statistics.

(12) Moroney, M. J., *Facts from Figures,* Penguin Books, 1956.
An excellent nonmathematical introduction to some basic statistical concepts.

Inventory Theory

(13) Arrow, K. T., Karlin, S., and Scarf, H., *Studies in the Mathematical Theory of Inventory and Production*, Stanford University Press, 1958.
A technical treatment of mathematical inventory models.

(14) Whitin, T. M., *The Theory of Inventory Management*, Princeton University Press, 1953.
One of the early comprehensive treatments of inventory problems.

Linear Programming

(15) Dantzig, George B., *Linear Programming and Extensions*, Princeton University Press, 1963.
Possibly the most comprehensive exposition on mathematical programming and related areas. Many examples and problems. The necessary theory is developed on the assumed knowledge of basic calculus.

(16) Gass, Saul I., *Linear Programming*, McGraw-Hill Book Company, New York, 1958.
One of the earliest full treatments of linear programming. Requires a knowledge of matrix algebra.

Dynamic Programming

(17) Howard, Ronald A., *Dynamic Programming and Markov Processes*, MIT Press, Cambridge, Massachusetts, 1960.
A 125-page book describing optimization by policy iteration in a discrete Markov process. Requires a knowledge of matrix algebra.

Queueing Theory

(18) Cox, D. R., and Smith, Walter L., *Queues*, Methuen's Monographs, London, 1961.
A brief treatment of several queueing situations. Requires knowledge of mathematical statistics.

(19) Morse, Philip M., *Queues, Inventory and Maintenance*, John Wiley & Sons, New York, 1963.
A thorough introduction to the theory of waiting line problems.

Sequencing Models

(20) Martino, R. L., *Project Management and Control*, Volumes 1, 2, 3, American Management Association, New York, 1964.

A very clear and detailed exposition of PERT scheduling and control techniques.

Game Theory

(21) Chernoff, Herman, and Moses, Lincoln E., *Elementary Decision Theory*, John Wiley & Sons, New York, 1959.
Introduction to statistical formulations for making decisions under uncertain conditions.

(22) Williams, J. D., *The Compleat Strategyst*, McGraw-Hill Book Company, New York, 1954.
An excellent nontechnical treatment of competitive strategies.

Simulation

(23) Conway, R. W., Johnson, B. M., and Maxwell, W. L., "Some Problems of Digital Systems Simulation," *Management Science*, Volume 6, No. 1, October, 1959.
A short description of some practical aspects in the use of simulation techniques.

(24) Conway, R. W., "Some Tactical Problems in Digital Simulation," *Management Science*, Volume 10, No. 1, October, 1963.

(25) Markowitz, H. M., Hausner, B., and Carr, H. W., *SIMSCRIPT: A Simulation Programming Language*, Prentice-Hall, Englewood Cliffs, New Jersey, April, 1963.
Programming manual for the SIMSCRIPT language. Contains a description of a generalized simulation model.

(26) Tocher, K. D., *The Art of Simulation*, D. Van Nostrand & Company, Princeton, New Jersey, 1963.
A monograph on the ideas underlying simulation models. A good introduction to this technique.

3 | Decision Models, Part 1

by James C. Emery

Man's ability to perform arithmetic calculations has probably expanded in recent years at a more rapid rate than any other form of technology (with the possible exception of his ability to blow himself up). Since the early 1940s, raw computational speed has increased by (at least) a factor of ten million, while the cost per calculation has decreased by considerably more than a thousandfold. Rapid progress has also been made in other aspects of information processing—e.g., input/output, data storage, and communications—but not nearly to the same extent as internal processing speeds.

In light of these technical developments, it is instructive to examine the various ways in which information processing can be applied within a management information system. The various applications can be classified (somewhat arbitrarily) as (1) routine data processing, (2) analytical decision models, and (3) simulation models.

Transaction Processing

Conventional data processing applications primarily deal with routine transaction processing. A transaction typically enters the system as a condensed description of such external events as the receipt of a sales order or check from a customer, adding a new item to inventory, or the receipt of material from a supplier. Transactions may also be triggered by the passage of time, resulting, for example, in the accrual of a depreciation charge for the accounting period.

Output from such processing consists of various working documents that serve the operating activities of the organization. Examples include invoices, checks, shipping papers, replenishment orders, and schedules. In addition, periodic reports are prepared on the basis of transaction activity (e.g., an income statement) and the resulting record status (e.g., a balance sheet).

Any successful MIS must be built upon the solid foundation of a transaction processing system. It is at this operations level that the bulk of data enter the system, are processed, and are then transformed into outputs. Furthermore, higher-level tactical decisions, such as those dealing with scheduling or inventory control, rely heavily on data inputs coming from transaction processing. Even high-level strategic decision making depends to some extent on periodic reports based on transaction processing.

Nevertheless, routine processing is not an ideal application for computers, since it tends not to exploit that part of information processing technology that has shown the greatest progress. Most routine applications involve reading and sorting of large files, but require relatively little internal computation (although exceptions obviously exist). Furthermore, a significant portion of the cost of implementing and operating routine processing systems involves high-priced labor in the form of system designers, programmers, operators, keypunchers, and so forth. It is fairly well understood by now that conventional transaction processing systems yield fairly marginal returns except in the relatively rare cases dealing with large volumes of repetitive transactions.

Current technology favors those applications that more fully exploit the capacity of the central processor. Such applications can often be combined with transaction processing. For example, the analysis of transaction data for management purposes (such as summarizing sales by product group), or handling special-purpose inquiries, can sometimes be incorporated within the routine file updating programs. The central processor in these cases is used as a filter between the detailed transaction data and management. This more sophisticated use of the computer begins to capitalize on the great efficiency of internal processing. The real payoff often comes, however, when the computer is used more directly in the decision process than merely supplying a decision maker with digested information.

Analytical Decision Models

Considerable effort has been spent in applying computers directly to the decision making process. Linear programming models, for example, have been used extensively, particularly in the petroleum industry. Some of these models can tax the internal computational capacity of even the largest computer.

The aim of the model builder is to describe the problem at hand in a mathematical form that permits the calculation of the *optimum* decision out of all possible alternative decisions. For example, one may wish to find the inventory ordering quantity that minimizes inventory costs, or the schedule that maximizes the value of production. The plan calculated is then executed in the real world, and hopefully leads to the results predicted by the model.

Three requirements must be met in order to develop an optimizing model: (1) It must be possible to duplicate the real world in mathematical form with sufficient accuracy that results from the model make sense, (2) there must exist an explicit measure of the objective to be optimized, and (3) there must be available a computationally feasible procedure for finding the optimum solution. Failure to meet any one of these requirements precludes the use of an optimizing model, and one must then be content with other means of decision making that normally involve more direct human participation.

One of the simplest optimizing models is the one used to calculate the economic order quantity (EOQ) of an inventory item. We can use it to illustrate the three requirements for optimization.

Expressing the problem in mathematical form. In the classical version of the EOQ model, only carrying cost and reordering cost are considered. Inventory is assumed to be received in a fixed-size order quantity, q, and is then withdrawn (e.g., sold or issued to production) in response to demands that arrive at a constant rate. It can be seen from Fig. 3-1 that the average inventory under these circumstances will be one-half the order quantity, or $q/2$. If it costs C dollars per year to carry one item in stock (which includes interest on the capital invested in inventory, incremental storage cost, obsolescence, etc.), the annual carrying cost is therefore $q \cdot C/2$.

There is assumed to be a fixed cost, R, of placing each replenishment order. Reordering cost includes such elements as the cost of the data processing to prepare a requisition; the cost of receiving, material handling, and inspection associated with each reorder; and setup costs (in the case of self-manufactured items) required to produce a reorder quantity. The expected number of orders per year is proportional to the total forecasted annual usage of the item, F, and is inversely proportional to the order quantity. Thus, the orders per year equals F/q, and the annual reorder cost is $R \cdot F/q$.

We have now developed a simple model of the inventory item. The total annual inventory cost of the item, T, can be expressed in the following equation:

$$T = \text{Annual Carrying Cost} + \text{Annual Reordering Cost} = q \cdot C/2 + R \cdot F/q$$

The cost in this equation is a function of the order quantity q (as well as C, R, and F). The values of C, R, and F are not subject to change—at least

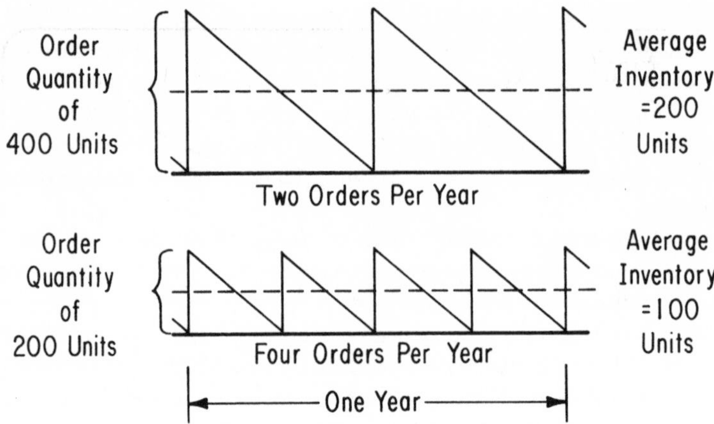

Fig. 3-1. Effect of order size and orders per year on average inventory level.

not as far as inventory decisions are concerned—and are therefore viewed as *parameters* of the model. The only *decision variable* subject to optimization is the order quantity q.

Determine an objective to optimize. The objective of the inventory model is quite simple: to minimize total annual inventory cost. The above equation for T expresses this cost as a function of decision variable q and parameters C, R, and F; it is said to be the *objective function* of the model.

Calculate the optimum decision. The simple inventory model permits the use of a well-known minimization procedure based on elementary calculus. Using this procedure it is possible to show that the value of q that minimizes annual inventory cost is equal to

$$\sqrt{2 \cdot F \cdot R/C}.$$

This is shown graphically in Fig. 3-2.

Total inventory cost is the sum of carrying cost and reordering cost. Suppose that annual usage is 800 units, reordering cost is $10 per order, and carrying cost is $0.40 per unit. If orders are placed for 200 units four times a year, the annual ordering cost will be $40; the annual carrying cost will be 200 X .40/2, or $40; and total cost will be $80. Total annual cost for other order quantities can be calculated similarly. It can be seen from the graph that the minimum cost occurs at an order quantity of 200 units. This agrees with the formula,

$$\text{EOQ} = \sqrt{\frac{2 \times \text{Forecasted Usage} + \text{Reorder Cost}}{\text{Annual Carrying Cost per Unit}}}$$

$$= \sqrt{\frac{2 \times 800 \times 10}{.40}} = 200$$

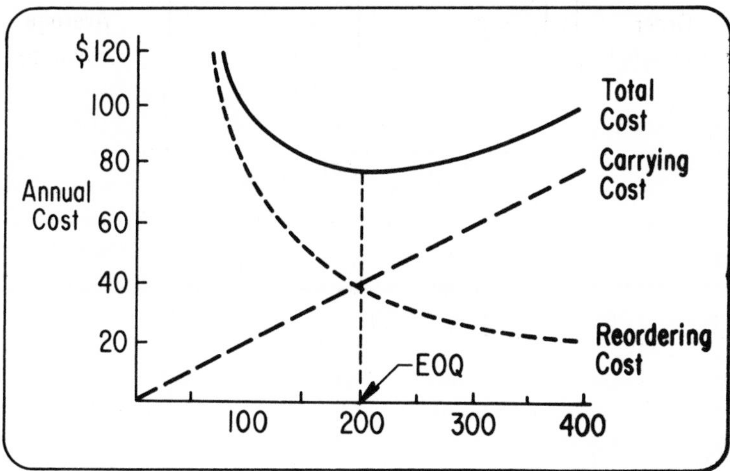

Fig. 3-2. Inventory costs as function of order quantity.

Linear Programming Model

Linear programming is probably the most widely used of the optimizing techniques. The technique requires that the objective function be expressed in linear form, which means that a change in a decision variable brings about a proportional change in the objective function. This implies, for example, that the profit per unit of an item being scheduled remains fixed over the range of production allowed by the scheduling model.

Suppose that we are interested in scheduling the production of two handmade products, rugs and blankets. The profit for each rug is $6, and for each blanket it is $9. The problem is to determine the schedule that maximizes profit. The decision variables are thus the quantities to produce of each of the products. Let x_1 represent the number of rugs scheduled, and x_2 the number of blankets. The objection function is therefore Profit = $6x_1 + 9x_2$.

The problem as it is now written is clearly incomplete, because otherwise one could make an unlimited profit by producing either product without limit. We must introduce *constraints* on the decision variables that recognize restrictions on production capacity.

Suppose that production of rugs and blankets requires skills of weavers and spinners. For a given scheduling period (a week, say) we have 1800 hours of weavers' time and 300 hours of spinners' time. Each product requires 2 hours per unit of weaving; while a rug or blanket requires .2 and .5 hours, respectively, of spinning. The capacity constraints can then be expressed as

Weavers: $2.0 \cdot X_1 + 2.0 \cdot X_2 \leqslant 1800$

Spinners: $0.2 \cdot X_1 + 0.5 \cdot X_2 \leqslant 300$

Two comments are in order regarding the constraints. First, the constraints, like the objective function, are linear equations (since each product requires a fixed unit capacity of each type of labor); this is a requirement of linear programming models. Second, the *inequalities*—in this example, a less-than-or-equal ($\leqslant$) relationship—express the fact that it is only necessary not to exceed the fixed capacity constraints; the model permits the use of only a portion of either resource (although in this problem it is not optimal to leave any unused resources).

Within the constraints, it can be shown that the optimal schedule is to produce 500 rugs and 400 blankets. This will result in the optimum profit of \$6,600. (See Fig. 3-3.)

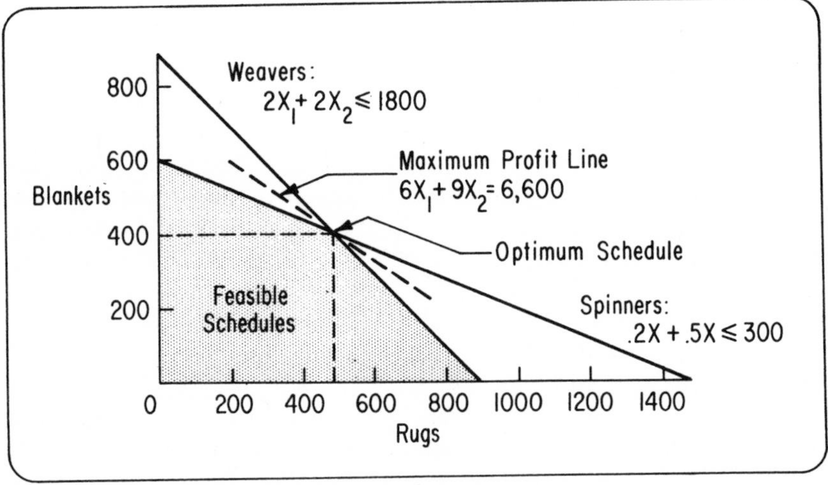

Fig. 3-3. Production scheduling using linear programming.

Requirements for Optimization

With these simple examples as illustrations, we can now examine in more detail the three requirements for using an optimizing model.

1. Expressing the problem in mathematical form. The first requirement is that the problem be expressible in mathematical form. Thus, one must develop equations that relate the consequences of actions (e.g., annual inventory cost) to decision variables (e.g., order quantity) and uncontrollable parameters (e.g., cost per reorder). In general form,

Consequences = f(Decision Variables, Parameters), where f(. . .) means "function of" or "dependence on."

The nature of the mathematical expression can vary from a quite simple equation (as in the inventory model) to exceedingly complex functions. Some of the complexities that the analyst must face are as follows.

Uncertainty. Often there exists considerable uncertainty about parameter values. In an inventory problem, for example, sales forecasts may be subject to fairly wide error. Even cost parameters, such as reordering cost, may be known only within a range of possible values. If the uncertainty significantly affects predicted results, one must consider introducing a *probabilistic* estimate in place of a single *deterministic* estimate.

The "pessimistic," "most likely," and "optimistic" estimates used in some PERT systems provide one way of representing probabilistic estimates. Uncertainty can also be represented in the form of a probability distribution having specified characteristics (such as mean and standard deviation). In a queueing model concerned with waiting lines in a supermarket, for example, we could represent the average interval between the arrival of customers at the checkout counter by a probability distribution of the sort shown in Fig. 3-4.

(Empirical observations [Fig. 3-4] can be made to determine the time at which customers arrive at a checkout queue. The time intervals between arrivals can then be represented in the form of a probability distribution [bottom figure]. The above distribution indicates, for example, that in 75% of the cases the interval between successive arrivals is less than 40 seconds.)

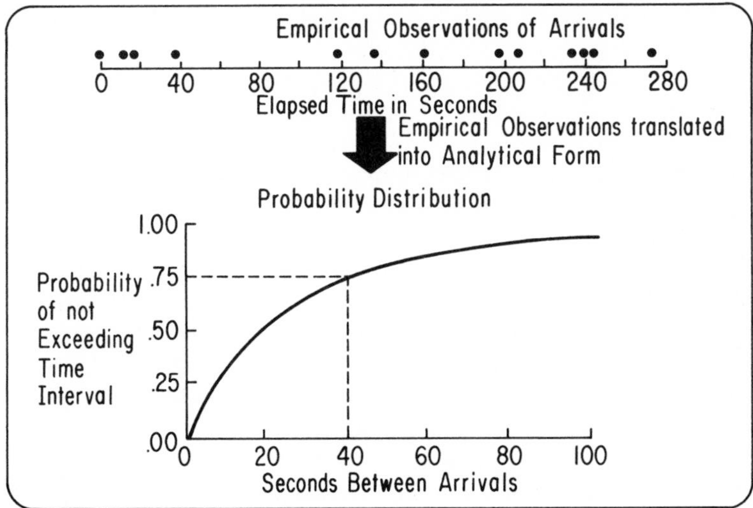

Fig. 3-4. Distribution of arrival intervals at checkout counter.

Large number of decision variables or parameters. Models often have many more variables and parameters than the simple examples given earlier. For instance, in a large scheduling model there may be several thousand decision variables, one for each product scheduled. There may similarly be a large number of parameters, such as individual product forecasts, processing times, capacity limitations, costs, and the like.

Constraints. We have seen from the linear programming example that a limitation on a physical resource such as labor can impose a constraint on the decision variables. Constraints can arise in other ways as well. For example, a decision variable may be constrained to fall within a given range over which the parameters of the model remain valid. In the previous linear programming example, the production of rugs might be limited to, say, 300 units because it is judged that sales cannot exceed that level at a price of $6 per unit. (This constraint would then shift the optimal schedule and thereby reduce the optimum profit to $6,120 from the unconstrained—but unobtainable—level of $6,6000.)

In other cases the underlying logic of the problem may constrain decision variables to nonnegative values (so that a negative output of a product cannot be produced, say) or to only integer values (so that 1.37 warehouses will not be built at site A, for instance). In still other models, a constraint may represent a policy decision rather than a physical restriction—as in a financial model that limits bank borrowing to, say, $5 million even though additional bank loans are available (but perhaps at undue cost or risk).

2. Determining the objective function. In the simple inventory and scheduling examples, finding a suitable objective function presented no problem. In many cases, however, the objective is by no means obvious. The problem arises because of the multidimensional nature of organizational goals: it is usually difficult, or even impossible, to find a reasonable *single* objective that can be optimized; it is particularly difficult in the case of higher-level decisions. And yet, optimization demands that a single objective function exist. (An operations researcher rebels at such policy statements as "Our goal is to provide the maximum possible service at the minimum possible cost.")

Even in the case of profit-making organizations, a single overall objective cannot be specified. Companies often devote some of their resources to such noneconomic goals as the support of education or the arts (although cynics can no doubt always find a profit motivation behind any corporate act). But even if we were bent solely on maximizing long-range profit, we would then be faced with the impossible task of actually measuring it. Operationally, we can only measure short-term (e.g., one year) profit as determined through a whole host of (often arbitrary) accounting conventions. In the absence of a single (measurable) objective, profit-making firms create supplementary goals such as growth in sales, share of markets and cost ratios.

Lower-level managers are also typically faced with multiple objectives. A plant manager, for example, concerns himself with production levels and costs, but he must also consider quality, safety, labor relations, community relations, and other "intangibles." The same sort of problem persists at the lowest decision-making level. For example, the objective in inventory control is usually not merely to minimize costs; it must normally also consider the risk of having stockouts.

If one can find a suitable trade-off among multiple goals it is then logically possible to optimize a single composite objective. For example, in dealing with an inventory problem we might be able to determine the cost of having a stockout (which includes such costs as customer ill will, disruption of production, and special costs of handling expedited orders). Knowing the trade-off between cost and service, we could then develop a composite cost objective to be minimized. Unfortunately, determining such explicit trade-offs tends to become increasingly difficult as one deals with higher-level problems. It is probably not feasible, for example, to obtain a general consensus about the appropriate trade-off between plant safety and profit.

In the absence of explicit trade-offs among objectives, one can introduce constraints on the objectives for which trade-offs are not available. The problem then becomes one of optimizing—to be more precise, *sub*optimizing—the remaining objectives. This approach is based on the perfectly sensible proposition that overall results are improved if one is as efficient as possible with respect to the unconstrained objectives, even if the constrained objectives are not set at their "true," but unknown, optimum value. The resulting suboptimization leads to a situation (called a *Pareto* optimum) in which performance cannot be improved without relaxing at least one of the constrained objectives.

Numerous examples exist of this approach. In an inventory problem with unknown stockout costs, one can minimize carrying and reordering costs subject to a maximum frequency of stockouts. In a financial model it is usually not possible to establish a trade-off between the cost of a bank loan and its risk, but it may be possible to minimize financing cost subject to an upper limit on short-term bank debt. These examples demonstrate that there tends not be a clear distinction between the objective function of a model and its constraints, since a constraint is often introduced in order to avoid the problem of specifying explicit trade-offs.

3. Calculating the optimum decision. The final requirement for optimization is the ability to manipulate the mathematical equations that form the model in order to determine the values of the decision variables that optimize the objective function. In some cases the manipulation is done analytically by hand. This was the means used, for example, in deriving the optimum order quantity from the simple inventory model. Once the analytic solution is available (such as

$$\mathrm{EOQ} = \sqrt{2 \cdot \mathrm{F} \cdot \mathrm{R/C}}),$$

a computer can then be used to calculate the optimum decision in a given case with specified parameter values.

The size and complexity of many models make it infeasible to derive general analytical solutions that merely require evaluation in a specific case. It may still be possible, however, to calculate the optimum solution using a suitable arithmetic procedure. Problems of this type can involve a great deal of computation, and almost always demand the use of a computer. Many of the best known optimization procedures, such as those used in linear programming, are of this type.

Despite the availability of very large modern computers, there exist a great many decisions that cannot be optimized because no computationally feasible procedure is currently available. This may be true even though both a suitable model and objective function are available. Certain scheduling problems fall into this class. For example, an integer programming model (a linear programming model in which all decisions variables must be integers) has been developed for scheduling a job shop, but it involves far too many variables to be computationally feasible for even small shops.

The feasibility of a given optimizing procedure depends on the state of the art in both computer technology and computational methods. As computers grow faster and bigger, and as more efficient computational procedures are developed, a wider and wider class of problems become tractable. Nevertheless, there will always remain still larger problems beyond the threshold of feasibility.

4 | Decision Models, Part 2

by James C. Emery

The Model as a Compromise

The requirements for an optimizing model are obviously very stringent. In fact, they can never be met completely. The real world is far too complex to be described faithfully with a series of equations; our objectives are far too ill-defined and diffuse to be captured precisely in the form of an explicit objective function; and the resulting model, even if it could be constructed, would present insuperable computational difficulty. It is therefore necessary to develop models that only approximate the real world in order to make them mathematically and computationally feasible. The real art in model making lies in the analyst's ability to find the simplest model that nevertheless captures the essence of the problem at hand.

There are numerous ways in which a model can be simplified. One way is to ignore the uncertainty that surrounds the estimate of a parameter by simply using a single fixed value. Another way is to use a relatively simple mathematical relationship in place of the much more complex relationship that may actually exist. Linear relationships are particularly popular because of the great computational efficiency of linear programming procedures. The world is not really linear, but frequently it is nearly enough linear within a restricted range of the decision variables that one is willing to give up some accuracy in order to gain substantial computational efficiency.

The scope and detail of a model govern the number of variables included in the mathematical representation. This in turn affects the complexity and

EDITOR'S NOTE: Reprinted with permission of Datamation®, copyright, Technical Publishing Co., Barrington, Illinois 60010, 1970.

computational requirements of the model. In order to make the model manageable one must normally deal (more or less independently) with small fragments of the total problem. It is also usually necessary to compress detail by dealing largely with aggregate variables.

Consider, for example, the case of scheduling the production within a multiplant firm. If significant interactions exist among the plants—if they supply one another with material, say, or if they share common resources or markets—then there may be substantial benefits from some degree of centralized scheduling. A detailed corporate model, in which each product at each plant is scheduled individually, would normally not be practical; instead, one would have to break the problem down and develop separate plant—or, more likely subplant—models that are suboptimized independently.

In order to partially *integrate* the separate models, it may be possible to develop an aggregate corporate model that sets constraints or adjusts the objective functions of the lower-level models. The process can even be repeated (or *iterated*) as a means of converging toward the corporate-wide optimum schedule. Hierarchies of linked models of this sort are not very common, but there is considerable current interests in extending their use. Their attractiveness lies in their ability to converge toward a global optimum through a series of independent (and hence simplified) suboptimized models.

Use of Heuristics

It is often possible to introduce nonoptimal simplifying procedures to reduce complexity and computational time. For example, in a multiwarehouse inventory model it may be very difficult to optimize the total distribution of items among all warehouses. A complete optimization would have to take account of such detailed matters as the relative cost of shipment by full versus less-than-truckload quantities.

Rather than considering this issue during the optimization calculation, it may be legitimate to use the LTL rates in a distribution model, and then to round up to a full truckload if a shipment approaches that quantity. One might, for instance, use the rule "When W (the fraction of a full truckload represented by a given shipment) exceeds 0.7, adjust all individual quantities of the items comprising the shipment by the factor 1/W." Such a rule will certainly not result in an optimum distribution, but it may be good enough to justify the very great simplification that this brings about.

Many large models find it convenient to use "common sense" rules, or heuristics, of this type. (A model builder may be a heuristic programmer without knowing it—much like the man who discovered at age 60 that he had been speaking prose all his life.) Indeed, for certain models for which a computationally feasible optimizing procedure is not available, the entire computational process may be based on such heuristics. This has been done, for example, in warehouse location and truck scheduling problems. The test of a heuristic procedure is not whether it yields optimal solutions—it does not—but whether it provides decisions that are superior to the best alternative approach.

Man-Machine Decision Systems

There exists a wide class of problems that cannot be formalized to the extent required to develop optimizing models or even explicit heuristic procedures. The preparation of annual operating budgets, for example, entails so many subjective judgments that its complete formalization is out of the question. On the other hand, budgeting deals with large masses of quantitative data that can easily swamp a human decision maker. The objective in the design of a *man-machine* decision system is to draw upon the best capabilities of both man and computer in dealing with problems too ill-defined and complex to be handled well by either partner alone.

Man in such a system normally has the task of conceiving of alternatives (for which he employs his own informal heuristics). The computer then predicts the consequences of each proposed alternative. It does this on the basis of a model.[1] For example, a planner may propose a budget that calls for an increase in marketing expenditures that he expects will result in, say, a 10 percent increase in sales. A model can be developed that considers such things as existing machine and labor capacity, current inventories, and various relationships among production volume and cost. On the basis of this model the consequences of the proposed budget can then be calculated in terms of cash flow requirements, additional labor requirements, changes in production costs, a projected income statement, and similar measures.

With such a system, the decision maker can exercise his judgment in assessing the relative merits of different alternatives. The models may not relieve him from the difficult task of making (implicit) trade-offs among goals (risk versus expected payoff, for example), but it at least provides him with predicted consequences that would otherwise be extremely difficult for him to estimate.

If the predicted consequences are unsuitable in some way (e.g., cash requirements exceed safe borrowing limits), he can revise the plan (e.g., lower marketing expenditure) in a way that he hopes will result in improved predicted consequences. The search for an improved plan can continue until the decision maker believes that further search will not yield sufficient benefits to justify its cost. To the extent that the decision maker is correct in this judgment, the plan obtained by the man-machine process can be viewed as the optimum that recognizes the cost of the decision process itself.

The effectiveness of a man-machine process is usually enhanced if it is implemented in a quick-response on-line system. The most obvious advantage is that it permits many more alternatives to be explored; it may also permit the man to retain a better grasp of the problem between evaluations. However, in the case of a complex model that requires extensive computing or protracted assessment by the man, an on-line system may offer relatively little advantage.

Sensitivity Studies

Very often a decision maker is less interested in the "optimum" solution from a model (which of course is only an approximation to the true optimum) than he is in gaining some insight into the effect on the objective function of changes in the model. A *sensitivity study* is aimed at providing a measure of the incremental effect (i.e., the *sensitivity*) of changes in the model.

The simplest type of change is to modify the value of a parameter. For example, one may wish to study the effects of a change in sales forecasts in an inventory model, the probability distribution of arrival times in a queueing model, or the capacity constraints in a scheduling model. In certain types of models sensitivity data of this sort can be obtained as a by-product of the optimization procedure. For example, the calculations used in solving linear programs yield directly the so-called *shadow prices* of the resources allocated by the model. The shadow price of a resource gives the incremental effect of a (small) change in the total amount of the resource available.[2] If sensitivity data cannot be obtained as a by-product of the optimization calculation, it may be feasible (but clearly more expensive) to introduce a changed parameter value into the model, recalculate the optimum solution, and then compare the two solutions.

More basic, structural changes to a model can also be studied, but with considerably more effort. For example, one may wish to explore the effect on the accuracy of a model of introducing simplifications of the sort discussed earlier. If it turns out, say, that the use of deterministic estimates for processing times in a scheduling model gives essentially the same result as probabilistic estimates, then there is little advantage in using the more elaborate version.

Sensitivity studies are employed in several different ways. For one thing, the construction of the model itself can often be aided by such studies. The model builder may first develop a very simple model, and then proceed to test which of the variables and parameters appear to be most sensitive. He can then expand and elaborate the more crucial parts of the model. This process can continue in hierarchical fashion until the total model is suitable enough for the purpose at hand.

Sensitivity studies are also very useful in interpreting the results of a model. The model is always imperfect to some degree, and therefore for important decisions it is imperative to impose human judgment on the model's solution.[3] Judgment is needed to assess such things as the effect of uncertainty in the parameter estimates and the effect of ignoring in the model certain intangible issues. Sensitivity studies provide valuable aid in such assessments. They can, for example, indicate the risk (i.e., the potential penalty) if sales turn out to be 50 percent less than planned, or the quantifiable cost of reducing inventory stockout probability from .10 to .05.

Finally, sensitivity data sometimes help in making higher-level decisions that impose constraints on lower-level decisions. For example, the shadow prices from a linear programming model for scheduling a refinery are useful in estimating the payoff from expanding plant capacity or shifting some production to an alternate facility. If the higher-level decision is formalized (in the form of a capital budgeting model or a corporate scheduling model, for example), sensitivity data provide the primary means of linking, or integrating, the hierarchy of models.

Simulation Models

The models discussed so far have all been of analytical form in which the objective function and constraints are expressed in a series of equations. With such a model, the consequences of a given alternative can be determined by evaluating the equations using the specified values of the decision variables. In some cases the evaluation is trivial, while in others it may be exceedingly difficult. (The determination of the *optimum* set of decision variables is still another matter, and may or may not be possible.)

In contrast to this, a simulation model does not allow the direct evaluation of the consequences of an alternative. A simulation model duplicates, more or less faithfully, the actual events that occur over time in the real world for a given set of parameters and decision variables. Certain consequences stem from the events that take place during the course of the simulation. The consequences are then presented to a decision maker, usually in highly aggregated form,[4] to aid him in predicting the consequences of implementing the specified alternative in the real world. Thus, a simulation model is run and the consequences are then *measured*, not *evaluated.*

Each event included in a simulator may entail the generation of a "random" variable drawn from a probability distribution provided as part of the parameters of the problem. Examples of random variables include daily demands or replenishment lead times in an inventory model, processing times in a scheduling model, and time intervals between arrivals in a queueing model.

Simulation models have been used widely. Inventory simulators, for example, are often used to test inventory policies. One might wish to test the consequences of a given order point and order quantity for an item. The events simulated include the arrival of withdrawal demands, the ordering of replenishment stock, and the receipt of stock. [See Fig. 4-1. The simulator duplicates the events in an inventory system. At the beginning of the simulation, decision variables Q (order quantity) and OP (order point) are read, along with cost parameters, demand and lead time parameters, and parameters that specify the number of days to be simulated (END). Some of the variables included in the model to keep track of current status (e.g., ON-HAND) are shown in capital letters. The model assumes that stock is issued until it is exhausted; after that further demand during a stockout condition is lost forever (i.e., no backorders are allowed). In this simulation time moves in equal increments from one day to the next. Each day's demand is handled in the aggregate, rather than treating separately individual orders that arrive during a day. Results at the end of the simulation are printed; they would include such measures as total cost (per year, say), ordering cost, carrying cost, and number of lost sales due to stockouts.] The consequences measured may include the cost of carrying inventory, cost of replenishing stock, and the number of stockouts. More detailed data, such as the average customer delay due to stockouts, may also be obtained.

Simulation models have also been widely applied to queueing problems. In choosing the number of checkout counters to provide in a supermarket, for example, one can simulate such events as the arrival of customers at the counter and the servicing of customers by the checkout clerk. Consequences might be measured by the cost of clerks, average wait time, maximum wait time, and the like.

The principal advantage of simulation is that it can cope with problems far too complicated to handle analytically. Analytical models are quite limited in dealing with complex relationships (particularly when probability distributions are involved), while simulation models are not. A simulation model can be developed for virtually any quantifiable problem; the cost of developing and running the model is the only serious limitation.

Simulator Versatility

Consider, for example, the versatility of an inventory simulator. It can deal with a variety of inventory schemes, such as an order point-order quantity, minmax, or periodic reorder policy. Demands and delivery lead times can be represented by any type of probability distribution. Complex backordering and expediting rules can be included. In short, any variety that exists in a real-world inventory system can be duplicated (at a cost) in a simulator.

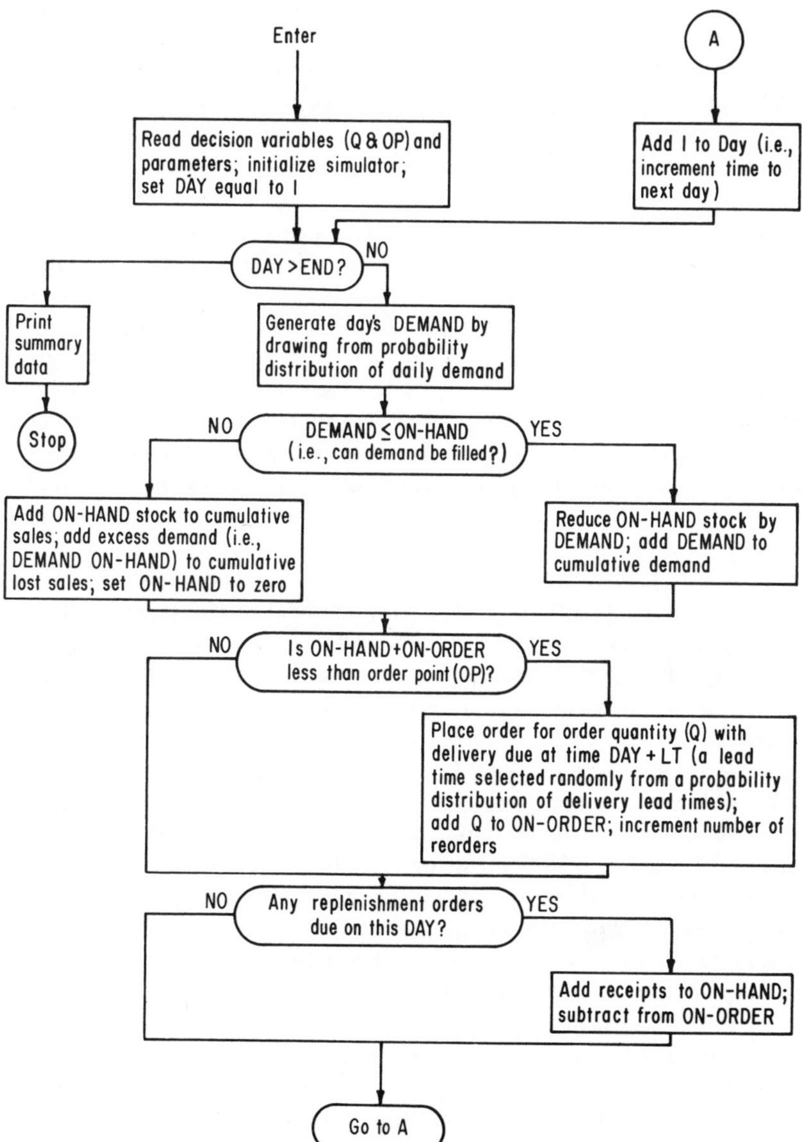

Fig. 4-1. Logic of an inventory simulator.

Simulation models, with rare exception, depend utterly on the computational capacity of a computer. They typically involve a large number of variables and deal with a large number—perhaps many thousands—of simulated events in order to gain greater statistical validity in measuring consequences. Dealing with each event may entail considerable complexity, such as the handling of an inventory demand or the determination of job priority in a job shop scheduling model. Clearly, models of this sort are only feasible when implemented on a computer.

The task of developing a simulator involves the identification of the significant events to be simulated and the specification of the logic required to handle each event. The logic is then expressed in some computer language. This is often facilitated by the use of a language specifically designed for simulation problems, such as GPSS or SIMSCRIPT. These languages make it especially easy to program (often, unfortunately, at a considerable penalty in computer efficiency) such tasks as the generation of random variables, keeping track of arrivals and departures from queues, and handling the *clocking* mechanism that controls the advancing of simulated time (either from event to event or in equal time increments).

A simulation model is typically used in the same way as a nonoptimizing analytical model—namely, as a predictor of the consequences of a proposed alternative. The search for the best alternative normally draws on a human decision maker to propose alternatives and evaluate consequences. In some cases, however, it may be possible to develop heuristics for doing this without direct human intervention.

The question often arises in model building whether one should develop an analytical or simulation model. An analytical model is generally to be preferred if a satisfactory one can be found. For one thing, it is often much cheaper to develop and operate than a simulation model. Furthermore, it provides useful insights about relationships among variables, and the computational procedure used to find the optimum (if one exists) often yields valuable sensitivity data. A simulation model, on the other hand, is often *too* life-like: underlying relationships are difficult to perceive in the jumble of simulated events, and random variation introduced to duplicate reality often makes it difficult to distinguish significant effects from mere random noise. And finally, an optimizing analytical model provides a specific decision, while a simulation model normally does not.

Simulation can thus be viewed as a brute force technique that one may resort to in the absence of a feasible analytical approach. The fact is, however, that very often appropriate analytical techniques are *not* available. The development of an analytical model may in many circumstances call for too many compromises with reality. The resulting "optimum" obtained from such a model is only optimum with respect to the alternatives permitted by the model; it may be a long way from the true optimum. A simulation model can be made as realistic as one is willing to pay for. In general it will not be possible to find the optimum solution from such a model, but it may yield a decision that is superior to the one obtained from an unrealistic analytical models. (See Fig. 4-2.)

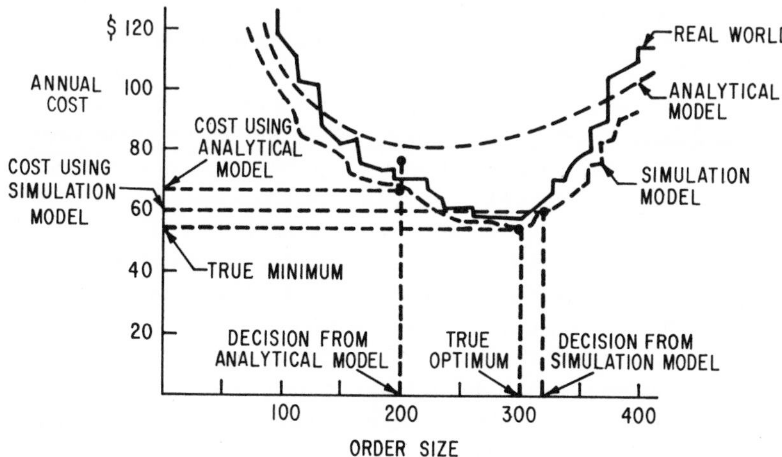

Fig. 4-2. Results achieved with optimizing versus simulation models for inventory.

Data for Decision Models

The implementor of a decision model must always face the critical task of obtaining such input parameters as forecasts, processing times, and costs. These data can come from ad hoc sources, or they can come from a direct link of the model with an on-going data base that is updated through routine transaction processing.

Ad hoc sources offer the great advantage of simplicity. No formal link need be developed to provide inputs in the precise form required by the model. Instead, the link is made informally by an analyst. The data may be collected specifically to support the model, or they may come originally from the existing data processing system. In any case, the analyst (or decision maker) performs any manipulation necessary to transform input data into the coding, format, sequence, and content demanded by the model.

Ad hoc data sources are certainly appropriate for one-shot or infrequent decision making. Plant location studies, major new investments, the launching of a new major product, and similar decisions may be adequately served by such sources. But in the case of repetitive decisions, particularly at the tactical level where decisions tend to be made often and demand high volumes of input data, ad hoc collection is quite unsatisfactory. The sheer cost of obtaining the data may be overwhelming, and—what is often worse—the possibility of obtaining accurate data may be slight indeed. Many a four-hour linear programming run has had to be repeated, for example, because of incorrect input data.

The real payoff from decision models has often come from embedding the model into the routine processing system. Inputs for such a model mostly come directly from the data base, with automatic transformation of transaction data into the form required by the model. For example, sales data may be transformed into forecasts that are in turn fed to an inventory model. (Parameters that are quite stable, such as standard costs, should normally be obtained from ad hoc sources and be updated periodically.) Outputs may be printed directly by the system in the form of such working documents as production schedules or purchase orders (monitored, to be sure, by a human, at least in aggregate form).

Linking decision models to the routine processing system is obviously very difficult. Integration through a common data base, accessed through a data management system, offers some real hope of better coping with the problem of obtaining transaction data to support the model. Perhaps more serious is the problem of automatically transforming the transaction data into the form required by the model. Unadjusted transaction data, such as past sales and actual production times, do not necessarily provide the best predictions for use in a model; they reflect nonstandard random events, abnormal conditions, and an environment that subsequently may have shifted. In order to be used in a model, transaction data should typically be smoothed, normalized, or adjusted to reflect expected future conditions. Achieving this automatically within the information system is not a trivial task.

The Human Decision Maker

An organization faces a whole spectrum of decisions that range all the way from extremely ill-structured ones to those that are susceptible to complete formalization. Although this article has focused on formal models, it should be obvious that for many of the most important decisions these models offer little aid. A problem may be too ill-defined to permit any significant formalization, or it may be handled well enough by informal means that the potential payoff from a complex model may not justify the large cost typically required for its development, implementation, and operation.

In an informal decision process the decision maker chooses an alternative unaided by a formal model. If the process is at all rational, however, he has an informal "model" that allows him to estimate the consequences of his acts. The model may be highly subjective, biased, and imprecise, but it may also incorporate some exceedingly powerful and effective heuristics for dealing with ill-structured problems. The information system may in this informal case only provide relatively undigested data in such form as sales or financial reports, production reports, and the like.

In the case of man-machine processes, the human receives much more direct aid from the formal information system. The decision process nevertheless relies heavily on human creative ability to discover attractive alternatives for evaluation, to perceive subtle patterns among decision variables, and their consequences, and to exercise judgment in assessing the relative merits of alternatives.

As more and more of the decision process is shifted to the model—and especially in the extreme case of an optimizing model that provides decisions that are executed with little direct human intervention—the locus of decision making changes. The decisions more and more come to be made by the model builder. Value judgments, insights about functional relationships, estimates of risk, the generation and assessment of alternatives—all become incorporated in the model.

If these decisions can best be made by technical experts, so be it (but the surrender of these responsibilities by management should at least be made explicit). It is much more likely, however, that the essential policy decisions made in the course of model development can best be made by managers that in the past have been successful in creating their own informal "models." The formal models merely make explicit human insights and experience.

The role of model formulator makes a manager no less a decision maker; in fact, by incorporating his decision *process* in a model he makes a much more fundamental contribution. But to play this role successfully the manager must view the model and the associated information system as a primary means of effecting decisions—which is to say that he must learn to manage through the system. This calls for sophisticated skills and a basic understanding of the systems on which he relies.

Notes

1. Probably most man-machine models are analytical, but they can also be simulation models (discussed below). Often an analytical model may employ a Monte Carlo technique to draw random samples from a probability distribution of a parameter (e.g., sales, cost of material, etc.) in order to generate a distribution of possible outcomes (e.g., net profit from a new product). This technique should be viewed as a computational method for dealing with compound probability distributions, rather than an example of simulation.

2. In the linear programming example in Part 1 it was shown that the incremental profit for additional weavers' time is $2 per hour; this is therefore the shadow price of weaving. However, a maximum of 3000 hours of weaving can be used because of the limit on spinning; therefore, weaving has a shadow price of zero beyond 3000 hours.

3. When the model is used for detailed, relatively unimportant decisions, such as the control of low-valued inventory items, one cannot afford to scrutinize individual decisions; only decisions in the aggregate can normally be given close attention once the model has been implemented.

4. As in the real world, one must choose which summary data are worth retaining as the best compressed description of results.

5 New Directions in Operations Research

by John Dearden and John Lastavica

Operations research is a discipline practiced by professionals in mathematics, statistics, economics, and other sciences. Unlike other professionals, such as lawyers, doctors, or accountants, operations researchers have to explain what their discipline is. In doing so, they face inordinate difficulties. One source of these difficulties is the fact that the definition and scope of operations research have changed substantially during the past decade. Difficulties arise in communications with business managers because they often do not understand the technical language, and because the developments of techniques in academic work have differed substantially from developments in business applications. Recognizing all of the problems facing it, one might conclude that operations research is at a crossroads.

The choices available to practitioners are few. It is possible to develop operations research into a body of theory, much like economic theory, and rationalize the developments in the real world *ex post facto*. Should this be attempted, operations research will be mainly of academic interest.

Operations research plays an important role in business. To be successful in business, both the practitioners and managers have to recognize that specialization is required, and that operations researchers are more effective when they are attached to operational departments, where their interaction with line decision makers is enhanced.

Just like any other management group, top management has to have an operations research staff to help solve technical problems. So operations research has developed specialized techniques in financial analysis, statis-

EDITOR'S NOTE: From *Financial Executive*, October 1970, pp. 24-33. Reprinted by permission of the publisher, Financial Executives Institute, and authors.

tics, optimizing techniques, and simulation, which are applicable to problems in information systems, marketing, logistics, and strategic planning. Further efforts to educate managements and to create an environment which fosters the use of these techniques will lead to increased attainment of corporate goals.

The Problem of Definition

Operations research is a wide and diversified area of activity. Observation of applications of research in business and education leads one to conclude that there is no clear agreement as to its precise role, a factor which contributes to the problems practitioners experience in applying OR techniques. They frequently have to explain what they do.

The definition of operations research can be developed in three different ways. Perhaps the most widely accepted technical definition is given in the classic textbook on operations research (Churchman, Ackoff, and Arnoff, *An Introduction to Operations Research*, Wiley, 1957):

> OR is the application of scientific methods, techniques, and tools to problems involving the operations of systems so as to provide those in control of operations with optimum solution to the problems.

This concept of operations research leads to several restrictive conclusions about the nature of the activity:

- It is homogeneous in that it attacks problems involving the operations of systems using a set of specified techniques and tools.
- The basic discipline of operations research is mathematics.
- The objective of an operations research study is to find an optimum solution.

This definition emerged at a time when linear programming was the principal tool of operations research. The definition of linear programming is actually not much different from this definition for operations research.

The difficulties with the definition appear when one approaches business managers, to whom it appears all inclusive. It leads managements to believe they are using scientific methods for problem solving irrespective of operations research. Further, it encourages management to view most business problems as systems problems. And finally, techniques which calculate the best possible solution are viewed with skepticism by managements who are intimately aware of the difficulties associated with making the assumptions on which the models are based.

In summary, the technical definition is unsatisfactory to both educators and businessmen. Therefore, a descriptive definition, which consists of the following elements, is frequently used:

- There is a team approach to problem solving.
- The members of the team represent different areas of expertise or scientific background.
- There is a mathematical model.
- There is interaction and involvement with the decision makers.

There are various implications in the descriptive approach. One is that operations research is the only multidiscipline problem-solving activity. This approach includes a multitude of activities not typically associated with operations research, such as value analysis and "brain storming." Further, this definition invites attempts to compare operations research with scientific management—a comparison not wholly warranted.

Perhaps the major difficulty with the descriptive definition is that the same definition is frequently used by the computer systems people. They also use a team approach, they also have different specializations represented, they also develop a computer program which is a mathematical model, and they also need the involvement of decision makers. The difficulty arises because operations research staffs are often associated with computer systems staffs in organizational structure. The need for distinction between the two functions is particularly strong because the types of problems handled and techniques used are completely different. Systems people are usually solving operational problems, but operations researchers are increasingly involved with decision problems.

There is a third approach to definition: operations research is what operations research people do. Of course, one now faces the need to define what one does. But this is easier because it can be explained in terms of the human relationship, power, and influence which is independent of formal organization and the technical definition. In this light, operations research may be described as the catalyst which is bringing the business and academic worlds closer to each other.

Traditional Models Ineffective

Although the formal technical definition of operations research implies a multitude of methods, techniques, and tools, actually there are only a few. If one is willing to consider families of tools which have some basic similarities, four categories are sufficient to describe them. These are financial models, statistical models, mathematical programming, and simulations.

Definite distinctions are possible within these categories. Thus, financial models include inventory models, capital budgeting, return on investment, financial statement analysis, and cash flow models; and simulation includes all those techniques where a computer is used to evaluate multiple alternatives, be they exhaustive or limited.

One can argue that the first two categories predate operations research. Financial models have been with us for some time; contemporary business would be inconceivable without them. Innovations in this field in the past two decades are the reflection mainly of socioeconomic changes and better insight. For example, new understanding of discounted cash flows, return on investment, and present value concepts, to name a few, can be attributed to developments in finance. Likewise, the use of economic profit and treatment of variable costs to correspond to the needs of decision models are applications of logic and better training provided by the business schools.

It is clear that the science and theory of statistics, sampling, and inference predate operations research. The use of statistics and experimentation in social sciences and business is new and unquestionably worthwhile, but even here one can argue that the developments are due to technological change. The ability to perform accounting audits of computer systems hinges on sampling methods, for example.

If one recognizes that simulation techniques did not appear until the late 1950s or early 1960s, it becomes clear why operations research was identified with mathematical programming in general and linear programming in particular. It is in this area, however, where a number of problems relating to the techniques' usefulness have appeared; namely, they have proved of limited value in solving practical business problems.

Ten to fifteen years ago, the limitations of the programming techniques were attributed to their relative newness. For example, Henderson and Schlaifer stated in 1954 ("Mathematical Programming: Better Information for Better Decisions," *Harvard Business Review,* May-June 1954):

> So far, very little has been accomplished toward the solution of *scheduling* problems, where certain operations must be performed before or after other operations . . . research is attempting to find procedures which will reduce even this problem to a straight-forward routine, and some progress in this direction is being made.
>
> Problem-solving precedures have been well developed only for problems where cost incurred or revenue produced by every possible activity is strictly proportional to the volume of that activity; these are the procedures that belong under the somewhat misleading title of *linear* programming. This limitation, however, is not as serious as it seems. Problems involving non-proportioned costs or revenues can often be handled by linear programming through the use of special devices or by suitable approximations, and research is progressing on the development of procedures which will handle some of these problems directly.
>
> As in the case of its other applications, however, mathematical programming is not a cure-all. Management can use it to great advantage in planning and policy making, but executives must first understand it correctly to be able to use it intelligently in combination with other tools of forecasting and planning. The fate of mathematical programming, in other words, lies today in management's hands. The scientist, the inventors, have done their work; it is now up to the users.

Current observations indicate that linear programming is still the only really useful technique for solving problems with a large number of variables, and this technique is still limited to solving problems where the relationships are linear. Other programming techniques such as dynamic or quadratic programming, although over 10 years old and the subjects of vast amounts of new research, are still largely of academic interest; their impact on business is infinitesimal. Quadratic programming has been developed as a tool for portfolio selection in the investment industry, and, even though substantial resources have been invested by a number of companies, the results are of little significance for the management of investments.

The only area where linear programming has resulted in definite improvements in performance are mix models, such as gasoline blending by oil refineries and the selection of plants and warehouses in the distribution industry. These problems are the prototypes of operational problems and should be distinguished from decision problems at the corporate level. Corporate decision problems, on the other hand, have been the typical goals of operations researchers in industry for some time.

If we exclude the simulation techniques, we are forced to conclude that operations research is useful only in solving operational problems in business.

In summary, then, doubts about the usefulness of optimizing techniques are based on two considerations: (1) present techniques can be used to solve only a limited kind of operating problem and are not adaptable at all to solving higher level management problems; (2) no real progress has been made in the last 10 or more years in developing techniques that are more useful to business. When Henderson and Schlaifer wrote in 1954 that research was being conducted to overcome some of the limitations in mathematical programming, it was a reasonable assumption *at that time.* After 15 years, however, can one continue to hold this belief? Back 15 years ago, those who questioned the usefulness of mathematical programming for top management were considered to be conservatives, unable to accept the truth of a changing environment.

To a considerable extent, this could have been true at that time. It was possible that linear programming was the first of a series of breakthroughs that would increase the effectiveness of management decision making. By 1969, however, one wonders if the proponents of mathematical programming are not the conservatives, unable to see the handwriting on the wall. At the very least, it is time to examine critically our assumptions concerning the potential impact of these techniques on business decision making. The fact that, after so many years, it is difficult to find a company where they are used above the operational level should give us cause for reflection.

Nonoptimizing Techniques

If practical developments in optimizing techniques have been insignificant, where have new developments occurred? New developments have occurred through the use of simulation techniques and time-sharing. These techniques have the following characteristics:

1. The mathematics involved are generally simple, most involving little more than an understanding of linear equations.
2. To use these techniques, it is necessary to have an intimate knowledge of the part of the business to which they are to apply.
3. They are dependent upon the computer for implementation.
4. In most cases these techniques are not designed to provide optimum solutions to problems. As a result, the adequacy of the solution depends on the ability of the people who develop the model.
5. The complexity of the models is in the aggregation of many simple relationships, all of which have some interdependencies.
6. The success of these techniques is due to the fact that the analysts have emulated closely the decision maker's frame of reference and decision structure and are introducing new thoughts and ideas very gradually.

Although the potential for using simulation techniques was developed prior to the availability of time-sharing systems, time-sharing has facilitated their expansion into the areas of decision making.

By recognizing the processes of simulation analysis, one can readily see the advantages of time-sharing in bridging the communication gap between analysts and decision makers. Typically, a model is developed by a team and validated against an existing situation which serves as a bench mark. A number of alternatives are then calculated and analyzed. In this process, the analysts are performing sensitivity analyses of the model, which is—hopefully—similar to the live system. The insight gained can lead to changes in the live system, since the changes in behavior of the system have, in effect, been predicted by the changes in the model.

When time-sharing is introduced in such a situation, the feedback between the model builders and the computer is reduced to such an extent that the decision maker becomes the analyst and in effect performs the sensitivity analysis. The decision makers can analyze and understand the alternatives much better than can the analysts, and their insight is evaluated without intermediaries.

From the analyst's point of view, there are numerous challenges: how to program a multitude of complex programs to interact, how to store substantial amounts of data at a reasonable cost, how to make the systems as fool-proof as possible, and how to introduce the appropriate decision models to the decision makers. There is ample evidence that a number of these problems have been solved successfully; for example, the growth in the time-sharing industry, the expansion in the teaching and use of these systems on campuses, and their adoption by operations research departments in industrial and financial enterprises.

In the banking industry, the expansion of time-sharing was in association with models which did little more than facilitate multitudes of algebraic manipulations; but the trend is to include numerous principles developed in decision theory.

In summary, the development of simulations and time-sharing has made the relationship between the researcher and the decision maker a much more important element in successful model building, for the following reasons:

1. It is possible to tackle a much wider range of problems. Consequently, the operations researcher is likely to be involved in more areas of management.
2. The effectiveness of the solution is more dependent upon the ability of the operations researcher. Consequently, it is necessary for operating management to have considerable confidence in the operations researcher.
3. A great understanding of the operations and decisions is necessary because the operations researcher is not restricted to a few mathematical models.

One is led to conclude that the expansion of operations research into the areas of corporate decision making will be linked intimately to the use of time-sharing systems, because these systems help bridge the gap between the decision maker and the analyst.

Failure of Operations Research

Business is not using the potential available from operations research techniques. This is true in inventory control, in asset management, and in investment management. Not only are decisions made on the basis of primitive decision rules, but very little attempt is made to evaluate the alternatives. There are areas of decision making where either linear programming or extended simulations are required to improve the quality of decisions made at the highest level in business. Yet operations researchers have not been successful in convincing top management that there is a superior approach. In most major corporations, one can find areas where either operations researchers have been unable to convince management of the desirability of using a more mathematical approach to decision making, or when models were tried, results were disappointing and far below those expected. Consequently, the models were either discontinued or, at least, further extensions were inhibited.

These conditions stem partly from the fact that operations researchers are usually a part of a staff group and are assigned to work on certain problems with operating managers. In this environment, one frequently finds that the people problem—the understanding and rapport between the technician and the manager—is a more serious problem than the operating problem. If one considers the decision problems at the top of the corporate pyramid, one finds that operations researchers typically do not have access to the top people and consequently are not in a position to develop the necessary models.

In spite of the development of superior tools readily adaptable to a multitude of problems, operations research is still not used as extensively as it should be. The answer, clearly, is to solve the people problem. Two things suggest themselves: one is to provide an organizational environment which facilitates communication, and the other is to structure studies so that communication flow is assured. These, in combination, will lead to more successful applications.

Developing a Structure for Decision Analysis

Operations research is not a homogeneous type of activity. Specialization in linear programming, statistics, simulation, or financial analysis has more direct application in some areas of business than in others. For example, linear programming is readily associated with the oil or food industries' manufacturing processes, and statistics and sampling are readily associated with marketing. This being so, it is logical to place the experts in each activity as closely as possible to the appropriate decision makers. To accomplish this would require the decentralization of the operations research function. Although there is a need for communication between the operations research people within an organization, the implementation of operations research analysis is better served by allowing operations researchers to report directly to line management.

The structure for decision analysis proposed below begins with the problem definition. If one is considering a simulation model, one has to model the decision maker's frame of reference which cannot be achieved without a very close contact between the researcher and the manager. Therefore, by and large, operations research will be more readily used if it is decentralized.

This puts the role of centralized operations research staffs in question. The solution, if there is one, is to reduce these staff groups to a very small number of people and to limit their function to selecting problems to be analyzed and convincing respective managers that techniques and talents can be secured to analyze the problems. The people who will remain in these roles will possess extraordinary managerial capabilities, as well as technical know-how, and their principal role in organizations will be that of change agents. In order to be effective, these staffs will have to act as consultants and advisors to the top managements of business organizations.

Organization alone will not assure success in operations research projects. It is essential that a structure for decision analysis follow principles which have been successful in the practice of the discipline. These are the principles:

- The change agent has to know what is the problem and what questions should be answered.
- The appropriate decision model has to be formulated to answer the questions.
- The data have to be gathered selectively according to the decision model needs.
- The information economics principle of diminishing returns should be observed throughout the analysis.

The first principle appears obvious. However, the questions initially asked by the decision makers are not always the questions which they would like to have answered, and a continuous interaction between the decision makers and the analysts is a necessity. The latter's role is to learn and understand the problem and then seek, explore, and explain the ideas which lead to better solutions.

The isolation and definition of problems, especially at the corporate level, is a formidable task because neither the decision makers nor the analysts have certain knowledge about future events or the multitude of implications.

The definition of the decision model is in the province of management science. It may be appropriate to use linear programming in certain situations while the ranking of alternatives based upon few criteria may be sufficient in others. An example of the former is the cash-alpha-thesis by R. Calman *(Cash Alpha, a Linear Programming Approach to Banking Relations,* MS thesis, MIT, 1967). It describes a corporation which is doing business with 15 banks and which maintains deposits in each for borrowing purposes. The balances are used in part to support the disbursement and collection activities for the corporation. Linear programming is used to allocate the activities to the various banks, considering the differentials in deposit earning allowances and the various types of fees charged by the banks. An example of the latter is a two-way ranking (by amount and rate of interest) of alternative sources of funds, used in banking to determine the appropriate transfer prices.

The management scientist gains corporate acceptance if his presentations define accepted cost and profit concepts. A simulation model can be used for one's understanding and evaluation of alternatives, but it need not be emphasized in presenting the solution to the users of the model. (See Lastavica, "Simulation of a Bank's Check Collection Process," *Bentley*

Business and Economic Review, June 1967.) It is more effective to present to the decision makers a financial evaluation of alternatives than to explain to them in detail the workings of the simulation model.

The next principle indicates that data should be subordinate to the model. An appropriate approach is to provide the capability to extract selective information from operational files and the capability to introduce information into the system from outside, which may be required for a particular decision according to the decision model. The data gathering process may be time consuming, but it is impossible to gather and maintain all the data for all possible problems at a reasonable cost.

The last pragmatical principle deals with information economics and diminishing returns. As one proceeds to extract more and more detailed information from an operational file, the information will be less and less useful for corporate decision makers. For example, a bank president needs to know the total demand deposits in his bank, but a complete list of all the depositors with their balances is not very useful to him.

A more formal approach to information economics has been described by Adrian McDonough from Wharton School of Finance *(Information Economics and Management Systems,* McGraw-Hill). He has reviewed the concepts of supply and demand for information and related them to traditional economic notions. He has developed the principle of diminishing returns and the value of information and cost of information curves and related them to the time period of the study.

The maximum net value of information is reached at the point where the difference between the value and the cost of information curves is the largest. The value and cost of information curves correspond to the total cost and total revenue curves in traditional economic notions, and the maximum net value of information corresponds to the point where marginal revenue equals marginal cost in traditional economics.

Managers and analysts often use the information economics principle in their daily decision making, although the process is frequently described as an intuitive one. The formal recognition of this principle in corporate decision making would lead to better communications and formalized decisions.

Fields of Specialization

There are four specific areas of operations research specialization. These areas are logistics, long-range planning, marketing, and information systems. These areas are not meant to be exhaustive. They are simply the four areas that we have observed to be most generally needed today. Other areas of specialization will be applicable to certain types of businesses, and new areas of specialization will appear in the future.

Logistics

We define logistics as the control of the flow of goods through a company. The logistics systems start with procurement of the raw materials and end with the delivery of the finished goods to the ultimate consumer. A company may have several logistics systems; e.g., one for each major product line.

Most of the early operations research activities were concerned with logistics systems. In the past, the responsibility for a single logistics system was often divided among several executives—a situation which was responsible for the notion that operations research provided overall systems solutions that crossed traditional functional lines. In fact, the logistics system is a single system that was subdivided because of the problems of communication. Now, with modern computer systems, particularly real-time systems, the logistics function is increasingly centralized.

As long as the logistics function is centralized, the operations research group specializing in logistics would report to the manager responsible for operating the logistic system. To the extent that the logistics system is still a divided responsibility, there will be a problem in placing the operations research group. In general, however, they should be assigned to the manager who has the most complex logistics problems.

In general, the logistics group will use more optimizing techniques than the other areas of specialty. Inventory control techniques are, of course, fundamental to a logistics control system. Linear programming can be successfully used in distribution. In addition, there are many linear programming applications within the typical plant. (It is probably in the intra-plant applications that linear programming is most neglected.) Besides optimizing techniques, simulation and heuristic programming also have potential applications in improving the logistics system. Note, however, it is vital that the logistics specialist have a thorough understanding of the particular logistics system with which he is working and an intimate acquaintance with the people operating it.

Strategic Planning

Operations research techniques can be of significant help to management in strategic planning. The technique most useful in strategic planning is simulation. For example, Company A is planning to double its manufacturing capacity in Europe. The problem is where in Europe to build what facilities. This involves a great many complex and interacting variables; e.g., population changes, tax laws, currency restrictions, economic stability in each country, to name a few. These variables are in addition to the usual problems of designing facilities to meet future needs. The usual way of solving such a problem is to make what seem to be reasonable assumptions and develop a plan based on these assumptions. With modern simulation techniques and the power of the digital computer, it is possible to build a digital model of the problem. This model permits use of a much greater number of variables, to test the impact of a much wider range of values for these variables, and to experiment with a much larger number of alternative plans. The result is a more complete and realistic analysis of the alternatives. In fact, one can argue that realistic strategic plans cannot be developed without operations research techniques.

With the exception of banking, where logistics systems for investments and strategic planning use very similar models, there is a vast difference in the expertise and techniques required in one compared with the other.

Although simulation is used to solve logistics problems, the simulation models used in logistics differ enormously from those used in strategic planning. There is a question about the usefulness of optimizing techniques for strategic planning because of the difficulty of expressing uncertainties in these models. Obviously, the knowledge required to understand a logistics system is almost entirely different from that required to develop strategic plans. Even the type of person required can be different. The logistics specialist must be able to communicate effectively with the operating manager, while the strategic planner is involved almost entirely with top management. To summarize, then, the strategic planner uses different techniques, requires a different kind of knowledge, and works with a different kind of person than the logistic specialist.

Marketing

The third area of business where operations research techniques have proved useful is marketing. The major use of operations research techniques is in marketing research. Here the traditional statistical techniques of sampling and forecasting are used. Of the newer techniques, simulation seems to be of the most value.

Although there is probably greater similarity between strategic planning and marketing research than between strategic planning and logistics, there are still significant differences. The techniques are different, the problems are different, the knowledge required is different, and the people are different. In fact, marketing research has tended to be a specialized field, apart from the usual operations research staff. An important reason for this, of course, is that the marketing manager must have control over marketing research. As a result, the newer operations research techniques have been somewhat slow in penetrating into this area.

Information Systems Groups

There is a substantial need for operations researchers associated with automation and systems project groups, in particular in the development of third-generation computer systems. This expertise is essentially in two areas: simulation of real-time systems and design of information flows which will enable managers to extract pertinent information from the automated systems. Skills required for simulation are not unlike those required for logistic problem solving, and queueing techniques are particularly useful to estimate the level of service that given units of computer equipment can provide. In banking, for instance, substantial analysis is required to estimate the demand and availability of check-handling equipment. Although this is a logistic problem on the operating side of the bank, one has to distinguish it from the logistics problem associated with the money position and short-term investments. It appears that the two experts required, who have vastly different interests, should report to the two distinct managers.

Design of information flows in automated systems is another role requiring a great deal of quantitative knowledge. The technician has to be versed in micro-economics and has to understand management objectives and goals. The latter is a problem which deals with values which have never been expressed by managers and yet are the foundation of behavior. Clearly, statements like "maximizing profits" are platitudes. The operations researcher's role is to conduct studies which lead to better definitions and understanding of management attitudes and to translate these into information requirements and into report structures which can be used by the systems and automation technicians. Operations research is the only discipline which can attempt to improve the flow of information between management and systems. The experts have to be attached to the computer's systems groups in order to accomplish this purpose.

Conclusions

Operations research involves an attitude directed towards problem solving in business. Although it is not dissimilar to the general approach taken by businessmen, there are differences in that an attempt is made to solve problems which have not been solved before or to solve them using the newest technology and the product of research in the academic world. Walter Wriston, president of the National City Bank of New York, in a speech before the International Chamber of Commerce in Copenhagen on October 24, 1968, pointed out that the developments in the business world in America include a rapprochement between the business and the academic world. Operations researchers can take pride in this recognition of one of their primary functions.

The questions we have been trying to answer deal with the more active performance of this function. We have seen developments in operations research which hinder this function, and we have seen others which provide a substantial impetus to this role. The hindrance comes from the development of sophisticated mathematical models in both academic and private research organizations and their publication in theoretical literature, without sufficient attempts made to communicate these to managers and to define practical situations where they might be applicable. On the other hand, time-sharing computer systems have made it possible to bring decision makers and researchers into a much more intimate contact. The researchers, in developing simulation models, are emulating the decision maker's thought processes and, consequently, are able to communicate much more readily than heretofore. The decision maker—the manager—finds that he can use his intuition—the basis of his judgment and his true expertise. But he also finds that, through simulation, he gets a superior evaluation of the outcome of his decisions. Because the evaluation is performed in real time, he finds that he can try various "strategies" and evaluate the results in short order and attain the level of knowledge which comes from sensitivity analysis. This being so, we attempt to answer the question "What should researchers do?" The answer appears obvious: "They should persuade more managers to use their superior technology." The best way to do this is to improve the communications between managers and researchers. An obvious way is to place them organizationally into a dependent relationship by making operations researchers directly responsible to the operating managers.

We attempt to answer a few other questions. Namely, is there a role for centralized operations research? There is, because there is a need to maintain the professional exchange which researchers have with each other. Also, centralized operations research has to assume those functions in which top management needs the advice of operations research. These deal with strategic planning and the human interactions associated with corporate goals.

There is also a message for the researchers, based on pragmatic experience associated with a number of successful projects in the field. These deal with the way in which successful studies can be developed and implemented. They point out, above all, the relative importance of the basic ingredients of research work and rank them as follows: problems, models, data, and values.

In summary, the advances in technology have made the job of operations researchers a little easier, and therefore more challenging.

Discussion Questions

1. Distinguish between the following terms:
   a. Model and Algorithm
   b. Linear and Nonlinear Programming
   c. Dynamic and Linear Programming
   d. Game Theory and Operational Gaming
   e. Operations Research and Operations Analysis
   f. Differential and Integral Calculus as used in Decision Models
   g. Zero-Sum and Non-Zero Sum Games
   h. Linear and Integer Programming
   i. Deterministic and Probabilistic Simulation Models
   j. Scientific Research and Operations Research
   k. Analytic and Simulation Models
2. What are the major steps in the scientific approach to problem solving? Which of these steps are most critical in developing acceptable solutions to operations research problems? Why?
3. What are the most difficult problems likely to be encountered in developing realistic operations research models? What measures can the analyst employ to minimize such difficulties?
4. What characteristics should a decision problem have in order for there to be a high probability that a successful solution can be developed using operations research techniques (e.g., simple vs. complex, functional vs. interdepartmental problem, operating vs. top management problem)? Why?
5. What benefits can managers expect to achieve by using operations research techniques to assist in the solution of operating, middle management, and top management problems? Are there any cases in which the limitations of developing and implementing operations research based solutions are likely to outweigh the benefits of such solutions? Explain fully.

6. Can operations research be best characterized as a philosophy, a pragmatic approach to problem solving, or a set of techniques drawn from diverse fields which can be used to evaluate and manipulate system behavior? Explain fully.

7. Under what circumstances is the development and testing of a system model likely to be more desirable than experimenting with the actual system? Are there ever cases in which experimentation with the real system may be preferable to developing and testing a system model prior to introducing changes in the system? When and why?

8. What is a measure of effectiveness? Give one or more examples applying to marketing, production, personnel, purchasing, engineering, and accounting or finance problems/systems. How can the analyst determine the best measure of effectiveness for a given problem and how can he balance conflicts between objectives?

9. What is the difference between optimization and suboptimization in operations analysis studies? When is the analyst justified in selecting a suboptimal alternative?

10. What role do constraints play in model development? How can the analyst evaluate the costs or consequences of changing one or more constraints?

11. How do electronic computers facilitate the use of operations research techniques? Are computers ever a handicap rather than an aid in operations analysis? Explain fully.

12. How important is it for the analyst to determine the range of conditions within which a model or a given solution will give valid results? What kinds of problems or systems are most likely to require that careful consideration be given to possible changes in environmental variables that could invalidate the model or a given problem solution?

13. Should the operations analyst attempt to develop an elaborate model initially which is an accurate representation of real world systems or start off with a simpler but more manageable model and gradually refine it? Why? (Note: consider carefully the benefits and limitations of each approach.)

14. Which of the major operations research models (i.e., allocation, competitive, inventory, queueing, PERT/CPM, simulation and gaming) are most likely to be useful in solving the kinds of problems given below? Why?

a. Personnel assignment.

b. Setting salesmen's quotas.

c. Allocating advertising expense budgets to various media.

d. Production scheduling of a seasonal product.

e. Inventory control for products with relatively fixed demand. With highly variable demand.

f. Equipment replacement.

g. Planning and controlling the development and testing of a new product.

h. Deciding how much money to invest in plant expansion.

i. Scheduling of preventative maintenance and repair operations.

j. Determining the number of clerks needed at a department store checkout counter.

15. For best long-range results, what should be the composition of the operations research task force? What factors should be given special attention by the OR team in order to ensure that its efforts will be successful? Explain fully.

16. What effect will the development of man-machine systems incorporating sophisticated decision models and high-speed computers have on the scope, timing, and validity of human decision making? Is the human decision maker's role likely to be more important in systems using analytic or simulation models? Why?

Bibliography

Ackoff, Russell L., "A Survey of Applications of Operations Research," *Proceedings of Conference on Case Studies in Operations Research,* Case Institute of Technology, 1956, pp. 9-17.

Brambilla, Francisco, "Operations Research as a Management Science," *Management International,* 1961, No. 4, pp. 45-61.

Bross, Irwin D. J., "Models," from *Design for Decision,* Macmillan Co., 1953, pp. 161-182.

Cockhill, G. L., "Operations Research in Process Development and Control," *Canadian Chartered Accountant,* May 1963, pp. 357-361.

Dearden, John, and John Lastavica. "New Directions in Operations Research," *Financial Executive,* October 1970, pp. 24-33.

Doherty, Philip A., "A Closer Look at Operations Research," *Journal of Marketing,* April 1963, pp. 59-65.

Dykman, F. C., "New Measurement Techniques Used in Financial Reporting," *Price, Waterhouse Review,* Spring 1969, pp. 39-49.

Edge, C. G. "Management Accounting and Operations Research," *Canadian Chartered Accountant,* April 1967, pp. 265-269.

Hammond, Robert A., "Making OR Effective for Management," *Business Horizons,* Spring 1962, pp. 73-82.

Hermann, Cyril C. and John F. Magee, "Operations Research for Management," *Harvard Business Review,* July-August 1953, pp. 100-112.

Jones, Curtis H., "Applied Math for the Production Manager," *Harvard Business Review,* September 1966, pp. 20-28, 180-184.

Kotler, Philip, "Operations Research in Marketing," *Harvard Business Review,* January-February 1967, pp. 30-44, 187-188.

Lazer, William, "The Role of Models in Marketing," *Journal of Marketing,* April 1962, pp. 9-14.

Philippakis, Andreas S., "Mathematical Analysis vs. Simulation Methods," *Journal of Systems Management,* May 1969, pp 28-31.

Reps, David N., and Morton Allen, "Mathematical Modelling with a Computer," *Ideas for Management, S&PA,* 1969, pp. 161-177.

Rodgers, Jack C., "An Introduction to Industrial Operations Research," *Data Processing Annual, DPMA,* Vol. XI, 1966, pp. 95-117.

Sandor, P. E., "Operations Research in Marketing," *Canadian Chartered Accountant,* May 1968, pp. 339-342 and *Management Controls,* July 1969, pp. 143-147.

Souder, William E., "Solving Budget Problems with Operations Research," *Budgeting,* July/August 1967, pp. 11-19.

Vatter, William J., "The Use of Operations Research in American Companies," *Accounting Review,* October 1967, pp. 721-730.

Wagner, Harvey M., "Practical Slants on Operations Research," *Harvard Business Review,* May-June 1963, pp. 61-71.

Walter, John R., "Operations Research in Production Planning," *Canadian Chartered Accountant,* March 1963, pp. 203-208.

Warrick, Walter H., "Planning—The Who, What, Where, When, and Why," *Production & Inventory Management,* 4th Quarter 1968, pp. 40-55.

Weinberg, Robert S., "The Uses and Limitations of Mathematical Models," *An Analytical Approach to Advertising Expenditure Strategy,* 1960, Association of National Advertisers, pp. 89-116.

PART II Mathematical Programming: Graphic, Simplex, Parametric, and Integer Programming Methods

Enrick points out that mathematical programming is particularly valuable in solving optimization problems subject to resource restrictions such as buying or making component parts, purchasing new or retaining old equipment, taking or ignoring volume discounts, planning long-range manpower requirements, and developing alternative sales or production programs. Simple problems can be solved graphically, whereas more complex problems require the use of matrix algebra and perhaps even a computer. Mathematical programming has been successfully utilized in product blending, minimum cost distribution scheduling, portfolio selection, advertising media selection, and personnel assignment.

Windal describes the simplex technique of linear programming, which requires a step by step iterative procedure that improves the solution at each stage until an optimal solution is reached. The optimal solution table indicates the number of units of each product to be produced, total profits, any underutilized resources, the effect on total profits of increasing the amounts of any fully utilized resource, and the impact on profits of substituting units of one product for another within given resource restrictions. Sensitivity analysis can be employed to determine the amount of change in scarce resources used, or product contribution margins needed, to change the optimal product program.

Hartley points out that sensitivity analysis can be applied to the objective equation coefficients, the constraining equation constants, and the constraining equation coefficients to determine how far these coefficients can vary without changing the optimal solution. Parametric programming is required to study the effect of simultaneous parameter changes on the problem solution. Opportunity costs yielded by linear programming are also valuable in variance analysis and joint costing.

Godfrey, Spivey, and Stillwagon demonstrate how parametric programming can be used to provide additional information about a linear programming problem solution helpful in integrating production and marketing planning. An optimal solution to the Apex production scheduling problem with three machines and three grades of paper is developed initially and the effects of changing certain restrictions are explored. The application of parametric programming to the scheduling problem indicates the effect of errors in sales forecasts, machine time estimates, and realized profits per ton on the problem solution. Finally, the dual variables are utilized to interpret the effects of different market strategies on total profits.

As Petersen indicates, mathematical programming problems can be classified as linear or nonlinear, as well as differentiated, on the basis of whether the variables are continuous or discrete (i.e., integers). Integer linear programming problems can be solved using cutting plane, shifted hyperplane, or truncated enumeration methods. Some of the most common integer programming problems are all-integer in nature, including fixed capital budgeting, traveling salesmen assignments, and multiple choice as well as fixed charge problems. A particularly interesting class of all-integer problems contains those whose variables can assume only the values of 0 or 1. Mixed-integer programming problems (i.e., those in which not all the variables are restricted to integers) include ordinary optimization, linear approximation to nonlinear functions, discrete alternative, and multiphase scheduling problems. The extension of integer programming to probabilistic as well as deterministic problems and the development of improved algorithms for computer solution are fruitful areas for further research.

Balsmeier proposes the use of integer programming to overcome some of the problems associated with the use of ranking procedures in the selection of capital investments. Using a sample problem, he demonstrates that ranking procedures may not result in allocation of resources to maximize the net return to the firm. Linear programming provides a better solution, but the fractional selection of one or more projects which typically occurs in such cases may not be feasible. Applying Gomory constraints to a primal simplex solution of the problem produces an optimal integer solution requiring selection of three of the four projects. The limitations of the model (e.g., it does not allow for the effects of risk and uncertainty or the inclusion of nonlinear or dynamic functions) are also pointed out.

6 Sales-Production Coordination through Mathematical Programming

by Norbert Lloyd Enrick

For any company that manufactures more than one product, the choice of a product mix requires careful balancing of anticipated costs and revenues. An analysis whose principal emphasis is on production costs may fail to take into account all the intricacies of sales forecasting and price variability. Or, more commonly, a sales-oriented analysis based on sales potential and unit profit margin may neglect the effect that various combinations of machines and facilities can have on costs.

Sometimes a product that seems to have a good profit margin may be relatively uneconomical to produce in large quantities because its production requirements create bottlenecks in a department or on a critical machine, thereby disproportionately limiting the production of other products. In such a case, production of apparently lower-margin products may contribute more to overall profits.

When a wide variety of products, models, styles, machines, and production facilities is involved, the calculation of the combination of products and quantities that will yield the maximum overall profit can be a complex task. Fortunately, new mathematical techniques are available that can greatly simplify the work, particularly when they are used in combination with electronic computers. This article describes how one of these techniques, mathematical programming, can be utilized to coordinate product and production planning.

Mathematics vs. Intuition

Often the results obtained from mathematical analysis are quite different from those that would probably emerge from a more intuitive form of decision making. Take the case illustrated in Table 6-1. (For the sake of simplicity, the 40 products actually manufactured by this electronic component producer and the one dozen processing stages actually used have been reduced in the table to four products, A, B, C, and D, and to four processing stages, machining, coil winding, mounting, and testing.) Table 6-1 shows the unit profit normally associated with each product, the normal productive capacity of each production department, and the production time requirements in each department for each product.

Table 6-1 Unit Profits and Production Requirements for Four Products

	Marketable Products				Normal Productive Capacity, hr/wk
	A	B	C	D	
a. Profit, $/piece	0.40	0.37	0.36	0.28	
b. Production time requirements, hr/1000 pieces					
Machining	30.6	30.6	32.6	22.4	250
Coil winding	72.0	64.8	72.0	79.2	720
Mounting	36.0	28.8	28.8	21.6	242
Testing	18.0	26.0	24.0	29.0	260

To the sales manager the choice of the product to be emphasized was obvious. "You can see," he pointed out, "that we make the greatest profit on Product A and the lowest profit on Product D. We don't need mathematics to show us the most desirable products to sell. Our problem is that people won't buy much of A."

The production manager, on the other hand, felt that some weight ought to be given to production balance. Despite its high unit profit, Product A had the disadvantage of requiring a relatively long time for mounting. Thus, it was likely to create a bottleneck in the mounting department, which would leave other machines idle while mounting was unable to meet the demands on it. The cost of this production imbalance could easily cancel out a good share of Product A's normal profit margin.

The pertinent data were put into linear equations and a computer was put to work calculating which products in which quantities would result in maximum overall profit for the company. The answer: 5,220 pieces a week of Product D, 3,790 pieces of Product B, 560 of Product A, and none of Product C. This combination would produce a total weekly profit of $3,088, higher than any other possible product combination, and would utilize the full productive capacity of every processing department except coil winding, where there would be a small but unavoidable under-utilization of 21 machine-hours a week.

The results were a surprise to the sales manager. Product A, which he had been trying to promote so vigorously, turned out to be a poor contributor to overall profit, and Product D, with the lowest unit profit, was shown to be the greatest contributor.

In the actual analysis, which included 40 products, company management gained a completely new perspective on its marketable products. Many past favorites lost out against previously overlooked items. As a result, the company was able to direct its sales and promotional efforts much more intelligently and decisively. In addition, plant morale was improved and costs reduced through better balanced production, more even flow of work, and less use of overtime and part-time workers.

Mathematical Programming

The company's conclusions about its product mix were reached by means of mathematical programming, a mathematical method of analyzing interrelated variables to determine the optimum combination. The required formulas are not particularly difficult to set up; their solution, tedious and time-consuming by manual methods, takes even a relatively small computer only a few minutes, even if a large number of variables are involved.

A large-scale problem, of course, can involve a staggering number of factors. In a large company several thousand products may be considered. A variety of market factors may be included in the problem, among them price-demand relationships, minimum product quantities or a complete line, maximum limits on marketability of specific products, long-term sales contracts limiting production capacity, and the extent of production for inventory in slack periods. The production side of the analysis may include a large number of processing departments—or even particular machine groups or machine types. For each processing department or machine the variables may include such factors as machine time, labor time, maintenance time, raw materials and supplies used, and skilled personnel needed. Other considerations may be introduced, such as whether to make or buy parts or completed components and assemblies, the desirability of new equipment purchases, the profitability of discount sales to large customers, and various alternative production or sales programs.

Such analyses can be used to aid management decision making in many areas. The following list includes only a few examples:

1. Considering the installation of new equipment because of limits on overall plant capacity
2. Planning to increase or trim managerial, administrative, staff, and operating personnel where either course appears desirable
3. Long-range planning to deal with anticipated technological and market developments
4. Integrating a variety of other tools for quantitative analysis and control

To illustrate how mathematical programming is applied, let us take a simplified example involving only linear factor combinations and variables (hence suitable for linear programming) and involving only two products (hence capable of being expressed graphically). This problem is based on a consulting engagement for a manufacturer of small metal parts.

Data concerning the two products, A and B, and the two most critical processing departments, polishing and plating, are given in Table 6-2. These include production rates and expected returns in terms of dollar contribution based on prices and market conditions. Contribution represents price less variable manufacturing cost. Variable manufacturing cost excludes fixed and selling costs.

At current prices Product A brings the higher contribution per gross. Theoretically, there is capacity to polish 40 gross of Product A weekly, but,

Table 6-2 Simplex Programming Problem

	Marketable Products A	B	**Productive Capacity hr/wk**	**Total**
a. Contribution, $/gross	6.00	5.00		
b. Production time requirements, hr/gross				
Polishing	3	4	120	
Plating	2	1	40	
c. Output if only Product A or Product B, but not both, are produced, gross/wk.				
Polishing*	(40)	30**		
Plating	20**	(40)		
d. Contribution from output in (c), found by multiplying (a) X (c), $/wk.	120	150	150***	

*Productive capacity divided by requirements in line b. Thus 120/3 = 40. Since only 20 gross can be plated, the 40 gross in polishing cannot be utilized beyond the plating bottleneck, and is therefore shown in parentheses.

**Bottleneck process for this product (A or B)

***Only Product A or Product B, but not both can be produced at this stage, so that the maximum contribution equals the highest contribution product, which is Product B at $150.

because there is plating capacity for only 20 gross of Product A per week, plating is a bottleneck. B's bottleneck is in polishing.

From Line *d* it is apparent that if only Product A is manufactured, production of 20 gross at $6 per gross profit contribution will result in a total weekly profit contribution of $120. If Product B is manufactured instead, production of 30 gross at $5 per gross profit contribution will result in a higher total profit contribution, $150 a week. The fact that the two products have different bottlenecks suggests that a combination of the two products should be produced.

The optimum product combination may be determined by graphing the possible quantities of Product A on one axis and Product B on the other, as in Fig. 6-1. The capacity if only Product A is polished (40 on the A axis) is connected by a line with the capacity if only Product B is polished (30 on the B axis). Similarly, plating capacity for Product A (20 on the A axis) is connected with plating capacity for Product B (40 on the B axis). The shaded portion of the graph represents feasible product combinations. For example, if 10 gross of B and 15 gross of A are produced, available plating capacity is exhausted. If 24 gross of B and 8 gross of A are produced, both plating and polishing capacities are exhausted.

Third Dimension

The data in Fig. 6-1 may also be shown as in Fig. 6-2, a three-dimensional form that permits addition of a new variable, the profit contribution associated with the various product combinations.

For the previously mentioned 15 gross of Product A and 10 gross of Product B, the total product contribution will be 15 times $6 plus 10 times $5, or $140. This amount is higher than the $120 for A alone but less than the $150 for B alone. If we produce, say, 8 gross of A and 10 of B, we will not be using all our capacity, and contribution will be only $98 a week (8 time $6 plus 10 times $5).

The trend of the heights of the dollar columns in Fig. 6-2 leads us to try the intersection point of the polishing and plating capacity, which corresponds to 8 gross of A and 24 gross of B, with a total profit contribution of $168 ($6 times 8 plus $5 times 24). Any movement away from this product combination yields lower total returns, as is shown in Fig. 6-3.

This simplified problem illustrates an important principle, valid for all mathematical programming with linear relationships: To find the maximum, investigate the corners. By analyzing the points 0, 20, 30 and the intersection of the two capacity lines, we have not only succeeded in constructing the dollar contribution dimension but also have found the optimum point.

Maximum profit does not always involve a combination of products, of

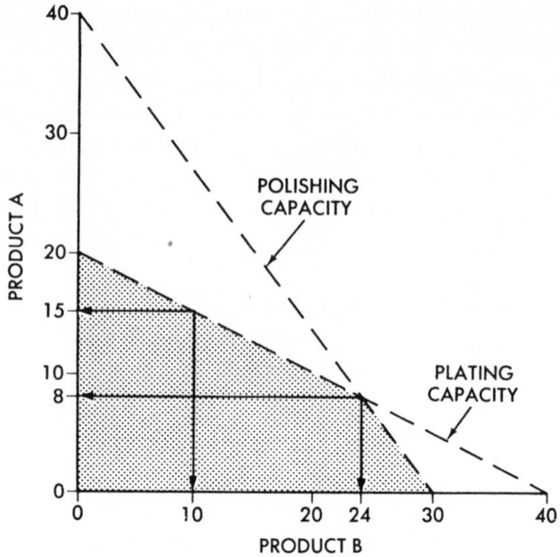

Fig. 6-1. Production capacities for two products. In this graphic presentation of the simplest programming example, the shaded area represents feasible production quantities of Products A and B. Beyond this area, bottlenecks in polishing and plating prevent further production.

course. For example, if Product A's contribution had been \$11, then production of 20 gross of A would have resulted in a total profit contribution of \$220, as against only \$208 from 8 gross of A (8 times \$11) plus 24 gross of B (24 times \$5).

The principle of investigating corners is crucial to solving the type of problem described here. It is applicable for all linear relationships of products and returns, no matter how many products are involved. However, with each product we add a dimension to the space structure to be investigated. Two products require three dimensions; three products need four dimensions; and ten products need eleven dimensions. Since humans have the ability to conceive only three-dimensional space, it is necessary to resort to mathematical investigation of corners in many-dimensional space.

Matrix Method

In actual practice, of course, few choices of product mix are simple enough to be expressed graphically. Such problems nearly always require matrix algebra, whether the solutions are obtained manually or with a computer. This technique will now be illustrated, using the same data previously presented for the polishing-plating contractor.

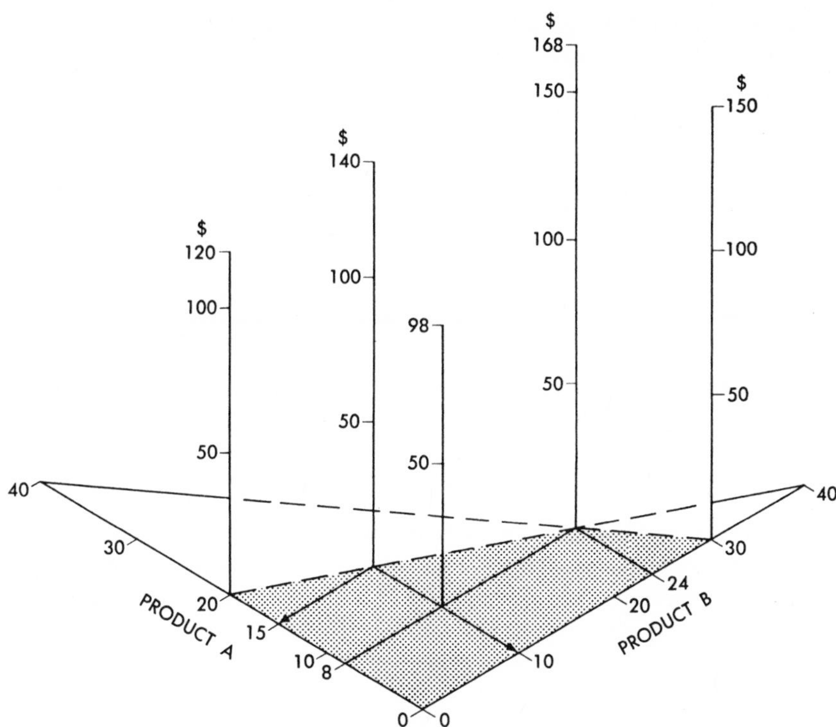

Fig. 6-2. Production capacities and profit contributions. In this three-dimensional representation, typical examples of various contributions from different quantities of Products A and B are shown: If 20 gross of A only are produced, contribution is 20 × \$6 = \$120. Producing 15 gross of A and 10 of B yields \$140 (15 × \$6 + 10 × \$5).

These data can be put into equations showing the objective of management and the controlling factors. The procedure is demonstrated in Table 6-3. There the equations are expressed in symmetrical form suitable for transfer into a block of numbers known as a matrix, as shown in Table 6-4. When the data are in matrix form, it is possible to solve for the optimum, following the matrix steps explained under the tables.

The first matrix shows that if only the two imaginary Products M and N are produced (in quantities of 120 and 40, respectively, as indicated in the results column), profit (Z) as expected will be zero. This first solution then represents the zero point of the diagram in Fig. 6-3. The evaluation row Z-P also contains negative entries, meaning that we are far removed from the optimum. A second matrix must be investigated, as in Table 6-5, using the transformation procedure of Fig. 6-4.

This new matrix tests production of 60 gross of imaginary Product M and 20 gross of actual Product A, with a profit of \$120. This result corresponds with the finding at the A side of the structure in Fig. 6-3. The matrix has investigated the corner represented by the Product A line and the plating capacity line at the base. However, since Z-P is negative for Column B of the matrix, we are not yet at optimum.

Table 6-3 Equations of Production and Profit-Optimizing Relationships

1. Objective Equation

   The overall objective is to maximize dollar profit, Z. Since Product A has a profit of $6 per gross and Product B has a profit of $5 per gross, maximum profit will result from producing that quantity A for Product A and that quantity B of Product B which yields the highest Z; or:

   $6A + 5B = Z$ Eq. 1

2. Production Equations

   Production of Products A and B is limited by the capacity of 120 hours per week in polishing and 40 hours in plating. At the production rates shown in Table 6-2, therefore, the quantities A and B of Products A and B that can be produced are:

   a. In polishing: $3A + 4B \leqq 120$ Eq. 2

   b. In plating: $2A + 1B \leqq 40$ Eq. 3

   The sign $\leqq$ means "equal to or smaller than," indicating that production cannot exceed capacity.

3. Symmetrical Equations

   The inequality signs in equations 2 and 3 are messy. But we can convert them to equal signs, by adding proper but as yet unknown magnitudes to the left-hand side of each equation. These magnitudes are known as "imaginary variables" representing imaginary production (of zero or greater quantity). Using "M" and "N" for these imaginaries and inserting zero values as shown below, we obtain symmetrical equations for the three expressions above:

   $6A + 5B + 0M + 0N = Z$ Eq. 1a

   $3A + 4B + 1M + 0N = 120$ Eq. 2a

   $2A + 1B + 0M + 1N = 40$ Eq. 3a

4. Solving for the Optimum

   The equations 1a to 3a can now be rewritten in a block of numbers or matrix (Table 6-4), which is convenient for solving them for the optimum profit, Z, sought.

Table 6-4 First Matrix

Row	Profit P	Products A	B	M	N	Result R	Evaluation R/A	Key Row
P		6	5	0	0			
M	0	3	4	1	0	120	120/3 = 40	
N	0	2	1	0	1	40	40/2 = 20	√
Z	—	0	0	0	0	0		
Z-P		−6	−5	0	0			

Key Column √

1. Columns A to R show the numerical coefficients of equations 1a to 3a for rows P to M. Column P shows the zero profits associated with the imaginary products M and N.
2. Row Z is the sum of the product quantities multiplied by their profits. For column A, 3 × 0 plus 2 × 0 totals 0.
3. Row Z-P is found by subtracting each entry in row P from row Z. Unless Z-P contains non-negative entries in all columns, maximum profit has not been reached. In fact, column R shows that when 120 units of imaginary Product M and 40 units of imaginary Product N are produced, profit will be zero (row Z).
4. The key column is A, since it contains the lowest Z-P. By dividing each entry under R by its corresponding A, R/A is obtained. In row M, R is 120 and A is 3, so that R/A is 120/3 or 40. The key row is N, since it contains the lowest R/A.
5. The intersection of key column and key row is the intersection of A and N, which yields the pivot entry, 2. This pivot, representing the lowest Z-P and the lowest R/A, is the basing point, from which a new matrix is formed next. This new matrix will seek to increase profits, until maximum profit is reached by successive "iterations" or matrix steps.

Table 6-5 Second Matrix

Row	Profit P	Product Columns A	B	M	N	Result R	Evaluation R/B
P		6	5	0	0		
M	0	0	5/2	1	−3/2	60	60/(5/2) = 24
A	6	1	1/2	0	1/2	20	20/(1/2) = 40
Z	—	6	3	0	3	120	
Z-P		0	−2	0	3		

1. Row M, columns B to R, is obtained from row M of the first matrix, using the transformation method shown in Figure 6-4. Column A, containing the pivot, becomes 0 for all product rows excepting the pivot row, where it becomes 1.
2. The other entries in row A are found from row N of the first matrix, by dividing each value in row N, from column A to R, by the pivot value, 2. Under column P, the unit-profit of $6 for Product A is shown.
3. Rows Z and Z-P are found from the steps previously shown for the first matrix. For column B, for example, Z = (5/2 × 0) + (1/2 × 6) = 3. Next, 3 minus 5 = −2.
4. The lowest Z-P entry is −2 under column B, which is therefore the new key column. Evaluating the ratio R/B for rows M and A, we find the new key row, M, corresponding to the lowest value of the ratio. At the intersection of new key column M and new key row A is the entry 5/2, which is the new pivot.
5. Although the present matrix yields a profit of $120, based on production of 60 units of Product M and 20 units of Product A (column R, rows Z, M, and A, respectively), this is not the maximum profit obtainable, since there is a negative value in the Z-P row. A third matrix must be formed, using the new pivot of 5/2.

The third and final matrix, shown in Table 6-6, yields the optimum solution of $168 for 24 gross of B and 8 gross of A, corresponding with the structure in Fig. 6-3. This is the maximum profit obtainable.

Table 6-6 Third Matrix

Row	Profit P	A	B	M	N	Result R
P		6	5	0	0	
B	5	0	1	2/5	−1/5	24
A	6	1	0	−1/5	1/5	8
Z	–	6	5	0.80	0.20	168
Z-P		0	0	0.80	0.20	

1. Row B, columns A to R, is obtained from M of the preceding matrix by dividing each entry in row M by the pivot value 5/2.
2. Rows A, Z, and Z-P are found from the second matrix, using the transformation steps previously shown.
3. There are no negative values in the Z-P row. Therefore the profit of $168 shown is the maximum attainable. No further matrix will be needed. By producing 24 units of Product B and 8 units of Product A (column R, rows B and A), the $168 optimum profit results.

For the two-product case illustrated here, the matrix method has little value. It is more rapid than trial and error and sometimes gives a more exact answer than can be read from a graph. But the real advantage of this method is that the matrix can easily be expanded to cover any number of products.

With a multiplicity of products the graphic method would fail and the trial and error approach would require a lifetime. Matrix algebra has neither disadvantage. To consider additional products, C and D, for example, it is necessary only to invent two other imaginary products, say, K and L, add corresponding columns and rows to the first matrix, and start the matrix procedure rolling. After several iterations the matrix that contains the solution will be reached.

Profitability Analysis

Linear programming provides a means of examining the relative profitability of various alternative production schedules. The method can be illustrated with the data previously presented for the polishing-plating contractor.

The first matrix, in Table 6-4, represents the equations 1a to 3a of Table 6-3. The matrix shows that if only Products M and N (the imaginary products) are manufactured, in quantities of 120 and 40 units, respectively,

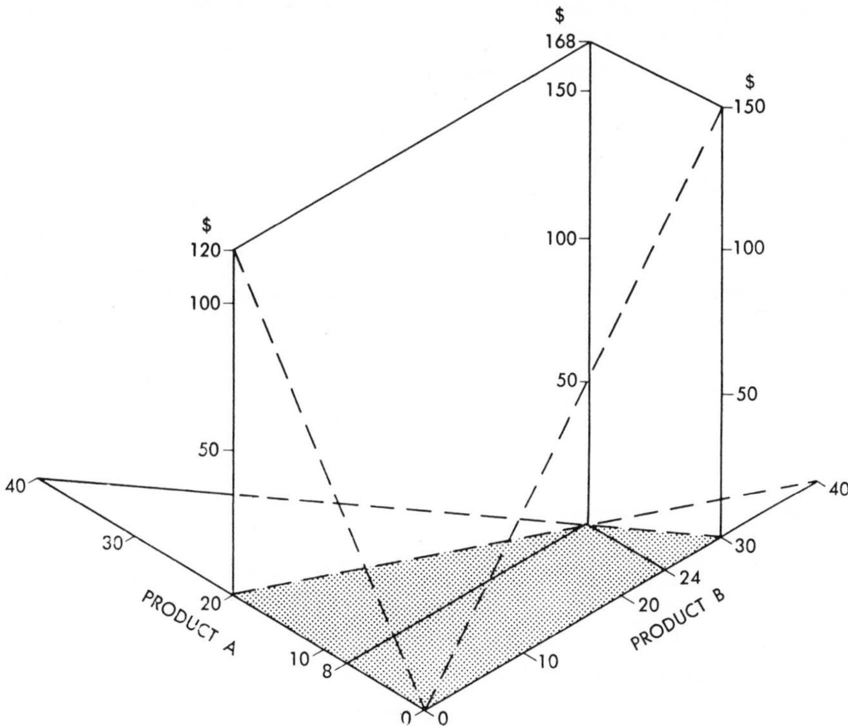

Fig. 6-3. Optimum product combination. Evaluation of the four corners of the base leads to discovery of the highest contribution. The first corner, O production, yields \$0. The second corner, 20 units of Product A at \$6 per unit, yields \$120; the opposite corner, 30 units of Product B at \$5 per unit, yields \$150. The farthest corner, for 8 units of A and 24 units of B, yields the maximum of \$168 (8 × \$6 + 24 × \$5).

capacity will be exhausted. But total profit will be zero. This is the least desirable position, from which one must look around to see what changes will produce better results.

The first step is to examine the entries in Rows M and N. The first entry in Row M under Column A is 3. This figure means in effect: If you wish to polish one unit of Product A, you must give up three hours of the imaginary Product M to obtain the requisite capacity. The adjoining entry calls for the surrender of four hours of M to obtain one unit of B. The entry 1 under Column M indicates that M is a substitute for itself, that is, that for each unit of M to be added an old unit of M must be dropped. No production of M need be given up to polish an additional unit of N because N does not need polishing; this explains the zero in the N column. The next row, N, may be analyzed in the same manner, this time for the plating process.

Row Z-P gives, for each product, the per-unit loss resulting if the product is not made. For example, $6 is lost for each unit of Product A that is not produced. Since this product shows the highest loss per unit, some amount of Products M and N should be replaced with some quantity of Product A. But how much?

The proper quantity of A may be found from the evaluation column. It shows that 40 units of A can be polished but only 20 can be plated. Plating is the bottleneck process for Product A.

We might investigate the effect of producing 20 units of A. Since this production exhausts plating capacity, we know that Product A replaces N. Therefore, we must substitute A for N in the matrix and insert the unit profit of $6 in the profit column. First, however, each new entry for the product and results columns must be divided by the pivot 2 before insertion. Because 2 hours of Product N must be given up for each unit of Product A added, the substitution of A for N means a change in the quantities of all entries by the ratio ½. This value also may be interpreted as the rate at which each unit of A is substituted for (the two units of) Product N.

Unlike Product N, Product A needs polishing. To permit this polishing Product M must be reduced. The formula in Fig. 6-4 shows the amounts involved. This formula again represents a substitution, but this time there is a subtraction: The corresponding key-row entry is adjusted for the substitution factor (in this case, multiplied by ½), and the resultant value is multiplied by the quantity shown by the key-column entry. The amount thus subtracted shows how much of Product M must be given up to produce the 20 units of Product A.

Take the results column as an example: For Row M the transformation is 120 minus (3 times 40/2). The 120 represents time now used in producing Product M. The ratio 40/2 represents the 20 units of Product A to be produced, and the 3 represents the units of Product M that must be given up for each unit of Product A that is polished. Thus, 3 times 20 is 60, which is subtracted from 120 to give the entry 60 found in the second matrix.

Optimum Contribution

The effect of substituting A for N in the second matrix is an increase in total profit from zero to $120. But we are not yet at a maximum. Imaginary Product M is using so much productive capacity that it causes a loss of $2 per unit of potential production of Product B. At least one more matrix is needed. Again the key column and row are determined, the pivot is found, a substitution is made (this time Row M is replaced with B), and the third matrix is obtained. As can be seen from the matrix, the introduction of B

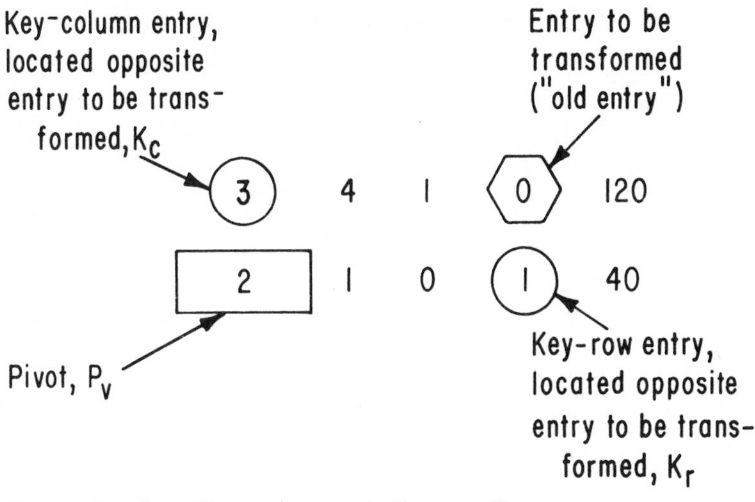

Formula for Transformed Entry, E_t

$$E_t = E_0 - \frac{K_c \times K_r}{P_v}$$

$$E_t = 0 - \frac{3 \times 1}{2} = -3/2$$

Fig. 6-4. Matrix transformation method. This is the method of matrix transformation illustrated for one of the entries in the First Matrix. The entire part of the matrix to be transformed, with key row and column, is shown above.

results in production of 24 units of this product. But to do so the quantity of Product A must be decreased by 12 (from 20 to 8). Total profit is now \$168. The absence of negative values in the Z-P row indicates that further substitutions would not bring a higher profit. The optimum has been reached.

Applications

The uses of mathematical programming are not limited to the product mix problem used as an example in this article. The technique is applicable to any optimization problem where a company, restrained by limitations on resources, must choose among many possible courses of action in such a way as to minimize costs or maximize revenues.

Some companies utilize mathematical programming in continuing computer decision-making systems. For the most part these systems cover functional areas of the company, such as distribution, advertising, or product processing—rather than overall corporate strategy.

Product Blending

Product blending in a process industry is one of the best known examples. Animal feed mixes, for example, must supply certain minimum daily requirements of basic vitamins, minerals, and other dietary elements to meed standards set by the U.S. Department of Agriculture. These requirements may be met by many possible combinations of such ingredients as corn, wheat, meat scraps, and soy beans. At any given time only one combination of ingredients will both conform to all specifications and minimize costs. Yet the optimum combination may change every time the price of one of the ingredients changes. Thus, feed producers have found it economical to set up operating systems by which computers regularly calculate new optimums based on new cost data.

Similarly, the oil industry has been among the earliest and heaviest users of linear programming. Many refineries have computers guiding the blending of fuel oil, gasoline, and other products to produce standard products at minimum cost. A large textile mill group uses mathematical programming to blend raw-stock fibers in various proportions (by fiber characteristics) to obtain fabrics of high strength and uniformity at the lowest cost consistent with these quality requirements.

Distribution Costs

Linear programming has also proved effective in minimizing distribution costs. Many companies have several plants and warehouses throughout the country to meet local consumer demand and provide temporary storage. The problem is which products to ship from which plants to which warehouses so as to minimize shipping and storage cost while at the same time meeting expected consumer demand. H. J. Heinz Company worked out a system for its plant-to-warehouse distribution. A computer, using mathematical programming, calculates an optimal schedule each week, saving many thousands of shipping dollars that might be wasted by rule-of-thumb allocations.

Operating systems based on mathematical programming are normally economical only for large companies—or for not so large companies in industries where prices of finished products or raw materials change frequently. Even a small company, however, can use the technique for occasional profitability analyses when a need arises to reallocate resources. Computer time can be rented from outside sources, or, if the problem can be simplified sufficiently, the equations can be solved manually.

Financial institutions have used mathematical programming to analyze their investment portfolios. Here the objective is to maximize yield while staying within strict limitations on maturity years for various groups of securities and other risk factors.

Media Selection

The technique also has been applied to the selection of advertising media. Here the problem is to select an optimal combination, from a great variety of alternative media, that fits within a limited budget but is consistent with sales estimates and marketing uncertainties. The results, as in all marketing applications, have been less clearly successful than in production because of the uncertain validity of the data available and of the assumptions used in structuring the problem.

A space company has worked out a method for optimal assignment of candidates with varying qualifications to highly demanding tasks, such as space program missions. Given the proficiencies and other qualifications of each candidate and the anticipated demands of each task, mathematical programming can be used to find that combination of men and tasks that would maximize the likelihood of success of the mission.

Conclusion

Mathematical programming is an effective technique for evaluating the cost and revenue effects of varying combinations of interrelated restricted alternatives. Thus, it can point the way to an optimal course of action.

Like all operations research techniques, however, mathematical programming does not provide final answers. Properly used, it can improve management's batting average in decision making. But its results can never be used as rigid directives, only as guides to an initial course continually subject to revision and adaptation based on new experience and evidence. Such a dynamic managerial process is in itself an optimum-oriented approach, continually enhancing the quality of planning, decision making, and control.

7 Linear Programming: Solution, Interpretation, and Sensitivity Analysis

by Floyd W. Windal

One of the major difficulties encountered in studying the new mathematical approaches to business decision making is the inclination of many authors to enmesh their presentation so completely in technical jargon and mystical symbols that it becomes virtually undecipherable. During my own period of wrestling with these new ideas, I resolved to translate at least some of the material into a form that the nonmathematician could understand. This article represents such an attempt.

One of the most widely discussed and utilized of the mathematical models proceeding out of the field of operations research is linear programming. It is a good starting point for the financial executive with a nonmathematical background who wishes to update himself through a program of self-study. An understanding of linear programming requires only the fundamentals of college algebra, yet it provides an insight into how mathematical models help solve business problems.

The following example is deliberately simple in order to reduce the complexity of the mathematical computations. It contains, however, sufficient facets to give the reader a good fundamental understanding of linear programming and to provide a basis for further study.

Formulating the Problem

The problem we shall consider involves the optimum allocation of limited resources to the production of several different products. Let us

EDITOR'S NOTE: FROM *Financial Executive,* April 1964, pp. 40—50. Reprinted by permission of the publisher, Financial Executives Institute, and author.

assume that we have the option of producing products 1, 2, and 3, which have respective contribution margins of \$5.00, \$7.00, and \$1.00 per unit. If we let X_1, X_2, and X_3 equal the unknown amounts of products 1, 2, and 3 we should produce, our total profit contribution, P, can be stated as the following "function." That is, P is a function of, or depends upon, the amounts of X_1, X_2, and X_3.

$$P = \$5X_1 + \$7X_2 + \$1X_3$$

Let us further assume that we have three resources to utilize in the production of our products. We have 500 of resource A, 350 of resource B, and 200 of resource C. The following table indicates how much of each resource is required to produce one unit of each product.

Resource	Product 1	Product 2	Product 3
A	20	10	25
B	10	7	15
C	5	8	5

Realizing that we have only a limited amount of each resource to use, we can state our restrictions (constraints) as follows:

$$20X_1 + 10X_2 + 25X_3 \text{ must be less than or equal to } 500$$
$$10X_1 + 7X_2 + 15X_3 \leqslant 350$$
$$5X_1 + 8X_2 + 1X_3 \leqslant 200$$

If we wished to convert these three constraints into equalities (equations), we would have to add unknowns for the amount of each resource which we do not use. Let's call A, B, and C the amounts of resources A, B, and C which we do *not* use. In linear programming jargon, these are called *slack* variables. Adding our slack variables to the inequalities stated earlier, we get the following equations (or equalities).

$$20X_1 + 10X_2 + 25X_3 + A = 500$$
$$10X_1 + 7X_2 + 15X_3 + B = 350$$
$$5X_1 + 8X_2 + 5X_3 + C = 200$$

Our profit contribution function stated earlier can also be stated in the same form through an algebraic manipulation. This function, referred to technically as the *objective function,* represents the amount we wish to maximize.

$$P = 5X_1 + 7X_2 + 1X_3$$
$$P - 5X_1 - 7X_2 - 1X_3 = 0$$

It can now be seen that we have a series of four equations—the objective function equation and our three constraint equations. We have seven unknowns: P, X_1, X_2, X_3, A, B, and C. This system of equations has an infinite number of possible solutions; i.e., we could produce many different combinations of products 1, 2, and 3 (represented by X_1, X_2, and X_3) and not violate our constraints. Because of the infinite number of possible solutions, we cannot get our answer through the traditional mathematical technique of solving a series of simultaneous linear equations. We must instead turn to the linear programming model, which systematically searches out the optimum solution.

Method for Beginners

The first step in our linear programming solution is to state the equations in tabular form (see Table 7-1). Note that there is a separate column for each variable, as well as an equals (=) column. Note also that the figures appearing in the body of the table are the "coefficients" of the various variables in each of the equations.

The format of a linear programming table and the particular solution technique followed vary widely. You will find almost as many variations as you find textbook illustrations on the subject. Frequently, these were devised with a computer solution in mind. The one we will use here is basically a hand-solution technique, which makes use of a traditional mathematical procedure for solving simultaneous linear equations. It is far easier to understand logically than most of the other methods.[1]

Looking at Table 7-1, it can be seen that one solution to our series of equations would be to let X_1, X_2, and X_3 equal zero, thus giving us zero profit and zero utilization of our resources. That is, A = 500, B = 350, C = 200, X_1 = 0, X_2 = 0, X_3 = 0, and P = 0. The variables with a value in the equals (=) column (P, A, B, and C) are called *basic* variables, and their coefficients are in boldface in the first table. Notice that each of the basic variables has only a single 1 coefficient in its column, signifying that one unit of each variable is equal to the amount in the equals (=) column. Note also that there are only as many basic variables as there are equations. The reason for the asterisk in row 3 of the X_2 column will be explained later.

More Profitable Solutions

From this point on, the solution technique consists of moving on to successive tables, each time reaching a more profitable solution, until an optimum is reached. As each new table is prepared, a new variable becomes basic and one of the previous basic variables drops out of the solution; i.e., becomes nonbasic. The following set of rules can be followed in determining which variable to make basic and which to remove from the solution.

- Make that variable basic which has the most negative figure in the zero row. In Table 7-1, this is the same as picking the variable of the product which is the most profitable per unit.
- Divide positive numbers (ignore zeros and negatives) in the column of the new basic variable into the numbers in the equals column.
- The basic variable in the row with the smallest answer becomes non-basic in the next table; i.e., that variable which most limits the amount of the new basic variable becomes non-basic.

Looking at Table 7-1, it can be seen that X_2 is the variable which has the most negative figure in the zero row (–7); i.e., product 2 is the most profitable per unit. By dividing the positive numbers in the X_2 column into the numbers in the equals column, we can determine which row has the most limiting variable. That is, we can determine in this first table which of the resources most limits our production of product 2.

$$\frac{500}{10} = 50 \qquad \frac{350}{7} = 50 \qquad \frac{200}{8} = 25$$

Row 3 is the most limiting row, giving the smallest answer (25), so the basic variable in that row (C) will become nonbasic in the second table. In other words, because it takes eight units of resource C to make one unit of product 2, we can produce only 25 units of product 2. If we had to concern ourselves only with resources A and B, we could produce 50 units of product 2. The fact that variable C becomes nonbasic in the next solution indicates that in that solution all of resource C is used up.

We now know that the X_2 column, row 3 block should have 1 in it in the next table (the asterisk in that block indicates this fact), and that the other blocks in the X_2 column should have zeros. The procedure for accomplishing this utilizes a technique for solving simultaneous linear equations. Essentially, what we do is change the form of the equations through multiplication and division, and adding one equation to another.

- Divide row 3, Table 7-1, by 8 and enter in row 3, Table 7-2.
- Multiply row 3, Table 7-2 by -7, add to row 2, Table 7-1, and enter in row 2, Table 7-2.
- Multiply row 3, Table 7-2 by -10, add to row 1, Table 7-1, and enter in row 1, Table 7-2.
- Multiply row 3, Table 7-2 by 7, add to row 0, Table 7-1, and enter in row 0, Table 7-2.

Table 7-1

P	X_1	X_2	X_3	A	B	C	=	Row
1	–5	–7	–1				0	0
	20	10	25	1			500	1
	10	7	15		1		350	2
	5	8*	5			1	200	3

Table 7-2

P	X_1	X_2	X_3	A	B	C	=	Row
1	$\frac{-5}{8}$		$\frac{27}{8}$			$\frac{7}{8}$	175	0
	$\frac{110^*}{8}$		$\frac{150}{8}$	1		$\frac{-10}{8}$	250	1
	$\frac{45}{8}$		$\frac{85}{8}$		1	$\frac{-7}{8}$	175	2
	$\frac{5}{8}$	1	$\frac{5}{8}$			$\frac{1}{8}$	25	3

Table 7-3

P	X_1	X_2	X_3	A	B	C	=	Row
1			$\frac{93}{22} = \$4.22\frac{8}{11}$	$\frac{1}{22} = \$.04\frac{6}{11}$		$\frac{9}{11} = \$.81\frac{9}{11}$	$\frac{2050}{11} = \$186\frac{4}{11}$	0
	1		$\frac{15}{11}$	$\frac{8}{110}$		$\frac{-1}{11}$	$\frac{200}{11} = 18\frac{2}{11}$	1
			$\frac{260}{8}$	$\frac{-9}{22}$	1	$\frac{-4}{11}$	$\frac{800}{11} = 72\frac{8}{11}$	2
		1	$\frac{-5}{22}$	$\frac{-1}{22}$		$\frac{2}{11}$	$\frac{150}{11} = 13\frac{7}{11}$	3

Optimal Solution

How do we know when we have arrived at the optimal solution? We check the zero row to see if there are any negative figures remaining. If not, we are at our optimal solution. If so, we know that our total profit contribution can be improved, and we proceed to the next table using the same rules as before.

Looking at Table 7-2, we can see that the basic variables are now P, X_2, A, and B. Their values are shown in the equals (=) column. As can be seen, this solution calls for the production of 25 units of product 2 (X_2), and our profit contribution (P) is \$175 (25 units × \$7.00 per unit). Note also that A = 250, which means that we still have 250 unused units of resource A. Likewise, we have 175 units of resource B still unused, indicated by the fact that B = 175. Note that X_1, X_3, and C are not in the basic solution and are therefore equal to zero. No units of products 1 and 3 are being produced, and there are no unused units of resource C.

The negative $5/8$ in the X_1 column of the zero row indicates to us that our profit contribution would increase by $5/8$ if we produced one unitof product 1. Thus, our next step is to move on to Table 7-3, making X_1 basic. Applying the rules previously stated, we find that variable A becomes nonbasic when X_1 becomes basic. The mathematical steps taken to get a 1 in row 1 of the X_1 column, and zeros in the other rows of that column, are as follows:

- Multiply row 1, Table 7-2, by 8/110 and enter in row 1, Table 7-3.
- Multiply row 1, Table 7-3 by $-5/8$ add to row 3, Table 7-2, and enter in row 3, Table 7-3.
- Multiply row 1,Table 7-3 by $-4\,5/8$ add to row 2,Table 7-2,and enter in row 2, Table 7-3.
- Multiply row 1, Table 7-3 by $5/8$, add to row 0, Table 7-2, and enter in row 0, Table 7-3.

Looking at Table 7-3, we see that there are no negative figures in the zero row, and we know we are at our optimal solution. The basic variables are P, X_1, X_2, and B, with X_3, A, and C not in the solution. Reading from the equals (=) column, we see that we are to produce 18 2/11 units of product 1 (X_1) and 13 7/11 units of product 2 (X_2). Our profit contribution (P) is \$186 4/11, and we have 72 8/11 unused units of resource B. It should be noted at this point that where it is impossible to produce fractional amounts of product, additional steps may be taken to derive an integer solution. Rounding the answers obtained from the noninteger model will not necessarily give an optimum integer solution. In some cases, however, especially where large numbers are involved, the rounded answer will be sufficiently accurate.

Imputed Values of Resources

The figures in the zero row of Table 7-3 are also of particular interest. The values in that row for the slack variables (A, B, and C) are the imputed values of one unit of each of those resources. Imputed value may be explained as follows. Given a certain contribution margin on each of the products, an optimum number of each product to produce, and the optimum utilization of the limited resources available to produce them, a per-unit value of those resources which are in short supply can be determined. Thus, resources A and C are fully utilized in the optimum production solution and are imputed a value of \$.04 6/11 and \$.81 9/11 per unit, respectively. Note that resource B, which is not fully utilized and thus is not in short supply, has a zero in the zero row, indicating no imputed value. Note that the optimal return of \$186 4/11 (P) is imputed in total to the two resources which are fully utilized: i.e., that are in short supply (Equation 1).

Resource	Imputed Value Per Unit	Number of Units		Total Value
A	$\frac{1}{22}\left(\$.04\frac{6}{11}\right)$	X 500	=	$\frac{500}{22}$
C	$\frac{9}{11}\left(\$.81\frac{9}{11}\right)$	X 200	=	$\frac{3600}{22}$

$$\frac{4100}{22} = \frac{2050}{11} = \$186\frac{4}{11}$$

Zero Row Values

The values in the zero row of the X_1, X_2, and X_3 columns indicate the difference between each product's contribution margin per unit, and the total imputed value of the resources required to produce it. For those products being produced (X_1, X_2), this difference is zero.

For example, let us examine the total imputed value of one unit of product 1. Referring back to the schedule shown earlier, we see that it takes 20 units of resource A, 10 units of resource B, and five units of resource C to produce one unit of product 1. Using the imputed values for resources A and C shown on Table 7-3, we get the total imputed value shown in Equation 2, which is the same as the contribution margin.

(20) (Imputed Value of Res. A) + (10) (Imputed Value of Res. B) + (5) (Imputed Value of Res. C)

$(20)(1/22) + (10)(\theta) + (5)(9/11)$

$20/22 + 45/11$

$110/22 = \$5$ = Contribution Margin on One Unit of Product 1

In the case of products not being produced, the total imputed value per unit, or total imputed cost, if you will, will exceed the per-unit contribution margin. That is, the production of these products would actually decrease the total profit contribution (P). Looking at product 3 (X_3), we find Equation 3.

(25) (Imputed Value of Res. A) + (15) (Imputed Value of Res. B) + (5) (Imputed Value of Res. C)

(25) (1/22) + (15) (θ) + (5) (9/11)
(25/22) + (45/11)

(115/22) =	$5.22 8/11	Total Imputed Value of One Unit of Product 3
	1.00	Contribution Margin on One Unit of Product 3
	$4.22 8/11	Negative Marginal Contribution of Product 3 (X_3)

Coefficients of Nonbasic Variables

The coefficients in the columns of the nonbasic variables, including the zero row coefficients, may be interpreted as follows. For every unit of a nonbasic variable made basic, the basic variables in each row will be reduced by the amount of the coefficient in that row. For instance, if X_3 were made basic to the extent of one unit (i.e., one unit of product 3 produced), the profit contribution (P) would be reduced by $4.22 8/11 (see preceding section). In addition, the basic variable in row 1 (X_1) would be reduced by the amount of the coefficient in the X_3 column, row 1, 15/11. That is, we would produce 15/11 less units of product 1.

The basic variable in row 2 (B) would be reduced by 260/8. This means that we would have fewer unused units of resource B. Finally, we would reduce the basic variable in row 3 by -5/22. In other words, we would *increase* the production of product 2 by 5/22 units. Thus, the decision to produce one unit of product 3 requires us to produce less of product 1, but producing less of product 1 released enough resources to enable us to produce more of product 2.

A similar kind of interpretation can be given to the coefficients in the columns of the slack variables which are nonbasic. For instance, if variable A were made basic, this would in effect be a reduction in the amount of resource A available. This is so because A is defined as the unused portion of resource A. For every unit of resource A taken away, the profit (P) would decrease in the amount of the coefficient in the zero row, $.04 6/11. In addition, X_1 would be reduced by 8/110, B would be increased by 9/22, and X_2 would be increased by 1/22. In other words, the effect of taking away one unit of resource A would be to reduce production of product 1, increase the amount of resource B unused, and increase the production of product 2.

Sensitivity Analysis

The discussion of the interpretation of the figures in the final table leads logically into the topic of sensitivity analysis. In fact, some of the previous discussion could be called by that name. Briefly, sensitivity analysis is the consideration of possible changes in the basic data of the problem, and the effect of such changes on the final result. Also included in the definition of sensitivity analysis is an examination of the magnitude of change required in the basic data before a new variable enters the final basic solution. Thus, the discussion in the previous section about the effect of a reduction in the amount of resource A available can be considered a form of sensitivity analysis.

Many other questions can be raised and answered using the data in the final table. Some of the these are:

- If the available amount of a scarce resource were reduced, how great would the reduction have to be in order to change which variables are basic and which are nonbasic?

This is merely a continuation of the discussion in the previous section. We said there that if variable A were made basic, this would in effect be a reduction in the amount of resource A available. We did not consider, however, how much of a reduction would be possible before a new variable entered the basic solution.

We can obtain this answer by dividing the positive coefficients in the A column into the figures in the equals (=) column and picking the smallest. A positive coefficient indicates a decrease in the basic variable of its row, and enough of a decrease will reduce the amount of that variable to zero and then to a negative, indicating the need for a different basic solution. No such limit is reached in the case of a negative coefficient, which indicates an increase in the amount of the basic variable in its row. In the case of resource A, the only positive coefficient is in row 1, so the limit of a reduction in resource A is

$$\frac{200}{11} \div \frac{8}{110} = 250$$

- How much would we be willing to pay for some additional units of a scarce resource? How many units would we be willing to buy at that price?

Looking again at resource A, we can reason that one additional unit would be worth \$.04 6/11, its imputed value. Just as a reduction in the amount of resource A available would reduce our profit contribution by that amount per unit, so some additional units of the resource would increase our contribution.

How much would we be willing to buy at that price? Again, we must look at the coefficients in column A and relate them to the corresponding figures in the equals (=) column. Every additional unit of resource A made available will cause an *increase* in each basic variable in the amount of the column A coefficient. Thus, the negative coefficients in the column will be the limiting ones. The smallest answer we get after dividing our negative coefficients into the equals (=) column figures will indicate the row of the basic variable which will first reach zero and then turn negative.

$$\frac{800}{11} \div \frac{9}{22} = 177\ 7/9$$

$$\frac{150}{11} \div \frac{1}{22} = 300$$

Thus, after we have purchased an additional 177 7/9 units of resource A, we will have used up all of resource B (the basic variable of row 2, which contains the -9/22 coefficient). Any purchase beyond that amount would result in a negative value for variable B and thus require a new variable in the basic solution. Note that the additional units of resource A would cause us to produce more of product 1 and less of product 2.

- How much would the contribution margin on a nonbasic product have to be increased in order to make it profitable to produce?

Looking at product 3 (X_3), which is not in the basic solution, we can see that the imputed value of the resources required to produce it exceeds its contribution margin by \$4.22 8/11.

Thus, an increase in its contribution margin of any amount greater than \$4.22 8/11 would make it profitable to produce. Looked at in a slightly different way, an excess of contribution margin over imputed value would mean a negative figure in the zero row for product 3 rather than a positive one, and following our solution rules learned earlier, we would proceed on to another table making X_3 basic and removing some other variable from the basic solution.

- How much could the contribution margin on a product being produced decrease before a new variable would enter the basic solution?

Looking at product 1 (X_1) we see that it has a zero in its zero row, indicating that its contribution margin is equal to the imputed value of the resources used to produce it. If the contribution margin on product 1 were to be reduced the imputed value would exceed the contribution margin and a positive figure would result in the zero row. In order to convert this positive figure into a zero (as in our solution technique followed earlier), we would multiply our row 1 coefficients by an equal negative amount, add the results to our old row zero figures, and enter these results as the new row zero in the table.

The limiting variable will be that one whose zero row coefficient is first converted to a negative as a result of the conversion process. This variable must be one which has a positive coefficient in row 1, as the procedure is to multiply row 1 by a negative figure and add it to the old row zero. Our limit will thus be the smaller of the following.

$$\frac{93}{22} \div \frac{15}{11} = 6\ 1/5 = \$6.20$$

$$\frac{1}{22} \div \frac{8}{110} = \frac{5}{8} = \$.625$$

Thus, any decrease in the contribution margin of product 1 of more than $.625 will result in a negative in the zero row of column A. This would mean that it would be profitable to make variable A basic, and to make some other variable nonbasic.

Summary

There is no pretention that this article covers the whole of linear programming. Many of the complications which might be found in an actual problem were deliberately avoided. Furthermore, the solution technique given would not be suitable for a very complex problem. The purpose of the article, however, is not to make the reader a linear programming expert. Rather, it is intended to introduce the technique, provide a basis for further self-study, and give the reader some understanding of the type of work being done in the broad field of operations research.

Note

1. Harvey M. Wagner, "The Simplex Method for Beginners," *Operations Research* (March-April 1958), pp. 190-199.

8 Linear Programming: Some Implications for Management Accounting

by Ronald V. Hartley

This article is intended to be a liaison between the scholars of quantitative methods (both accountants and operations researchers) and management accountants, concerning the practical implications of linear programming (LP). The purpose here will be to interpret and define: (1) the data needed for LP, (2) the sensitivity of the data and the value of such knowledge, (3) LP and its value in variance analyses and (4) the use of LP in joint costing procedures.

ACCOUNTING DATA NEEDED FOR LP

Linear programming requires three basic kinds of data:

1. Coefficients for the objective equation
2. Coefficients of substitution (for the constraining equations)
3. The capacities or requirements (for the constraining equations)

Most frequently the accountant will be requested to supply objective equation coefficients—revenues, costs or "profits." Although obvious when examining the nature of the LP model, it is nevertheless important to point out that the revenue and costs which are necessary for the objective equation must be those that are variable (and, of course, linear).

In addition to the above requirement, the data must be relevant (future data that differ among the alternatives) and reliable (more to be said about this later). In some cases, the data must include more than conventional accounting data. Specifically, accountants need to consider opportunity

EDITOR'S NOTE: From *Management Accounting*, November 1969, pp. 48-51. Reprinted by permission of the publisher, National Association of Accountants, and author.

costs and their orderly collection within an information system. LP itself generates opportunity costs which are useful for various purposes, some of which are discussed later.

It should be emphasized that in the classification of revenue and cost data, the primary factor of consideration should be their behavior rather than their functional relationships. The cost accounting system and reports should be designed with this requirement in mind if they are to be of any value to linear programming and other quantitative methods.

SENSITIVITY OF DATA

Sensitivity analyses are investigations dealing with changes in data and the effect of these changes on the optimal solution to a problem. A sensitivity analysis can be made of the three parameters used in a LP model—the objective equation coefficients, the constraining equation constants and the constraining equation coefficients. An analysis of the first will be discussed here since these coefficients are the parameters of greatest concern to the management accountant. In other words, the accountant should be concerned in knowing how much a cost or contribution margin figure can vary from the estimate without changing the optimal solution. A simple example will now be introduced to illustrate sensitivity analysis with respect to the objective equation coefficients.

Example

Let us assume that there are three products (X_1, X_2, and X_3) that can be produced and that each of them uses the same facilities. According to the best estimates, these products yield a per unit contribution margin of $90, $100 and $80 respectively. Assume there are only two limiting factors—labor hours and machine hours. There are 26 units of labor time and 38 units of machine time available per day, Product X_1 requires 2.7 units of labor time per unit of product and 0.9 units of machine time. Product X_2 requires 2.0 units of each and X_3 requires 0.8 of labor and 3.2 of machine time.

The initial and optimal LP tableaus[1] are given in Table 8-1 and 8-2. (S_1 and S_2 are the slack variables.)

The first thing to note is the significance of the implicit values associated with the slack variables (the last row of the optimal matrix). The $33.33 (ignore the sign) means that if another unit of labor time was available, the total contribution margin could be increased by $33.33. Conversely, if there was one less unit, the profits would be reduced by $33.33.

Table 8-1 Original Problem—Initial Tableau

			90.00	100.00	80.00	0.0	0.0
			X_1	X_2	X_3	S_1	S_2
0.0	S_1	26.0	2.7	2.0	8.0	1.0	0.0
0.0	S_2	38.0	0.9	2.0	3.2	0.0	1.0
		0.0	0.0	0.0	0.0	0.0	0.0
			90.00	100.00	80.00	0.0	0.0

Table 8-2 Original Problem—Optimal Tableau

			90.00	100.00	80.00	0.0	0.0
			X_1	X_2	X_3	S_1	S_2
100.00	X_2	11.0	1.650	1.0	0.0	0.667	−0.167
80.00	X_3	5.0	−0.750	0.0	1.0	−0.417	0.417
		1,500.00	105.00	100.00	80.00	33.33	16.67
			−15.00	0.0	0.0	−33.33	−16.67

Tables 8-3 and 8-4 show this via the simplex method. A comparison of Table 8-4 with Table 8-2 indicates that the profit is increased from $1,500 to $1,533.33 and that the solution is 11.667 of X_2 and 4.583 of X_3. The related value of machine time is $16.67.

The implicit value of the restraints is also an indication of the maximum premium per unit that one would be willing to pay to reduce the bottleneck.

Table 8-3 One Additional Unit of Labor—Initial Tableau

			90.00	100.00	80.00	0.0	0.0
			X_1	X_2	X_3	S_1	S_2
0.00	S_1	27.0	2.7	2.0	0.8	1.0	0.0
0.00	S_2	38.0	0.9	2.0	3.2	0.0	1.0
		0.0	0.0	0.0	0.0	0.0	0.0
			90.00	100.00	80.00	0.0	0.0

Table 8-4 One Additional Unit of Labor—Optimal Tableau

			90.00	100.00	80.00	0.0	0.0
			X_1	X_2	X_3	S_1	S_2
100.00	X_2	11.667	1.650	1.0	0.0	0.667	−0.167
80.00	X_3	4.583	−0.750	0.0	1.0	−0.417	0.417
		1,533.33	105.00	100.00	80.00	33.33	16.67
			−15.00	0.0	0.0	−33.33	−16.67

This value is only valid over a limited range of additions however. At a certain point an additional unit will not be worth as much as before because the relationship of the constraints to each other will change or there may even cease to be a bottleneck with respect to the given resource.

Next to be considered is the sensitivity of the contribution margin estimates for the product(s) not in the optimal product mix. In other words, assuming all other factors constant, what must the contribution margin be on such a product before it will enter the optimal product mix.

The key to the answer is found in the last row of the optimal tableau (Table 8-2) for product X_1. The -\$15.00 figure indicates that the opportunity cost of introducing X_1 (the lost profits resulting from reallocation of resources) exceeds its unit contribution margin.

The opportunity cost is computed as follows. If one unit of X_1 was to be added, the coefficients of substitution from Table 8-2, the column for X_1, indicate that X_2 would have to be decreased by 1.65 units and X_3 increased by .75 units (the negative sign indicates an increase).

Thus, the lost profit on X_2 is \$165 (1.65 x \$100) and the increased profit from X_3 is \$60 (.75 x \$80), so that the net opportunity cost is 105 (\$165-\$60). Hence, if the contribution margin was greater than \$105 (\$90 + \$15), product X_1 would enter the solution. It would enter because the opportunity cost would still be \$105 since the profits on X_2 and X_3 from which the previous calculation was made, remain the same. Therefore, with a new profit greater than \$105 and the same opportunity cost the P_j-z_j value would be positive indicating the optimal solution had not been found.

Tables 8-5 and 8-6 show the optimal results when the contribution of X_1 is \$104 and then \$106. Thus, the accountant should be statistically certain

Table 8-5 Contribution Margin of X_1 = \$104—Optimal Tableau

			104.00 X_1	100.00 X_2	80.00 X_3	0.0 S_1	0.0 S_2
100.00	X_2	11.0	1.650	1.0	0.0	0.667	−0.167
80.00	X_3	5.0	−0.750	0.0	1.0	−0.417	0.417
		1,500.00	105.00	100.00	80.00	33.33	16.67
			−1.00	0.0	0.0	−33.33	−16.67

Table 8-6 Contribution Margin of X_1 = \$106—Optimal Tableau

			106.00 X_1	100.00 X_2	80.00 X_3	0.0 S_1	0.0 S_2
106.00	X_1	6.667	1.0	0.606	0.0	0.404	−0.101
80.00	X_3	10.000	0.0	0.455	1.0	−0.114	0.341
		1,506.67	106.00	100.61	80.00	33.74	16.57
			0.0	−0.61	0.0	−33.74	−16.57

that there is not a \$15 understatement of product X_1's contribution margin. Reliability statistics will be discussed later.

Next to be considered is an analysis of the sensitivity of the contribution margins for the products in the optimal mix. It can be shown[2] that the optimal mix will not change if all other factors are constant and if the change in the contribution margin, dp_k, of product X_k is confined between the upper and lower limits given by the following relationship:

$$\text{maximum overall positive } h_{kj} \text{ and j not in the mix } \frac{p_j - z_j}{h_{kj}} \leqslant dp_k \leqslant$$

$$\text{minimum overall negative } h_{kj} \text{ and j not in the mix } \frac{p_j - z_j}{h_{kj}}.$$

where:

p_j = profit on the jth product
z_j = opportunity cost of the jth product
h_{kj} = coefficient of substitution from the optimal matrix using the row representing the kth product, j representing the column.

Product X_2 in the original problem has its base in the first row of the optimal tableau (see Table 8-2). Thus:

$h_{21} = 1.650$
$p_1 - z_1 = -15.00$
$h_{22} = 1.0$
$p_2 - z_2 = 0.00$
(X_2 in the solution)
$h_{23} = 0.0$
$p_3 - z_3 = 0.00$
(X_3 in the solution)
$h_{24} = 0.667$
$p_4 - z_4 = -33.33$
$h_{25} = -0.167$
$p_5 - z_5 = -16.67$

The limits for dp_2, maximum to minimum, are:

$$\left(\frac{-15.00}{1.650}, \frac{-33.33}{0.667}\right) \leqslant dp_2 \leqslant \left(\frac{-16.67}{-0.167}\right)$$

$$(-9.09, -50.00) \leqslant dp_2 \leqslant (100)$$
$$-9.09 \leqslant dp_2 \leqslant 100$$

The contribution margin of product X_2 could be reduced to \$90.91 (\$100.00-\$9.09) or increased to \$200 (\$100+\$100) and the optimal solution would still be $X_2 = 11$ and $X_3 = 5$. The profit would obviously change but not the mix. Thus, if the \$100 estimate for X_2 was in error and if the true contribution was between \$90.91 and \$200, the optimal action would still have been taken.

Tables 8-7 and 8-8 show this relationship by changing the contribution

Table 8-7 Contribution Margin of X_2 = \$91—Optimal Tableau

			90.00 X_1	91.00 X_2	80.00 X_3	0.0 S_1	0.0 S_2
91.00	X_2	11.0	1.650	1.0	0.0	0.667	−0.167
80.00	X_3	5.0	−0.750	0.0	1.0	−0.417	0.417
		1,401.00	90.15	91.00	80.00	27.33	18.17
			− 0.15	0.0	0.0	−27.33	−18.17

Table 8-8 Contribution Margin of X_2 = \$90—Optimal Tableau

			90.00 X_1	90.00 X_2	80.00 X_3	0.0 S_1	0.0 S_1
90.00	X_1	6.667	1.0	0.606	0.0	0.404	−0.101
80.00	X_3	10.000	0.0	0.455	1.0	−0.114	0.341
		1,400.00	90.00	90.91	80.00	27.27	18.18
			0.0	−0.91	0.0	−27.27	−18.18

on X_2 to \$91 and then to \$90. Note the product mix in Table 8-7 is equal to the one in Table 8-2.

Limitations

A major limitation with this analysis is that it fails when the contribution figures for the products change simultaneously. For example, if the payoff for X_1 was changed to \$104 (which is below its entry point) and X_2's payoff was changed to \$91 (which is above its exit point), the mix does change (see Table 8-9). Nevertheless, this analysis indicates the sensitivity of the data and may suggest areas in which the adequacy of the data might want to be carefully considered.

Should it be desired to study the effect of simultaneous changes of the parameters, parametric programming can be used. Parametric programming involves the orderly changing of parameter values while observing the effects on the optimal solution.

The analysis for X_3 is as follows:

$$\left(\frac{-16.67}{0.417}\right) \leqslant dp_3 \leqslant \left(\frac{-15.00}{-0.750}, \frac{-33.33}{-0.417}\right)$$

$$-40.00 \leqslant dp_3 \leqslant 20.00$$

Table 8-9 CM of X_1 = \$104, CM of X_2 = \$91—Optimal Tableau

			104.00	91.00	80.00	0.0	0.0
			X_1	X_2	X_3	S_1	S_2
104.00	X_1	6.667	1.0	0.606	0.0	0.404	–0.101
80.00	X_3	10.000	0.0	0.455	1.0	–0.114	0.341
		1,493.33	104.00	99.39	80.00	32.93	16.77
			0.0	–8.39	0.0	–32.93	–16.77

Implications

What are the implications of sensitivity analyses for the cost accountant? Primarily he should be sure that the risk of the actual data falling outside the range of values determined by sensitivity analysis is low. In fact, it would be useful to a study of this type if the reliability of the data be established as part of the original estimates. For example, the contribution margin for product X_1 might be communicated as follows: "95% of the time it will be between \$85 and \$95 with a mean of \$90." If these were the reliability statistics for the original problem the risk would be nil that product X_1's contribution would exceed \$105. It should be noted that the data for this problem were randomly chosen and may not be as sensitive as real world data.

How does one arrive at the reliability estimates suggested above? This depends upon the conditions under which the cost estimates are made. If, (1) the conditions of the recent past have been relatively constant and (2) if it is reasonable that such conditions will prevail into the near future, then classical statistics can be used. That is, data for the last nine months (for example) can be analyzed as to the average contribution margin. Since nine is a small sample, the *t* distribution can be used to determine the confidence interval for a desired confidence coefficient. In other words, the contribution margin is a random variable which can be communicated as an expected value and a measure of its dispersion around the mean.

If conditions of the future are significantly different from the past, or if the process for which data are to be determined is a new one, then classical statistics fail. Thompson and Kemper[3] suggest a methodology for dealing with this type of situation. Again, without going into an example, the process involves determining a subjective estimate of the contribution margin as well as a subjective estimate of the standard deviation. The latter is determined by asking the estimator a series of questions and using his responses to compute an implied standard deviation. After estimating these data, classical approaches are used to establish confidence intervals.

LP AND VARIANCE ANALYSIS

Another area in which there is a relationship between LP and management accounting is that of "gross profit analysis." Joel S. Demski suggested the use of LP in this area to obtain additional information of an opportunity cost nature.[4] Traditionally, these analyses are performed to determine the causes of the difference between actual income and budgeted income. Using LP in retrospect enables the determination of the opportunity cost of not choosing the optimal solution implied by the actual relationships that existed (and which probably differed with those projected during the planning phase).

Using LP as suggested adds a third dimension to the analysis:

1. Budgeted volume @ budgeted unit profits = budgeted income
2. Actual volume @ actual unit profits = actual income
3. Post-optimal volume @ actual unit profits = post-optimal income

Conventional analysis involves the equation:

Budgeted income — actual income

and refines the variance to that portion caused by mix and volume and that caused by nonstandard performance. The analysis can be extended to:

Total variance = (Budgeted — Post-optimal income)
+ (Post-optimal — Actual income)

where the first term is an indicator of the effectiveness of the budgeting process and the second is the opportunity cost of not adopting the optimal plan for the actual relationships.

If it is assumed that the decision process is such that LP can be used to determine the budgeted volume[5], then the post-optimal analysis is done by linear programming using the parameters actually experienced. It is then solved to determine the optimal course of action that should have been taken. This, in turn, will give the post-optimal income.

Examples

To illustrate, assume that in the planning phase the available information was that which was used in the original problem and, accordingly, the budgeted product mix was given by the solution in Table 8-2 (budgeted profit = \$1,500). Further, assume that after the period started an unavoidable change in the profit of X_2 took place, the new amount being \$90. It was too late to change the mix so the actual results were:

11 of X_2 @ \$90 =	\$ 990
5 of X_3 @ \$80 =	400
Total profit	\$1,390

Post-optimal analysis would reveal that the mix should have been according to Table 8-8 yielding a profit of \$1,400. Therefore:

1. Budgeted income = \$1,500
2. Post-optimal income = \$1,400
3. Actual income = \$1,390

The difference between budgeted and actual due to sub-par planning is \$100 (1-2) and the opportunity cost of using a non-optimal product mix is \$10 (2-3).

Consider a second example. Again assume that at the planning phase the original data was available and after production was started the profit of X_1 changed to \$106. The actual income is:

11 of X_2 @ \$100 =	\$1,100
5 of X_3 @ \$ 80 =	400
Total profit	\$1,500

The post-optimal solution is given by Table 8-6 so that:

1. Budgeted income = \$1,500.00
2. Post-optimal income = \$1,506.67
3. Actual income = \$1,500.00

Note that, in this case, traditional analyses would not have signaled a variance. Finally, it should be noted that each of the two variances can be analyzed in further detail but will not be done here.

LP AND JOINT PRODUCT COSTING

Consider briefly one final relationship between LP and management accounting. The assignment of joint costs has always been a problem to accountants. The methodology for doing this has normally been some version of the relative sales value method given the *actual* combination of joint products resulting from production.

It is contended here that an allocation of joint costs can be made which adheres closer to the concept of standard cost if it is done on the basis of a post-optimal solution to the joint product problem. In other words, LP can be used in the same way as suggested by Demski and discussed in the previous section. Given raw material availabilities, sales values at split-off, revenues and costs if processed beyond split-off point, market constraints, production coefficients and production capacities actually observed during the period, LP could be used to find the optimal combination of joint products implied by the actual conditions. Conventional methods would then be used to allocate joint costs based on the post optimal LP solution instead of the actual combination.

It is contended that these costs would be a better indication of value added than would costs allocated on the basis of actual production. Furthermore, the solution to such an LP problem should be beneficial to the planning process when joint products are involved.

CONCLUSION

Although it has limitations, LP is a powerful tool. Many of the limitations can be circumvented with some imaginative thinking. The accounting department can "make or break" an LP study or it can make such a study easier or more difficult. The challenge is there (not only with LP but also with other operations research techniques) and it is hoped that management accountants will accept it.

Notes

1. The reader is referred to Frederick S. Hiller and Gerald J. Lieberman, *Introduction to Operations Research,* (Holden Day, Inc., 1967) for a discussion of the LP simplex method. In the format used here the first column is the per unit contribution margin of the products in the solution, column two is the name of the products in the solution, column three is the solution and the resulting profit. The remaining columns contain the per unit contribution margin, the name, the coefficients of substitution (2 each), the per unit opportunity cost and the difference between the contribution margin (p_j) and opportunity cost (z_j) for each of the products and slack variables.

2. See Saul I. Gass, *Linear Programming,* McGraw-Hill Book Co., New York, 1964, pp. 132-133.

3. William W. Thompson, Jr., and Earl L. Kemper, "Probability Measures for Estimated Data," *Accounting Revenue,* July 1965, pp. 574-578.

4. Joel S. Demski, "An Accounting System Structured on a Linear Programming Model," *Accounting Review,* October 1967, pp. 701-712.

5. Other situations might warrant the use of another quantitative technique, but the process would be the same using the applicable technique the same way as LP is used here.

9 Production and Market Planning with Parametric Programming

by James T. Godfrey, W. Allen Spivey, and George B. Stillwagon

Introduction

Linear programming and its extensions have been applied to many business problems. One of the earliest applications was to problems of production allocation in the short run, where the main emphasis was on determining an optimal allocation of resources for a planning period. The purpose of this paper is to show how parametric programming (or sensitivity analysis) can be used to go beyond the determination of optimal allocation of production to provide management with tools for integrating production planning and market planning.

By means of duality properties of linear programming, we first examine systematically questions of model refinement by determining the "value" of each constraint in the model and using this value to study the effects of changing a constraint. As is well known, a linear programming model requires certain "givens" relative to which an optimal solution is determined. In production allocation problems, these givens can be estimates of machine capacity and machine rates, demand forecasts, etc., which are subject to change within the decision period. We use parametric programming to investigate the effects of changing givens in such a model. In particular, interactions between alternate sales forecasts and optimal production allocations are considered in detail. Parametric programming is also used to examine alternate profit-volume strategies in the short run, thus relating marketing and production decisions directly. Finally, the presentation is developed largely in terms of a question and answer dialogue

EDITOR'S NOTE: From *Industrial Management Review,* Fall 1968, pp. 61-75. Reprinted by permission of the publisher, Industrial Management Review Association, and authors.

between a manager and a model builder. By limiting the use of mathematical terms, it is hoped that the flexibility and practical usefulness of these concepts may be readily apparent and more easily understood.

Model Development

The Apex Corporation provides the setting for our linear programming model. To simplify both our description of the model in this section and our use of it in later sections, we will assume that Apex has three machines and produces three grades of paper. Although the size of this model is small relative to the very large models of the same type which the authors have designed, the decision-making interpretations of this model are representative of those available and operational in larger and more complex models. Indeed, the latter, through their greater complexity, provide management with even more flexibility than the simple model used in our exposition below.

Table 9-1 sets forth the production characteristics of the three machines. Machine 3 is older than the others, breaks down more frequently, and requires more maintenance. As a result, machine time availability for Machine 3 is less than that for the others.

Table 9-2 contains market data on the three grades of paper. All three grades have forecasts of upper limits on demand for the planning period and Grade B has a production limit which insures that at least the indicated amount of this grade will be made during this period. The size of the profit for each grade depends on the machine used, since the machines are not of

Table 9-1 Production Data: Machine Characteristics

Machine	Production Hours Available	Hours Required to Make One Ton		
		Grade A	Grade B	Grade C
1	60	1.0	2.0	1.5
2	60	1.5	2.5	2.0
3	40	1.0	2.5	2.0

Table 9-2 Market Data on Paper Grades

Paper Grade	Upper Sales Forecast (Tons)	Lower Production Limit (Tons)	Profit Per Ton by Machine		
			1	2	3
A	20	0	$3.00	$2.50	$0.00
B	40	20	1.00	0.90	0.00
C	40	0	2.50	2.00	0.00

uniform efficiency. There is no unit profit associated with using Machine 3; in fact, the age of the machine and the maintenance costs appear to indicate that it would be unprofitable to use this machine at all.[1]

In textbook-type examples of linear programming, the input and output data in Tables 9-1 and 9-2 constitute the basis of problem definition. The corresponding linear programming problem is set up with the appropriate linearity assumptions, and an optimal decision vector obtained. This decision vector is then management's "best" course of action and the problem ends. Actually, the "physical" input-output data constitute the beginning of the model building problem, not its end. In addition to the physical conditions of the problem, management can and often does impose requirements, some based on operational procedures that have been successful in the past and some arising from past sales experience and logistical aspects of the business. Suppose, for example, that in the past the sales (in tons) of Grades B and C have been about the same and management specifies that any production allocation should maintain this balance. Furthermore, suppose some customers regularly specify that Grade A must be made on Machine 2 because they buy paper in less than carload lots and freight charges to them are lower when the paper is delivered from Machine 2. Management therefore specifies as a second condition that at least 20 percent of the total production of A must be made on Machine 2.

Let X_{ij} denote the amount of production of grade j on machine i, where i = 1, 2, 3, and j represents A, B, C. The objective is to maximize profit per ton. Model 1 below is a mathematical statement of the problem.

Maximize $3X_{1A} + 2.5X_{2A} + 0X_{3A} + 1X_{1B} + .9X_{2B} + 0X_{3B} + 2.5X_{1C} + 2X_{2C} + 0X_{3C}$ (1)

subject to:

$$X_{1A} + 2X_{1B} + 1.5X_{1C} \leqslant 60 \quad (2)$$
$$1.5X_{2A} + 2.5X_{2B} + 2X_{2C} \leqslant 60 \quad (3)$$
$$X_{3A} + 2.5X_{3B} + 2X_{3C} \leqslant 40 \quad (4)$$
$$X_{1A} + X_{2A} + X_{3A} \leqslant 20 \quad (5)$$
$$X_{1B} + X_{2B} + X_{3B} \leqslant 40 \quad (6)$$
$$X_{1C} + X_{2C} + X_{3C} \leqslant 40 \quad (7)$$
$$X_{1B} + X_{2B} + X_{3B} \geqslant 20 \quad (8)$$
$$X_{1B} + X_{2B} + X_{3B} - X_{1C} - X_{2C} - X_{3C} = 0 \quad (9)$$
$$-.2X_{1A} + .8X_{2A} - .2X_{3A} \geqslant 0 \quad (10)$$
$$X_{ij} \geqslant 0 (i = 1, 2, 3); (j = A, B, C). \quad (11)$$

Constraints (1) through (8) present the data in Tables 9-1 and 9-2 in mathematical form. Equation (9), called a force equation, represents the first of the two conditions imposed by management, and equation (10) the second, or locational, condition. An optimal allocation for the period is then determined by an optimal solution to the linear programming problem above, and the objective function (1) gives the corresponding optimal profit. It is important to observe that such an allocation is optimal if and only if all relevant aspects of the model above remain unchanged during the decision period. Some of the givens in this model are sales forecasts (see Table 9-2); others are based on past experience, such as estimates of production time available in a period; and still others are profit per ton figures that are actually *anticipated* profits per ton. A good manager will want a model that suggests how to move to alternate optimal allocations when givens based on estimates undergo change. Moreover, management might want to prepare itself to anticipate problems more effectively by deliberately changing some of the givens in order to see what might happen to the optimal outputs of the model. In other words, management could use the model as a learning device. Varying the givens in a linear programming problem has the technical name of parametric programming.[2] We will consider some of these features in detail in a later section.

Table 9-3 Comparison of Models I and II: Optimal Allocation (Tons)

Activity Level	Model I With Machine 3	Model II Without Machine 3
X_{1A}	16.00	16.00
X_{2A}	4.00	4.00
X_{1B}	0.00	3.31
X_{2B}	17.93	21.60
X_{3B}	16.00	0.00
X_{1C}	29.33	24.91
X_{2C}	4.59	0.00
Optimal Profit	$156.65	$143.04

Model Refinement

Since our purpose is to examine interpretations of models and decisions based on them rather than mathematical properties, we will display flexibilities of linear programming by means of a question and answer dialogue between the manager and model builder. A manager looking at the data in Tables 9-1 and 9-2, without referring to Model I, might raise questions about the feasibility of operating Machine 3. Indeed, he might pose the following question: Should we continue to operate Machine 3 or should it be scrapped? In order to answer this question, a second model, Model II can be formulated which does not contain Machine 3. The two optimal allocations and corresponding profits from Model I and Model II can then be compared. These data are summarized in Table 9-3. Table 9-3 shows clearly that it is worthwhile to use Machine 3, at least in the short-run period for which the models are assumed to be applicable. In fact, the entire capacity (40 hours) of Machine 3 is used in an optimal solution to Model I since 16 tons of Grade B are allocated to Machine 3 and the machine time required is 2.5 hours per ton. This allocation results from the force equation (9) which, it will be recalled, represents management's requirement that equal amounts of Grades B and C be produced. In the absence of this constraint, perhaps no more than the lower production limit of 20 tons for Grade B might be produced. More than this lower limit of B would be made only if the demands for A and C were filled because B has the lowest unit profit. Thus, the paradoxical result of using a machine having zero profit contribution is a consequence of an *ad hoc* judgment by management to perpetuate an operational characteristic from the past. In other words, a constraint has a strong "forcing" influence on an optimal decision and therefore interacts with the latter in an important way. One of the advantages of a model such as the one above is that the forcing effects can be made explicit.

Given this information, management might be led to examine the requirement that Grade B and Grade C be produced in equal amounts. A model could be formulated without this constraint, or the constraint could be "sensitized" by changing the proportions of B and C to be produced and observing the corresponding impact on optimal allocation and profit. We could determine how much more of Grade C to produce relative to Grade B and how much larger the alternate optimal profit would become. Moreover, once we have determined the proportions of B and C which yield the largest optimal profit, we might then examine the marketing and distributional aspects of these proportions. It could be, for example, that the sensitization of the constraint would indicate that 10 times more Grade C paper should be produced than Grade B but that the sales of B and C are so closely related that it is not feasible to sell 10 tons of C for each ton of B. We will return to a consideration of these matters later in the paper.

Suppose now management wants to consider some "what if" questions concerning the impact of variations in the givens of the model on optimal allocation and profit (parametric programming). To examine such questions, it will be necessary to elaborate our discussion of the model of linear programming.

We have already described how an optimal solution to the linear programming model provides us with an optimal allocation and an optimal profit for a period. Each X_{ij} in an optimal solution represents an (optimal) quantity of paper grade j that should be produced on machine i. From an operational viewpoint, we can regard the "ij" combinations as "activities" in which the corporation can engage during a period. For example, activity 1A denotes using Machine 1 to produce Grade A. The production operations of Apex during a period depend on which activities are to be used as well as on the quantity of paper to be made by each activity. When an X_{ij} in an optimal allocation is positive, the corresponding activity will be in use during the period and operated at a level determined by the size of X_{ij}. When an X_{ij} is zero, the corresponding activity will not be operated. Thus, an optimal solution to our linear programming model provides an optimal set of (basic) activities as well as an optimal allocation and profit. Knowing what to produce on each machine (the basic activities) and how much to produce (an optimal allocation or level at which to operate each activity), management can develop an optimal production schedule for the planning period.

It is an important property of linear programming that X_{ij}'s in an optimal solution satisfy some of the constraints (2) through (10) as equalities. For example, if we substitute an optimal solution to Model 1 (see Table 9-3) into constraint (2) we have:

$$16 + 2(0) + 1.5(29.33) \leqslant 60$$

that is,

$$60 \leqslant 60.$$

When an inequality is satisfied as an equality in a constraint, we say that the constraint is *binding*. Note that some of the constraints (2) through (10) are not binding with respect to the optimal solution above. For example, substitution of the same optimal solution in (6) gives:

$$0 + 17.93 + 16 \leqslant 40$$

that is,

$$33.93 \leqslant 40.$$

It is an interesting feature of the mathematics of linear programming that we can readily determine how many of the constraints will be binding and how many will not be binding.

Suppose we consider changing the givens on the right-hand sides of constraints (2) through (10). If a given is changed on the right-hand side of a constraint that is not binding, we can determine a range for this given within which optimal allocation, optimal profit, and optimal activities do not change at all. On the other hand, changing the right-hand side of a binding constraint will change the values of the X_{ij}'s and corresponding optimal profit but will not necessarily change the optimal activities. For some such changes, we still engage in the same basic activities but at different levels. For changes beyond these we must both change basic activities (that is, select a new set of basic activities) and change the X_{ij}'s. Parametric programming enables us to calculate a range for changing each given on the right-hand side such that for any value in a specified range, the original basic activities are still engaged in, and the optimal levels X_{ij} can be quickly recomputed without resolving the entire problem. This is no small advantage when one recalls that the number of equations in some problems is in excess of 1,500 and the number of unknowns can go as high as 5,000. If we wish to change the givens beyond this range, parametric programming enables us to calculate a new set of basic activities, a new optimal allocation, and a new optimal profit directly from the old optimal situation without resolving the entire problem.

Parametric Programming

Suppose management asks: What would happen if sales forecasts or machine time estimates turn out to be in error? Table 9-4 contains a range (described above) of values for each of the right-hand side elements of (2) through (10). Constraint (2) is the capacity restriction of time available on Machine 1. A time estimate of 60 hours was originally entered in our linear programming model and an optimal solution to that model indicates that the total time of 60 hours should be used. The range given, 16.0 – 72.4, means that the actual time available on Machine 1 can vary anywhere in this range without necessitating a change in our basic activities. However, this range is for a binding constraint; the levels of the basic activities will have to be changed for any machine time other than 60 hours. This could be valuable information if Machine 1 should break down during the period. Suppose that for some reason only 40 hours of time will be available on Machine 1 during the period. Since 40 is in the range 16.0 – 72.4 the basic activities do not change but the levels of the basic activities would change. Table 9-5 displays the nature of these changes. Activities 2B and 1C undergo decreases in level and 2C is increased, with a loss in profit of $23.85 for the period. Note also that this is a *minimum loss* in the sense that the adjustments shown in Table 9-5 are *optimal adjustments.* In other words, if time on Machine 1 is reduced to 40 hours and some other plan adopted, the loss would be equal to or greater than that above.

Table 9-4 Right-Hand Side Ranges

Constraint	Optimal Allocation	Given Value	Lower Range	Upper Range
(2)*	60.00	60	16.00	72.40
(3)*	60.00	60	39.33	87.33
(4)*	40.00	40	19.33	67.33
(5)*	20.00	20	0.00	65.85
(6)	33.93	40	31.70	40.00
(7)	33.93	40	31.70	40.00
(8)	33.93	20	31.70	40.00
(9)	0.00	0	−10.93	8.27
(10)	0.00	0	−4.00	6.53

Table 9-5 Comparison of Models I and III

Model I Machine 1 at 60 Hours Capacity		Model III Machine 1 at 40 Hours Capacity	
Basic Activities	Activity Level (X_{ij})	Basic Activities	Activity Level (X_{ij})
1A	16.00	1A	16.00
2A	4.00	2A	4.00
2B	17.93	2B	12.00
3B	16.00	3B	16.00
1C	29.33	1C	16.00
2C	4.59	2C	12.00
Optimal Profit	$156.65		$132.80

Now suppose we go below the indicated range and set the time available on Machine 1 at 15 hours. A new set of basic activities must be determined; we cannot compensate for this new value of machine time available on Machine 1 by adjusting the old basic activity levels. Table 9-6 presents the new basic activities and their operating levels for our model having 15 hours of time available on Machine 1. The old basic activities and their levels are also presented so that they may be compared with the new.

Constraints (6) and (7) are examples of non-binding constraints (sales forecasts for Grades B and C, respectively). Our optimal allocations for these grades (33.93 tons each) are less than their forecasts (40 tons each), and variations of actual sales from the forecasts cannot affect our basic activities or their levels if they are between 33.93 and 40.00. If the actual sales are between 31.70 and 33.93, however, activity levels will change but not the set of basic activities (31.70 is the lower end of the range identified in Table 9-4). If actual sales go to 31.70 tons or below, changes in both optimal allocation and basic activities will be required.

Table 9-6 Comparison of Models I and IV

Model I Machine 1 at 60 Hours Capacity		Model IV Machine 1 at 15 Hours Capacity	
Basic Activities	**Activity Level**	**Basic Activities**	**Activity Level**
1A	16.00	1A	15.00
2A	4.00	2A	5.00
2B	17.93	2B	4.56
3B	16.00	3C	16.00
1C	29.33	2C	20.56
2C	4.59		
Optimal Profit	$156.65		$102.71

Table 9-7 Profit Ranges Per Ton

Activity	Estimated Profit	Lower Range	Upper Range
1A*	$3.00	$2.73	infinity
2A*	2.50	−6.26	$2.77
3A	0.00	minus infinity	2.09
1B	1.00	minus infinity	1.67
2B*	0.90	0.25	2.50
3B*	0.00	−0.71	infinity
1C*	2.50	1.99	2.91
2C*	2.00	1.61	2.52
3C	0.00	minus infinity	1.28

The constraint (5) on Grade A sales is binding and an analysis similar to that for the Machine 1 time estimate could be made. Actual sales of A can vary between zero and 65.85 tons without changing the basic activities, although their operating levels would change.

Suppose management asks: What would happen if any of the actual realized profits per ton were different from the original estimates? Table 9-7 contains ranges for each of the profit estimates in the original problem. The interpretation of profit ranges is different from that of the constraint ranges given above. The profit for a grade can vary within the given range without necessitating changes either in basic activities *or* in operating levels. For example, the profit for basic activity 1C can vary between $1.99 and $2.91, with only optimal profit being affected. If its actual unit profit should be $2.00 rather than its estimate of $2.50, then optimal profit for the period would be reduced by $0.50 (profit reduction) times $29.33 (allocated tonnage) or $14.67. No changes in basic activities would be necessary since $2.00 is in the specified profit range for 1C. But if actual profit for 1C should be less than or equal to $1.99, changes in basic activities and their operating levels must be made in order to make optimal use of resources. Table 9-8 presents a comparison between our original Model I and Model V, having profit for 1C equal to $1.80 (i.e., outside the range $1.99-2.91, presented in Table 9-9). Now the activity level of 1C decreases, that of 2C increases, and 1B replaces 2B as a basic activity.

Changes in profit (within the specified range) for nonbasic activities do not affect optimal profit, basic activities, or operating levels. For example,

Table 9-8 Comparison of Models I and V

Model I 1C Profit = $2.50		Model V 1C Profit = $1.80	
Basic Activities	**Activity Level**	**Basic Activities**	**Activity Level**
1A	16.00	1A	16.00
2A	4.00	2A	4.00
2B	17.93	1B	17.29
3B	16.00	3B	16.00
1C	29.33	1C	6.29
2C	4.59	2C	27.00
Optimal Profit	$156.65		$140.61

Table 9-9 Comparison of Models I and VI

Model I 3C Profit = $0.00		Model VI 3C Profit = $1.28	
Basic Activities	**Activity Level**	**Basic Activities**	**Activity Level**
1A	16.00	1A	16.00
2A	4.00	2A	4.00
2B	17.93	2B	21.60
3B	16.00	3B	12.33
1C	29.33	1C	29.33
2C	4.59	3C	4.59
Optimal Profit	$156.65		$156.65

nonbasic activity 3C has a profit range of minus infinity to \$1.28. Its profit can be as low as possible without affecting optimal profit, allocation, and activities. But if its profit becomes \$1.28 or higher, then 3C is a worthwhile activity to operate and changes in basic activities and levels will be needed. Table 9-9 presents a comparison of our original optimal profit, activities, and operating levels (Model I with zero profit for 3C) with those for a model with profit of \$1.28 per ton for 3C (Model VI). Notice that optimal profit is the same for each model. We can describe the \$1.28 profit for 3C as a point of indifference; that is, if our only objective is profit, then we should be indifferent between Models I and VI. If profit for 3C becomes greater than \$1.28, optimal profit will be raised.

Before considering more management questions, it will be necessary to discuss interpretations of duality in linear programming. The problem (1) through (11) has a dual problem:

$$\text{Minimize } 60y_1 + 60y_2 + 40y_3 + 20y_4 + 40y_5 + 40y_6 - 20y_7 + 0y_8 + 0y_9 \tag{12}$$

subject to:

$$y_1 + y_4 + .2y_9 \geqslant 3.0 \tag{13}$$

$$1.5y_2 + y_4 - .8y_9 \geqslant 2.5 \tag{14}$$

$$y_3 + y_4 + .2y_9 \geqslant 0.0 \tag{15}$$

$$2y_1 + y_5 - y_7 + y_8 \geqslant 1.0 \tag{16}$$

$$2.5y_2 + y_5 - y_7 + y_8 \geqslant 0.9 \tag{17}$$

$$2.5y_3 + y_5 - y_7 + y_8 \geqslant 0.0 \tag{18}$$

$$1.5y_1 + y_6 - y_8 \geqslant 2.5 \tag{19}$$

$$2y_2 + y_6 - y_8 \geqslant 2.0 \tag{20}$$

$$2y_3 + y_6 - y_8 \geqslant 0.0 \tag{21}$$

$$y_1, \ldots, y_7 \geqslant 0;\ y_8 \text{ unrestricted};\ y_9 \geqslant 0. \tag{22}$$

The maximization problem (1) through (11), sometimes called the *primal problem,* is one of resource allocation; the dual problem (12) through (22) is a pricing or resource (input) valuation problem. The dual values y_k, $k = 1, \ldots, 9$ (called shadow prices) are values per unit of resource k when the resource is used optimally; for example, y_i is the price or value of one unit of time on Machine 1, y_2 is the value of one unit of time on Machine 2, etc. The values y_k are also called *marginal values.* Roughly speaking, they indicate the change in profit that would occur if one additional unit of resource k were available and used optimally in the firm.[3] Finally, an optimal solution to the primal can be used to develop an optimal solution to the dual, and most computer codes print out optimal solutions to both problems. An optimal solution to the dual problem of Model I is

y_1 = \$1.19, y_2 = \$0.64, y_3 = \$0.28, y_4 = \$1.75, y_5 = \$0.00, y_6 = \$0.00,
y_7 = \$0.00, y_8 = \$–0.71, y_9 = \$0.27.

These comments on duality enable us to assess more carefully the comments made earlier concerning managerial interpretations of the force equation (9). This equation specifies that production of Grade B and Grade C be equal. The dual value associated with equation (9) in Model I is y_8 = \$-0.71. This means that if the right-hand side of (9) increases from zero to 1, optimal profit will change by \$-0.71 (i.e., it will decrease by \$0.71). Also, this one ton increase in (9) means that production of Grade B will exceed Grade C by one ton. We conclude that we could *increase* optimal profit by \$0.71 if we allow production of Grade C to exceed Grade B by one ton.

Table 9-4 shows ranges for all the right-hand sides of Model I. The right-hand side of (9) which is a binding constraint, has a range of -10.93 to +8.27. The production of Grade B can exceed that of Grade C by up to 8.27 tons or the production of Grade C can exceed that of Grade B by up to 10.93 tons without requiring changes in basic activities; only the activity levels would change. Now, using the dual value of \$-0.71, management can quickly evaluate this information. The production of C could exceed that of B by up to 10.93 tons for an increase in optimal profit of \$0.71 per ton. Given this opportunity for an increase in profit, management must determine if it is possible to sell 10.93 more tons of Grade C than of Grade B.

Force equation (10), with a dual value of \$0.27 might also be a matter for examination by management. This force requirement was that at least 20 percent of the total production of Grade A be produced on Machine 2. In an optimal solution to Model I, constraint (10) is binding because 16 tons of A were allocated to Machine 1 and four tons, exactly 20 percent of the production of A, were allocated to Machine 2. An interpretation of the dual value (\$0.27) is that for every ton of production of A that we transfer from Machine 2 to Machine 1 (therefore violating our force requirement), we could increase optimal profit by \$0.27 per ton. If we transfer the entire four tons of A initially allocated to Machine 2 to Machine 1, we could increase optimal profit by 4 × \$0.27 = \$1.08. With this knowledge, management might question whether the constraint is necessary. The reason given for it was that some customers buy in less than carload lots and freight charges are lower when Grade A is produced on Machine 2. Suppose Apex has the following policy for freight charges: (1) when customers buy in carloads, Apex absorbs the freight charges; (2) when customers buy in less than carload lots, the customer pays the difference between carload and less than carload rates. It is this differential D that some customers would like to minimize by having Grade A produced on Machine 2. If D < \$0.27, it would be profitable for Apex to violate constraint (10), that is, eliminate this force requirement, by transferring the production of four tons of A from Machine 2 to Machine 1 and absorbing the freight differential D. Optimal profit would then be increased by 4(\$0.27 — D).

To obtain an estimate of the combined impact of the two force requirements on an optimal use of production facilities, we can remove the two constraints (9) and (10) from Model I and obtain an optimal solution to a new model. This reduced model would produce an optimal profit of \$165.33, compared to \$156.65 for Model I with the force requirements. The difference in total profit is \$165.33 – \$156.65 = \$8.68; the negative of this, \$–8.68, can be regarded as the "cost" of the force requirements. Given this, management can compare the cost with its estimate of the advantage to the business of having the force requirements as part of the decision model.

Table 9-10 Comparison of Models I and I′

Activities	Optimal Activity Levels (Tons) Model I	Model I′	Change in Optimal Activity Levels	Profit Per Ton	Incremental Change in Profit
1A	16.00	16.80	+0.80	\$3.00	\$+2.40
2A	4.00	4.20	+0.20	2.50	+0.50
3A	0.00	0.00	0.00	0.00	0.00
1B	0.00	0.00	0.00	1.00	0.00
2B	17.93	17.62	–0.31	0.90	–0.28
3B	16.00	16.00	0.00	0.00	0.00
1C	29.33	28.80	–0.53	2.50	–1.33
2C	4.59	4.82	+0.23	2.00	+0.46
3C	0.00	0.00	0.00	0.00	0.00
					\$+1.75*

Suppose management asks: Would other profit-volume strategies be more profitable? Our linear programming model presupposes a particular relationship between the profit and sales forecasts for each paper grade. To answer management's question, we will use some of the dual values for Model I given above.

The three grades of paper in Model I have dual variables (y_4, y_5, y_6), with values (1.75, 0,0). For each additional ton of Grade A that we can sell (over our forecast and allocation which are equal), optimal profit can be raised by y_4 = \$1.75. Grades B and C have zero dual values ($y_5 = y_6 = 0$). This means that even if it were possible to sell more of B or C than forecasted, we would not do so because this would not be using our resources in an optimal way. Our optimal allocations of B and C are less than forecasted already; therefore, even if the marketplace provides an opportunity to sell more of B and C than forecasted, the restrictions on our production facilities tell us that we should not do so. This is essentially what zero dual values mean to management in this case.

In such situations, management sometimes asks: if we sell an additional ton of Grade A, why is optimal profit raised by \$1.75 (the dual value) rather than by \$3.00 or \$2.50, which are the profits per ton of Grade A when produced on Machines 1 and 2, respectively? Table 9-10 provides an answer to this question. Model I is as above and Model I′ is the same as Model I except that the forecast for Grade A is 21 tons instead of 20 (Model I′ essentially "increments" Grade A by one ton).

The positive dual value for Grade A suggests that we might exploit our production facilities to yield greater profits. To be realistic, however, we should expect that selling more of A will incur a cost to the business. Let us assume a linear relationship so that for every additional ton of A we

Table 9-11 Profit-Volume Strategies

Grade A Demand Forecast	Profit Reduction	Profit Per Ton X_{1A}	X_{2A}	X_{3A}	Optimal Profit
20	\$0.00	\$3.00	\$2.50	\$0.00	\$156.65
21	0.05	2.95	2.45	−0.05	157.35
22	0.10	2.90	2.40	−0.10	157.96
23	0.15	2.85	2.35	−0.15	158.46
24	0.20	2.80	2.30	−0.20	158.86
25	0.25	2.75	2.25	−0.25	159.16
26	0.30	2.70	2.20	−0.30	159.37
27	0.35	2.65	2.15	−0.35	159.47
28	0.40	2.60	2.10	−0.40	159.47
29	0.45	2.55	2.05	−0.45	159.38
30	0.50	2.50	2.00	−0.50	159.18
31	0.55	2.45	1.95	−0.55	158.88
32	0.60	2.40	1.90	−0.60	158.48
33	0.65	2.35	1.85	−0.65	157.99
34	0.70	2.30	1.80	−0.70	157.39
35	0.75	2.25	1.75	−0.75	156.69
36	0.80	2.20	1.70	−0.80	155.89
37	0.85	2.15	1.65	−0.85	155.00

Table 9-12 Comparison of Models I and VII

Model I		Model VII	
Basic Activities	**Activity Level**	**Basic Activities**	**Activity Level**
1A	16.00	1A	22.40
2A	4.00	2A	5.60
2B	17.93	2B	15.50
3B	16.00	3B	16.00
1C	29.33	1C	25.07
2C	4.59	2C	6.43
Optimal Profit	$156.65		$159.47

desire to sell, we must reduce its price, and therefore our profit, by $0.05. Grade A can be produced by Machines 1, 2, and 3 with profits of $3.00, $2.50, and $0.00 per ton, respectively, and its original forecast was 20 tons. If we desire to raise its forecast to 21 tons, we must, under our assumption above, decrease its price and profit by $0.05 per ton. A new model then would have 21 tons as the forecast for A and profits of $2.95, $2.45 and $0.05 for production by the three machines. We can now analyze this profit-volume relationship of Grade A within the context of our linear programming Model I. Relative to Model I, we allow the forecast of demand of 20 tons for Grade A to increase and the corresponding profits ($3.00, $2.50, and $0.00) to decrease simultaneously in the ratio described above. Our objective is to observe what happens to optimal profit so that we may determine if it is a worthwhile strategy to sell more of Grade A by reducing its profit per ton.

Table 9-11 presents the estimated optimal profits that we could obtain by allowing the simultaneous changes in the forecast and profit for Grade A. We observe that at a forecast of 28 tons and a profit reduction of $0.40 per ton, our optimal profit reaches a maximum value of $159.47 (rounded). Thus, the strategy of reducing the profit of Grade A by $0.40 per ton in order to sell 28 tons is better than the original strategy of Model I. Let us call a model using this new strategy Model VII. Optimal allocations for Models I and VII are presented in Table 9-12. The basic activities for Model VII are the same as they were for Model I; to implement the new strategy, we simply operate the same basic activities at the new levels indicated for Model VII in Table 9-12.

Concluding Remarks

We have presented a few of the managerial questions that can be dealt with by means of parametric programming assisted by an appropriate computer program. The all-important dialogue between manager and model builder can be carried out in these and other ways and can hopefully result in better mutual understanding and better decisions.

References

(1) Baumol, W. *Economic Theory and Operations Analysis*, 2d ed. Englewood Cliffs, N.J., Prentice-Hall, 1965.

(2) Dantzig, G. *Linear Programming and Extensions.* Princeton, N.J., Princeton University Press, 1963.

(3) Gass, S. *Linear Programming,* 2d ed. New York, McGraw-Hill, 1964.

Notes

1. Profit per unit is defined as revenue per unit minus variable cost per unit. Fixed costs are excluded from this short-run analysis.
2. In the language of linear programming, the givens we will be examining and changing will be coefficients in the objective funtion (1) and elements of the vector comprising the right-hand sides of (2) through (10).
3. See Baumol [1], pp. 103-128; Dantzig [2], pp. 120-139, 254-264; Gass [3], pp. 83-94.

10 Integer Linear Programming

by Clifford C. Petersen

In its most general sense, mathematical programming is the solution of optimization problems where inequalities are involved. For centuries mathematicians have directed appreciable attention to the solution of problems involving systems of equations, and only in recent decades has intensive effort been applied to problems based on inequalities. This has probably been caused by the greater emphasis given economic problems and the emergence of electronic computers to speed up the onerous calculations. The kinship of inequalities and economic problems is illustrated in the following example. If a manufacturer has a limited supply of labor and of materials, and a certain number of product types that he can make, he can plan the production quantities of each type of product in a way that will maximize his profit, regardless of the fact that he may have some material left over or some labor unexpended. Planning in a way that will expend all of his resources may not maximize his profit. The mathematical expressions (inequalities) that state the limits of his resources may be called constraints, and the expression that states how his optimized criterion (profit in this case) is calculated is usually called the criterion or objective function. The constraints and the criterion function are expressed in terms of variables x_1, $x_2, \ldots, x_n$ (quantity of each product, in the example just cited) to which values are to be assigned in an optimal though constrained manner.

Any constraints that are in the form of equalities can be accommodated by expressing each equation as a pair of opposing inequalities.

Depending upon whether the mathematical expressions for the constraints and criterion function are linear, or contain higher order terms, the mathematical programming techniques are classified as linear or non-linear.

EDITOR'S NOTE: From *The Journal of Industrial Engineering,* August 1967, pp. 456–464. Reprinted by permission of the publisher, American Institute of Industrial Engineers, Inc., and author.

LINEAR PROGRAMMING

A brief graphic review of the linear programming process will lend clarity to the discussion of integer programming which is the main topic to be considered here. Consider the following simple, two-variable problem:

Maximize $Z = 5x_1 + 7x_2$

subject to the constraints

$8x_1 + 14x_2 \leqslant 63$ (Constraint 1)

$10x_1 + 4x_2 \leqslant 45$ (Constraint 2)

As shown in Fig. 10-1, the optimal solution is where the Z-line (which would be an n-dimensional hyperplane if there were a larger number of variables) touches an extreme point of the feasible region; $x_1 = 3.5$ and $x_2 = 2.5$. Highly efficient algorithms exist for the mathematical solution of problems of this type.

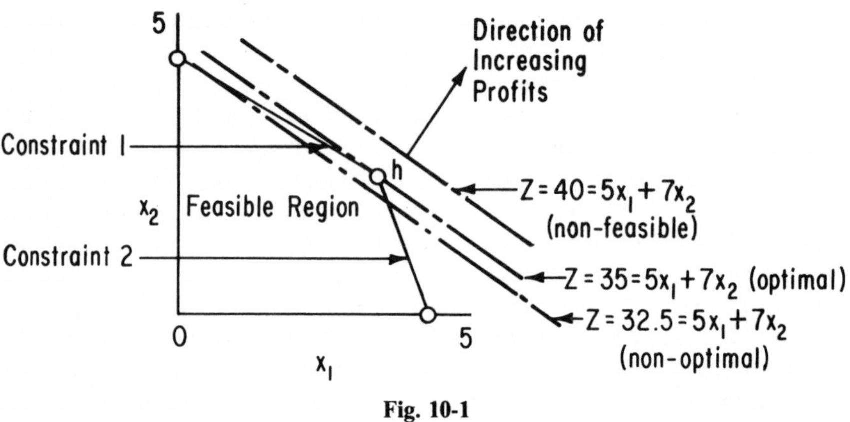

Fig. 10-1

NON-LINEAR PROGRAMMING

If any of the mathematical expressions for the constraints or criterion function are non-linear, the solutions become much more difficult. Methods for solving such optimization problems are at the forefront of present research, progress having been made on simple types only (10). Quadratic programming, methods using Lagrangian multipliers, and dynamic programming (3) are some of the most used techniques.

CONTINUOUS AND DISCRETE VARIABLES

Mathematical programming problems are further classified on the basis of whether the variables are continuous or whether they are restricted to discrete values. This distinction is primarily applicable to linear problems where techniques for handling the discrete integer case are evolving.

INTEGER LINEAR PROGRAMMING

Integer linear programs (also called discrete or diophantine programs) are sometimes considered to be non-linear programming problems which would be linear if some or all of the variables were not restricted to integral values. They may also be considered as a subclass of linear programming problems having some or all of the variables restricted to integral values. If all of the variables are so restricted, the problem is classified as "all-integer"; if only some of the variables are so restricted the problem is classified as "mixed."

Solving a linear integer programming problem as if it were a continuous linear programming problem, and then rounding the solution to the nearest integers gives generally satisfactory results if the values are large so that rounding has negligible effect. However, the most interesting integer programming problems are those in which the variables must be small whole numbers, often zero or one.

If the example shown in the previous figure is considered to be restricted so that only integral values of x_1 and x_2 are permissible, rounding the previously shown solution would give $x_1 = 3$, $x_2 = 2$, and $Z = 29$. As shown in Fig. 10-2, the optimal integer solution is actually $x_1 = 2$ and $x_2 = 3$ (point m), with Z maximized at 31.

This simple illustration shows how deceptive rounding may be with small values of variables. The optimal integer solution of such a small problem may easily be found by trial and error, but it should be remembered that typical problems involve many variables and many constraints; general methods are thus very desirable.

FUNDAMENTAL INTEGER PROGRAMMING TECHNIQUES

Cutting Plane Methods

As early as 1958, R.E. Gomory published a method applicable when all variables are constrained to integer values (8). The early Gomory algorithm started with an optimal solution (such as obtained by the Simplex Method) for the given problem, and, assuming that all variables were not integers in that solution, proceeded by generating additional constraints or cuts. Each of these cuts excluded certain feasible solutions without excluding any with certain variables having integer values. After the creation of each new constraint, in accordance with the rules of the algorithm, an iterative procedure was implemented to obtain a new feasible solution which came closer to an all-integer solution. The new constraints were all retained and the problem grew in size as the iterations progressed. Mathematically it was shown that the procedure converged in a finite number of steps if the criterion function had a lower as well as an upper bound, but computer experience showed that the method was somewhat unpredictable, often requiring a tremendous amount of calculation. In addition, because of the multiplication involved, rounding errors occurred making exact solutions difficult to achieve.

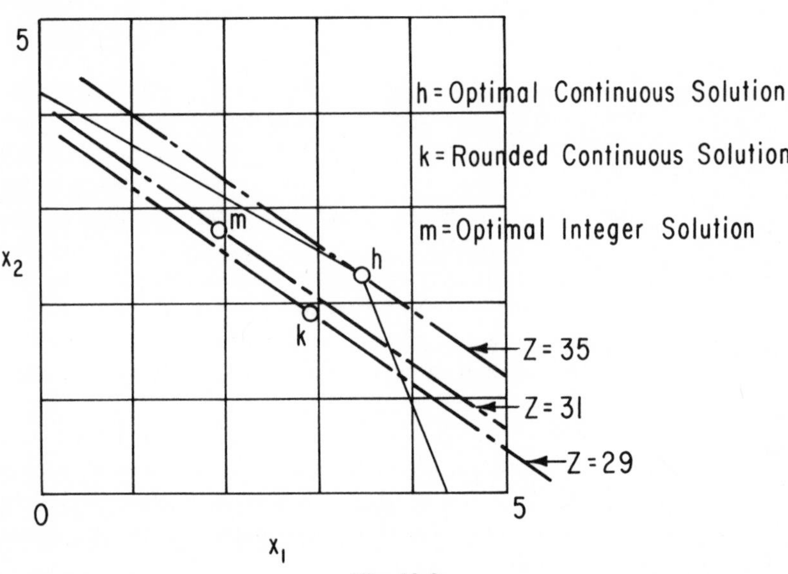

Fig. 10-2

An improved "all-integer integer programming algorithm" was described by Gomory in 1963 (9) for application to the same kind of problems as his older algorithm. In the new algorithm each constraint is used for an iteration, then discarded in favor of the next newly generated constraint. This algorithm also has been shown to terminate in a finite number of steps, but the actual number required has been found to be highly variable and unpredictable. Work is being done by numerous researchers to implement and refine cutting plane methods as typified by Gomory's algorithms. Existing computer programs utilizing the all-integer algorithm are being applied to various test problems. The current literature contains numerous papers describing the results and comparing the algorithm's efficiency with that of other techniques.

Shifted Hyperplane Methods

A typical method using the shifted functional hyperplane technique is that described by Land and Doig in 1960 (14). The method operates on an optimal fractional solution. In other words, it starts after one has first with standard techniques reached a solution where the variables have been assigned values (not necessarily integral) that optimize the criterion function while remaining just within the constrained region. The hyperplane defining the criterion function is then methodically shifted so it cuts into the space representing the feasible region. This differs from the cutting plane method which defines new feasible space and then seeks a position of the hyperplane that just touches the new space at a point. In the Land and Doig method the hyperplane is pushed down until it meets an integral point of one of the variables; the effect of varying the other variables to their bracketing integer values is systematically explored and the optimal integer solution is determined. This method has an advantage when only some of the variables are required to be integers and others are not so restricted.

Truncated Enumeration Methods

An obvious technique for solving integer programs is complete enumeration. By assigning all integer combinations of the variables, selecting only values available within the space representing the feasible region, the optimal assignment may be found by comparison. With practical problems, however, the number of variables and constraints produces an astronomical number of combinations to be explored, and thus requires techniques for excluding most of the combinations. Glover (7) has neatly summarized the great amount of work done to devise truncated enumeration techniques.

Egon Balas in 1965 (1) published an interesting algorithm of this class that applies to the special case when all variables are restricted to the values of zero or one. This technique is very useful because many economic problems resolve into a question of choice, where a value of one may be taken to mean selection of an alternative designated by a particular variable, and the value of zero, rejection of the alternative. Furthermore, in other types of problems, variables that may attain values larger than one, but are bounded, may be represented in binary form and solved with the zero-one algorithm. The Balas algorithm is completely additive, thus free of the rounding errors usually resulting from multiplication. It is a systematic search method where branches of the combinatorial "tree" are examined and, with the use of certain tests, are determined to be either useless for further search (in which case they are abandoned) or possible sources of improved, lower cost, feasible solutions (in which case the search continues along such branches). In a problem of n variables, each of which must be assigned a value of zero or one, there are 2^n possible feasible and non-feasible solutions. The efficiency of the algorithm in avoiding complete enumeration depends on the discerning power of the applied tests. Balas' original tests proved effective in solving problems of up to 30 variables in reasonable lengths of time. Other tests have been suggested and implemented to solve 50-variable problems of the capital budgeting type (15) and up to 159-variable problems of other types (5).

TYPICAL INTEGER PROGRAMMING PROBLEMS: ALL-INTEGER

Some of the most frequently occurring all-integer problems are those involving choice or selection. Some of these are described here.

Capital Budgeting Problem

This type of problem requires the selection from numerous profitable ventures, each having a cost in future time periods, a combination of ventures that will maximize profit while remaining within cost budgets established for each of the future time periods. The choosing of research projects having predictable future investment demands, or the selection of investment programs, each requiring cash outlays in future time periods, typify the capital budgeting problem. (The minimization of cost in purchase of ventures having income in future time periods, in such a way as to equal or exeed stipulated total income requirements for these future time periods, would be the inverse problem, and would be solved in a similar manner.)

The single time period problem is trivial, but will serve to illustrate the elementary concept. The following one-year development projects are all considered desirable but there are insufficient funds to pursue them all.

If the profit /cost ratios are calculated for each project in Table 10-1, the projects would rank 3, 4, 2, 1, with the most profitable first. The optimum choice is achieved by funding the most profitable projects until available funds are depleted (that is, choose projects 3, 4, and 2).

If multiple time periods are made a part of the problem, the problem is not so trivial. Assume that the projects run three years.

Table 10-1

Project	Thousands of Dollars: Expected Profit	Cost	
1	90	30	
2	60	15	Available Funds:
3	180	30	$75,000
4	100	20	
	430	95	

Table 10-2

Project	Expected Profit	Cost Year 1	Cost Year 2	Cost Year 3
	Thousands of Dollars			
1	90	8	10	12
2	60	2	5	8
3	180	15	10	5
4	100	10	5	5
	430	35	30	30
Maximum Allowable Budget:		25	25	25

This problem shown in Table 10-2 is set up in the following manner and is easily solved by use of a zero-one algorithm:

Maximize

$$90x_1 + 60x_2 + 180x_3 + 100x_4$$

Subject to:

$$8x_1 + 2x_2 + 15x_3 + 10x_4 \leqslant 25$$

$$10x_1 + 5x_2 + 10x_3 + 5x_4 \leqslant 25$$

$$12x_1 + 8x_2 + 5x_3 + 5x_4 \leqslant 25$$

All $x_j = 0$ or 1

The solution will give values of one or zero for each x_j, $x_j = 1$ meaning Project j is chosen, $x_j = 0$ meaning it is rejected. All budgeted funds will not necessarily be spent, but the profit will be maximized under the constraint of the three annual budgets.

Traveling Salesman Problem

A much publicized problem that, practically speaking, is a general formulation for determining an optimum sequence of n items or events all having linear interrelations, is stated as follows.

A salesman starts from a certain town and must visit all the other n - 1 interconnected towns just once and return to the starting point in such a way that the total distance traveled is as short as possible. Each town is directly accessible from all the others and the direct distance between each pair is given as d_{ij}. There are $(n - 1)!$ different tours possible, half of which are unique sequences and half being their inverse. One of several possible formulations, as described by Vajda (16) and Hadley (10), is illustrated with the following simplified four-city example, having $(4 - 1)! = 6$ possible circuits, and four legs to a tour. Note that while one can readily solve such a simple problem by complete enumeration of the six tours and selection of the shortest by inspection, this would not be true of large problems.

For this example one is given the input shown in Fig. 10-3. The zero-one variable x_{ijk} is defined to represent the selection of a traverse from city i to city j as the kth leg of the tour. In this example, starting at City 1 will be assumed although the optimal sequence will be the same regardless of where one starts.

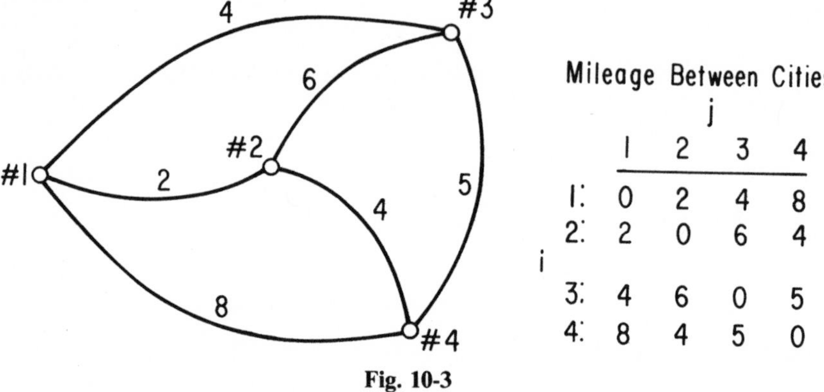

Mileage Between Cities

i \ j	1	2	3	4
1:	0	2	4	8
2:	2	0	6	4
3:	4	6	0	5
4:	8	4	5	0

Fig. 10-3

The first set of constraints is formulated from the requirement that for the kth leg of the itinerary only one span is traversed:

$$x_{121} + x_{131} + x_{141} = 1 \quad \text{for the 1st leg}$$

$$x_{232} + x_{242} + x_{322} + x_{342} + x_{422} + x_{432} = 1 \quad \text{for the 2nd leg}$$

$$x_{233} + x_{243} + x_{323} + x_{343} + x_{423} + x_{433} = 1 \quad \text{for the 3rd leg}$$

$$x_{214} + x_{314} + x_{414} = 1 \quad \text{for the 4th leg}$$

The first and fourth constraints are curtailed because starting and ending at City 1 was required. In these four constraints all the needed variables have been defined and entered into the problem. However, these variables must be regrouped into other constraining expressions according to the logic of the problem.

The second set of constraints is based on the requirement that for all towns there is just one other town that will be reached from it on some leg.

$x_{121} + x_{131} + x_{141} = 1$ (redundant; omit) from City 1

$x_{232} + x_{242} + x_{233} + x_{243} + x_{214} = 1$ from City 2

$x_{322} + x_{342} + x_{323} + x_{343} + x_{314} = 1$ from City 3

$x_{422} + x_{432} + x_{423} + x_{433} + x_{414} = 1$ from City 4

A third set of constraints is deduced from the fact that for all towns there is just one other town from which it will be reached on some leg.

$x_{214} + x_{314} + x_{414} = 1$ (redundant; omit) to City 1

$x_{121} + x_{322} + x_{422} + x_{323} + x_{423} = 1$ to City 2

$x_{131} + x_{232} + x_{432} + x_{233} + x_{423} = 1$ to City 3

$x_{141} + x_{242} + x_{342} + x_{243} + x_{343} = 1$ to City 4

To provide continuity and prevent a solution comprising several disconnected circular tours, it is required that when a town is reached on the kth leg, it must be left on the $(k + 1)$th leg (or first leg if $k = n$).

$x_{121} = x_{232} + x_{242}$ If City 2 is reached on 1st leg

$x_{131} = x_{322} + x_{342}$ If City 3 is reached on 1st leg

$x_{141} = x_{422} + x_{432}$ If City 4 is reached on 1st leg

$x_{322} + x_{422} = x_{233} + x_{243}$ If City 2 is reached on 2nd leg

$x_{232} + x_{432} = x_{323} + x_{343}$ If City 3 is reached on 2nd leg

$x_{242} + x_{342} = x_{423} + x_{433}$ If City 4 is reached on 2nd leg

$x_{323} + x_{423} = x_{214}$ If City 2 is reached on 3rd leg

$x_{233} + x_{433} = x_{314}$ If City 3 is reached on 3rd leg

$x_{243} + x_{343} = x_{414}$ If City 3 is reached on 3rd leg

$x_{214} + x_{314} + x_{414} = x_{121} + x_{131} + x_{141} = 1$ (redundant; omit)

When City 1 is reached on 4th leg.

Because minimizing the total tour distance is desired, the criterion function is

Minimize

$$\sum_i \sum_j \sum_k d_{ij} x_{ijk},$$

where the x_{ijk} are restricted to zero or one. Using the distances of Fig. 10-3, and eliminating the $d_{ij}x_{ijk}$ forced to zero because it was required that the tour start and end at City 1, the criterion function becomes

Minimize

$$\begin{aligned} Z = {} & 2x_{121} + 4x_{131} + 8x_{141} + 6x_{232} + 4x_{242} + 6x_{322} + 5x_{342} + 4x_{422} + 5x_{432} \\ & + 6x_{233} + 4x_{243} + 6x_{323} + 5x_{343} + 4x_{423} + 5x_{433} + 2x_{214} + 4x_{314} \\ & + 8x_{414} \end{aligned}$$

In this problem there are 18 variables and 19 constraints for a four-city problem, a degree of complexity easily manageable with present zero-one algorithms. When all constraints are satisfied simultaneously with a least-distance solution one has $Z = 15$, with the sequence 1,3,4,2,1 (or its inverse, 1,2,4,3,1).

In general this type of problem with this formulation will require $2(n-1) + (n-1)(n-2)^2$ variables and $3n + (n-1)^2 - 2$ constraints. A 20-city problem, with $n = 20$, will become grossly difficult with 6,194 variables and 419 constraints. Other formulations and decomposition methods are used for large problems.

Multiple Choice Problems

An interesting type of problem in which a number of groups of alternatives are posed, and wherein one alternative must be chosen from each group, has been discussed by Healy (13). Healy has devised a convenient technique, which he calls Multiple Choice Programming (basically a variant of the cutting plane class), but other integer algorithms will also solve problems of this type.

The following oil well drilling example will illustrate the multiple choice type of problem. There are three drilling sites and four underground targets (see Fig. 10-4). Each target is to be reached from only one site, the problem being to determine which site is to be used for each target so as to minimize cost.

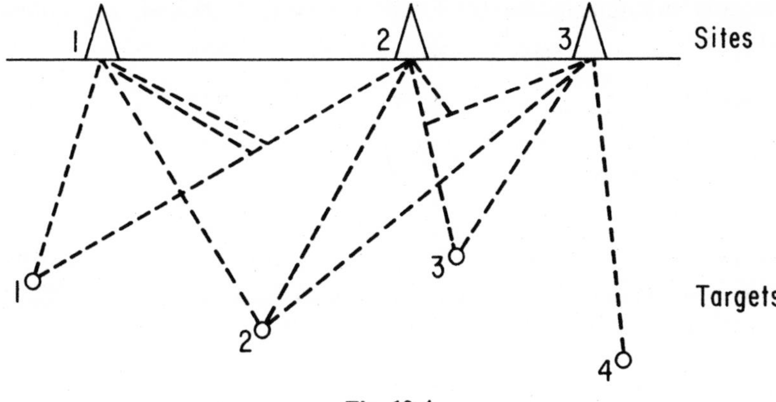

Fig. 10-4

Drilling costs from each site to each target are given, and, in addition, a site preparation cost is involved. If, for example, all targets were reached from Site 2, one would not incur the site preparation costs on Sites 1 and 3. Typical data might be as given in Table 10-3.

Table 10-3

	Cost of Drilling to Target				Site
Site	**1**	**2**	**3**	**4**	**Preparation Cost**
1	2.3	0.6	1.0	6.6	4.3
2	3.7	6.3	4.2	6.3	1.0
3	1.0	8.1	8.6	9.9	3.5

The variables x_{ij} can be defined to indicate the drilling from site i to target j, their values restricted to zero or one, and in the eventual solution a value of one interpreted to mean "drill," and a value of zero to mean "do not drill." Similarly, one can define y_i relative to preparation of site i, with similar interpretations of the values of zero and one. One has

Minimize

$$4.3y_1 + 2.3x_{11} + 0.6x_{12} + 1.0x_{13} + 6.6x_{14} + 1.0y_2 + 3.7x_{21} + 6.3x_{22}$$
$$+ 4.2x_{23} + 6.3x_{24} + 3.5y_3 + 1.0x_{31} + 8.1x_{32} + 8.6x_{33} + 9.9x_{34}$$

The constraints which comprise the multiple choice aspect are

$x_{11}+x_{21}+x_{31}=1$ Target 1 is reached from only one site

$x_{12}+x_{22}+x_{32}=1$ Target 2 is reached from only one site

$x_{13}+x_{23}+x_{33}=1$ Target 3 is reached from only one site

$x_{14}+x_{24}+x_{34}=1$ Target 4 is reached from only one site

The crux of the problem is to determine the site for each of the preceeding constraints. If fractional solutions were permitted, an answer such as $1/3+1/3+1/3 = 1$ would obviously be nonsensical; hence the need to employ integer methods, and to restrict the x_{ij} to integers.

Additional constraints, bringing the variables y_i into the picture, are

$x_{11}+x_{12}+x_{13}+x_{14} \leqslant 4y_1$ and $y_1 \leqslant 1$; for Site 1

$x_{21}+x_{22}+x_{23}+x_{24} \leqslant 4y_2$ and $y_2 \leqslant 1$; for Site 2

$x_{31}+x_{32}+x_{33}+x_{34} \leqslant 4y_3$ and $y_3 \leqslant 1$; for Site 3

These constraints recognize that the largest number of drilling operations that can be launched from any site is $4y_i$. If y_i is zero, indicating no site preparation activity, then all of the x variables directed from Site i must be zero. Conversely, if any or all of these x variables are one, then y_i cannot be zero and hence must be one.

The three constraints just described make this problem resemble the "fixed charge" problem which is discussed next in its most typical form.

Fixed Charge Problem

Assume that 1,000 units of a product must be produced and three machines are available on which to produce them. The machines are of differing efficiency and capacity, as characterized by Table 10-4.

Except for the capacity limitation it is obvious that the process plan resulting in least cost would be to make all 1,000 units on Machine 2 at a cost of $8,000. The problem, in view of the capacity limits, is to determine the quantity, x_j, to produce on each machine so as to minimize cost. The

Table 10-4

Machine	Start-up Cost	Cost per Unit Processed	Capacity
1	$3000	$6	700
2	1000	7	400
3	400	9	1000

problem is formulated as follows and is readily solved by all-integer techniques (10):

Let

$$d_j = \begin{cases} 0 & \text{if } x_j = 0 \\ 1 & \text{if } x_j > 0 \end{cases}$$

Minimize

$$3000d_1 + 6x_1 + 1000d_2 + 7x_2 + 400d_3 + 9x_3$$

Subject to:

$$x_1 + x_2 + x_3 \geqslant 1000$$

$$x_1 \leqslant 700d_1$$

$$x_2 \leqslant 400d_2$$

$$x_3 \leqslant 1000d_3$$

with d_1, d_2, and d_3 constrained to values of zero or one. It is assumed here that fractional quantities of product are invalid, and that all x_j must be integers; otherwise this would be classified as a mixed integer programming problem. The fixed charge problem can also be restated in terms of minimizing manufacturing time, or in terms of maximizing output (11) in a fixed time period.

TYPICAL INTEGER PROGRAMMING PROBLEMS: MIXED

The following selection of examples of mixed integer programming problems is not intended to be exhaustive, but is for the purpose of illustrating the versatility and usefulness of integer programming techniques.

Ordinary Optimization

Many of the multitude of linear optimization problems that have become classics in non-integer programming are candidates for mixed integer programming methods as soon as the requirement is added that some of the variables are restricted to integers. Danzig described many such problems as early as 1957 (4), and Balinski published a very comprehensive survey on integer programming in 1965 (2). The empty container problem, if applied to discrete objects, seeks to minimize the number and variety of containers required for shipment of the produced items. The paper trim problem seeks minimization of waste in the slicing of newsprint rolls into rolls of lesser width to fill specific quantity requirements. The flight scheduling problem seeks an efficient schedule when specified quantities of cargo must be flown to a number of destinations. Allocation problems can take on integer requirements and thus complicate the usual process of determining optimal allocation. Formulations will not be shown for these classes of problems. Instead, a few examples will be given to illustrate some of the unique features which permit mixed integer programming to extend the scope of linear programming.

Linear Approximation to Non-Linear Problems

When the criterion function is non-linear it may be broken into a series of straight line segments and solved by linear programming methods. The method becomes complicated even with linear constraints. In this example the criterion function is expressed in terms of only one variable, x_1, and is easily plotted and solved by inspection. In a practical problem the criterion function would be expressed in terms of several variables and the solution would not be so obvious.

Assume that one wishes to maximize the efficiency, y, of a machine, and that the efficiency varies as a function of the speed, x_1, as plotted in Fig. 10-5. The criterion function is

$$\text{Maximize } y = f(x_1).$$

Also assume that the speed limits are such that the following linear constraints hold:

$$x_1 \geqslant .1$$

$$x_1 \leqslant .4$$

The curve may be approximated by any number of straight line segments, two in this example, and terminology assigned as shown in Fig. 10-6.

Assigning b values from the y axis and a values from the x_l axis of the original curve, this approximation to the original criterion function may be expressed as:

$$x_1 = .1t_0 + .2t_1 + .4t_2$$

$$y = .2t_0 + .1t_1 + .3t_2$$

These expressions define the new function if it is insured that only two successive values of t_i come into the solution, and provided it is also required that $t_0 + t_j + t_2 = 1$.

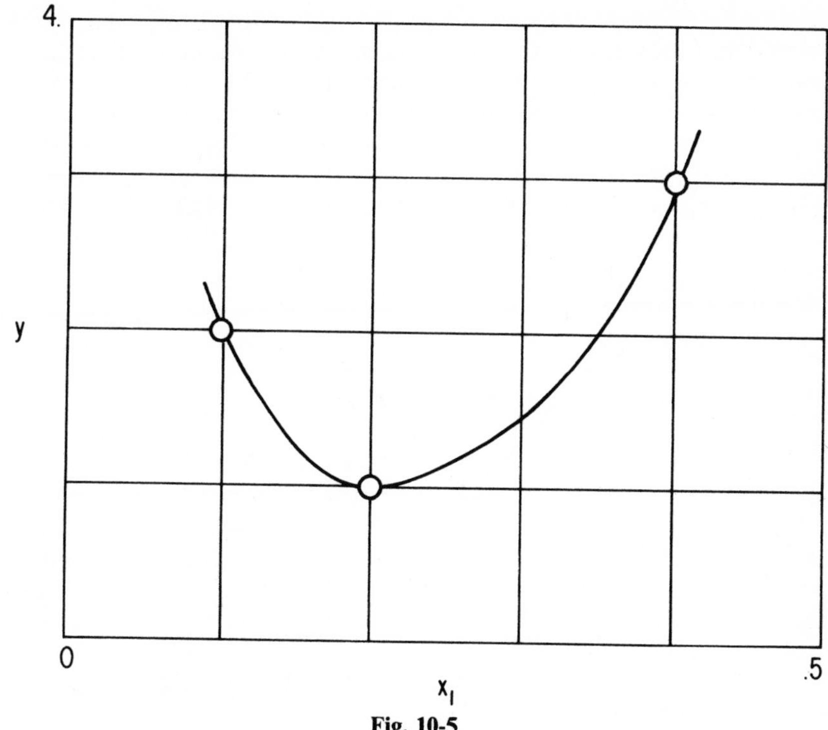

Fig. 10-5

To insure that only two successive values of t_i are non-zero, the original constraints must be supplemented by constraints containing zero-one variables (d_i) in an appropriate manner. The full set of constraints then become

Constraint 1 $\quad x_1 \geqslant .1$

2 $\quad x_1 \leqslant .4$

3 $\quad d_0 \geqslant t_0$

4 $\quad d_0 + d_1 \geqslant t_1$

5 $\quad d_1 \geqslant t_2$

6 $\quad d_0 + d_1 = 1$

7 $\quad t_0 + t_1 + t_2 = 1$

where all d_i are constrained to values of zero or one, but the t_i variables may be fractional.

The logic of this formulation may be tested by assuming that a solution

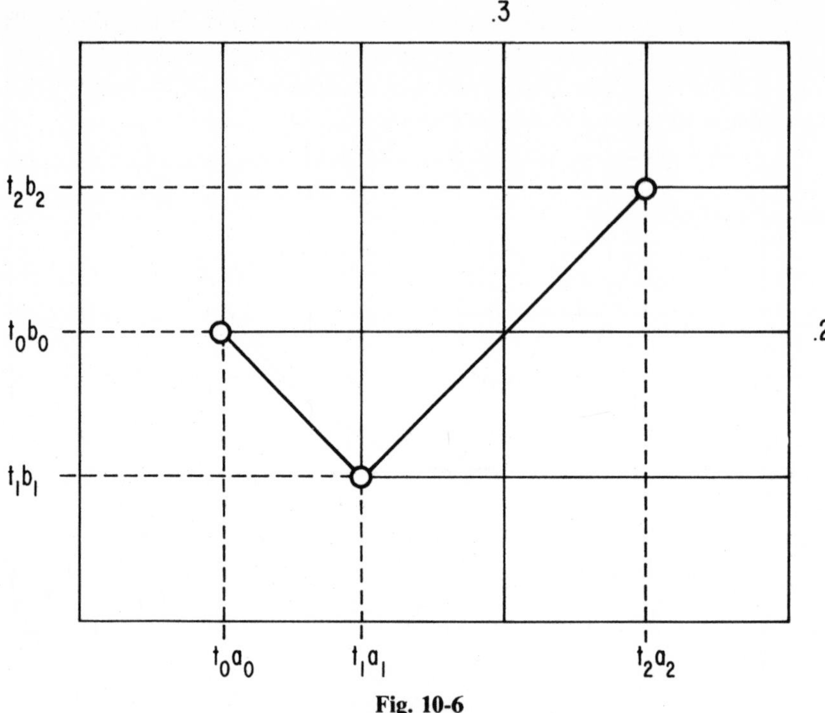

Fig. 10-6

indicated $d_i = 1$. Then the sixth constraint forces $d_0 = 0$, the third forces $t_0 = 0$, and the fourth and fifth permit t_1 and t_2 to take on values $\leqslant 1$ such that they total one in conformity with the seventh constraint. If one arbitrarily asigns the value 1/2 to t_1 and t_2, it is seen from Fig. 10-6 that $x_1 = .2\ (1/2) + .4\ (1/2) = .3$, and $y = .1\ (1/2) + .3\ (1/2) = .2$ does produce a point on the segmented plot.

In summary, the efficiency, y, has been approximately expressed in linear terms involving the variables t_i so that ordinary linear programming methods may be used to obtain maximization ($t_0 = t_1 = 0$; and $t_2 = 1$; and $y = .3$ for this example.) To do this, a problem with a non-linear criterion function, with two linear constraints, and one continuous variable became a linear problem of seven linear constraints, three continuous variables (t_0, t_1, and t_2) and two zero-one variables (d_0 and d_1). If the criterion function had been broken into more segments to give a better approximation, the problem would have grown even more in complexity (10).

Methods for handling non-linear constraints are also available. One technique devised by H.O. Hartley (12) converts each non-linear constraint into m^n linear constraints, where n is the number of variables and m is the number of linear segments used to approximate the non-linear constraint.

The method is tedious and will not be illustrated here.

The preceding discussion of approximation problems should convey the message that while mixed integer programming can be used to solve nonlinear problems, satisfactory degrees of approximation will usually cause the problem to take on huge dimensions.

Discrete Alternatives

The following simple problem illustrates the use of mixed integer programming in formulations (10) where any k of q constraints (but not all of them, since $q > k$), must be observed. Assume that \$100,000 is to be invested in a manner that maximizes annual interest income. Expected returns are:

Bonds—5 percent per year,
Blue chip stocks—6 percent per year,
Electronic stocks—8 percent per year.

If x_1, x_2, and x_3 are defined as the number of dollars to be invested in these three categories, respectively, one has the criterion function

Maximize

$$.05\,x_1 + .06\,x_2 + .08\,x_3$$

and the obvious constraint

$$x_1 + x_2 + x_3 \leqslant 100{,}000$$

(Other mandatory constraints, such as those that would relate to the existing investments could also be present, but are omitted here for simplicity.) It will be assumed, furthermore, that the investment policy requires that any two of the following three rules must be observed:

Rule 1: $x_2 + x_3 \leqslant 3/4$ of the sum to be invested at any one time.

Rule 2: $x_3 \leqslant 1/2$ of the sum to be invested at any one time.

Rule 3: $x_2 \leqslant 1/8$ of the sum to be invested at any one time.

For this particular investment these rules may be written as

$$x_2 + x_3 - 75{,}000 \leqslant d_1\,(100{,}000)$$

$$x_3 - 50{,}000 \leqslant d_2\,(100{,}000)$$

$$x_2 - 12{,}500 \leqslant d_3\,(100{,}000)$$

where the d_i are zero-one variables, the 100,000 represents the upper bound, and where the following added constraint applies:

$$d_1 + d_2 + d_3 = 1.$$

Since the d_i must equal zero or one in the optimal solution, the latter constraint permits just one of them to equal unity. If, for example, $d_2 = 1$, then the effect on the constraint $x_3 - 50{,}000 \leqslant d_2(100{,}000)$ is to open up Rule 2 and make it non-binding ($x_3 \leqslant 150{,}000$), whereas the constraints based on Rules 1 and 3 are binding.

The solution to this problem, using mixed integer techniques, will determine values, denoting amounts to be invested, for the continuous variables x_i, and will, as a by-product, show the zero or one d_i values which produced the maximum yearly interest income.

Three-Machine Scheduling Problem

Multiphase scheduling problems are typified by the following job scheduling problem occurring in a machine shop. There are n items (jobs) to be scheduled through three operations that must be performed in a given order by Machines I, II, and III; that is, the first item scheduled must have its Machine I operation completed before the next item can be fed to Machine I, and items finishing the Machine I operation must go through Machine II before going to Machine III. The required time on the various machines is not the same for all items; therefore, various sequences of scheduling the items will result in varying machine idle times *(s)* and varying item waiting times *(u)*, and will affect the total time needed to finish all items.

Figure 10-7 shows a possible three-job situation where Jobs 3, 1, and 2 are scheduled in that order, where circled numbers are time durations, and where

$s_k{}^h$ indicates the idle time on machine h following the job in sequence position k.

$u_k{}^h$ indicates the waiting time of the job in sequence position k after completion of processing on machine h.

L_i, M_i, and N_i are the processing times of the ith job on Machines I, II, and III, respectively.

The objective is to determine a job sequence that will minimize the overall time. If Machine III is observed it will be noted that it cannot start until the L and M of the first job scheduled have elapsed. If a sequence is selected that will minimize that delay in starting on Machine III, and

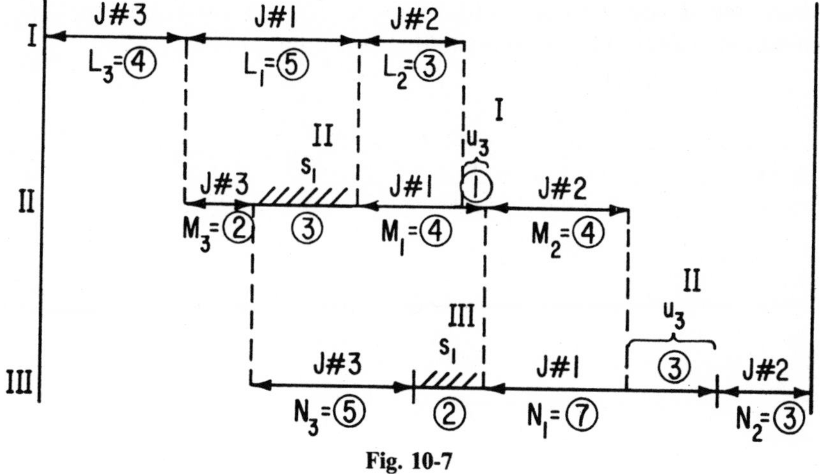

Fig. 10-7

minimize the idle time on Machine III following all jobs but the last one scheduled, the objective will have been accomplished.

The formulation is started by defining a set of variables, x_{ij}, where i indicates the job number and j the sequence position. Each of the x_{ij} variables will be restricted to values of one or zero in the resulting solution.

$$x_{ij} = \begin{cases} 1 \text{ if job } i \text{ occupies the } j\text{th position of input sequence} \\ 0 \text{ if otherwise} \end{cases}$$

Because each job can occupy only one position in the sequence, and because each position can be held by only one job, one can write the following six preliminary constraining equalities:

$$x_{11} + x_{12} + x_{13} = 1 \qquad x_{11} + x_{21} + x_{31} = 1$$

$$x_{21} + x_{22} + x_{23} = 1 \qquad x_{12} + x_{22} + x_{32} = 1$$

$$x_{31} + x_{32} + x_{33} = 1 \qquad x_{13} + x_{23} + x_{33} = 1$$

All $x_{ij} \leqslant 1$; require integer solution.

To form the criterion function the L and M of the first job scheduled is needed, plus the idle time on Machine III. For the three-job example used here this is expressed as:

$$\text{Minimize } (L_1 + M_1)x_{11} + (L_2 + M_2)x_{21} + (L_3 + M_3)x_{31} + S_1^{\text{III}} + S_2^{\text{III}}$$

and the total time will be this minimized quantity plus the constant sum

$N_1+N_2+N_3$. Because only one of the x_{i1}, the one corresponding to the job in the first sequence position, can equal one, the inappropriate L_i and M_i will be cancelled from the criterion function. (If there were n jobs, there would be n terms of the form $(L_i+M_i)x_{i1}$, and n - 1 terms of s_k^{III}.)

The following additional constraining equalities must also be satisfied. The first two (n-1) are based on examination of the relationship between Machines II and III; the second two (n-1) based on Machine I and II.

$$s_1^{\text{II}} + [M_1x_{12} + M_2x_{22} + M_3x_{32}] + u_2^{\text{II}}$$
$$= \textcircled{u_1^{\text{II}}} + [N_1x_{11} + N_2x_{21} + N_3x_{31}] + s_1^{\text{III}}$$

$$s_2^{\text{II}} + [M_1x_{13} + M_2x_{23} + M_3x_{33}] + u_3^{\text{II}}$$
$$= u_2^{\text{II}} + [N_1x_{12} + N_2x_{22} + N_3x_{32}] + s_2^{\text{III}}$$

$$\textcircled{s_1^{\text{I}}} + [L_1x_{12} + L_2x_{22} + L_3x_{32}] + u_2^{\text{I}}$$
$$= \textcircled{u_1^{\text{I}}} + [M_1x_{11} + M_2x_{21} + M_3x_{31}] + s_1^{\text{II}}$$

$$\textcircled{s_2^{\text{I}}} + [L_1x_{13} + L_2x_{23} + L_3x_{33}] + u_3^{\text{I}}$$
$$= u_2^{\text{I}} + [M_1x_{12} + M_2x_{22} + M_3x_{32}] + s_2^{\text{II}}$$

In general, 2(n-1) constraining equalities of this construction would be written.

It is apparent that even a simple three-job example of a three-machine scheduling problem gets very complex, involving eight variables of the s and u type (the circled ones above are logically equal to zero), nine variables of the x type, and nine constraints (one of the first six stated may be omitted, as satisfying five of the constraints will force satisfaction of the sixth). In general, $n^2+4(n - 1)$ variables and $4n - 3$ constraints are involved.

In the final solution, the x_{ij} variables must be integers (restricted to zero or one) but the s and u variables can usually be fractional. When dealing with small, discrete units of time the s and u variables may also be restricted to integers in which case the problem becomes one of the all-integer variety. Extensive work has been performed by Giglio and Wagner in solving three-machine scheduling problems with presently available algorithms (6).

CONCLUSION

It is hoped that this review of integer programming has not offended the mathematical purist by its avoidance of generalized notation. While such notation is valuable shorthand, it often needs concrete expression, in terms of examples, to be clear to the practitioner.

The simplicity of the examples may mislead the reader; he is warned that, as real problems are formulated, many intricate dependencies tend to get inserted into the mathematical model. Even in circumstances where linearities exist for all variables, problems can become quite complicated.

It is also worth noting that only purely deterministic problems have been reviewed. Many situations involve probabilities, and this leads to a branch of programming often called stochastic programming, which is a subject deserving independent treatment.

There is a clear need for improved integer programming algorithms that will efficiently handle several hundred variables. Apparently this need has been recognized by numerous mathematicians who are active in this field. However, there is also a great need for communicating the scope of what is now available to the many persons who encounter real problems day by day. Integer programming techniques are of real value only when applied to such problems.

References

(1) Balas, E., "An Additive Algorithm for Solving Linear Programs with Zero-One Variables," *Operations Research,* Volume 13, No. 4, July-August, 1965.

(2) Balinski, M.L., "Integer Programming: Methods, Uses, Computation," *Management Science,* Volume 12, No. 3, November, 1965.

(3) Bellman, R., and Dreyfus, S., *Applied Dynamic Programming,* Princeton University Press, New Jersey, 1961.

(4) Danzig, G.B., "Discrete Variable Extremum Problems," *Operations Research,* Volume 5, No. 2, April, 1957.

(5) Fleischmann, B., "Computational Experience with the Algorithm of Balas," *Operations Research,* January-February, 1967.

(6) Giglio, R.J., and Wagner, H.M., "Approximate Solutions to the Three-Machine Scheduling Problem," *Operations Research,* Volume 12, No. 2, March-April, 1964.

(7) Glover, F., "Truncated Enumeration Methods for Solving Pure and Mixed Integer Linear Programs," Working Paper, Operations Research Center, University of California, Berkeley, May, 1966.

(8) Gomory, R.E. "Outline of an Algorithm for Linear Solutions to Linear Programs," *Bulletin of the American Mathematical Society,* Volume LXIV, September, 1958.

(9) Gomory, R.E., "All-Integer Integer Programming Algorithm," in *Industrial Scheduling,* J.F. Muth and G.L. Thompson, editors, Prentice-Hall, New Jersey, 1963.

(10) Hadley, G., *Non-Linear and Dynamic Programming,* Addison-Wesley, Reading, Massachusetts, 1964.

(11) Haldi, J., "Twenty-five Integer Programming Test Problems," Working Paper No. 43, Graduate School of Business, Stanford University, December, 1964.

(12) Hartley, H.O., "Nonlinear Programming by the Simplex Method," *Econometrica,* Volume 29, 1961.

(13) Healy, W.C., Jr. "Multiple Choice Programming," *Operations Research,* January-February, 1964.

(14) Land, A.H., and Doig, A.G., "An Automatic Method of Solving Discrete Programming Problems," *Econometrica,* Volume 28, 1960.

(15) Petersen, C.C., "Computational Experience with Variants of the Balas Algorithm Applied to the Selection of R&D Projects," May, 1966, *Management Science,* Volume 13, No. 9, May, 1967.

(16) Vajda, S., *Mathematical Programming,* Addison-Wesley, Reading, Massachusetts, 1961.

11 Linear and Integer Programming Applied to Capital Budgeting

by Phillip W. Balsmeier

This paper describes how a typical resource allocation problem can be resolved using an integer programming computer program. The program is presently set up to handle a problem of up to 40 rows and columns (structural variables plus negative slacks which are automatically generated for $\geqslant$ type rows) and can easily be modified to handle a larger problem.

The first phase of the program minimizes a "sum of infeasibilities" using the method as outlined in most LP textbooks.[1] This procedure interatively drives out the artificial variables, and eventually reaches a feasible solution. At that point, control is passed to the second phase which proceeds to find an optimum solution (maximizing the objective function). This optimal solution is printed and the reduced costs of slack and structural variables not in the solution are printed. The optimal solution report includes cost ranging for variables in the solution. Once the optimum feasible solution has been achieved, the third phase proceeds to use Gomory constraints, which forces an integer solution. Either the noninteger or integer solution can be produced.

The sample problem selected is a problem in capital budgeting which is concerned with the allocation of the firm's limited resources to competing (future) projects which, when developed, offer prospective returns of "net present value" of future returns for each project, and then allocate resources among the projects by some decision rule to the point where available resources are consumed.

Joel Dean[2] recommends that the projects be ranked in a hierarchy, beginning with the project having greatest pay-off/cost ratio, followed by the project having next greatest ratio; and so on, until all projects are listed. Available resources are then allocated down the hierarchy, and the last project to be fully funded is the last one to be considered. The remaining projects are not considered.

Such a procedure may *not* result in an optimal allocation of resources which will maximize the net return to the firm.[3] In fact, in the simple example which follows, Dean's ranking does not produce an optimal allocation and return is not maximized.

An alternative procedure, with more promising possibilities, results when linear programming techniques are used.

Example

Let X_1, X_2, X_3, X_4 be four projects under consideration, which are "competing" for a scarce capital resource (money for development).

Using the special case (0 – 1) of integer programming, one says that if

$$x_j = 0$$

then project X_j is not accepted for allocation, and if

$$x_j = 1$$

then X_j receives an allocation of necessary funds for initiating and funding the project.

Now, let each project "pay" a return of a unique amount (return = capital + profit to the firm):

e_j = pay-off coefficient for the jth project
e_1 = \$40
e_2 = \$30
e_3 = \$50
e_4 = \$60

Let "costs" also be associated with each project:

c_j = "cost" to develop jth project
c_1 = \$30
c_2 = \$20
c_3 = \$40
c_4 = \$50

If one used Dean's procedure, he would rank the projects in order of decreasing e_j/c_j and allocated available resources:

x_j	e_j	c_j	e_j/c_j
2	\$30	\$20	\$1.50
1	40	30	1.33
3	50	40	1.25
4	60	50	1.20

Assume now that available resources are only \$100. According to Dean's procedure, we would allocate \$20 (c_j) to x_2, \$30 to x_1, and \$40 to x_3, at which point \$90 would be "used." One could not allocate further, as only \$10 (resources) remain, and there is no project with $c_j \leqslant \$10$. Thus, only three projects would be allocated funds, and the prospective pay-off would be

$$e_2 + e_1 + e_3 = \$30 + \$40 + \$50 = \$120$$

This is not an optimal allocation, as one shall presently see.

Now, let an objective function, expressing the firm's prospective total return, be written in the form

$$z = \sum_{j=1}^{j} c_j x_j$$

which is to be maximized by integer LP techniques, subject to certain constraints. In this case,

$$z = 40x_1 + 30x_2 + 50x_3 + 60x_4$$

The initial constraints are written from the cost coefficients and the *initial* requirement that each x_i be some number *between* 0 and 1, but *not necessarily* either 0 or 1. This latter requirement is *to permit optimization* with primal simplex rules, in which the optimal solution will be *primal optimal* but not necessarily integer. The integer constraints will be applied later.

Accordingly, the initial constraints are:

$$\left.\begin{array}{l} R \geqslant \sum^{j} c_j x_j \\ 30x_1 + 20x_2 + 40x_3 + 50x_4 \leqslant 100 \end{array}\right\} \text{Resource Limitation}$$

$$0 \leqslant x_i \leqslant 1 \} \text{ Feasible Projects} = +1 \text{ or less}$$

Introducing the necessary slack variables to convert the constraint inequalities to equations:

$30x_1 + 20x_2 + 40x_3 + 50x_4 + s_0 = 100$

$x_1 + s_1 = 1$

$x_2 + s_2 = 1$

$x_3 + s_3 = 1$

$x_4 + s_4 = 1$

Rewriting the objective function to convert to matrix form:

$$z - 40x_1 - 30x_2 - 50x_3 - 60x_4 + s_0(0) + s_1(0) + s_2(0) + s_3(0) + s_4(0) = 0$$

The initial tableau, now initially *feasible* but *not optimal,* can now be written (Gauss-Jordan Matrix), which is then iterated to an *optimal primal solution* by the conventional *primal simplex* rules:

Tableau 11-1

z	x_1	x_2	x_3	x_4	s_0	s_1	s_2	s_3	s_4	b	0
	30	20	40	50	1					100	2
	1					1				1	—
		1					1			1	—
			1					1		1	—
				(1)					1	1	1 ← r
1	−40	−30	−50	−60							
				↑ k							

Tableau 11-2

x_1	x_2	x_3	x_4	s_0	s_1	s_2	s_3	s_4	b	θ
30	20	40	0	1				−50	50	$\frac{5}{4}$
1					1				1	—
	1					1			1	—
		(1)					1		1	1 ← r
			1					1	1	—
−40	−30	−50	0					60	60	
			↑ k							

Tableau 11-3

x_1	x_2	x_3	x_4	s_0	s_1	s_2	s_3	s_4	b	θ
30	20	0	0	1			−40	−50	10	$\frac{1}{3}$ ← r
1					1				1	1
	1					1			1	—
		1					1		1	—
			1					1	1	—
−40	−30	0	0				50	60	110	
↑ k										

Tableau 11-4

x_1	x_2	x_3	x_4	s_0	s_1	s_2	s_3	s_4	b	θ
1	$\frac{2}{3}$	0	0	$\frac{1}{30}$	0	0	$-\frac{4}{3}$	$-\frac{5}{3}$	$\frac{1}{3}$	—
	$-\frac{2}{3}$			$-\frac{1}{30}$	1		$\frac{4}{3}$	($\frac{5}{3}$)	$\frac{2}{3}$	$\frac{2}{5}$ ← r
	1					1			1	—
		1					1		1	—
			1					1	1	1
0	$-\frac{10}{3}$	0	0	$\frac{4}{3}$	0	0	$-\frac{10}{3}$	$-\frac{20}{3}$	$\frac{370}{3}$	
								↑ k		

Tableau 11-5

x_1	x_2	x_3	x_4	s_0	s_1	s_2	s_3	s_4	b	θ
1					1				1	—
	$-\frac{2}{5}$			$-\frac{1}{50}$	$\frac{3}{5}$		$\frac{4}{5}$	1	$\frac{2}{5}$	—
	1					1			1	1 ← r
		1					1		1	—
	$\frac{2}{5}$		1	$\frac{1}{50}$	$-\frac{3}{5}$		$-\frac{4}{5}$		$\frac{3}{5}$	$\frac{3}{2}$
0	$-\frac{18}{3}$	0	0	$\frac{6}{5}$	4	0	2	0	$\frac{378}{3}$	
	↑ k									

Tableau 11-6

x_1	x_2	x_3	x_4	s_0	s_1	s_2	s_3	s_4	b	θ
1	0	0	0	0	1	0	0	0	1	
0	0	0	0	$-\frac{1}{50}$	$\frac{3}{5}$	$\frac{2}{5}$	$\frac{4}{5}$	1	$\frac{4}{5}$	←
0	1	0	0	0	0	1	0	0	1	
0	0	1	0	0	0	0	1	0	1	
0	0	0	1	$\frac{1}{50}$	$-\frac{3}{5}$	$-\frac{2}{5}$	$-\frac{4}{5}$	0	$\frac{1}{5}$	
0	0	0	0	$\frac{6}{5}$	4	6	2	0	$\frac{396}{3} = 132$	

Tableau 11-6 is now the *primal, feasible optimum* solution since

(1) no negative e_j remain (→ optimal)
(2) all $b_i \geqslant 0$ } feasible
(3) all $s_j \geqslant 0$ } feasible

However, all x_j are *not* integer-valued:

$x_1 = 1$

$x_2 = 1$

$x_3 = 1$

$x_4 = \frac{1}{5}$

It is now desired to "force" an integer solution (all $x_j = 0,1$), which can be done by the *Gomory-Baumol* method of introducing an integer constraint and "back-pivoting" to an optimal solution in which all structural variables (x_j) become integers.[4]

This method uses the so-called dual simplex rules for pivoting, which are different from the *primal* simplex rules. To introduce the new integer constraint and then back-pivot, the solution matrix must first be in *dual-feasible* form. The first primal matrix which is also dual-feasible is the primal optimal; i.e., the non-integer primal optimal Tableau 11-6. Once this matrix (primal *optimal)* has been developed, then the integer constraint can be written and the back-pivoting started.

The new integer constraint is developed as follows:[5]

(1) Choose any *row* in the primal optimal tableau, for which b_i is noninteger. Rewrite this row as

$$b_i' = a_{it}'x_t + a_{ir}'x_r + \ldots\ldots\ldots + a_{iq}'x_q + x_s$$

(The prime indicates the equation is from the primal optimal tableau; x_s is the variable *in solution.)*

In Tableau 11-6, choose the second row (custom is to choose the *greatest* factional b_i' since one wishes to remove from the solution the "most infeasible" variable (x_s) whose value is b_i').
Thus:

$$\frac{4}{5} = \frac{4}{5}s_3 + \frac{2}{5}s_2 + \frac{3}{5}s_1 - \frac{1}{50}s_0 + (1)\,s_4$$

Rearrange the equation so that all terms except s_4 are on the left-hand side:

$$\frac{4}{5} - \frac{4}{5}s_3 - \frac{2}{5}s_2 - \frac{3}{5}s_1 + \frac{1}{50}s_0 = s_4$$

By the method of "fractional parts,"[6] s_4 can be constrained to be integer by forcing the left-hand side to be congruent to zero.

$$f\left(\frac{4}{5}\right) + f\left(-\frac{4}{5}\right)s_3 + f\left(-\frac{2}{5}\right)s_2 + f\left(-\frac{3}{5}\right)s_1 + f\left(\frac{1}{50}\right)s_0 \equiv 0;$$

or, transposing $f\left(\frac{4}{5}\right)$ to the right-hand side:

$$f\left(-\frac{4}{5}\right)s_3 + f\left(-\frac{2}{5}\right)s_2 + f\left(-\frac{3}{5}\right)s_1 + f\left(\frac{1}{50}\right)s_0 \equiv -f\left(\frac{4}{5}\right) \equiv f\left(-\frac{4}{5}\right)$$

Then:

$$f\left(\frac{1}{5}\right)s_3 + f\left(\frac{3}{5}\right)s_2 + f\left(\frac{2}{5}\right)s_1 + f\left(\frac{1}{50}\right)s_0 \equiv f\left(\frac{1}{5}\right),\ f\left(\frac{6}{5}\right),\ f\left(\frac{4}{5}\right)$$

or

$$\frac{1}{5}s_3 + \frac{3}{5}s_2 + \frac{2}{5}s_1 + \frac{1}{50}s_0 \geqslant \frac{1}{5}$$

which is the *new* integer constraint inequality.

To simplify the inequality, multiply through by 50:

$$10s_3 + 30s_3 + 20s_1 + s_0 \geqslant 10$$

Subtract a *new* slack variable, s_5, to convert to an equality:

$$10s_3 + 30s_2 + 20s_1 + s_0 - s_5 = 10$$

and multiply by -1 to convert the new constraining equality to dual-feasible form:

$$-10s_3 - 30s_2 - 20s_1 - s_0 + s_5 = -10$$

(2) This new constraining equation is now introduced as an additional constraint in the dual-feasible (=primal optimal) Tableau 11-6. This tableau thus becomes *primal* *in*feasible (since $b_i = -10$), but *still optimal.* In this manner, *in*feasibility is introduced, while at the same time, optimally is preserved:

Tableau 11-6A

x_1	x_2	x_3	x_4	s_0	s_1	s_2	s_3	s_4	s_5	b	
				-1	-20	-30	-10		$+1$	-10	The new ← constraint equality
1					1					1	
				$-\frac{1}{50}$	$\frac{3}{5}$	$\frac{2}{5}$	$\frac{4}{5}$	1		$\frac{4}{5}$	
	1									1	
		1								1	
			1	$\frac{1}{50}$	$-\frac{3}{5}$	$-\frac{2}{5}$	$-\frac{4}{5}$			$\frac{1}{5}$	
				$\frac{6}{5}$	4	6	2			132	

One now *re*-optimizes, hopefully removing the infeasibility by the *dual simplex* rules. Whereas, the *primal* simplex rules first choose an *incoming* variable to produce greatest advance toward an optimum (by selecting $k = \max(e_j - z_j)$), and second, they choose the *exiting* variable so as to maintain feasibility (by selecting $r = \min 1 + j$), the *dual simplex rules do just the opposite.* What one wishes to do by the dual simplex is:

(1) *First,* choose the "most infeasible" variable as the one to *exit* (this leads to a restoration of feasibility);

(2) *Second,* choose the *incoming* variable as the one which maintains optimality.[7]

Accordingly, the *dual simplex* rules are:

(a) Choose the *row* first, corresponding to

$$b'_r = \underset{i}{\text{MIN}}\ (b'_i), \text{ (By minimum, one means most negative)}$$

(b) Choose the *column* next, in which

$$\delta_k = \underset{j}{\text{MIN}} \left| \frac{e_j - z_j}{a_{rj}} \right|, \ a_{rj} < 0.$$

(If a *tie* results between several

$$\delta_k = \underset{j}{\text{MIN}} \left(\frac{e_j - z_j}{a_{rj}} \right),$$

choose k as the column with $\underset{j}{\text{MIN}}\ (e_j - z_j)$ among the tied δ_k.)

In this fashion, one chooses the pivot element in Tableau 11-6B as follows:

Tableau 11-6B

x_1	x_2	x_3	x_4	s_0	s_1	s_2	s_3	s_4	s_5	b
				-1	-20	-30	-10		1	-10
1					1					1
				$-\frac{1}{50}$	$\frac{3}{5}$	$\frac{2}{5}$	$\frac{4}{5}$	1		$\frac{4}{5}$
	1					1				1
		1					1			1
				$\frac{1}{50}$	$-\frac{3}{5}$	$-\frac{2}{5}$	$-\frac{4}{5}$			$\frac{1}{5}$
				$\frac{6}{5}$	4	6	2			132
	$e_i - f_i$			$-\frac{6}{5}$	$-\frac{1}{5}$	$-\frac{1}{5}$	$-\frac{1}{5}$			$\leftarrow \delta_i$

The pivot element is -10, at the intersection of the *r*th *row* and the *k*th *column.*

One can now iterate *in the normal primal manner*, using *primal* rules for the iteration:

Tableau 11-7A

z	x_1	x_2	x_3	x_4	s_0	s_1	s_2	s_3	s_4	s_5	b
					$+\frac{1}{10}$	+2	+3	+1		$-\frac{1}{10}$	1
	1					1		0			1
					$-\frac{1}{10}$	−1	−2	0	+1		0
		1					1	0			1
			1		$-\frac{1}{10}$	−2	−3	0		$+\frac{1}{10}$	0
				1	$+\frac{1}{10}$	+1	+2	0		$-\frac{4}{50}$	1
					1	0	0	0	0	$\frac{2}{10}$	130

The Tableau is *optimal* (all $e_j - z_j \geqslant 0$)
The Tableau is *feasible* (all $b_i \geqslant 0$, all $s_i \geqslant 0$)
The Tableau is *integer* (all $x_i = 0, 1$)

The solution variables can now be read out:

$x_1 = 1$ $s_0 = 0$
$x_2 = 1$ $s_1 = 0$
$x_3 = 0$ $s_2 = 0$
$x_4 = 1$ $s_3 = 1$
$s_4 = 0$
$s_5 = 0$
z opt. = \$130

Is the original resources constraint satisfied?

$$\Sigma c_{ij}x_{ij} = 30(1) + 20(1) + 40(0) + 50(1) = \textit{\$100}$$

Yes, since $(\Sigma c_{ij}x_{ij} + 100) \leqslant (R = 100)$.

The conclusion is that Tableau 11-7A is an *optimal, feasible, integer* solution to the problem.

Note that the optimal LP method results in z = \$130, whereas Dean's ranking method resulted in z = \$120.

Comments

Whereas, the introduction of only one integer constraint (in the primal optimal tableau) resulted here in an integer optimum with only one "back-pivot" dual operation, one should not imply that this is always guaranteed. If, after reoptimizing using the dual rules, another *noninteger* optimal solution resulted, then *another* integer constraint would be generated and introduced in the *last* optimal noninteger tableau. This tableau, with the additional constraint incorporated, would then be again reoptimized (using dual rules), and the process continued until a final optimal, feasible integer solution is obtained.[8]

Because the *dual* simplex method is based on a rigorous mathematical proof (Gomory), one is assured of maintaining optimality while removing the noninteger infeasibility.[9]

Future Research

The model as written provides an optimizing solution procedure rather than a predicting method. With the addition of Bayesian statistics to develop a pay-off table for the projects, one could introduce a measurement of risk and uncertainty. With this addition to the model, it may be possible to use it as a predicting model. Much research would still be required before one could determine the real value of the addition of statistics.

The program also has the limitations of being a linear model which is not the answer to all of the optimizing problems. To handle the nonlinear problem, a new model in dynamic programming would have to be developed or at least extensive modification made to this one. Linear programming has been used successfully for many years in problems concerning product mix, blending, refineries, production runs, equipment use, location or warehousing problems, and scores of variations of economic, financial, and marketing types of former enigmas. However, little has been done with the removal of risk and uncertainty from the technique.

Notes

1. Saul I. Gass, "Linear Programming," *Methods and Applications*, Second Edition (McGraw-Hill, 1958), pp. 71-73.
2. Joel Dean, *Capital Budgeting* (New York: Columbia University Press, 1951).
3. H. Martin Weingartner, *Mathematical Programming and the Analysis of Capital Budgeting Problems* (Ford Foundation Award-Winning Doctoral Dissertation Series; Englewood Cliffs, New Jersey: Prentice-Hall, Inc., 1963).
4. Robert W. Llewellyn, *Linear Programming* (New York: Holt, Reinehard and Winston, 1964), pp. 201-204, 269.

5. Ibid., p. 269.
6. $f(d) = a_i$; $0 \leqslant a < 1$; where $d - a$ = an integer.
7. Op. cit., pp. 201-204.
8. Ibid., p. 270.
9. Ibid., pp. 201-204.

Discussion Questions

1. What advantages does graphic linear programming have over intuitive approaches to resource allocation for simple problems? At what point should the user shift from graphic to more sophisticated linear programming techniques? Why? Explain fully.

2. How does the simplex method differ from graphic approaches to solving linear programming problems? Does the simplex method provide any information not obtainable from graphic formulations? If so, what?

3. How does one test for optimality in the graphic linear programming problem? In the simplex algorithm? If the solution is not optimal, what procedure should be followed in each case?

4. Is sensitivity analysis likely to be helpful in any of the following cases? Explain fully.

a. The values of several key decision variables are subject to considerable uncertainty but the penalties for delaying the decision are high.

b. Estimates of parameter values are uncertain and the costs of additional data collection and analysis are high.

c. A decision is to be made on acceptance or rejection of a project very similar to many past projects in which actual revenue and cost factors have not varied from estimated figures by more than 5 percent.

d. Management wishes to test out the feasibility of proposed production and inventory scheduling programs under conditions of variable demand and supply restrictions using mathematical programming.

e. Key decision variables are subject to moderate uncertainty but the consequences of a wrong decision are likely to be severe and the costs of collecting and analyzing additional information about decision parameters is high.

5. What is parametric programming? How does it differ from sensitivity analysis? Explain fully.

6. How does the dual problem differ from the primal problem in linear programming? What information does the dual problem provide which may be helpful in applying sensitivity analysis to a problem solution?

7. Is it necessary to completely resolve a linear programming problem when one or more variables, coefficients, or constraints are changed? Why?

8. Under what conditions is it desirable to solve for the optimal integer solution rather than rounding off to the nearest whole number a linear programming problem solution? In what circumstances would cutting plane, shifted hyperplane, and truncated enumeration methods be most suitable for solving integer programming problems?

9. What problems commonly arise in applying sensitivity analysis to integer programming problems? How can these problems be overcome?

10. What are the benefits and limitations of using matrix inversion techniques in solving linear programming problems when computer processing is not possible? Would your answer be different if computer processing was to be employed? Why?

Bibliography

Balinski, M.L., "Integer Programming: Methods, Uses, Computation," *Management Science*, November 1965, pp. 253-313.

Beale, E.M.L., "Survey of Integer Programming," *Operational Research Quarterly*, June 1965, pp. 219-228.

Beale, E.M.L., P.A.B. Hughes, and R.E. Small, "Experiences in Using a Decomposition Program," *Computer Journal*, April 1965, pp. 13-18.

Beckmann, Martin J., "A Technical Note: Alternative Approaches to the Production Programming Problem," *Engineering Economist*, Spring 1968, pp. 173-187.

Beged Dov, A.G., "Optimal Assignment of Research and Development Projects in a Large Company Using an Integer Programming Model," *IEEE Transactions on Engineering Management*, December 1965, pp. 135-142.

Beightler, Charles S., Robert M. Crisp, Jr. and Wilbur L. Meier, Jr., "Organization by Geometric Programming," *Journal of Industrial Engineering*, March 1968, pp. 177-120.

Byrne, R., A. Charnes, W.W. Cooper, and K. Kortznek, "Some New Approaches to Risk," *Accounting Review*, January 1968, pp. 18-37.

Chaiho Kim, "Decomposition of Planning Systems," *Decision Sciences*, July-October 1970, pp. 397-422.

Charnes, A., and W.W. Cooper, "Management Models and Industrial Applications of Linear Programming," *Management Science, 1957,* pp. 38-91.

Courtillot, M., "Varying All the Parameters in a Linear Programming Problem," *Operations Research*, July 1962, pp. 471-475.

Dantzig, George B., "On the Status of Multi-stage Linear Programming Problems," *Management Science*, October 1959, pp. 53-72.

Dantzig, George B., and Philip Wolfe, "Decomposition Principles for Linear Programs," *Operations Research*, February 1960, and "The Decomposition Algorithm for Linear Programs," *Econometrica*, October 1961.

Demski, Joel S., "Some Considerations in Sensitizing an Optimization Model," *Journal of Industrial Engineering*, September 1968, pp. 463-467.

Dorfman, Robert, "Mathematical, or 'Linear' Programming: A Non-mathematical Exposition," *American Economic Review*, December 1953, pp. 797-825.

Dorn, W.S., "Non-Linear Programming—A Survey," *Management Science*, January 1963, pp. 171-208.

Geoffrin, A.M., "Elements of Large Scale Mathematical Programming," *Rand Corporation Reports*, R-481-PR, November 1969, 83 pp.

Glover, Fred, "Management Decision and Integer Programming," *Accounting Review*, April 1969, pp. 300-303; "A New Foundation for a Simplified Primal Integer Programming Algorithm," *Operations Research*, July-August 1968; and "A Multiphase Dual Algorithm for the Zero-One Integer Programming Problem," *Operations Research*, November-December 1965, pp. 879-919.

Gomory, R.E., and W.J. Baumol, "Integer Programming and Pricing," *Econometrica*, July 1960, pp. 521-550.

Harris, Paula M.J., "An Algorithm for Solving Mixed Integer Linear Programming Problems," *Operations Research Quarterly*, June 1964, 117-132.

Hartley, Ronald V., "Some Extensions of Sensitivity Analysis," *Accounting Review*, April 1970, pp. 223-234.

Jensen, Robert E., "Sensitivity Analysis and Integer Linear Programming," *Accounting Review*, July 1968, pp. 425-446.

Jewell, W.S., "A Classroom Example of Linear Programming," *Operations Research*, July-August 1960.

Mulligan, James E., "Basic Optimization Techniques—A Brief Survey," *Journal of Industrial Engineering*, May-June 1965, pp. 192-197.

Parsons, James A., "MATRIX METHODS: Solving Systems of Equations with Matrix Techniques," *Systems and Procedures Journal*, January-February 1968, pp. 8-9; March-April 1968, pp. 8-9; "Processing Configuration Data with Matrices," *Systems and Procedures Journal*, May-June 1968; and "Simplifying Matrix Operations by Partioning," *Systems and Procedures Journal*, July-August 1968, pp. 31-32.

Pritzker, A.A.B., and L.J. Watters, "A Zero-One Programming Approach to Scheduling with Limited Resources," *Rand Corporation Reports*, RM-5561-PR, January 1968, 49 pp. See also "Multiproject Scheduling with Limited Resources, A 0-1 Programming Approach," P-3800, February 1968, 35 pp.

Rappaport, Alfred, "Integer Programming and Managerial Analysis,"

Accounting Review, April 1969, pp. 297-299; "Sensitivity Analysis in Decision Making," *Accounting Review*, July 1967.

Russell, Edward, "Lessons in Structuring Large LP Models," *Industrial Engineering*, March 1970, pp. 12-18.

Rustay, R.C., "Optimization for Beginners," *Machine Design*, October 29, 1970, pp. 69-74.

Spivey, W. Allen, "Decision Making and Probabilistic Programming," *Industrial Management Review*, Winter 1968, pp. 57-67.

Trainor, Richard J., "Mathematical Programming," *Interdisciplinary Studies in Business Behavior*, Joseph W. McGuire, editor, Southwestern Publishing Co., 1962, pp. 117-131.

Trauth, C.A. Jr. and R.E. Woolsey, "Integer Linear Programming: A Study in Computational Efficiency," *Management Science*, May 1969, pp. 481-493.

Wagner, Harvey, "An Integer Linear Programming Model for Machine Scheduling," *Naval Research Logistics Quarterly*, 1959, pp. 131-140. See also "The Simplex Method for Beginners," *Operations Research*, 1958, 7 pp.

Wegner, Peter, "A Non-Linear Extension of the Simplex Method," *Management Science*, October 1960, pp. 43-55.

Young, R.D., "A Simplified Primal (All-Integer) Integer Programming Algorithm," *Operations Research*, July-August 1968.

PART III Mathematical Programming: Transportation and Assignment Methods

Szandtner emphasizes the usefulness of the relatively simple transportation method of linear programming in determining minimum cost distribution patterns. The basic transportation problem generally involves a number of demand and supply points, known demand requirements, and supply capacities which are not to be exceeded. There are a number of alternative ways of supplying demand at varying costs as well. Some common applications of the transportation method include allocation of units of raw material to processing plants, of warehouse stock to multiple plants, and of final customer demand to either plants or warehouses. Once an optimal solution has been reached, it is possible to determine the effects of changes in supply point capacity, transportation costs, or demand patterns, etc., on total distribution patterns and costs. Forbidden routes, overtime production, and transshipment can be accommodated by slight modifications in the basic model. Other extensions (e.g., multiple product cases) can be solved using the general linear programming model.

VAM (Vogel's approximation method) frequently leads to an optimal solution more rapidly with less manual effort than other solution methods (e.g., Northwest Corner), as Steiner[13] observes. The use of an efficient solution procedure is particularly important in cases where there are a large number of sources and destinations. It is possible to test for optimality after each allocation by evaluating all unused cells of the transportation tableau to determine if the solution can be improved by shifting units from occupied cells to any unused cell. If degeneracy occurs (i.e., there are not enough occupied cells with allocations), an arbitrary allocation can be used to keep the solution from cycling away from the optimum one. When all unoccupied cells yield a positive sum during the optimality test, the optimal solution has been reached.

Perry examines the problem of controlling production costs when manufacturing demand temporarily exceeds shop capacity. A transportation model is used to determine a production schedule that will hold the total increase in production costs to a minimum. In such cases it is ordinarily necessary to increase the capacity of bottleneck machine centers and schedule various products at the least possible total cost for manpower and facilities utilized. Production rates for each machine are translated into relative production hours for problem solution and are then converted back to actual production hours or product units. The model as given can be extended to handle inventory requirements, multiple production periods, or lateness penalties.

Transshipment transportation models are useful in formulating and solving production or procurement scheduling problems involving period unit costs, carrying costs, storage capacity, safety stock, and maximum and minimum inventory restrictions, as Tummins and Page demonstrate. Optimum periodic inventory levels and acquisition schedules can be determined using a format that incorporates upper and lower bounded cells, transshipment cells, and bounded transshipment cells. The transshipment cells insure that all purchases plus beginning inventories are used in a given period or are transferred to a succeeding period. This type of model has considerable promise for use in such applications as production planning, distribution analyses, multiplant capital budgeting, and market research.

The assignment method of linear programming, discussed by Carter and Gould is useful in assigning men or machines to jobs when many alternative possibilities exist and when it is desired to minimize total costs, working time, etc. So long as cost per unit output is known and relative efficiency varies from one job to another, the assignment algorithm permits systematic development of the minimum cost allocation scheme. When selection criteria can be boiled down to a single figure for each material-job combination, assignment methods can be used in design work to select the best mix of materials. With some modification, the basic assignment method can also be used to evaluate alternative improvement schemes, to determine manpower and machine assignments to jobs, to make vehicle assignments, or to determine optimum equipment locations within plants.

Windall introduces the subject of dynamic programming by using a cost minimization problem as an example. A manufacturer can use three possible shipping methods: barge, truck, or rail, for transporting his product from the production site to a specified destination. It is possible to change from one shipping method to another at two intermediate points and either a forward or backward approach may be used to determine the combination of shipping methods for the three problem stages which will minimize total shipping costs. As noted, dynamic programming can be applied to other multistage or multiperiod processes such as economic order quantity determination, capital investment, variable production processes, advertising expenditures, and sales effort allocation.

12 The Transportation Problem— A Special Case of Linear Programming

by T. A. B. Szandtner

Linear programming is a powerful mathematical technique that has found numerous applications in industry in recent years. This article attempts to provide a non-mathematical introduction to this technique, starting with the more specialized transportation method and indicating how its application relates to and often leads to more general linear programming models. Emphasis is laid on the structure of this type of problem, how to collect the necessary data, how to interpret the results, and how to organize the reporting system to ensure that the results can be implemented. The way in which the method can be used as a simulation tool to assist management evaluate alternative policies is also illustrated.

Basic Transportation Problem

The basic transportation problem applies to any typical distribution situation in which there are a number of *demand points,* each with known requirements for a given product, to be supplied from a number of *supply points,* each of which has a known capacity of this product. Linking the supply and demand points are a number of possible routes, each of which has a distribution cost.

The objective is to determine the distribution pattern which will minimize total cost. In other words, we are trying to decide how much product

EDITOR'S NOTE: From *Canadian Chartered Accountant,* February 1970, pp. 127-130. Reprinted by permission of the publisher, The Canadian Institute of Chartered Accountants, and author, T.A.B. Szandtner of Woods, Gordon & Co., Toronto, Canada.

should be shipped over each possible route in order to satisfy all demand point requirements while not exceeding the capacity limitations of any supply point.

Using the following definitions, we can look at this problem schematically in Fig. 12-1.

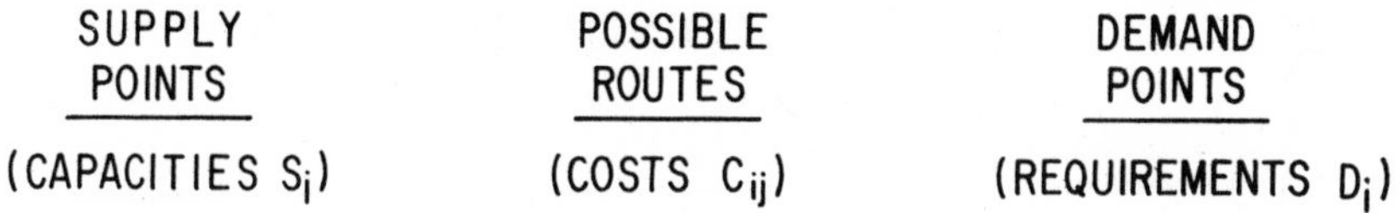

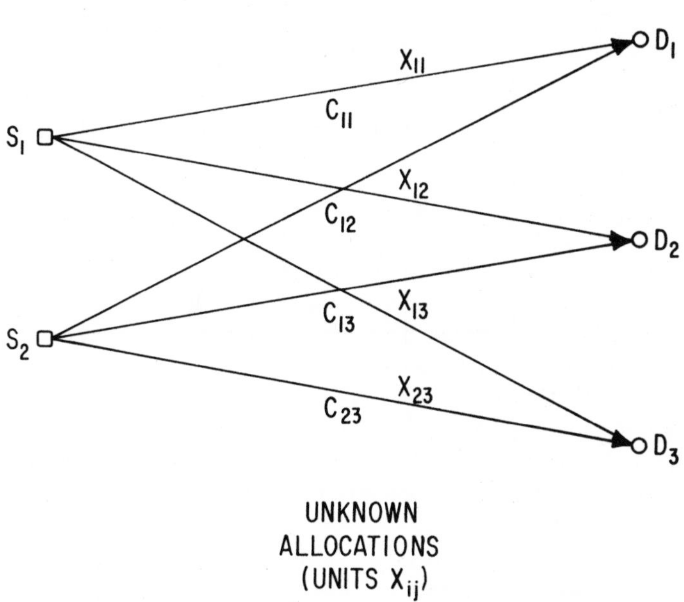

Fig. 12-1. The basic transportation problem.

S_i—capacity at supply point i

D_j—requirement at demand point j

C_{ij}—the cost of transferring one unit of production from supply point i to demand point j

X_{ij}—the number of units of production to be moved from supply point i to demand point j.

Figure 12-2 represents a sample transportation problem with three supply points (A, B, and C) and four demand points (1, 2, 3, and 4). The capacities or requirements are indicated in the column and row labelled 'Total'. The costs C_{ij} are indicated in the corner of each matrix cell. Thus, all the known information relating to the sample problem is displayed in the table and it is required to deduce the X_{ij}. These can be entered in the top left corner of each matrix cell. If the problem is not too large an iterative manual method can be used to generate a series of solutions to the problem starting with a feasible solution and gradually leading to the ultimate solution.

DEMAND POINTS

SUPPLY POINTS		1	2	3	4	TOTAL
	A	10	5	6	7	25
	B	8	2	7	6	25
	C	9	3	4	8	50
	TOTAL	15	20	30	35	

Fig. 12-2. Sample transportation problem.

There are a number of ways of finding an initial feasible solution described in the literature.[1] The Northwest Corner Rule has been used to derive the initial solution shown in Fig. 12-3, for which the value of the objective function is found to be 665. By working through a series of very simple steps, this initial solution can be transformed into the optimal solution which is displayed in Fig. 12-4. Here the value of the objective function is 535 and it can be mathematically proven that no other solution will give a lower total cost.

A close study of the resulting table shows that the optimal solution contains some surprising allocations. For example, the 25 units available at supply point A are all allocated to demand point 4 at a cost of 7 per unit, which is a relatively expensive way of moving the product from this supply point. In addition, it can be seen that 10 of the 50 units available at supply point C are allocated to demand point 1 at an extremely high cost of 9 units when other, much less expensive, links from supply point C are available.

DEMAND POINTS

		1	2	3	4	TOTAL
SUPPLY POINTS	A	<u>15</u> 10	<u>10</u> 5	6	7	25
	B	8	<u>10</u> 2	<u>15</u> 7	6	25
	C	9	3	<u>15</u> 4	<u>35</u> 8	50
	TOTAL	15	20	30	35	

INITIAL SOLUTION COST=665

Fig. 12-3. Sample transportation problem.

This indicates a complex interation between the supply and demand point and that simply putting as much as possible into the cheapest cells is not likely to result in the optimal solution. If this is true for a small sample problem it is easy to imagine how far from the optimum it can be in a very large distribution system.

Using the same symbols, Fig. 12-5 shows a mathematical formulation of the problem. An objective function Z represents the total cost of the distribution pattern selected, followed by a number of constraint equations. The first set of equations reflects the need of not exceeding the capacity of any supply point, while the second set reflects the condition that the requirements at all demand points must be met. The last constraint equation simply means that a negative quantity cannot be sent along any possible route.

This set of equations demonstrates that the transportation problem is in fact a linear programming problem—i.e., there is a linear function of X to be optimized with a number of linear constraints on the possible values of the X's. This problem can be solved using the simplex method. However, the fact that all the coefficients of X in the constraint equations are unity, and that the X's are arranged in a special way permits the problem to be

DEMAND POINTS

	1	2	3	4	TOTAL
A	10	5	6	25 / 7	25
B	5 / 8	10 / 2	7	10 / 6	25
C	10 / 9	10 / 3	30 / 4	8	50
TOTAL	15	20	30	35	

SUPPLY POINTS

FINAL SOLUTION COST=535

Fig. 12-4. Sample transportation problem.

Specifying Equations

Minimize Total Cost

$$X_{11}C_{11} + X_{12}C_{12} + X_{13}C_{13} + X_{21}C_{21} + X_{22}C_{22} + X_{23}C_{23}$$

Subject to:

$$\left.\begin{array}{l} X_{11} + X_{12} + X_{13} = S_1 \\ X_{21} + X_{22} + X_{23} = S_2 \end{array}\right\} \text{ SUPPLY CONSTRAINTS}$$

$$\left.\begin{array}{l} X_{11} + X_{21} = D_1 \\ X_{12} + X_{22} = D_2 \\ X_{13} + X_{23} = D_3 \end{array}\right\} \text{ DEMAND CONSTRAINTS}$$

Fig. 12-5.

written down in the tabular form of the example and to be solved by the simpler transportation method.

Extensions to Basic Problem

The sample problem had a number of restrictive assumptions which can be removed quite simply. It was assumed that total supply is exactly equal to total demand in the distribution system, which is not usually the case. This problem is resolved by introducing either dummy demand or dummy supply points as necessary to absorb the excess of supply or demand.

Also, the sample problem considered distribution costs only, which ignores the fact that unit production costs often differ from one supply point to another. This problem is easily resolved by adding the unit production cost at each supply point into the relevant cost, so that C_{ij} represents the cost of producing one unit of the product at supply point i and transporting it to demand point j. Further extensions to the basic problem can be made and are discussed later in this article.

Example of Application Areas

Applications of the transportation method can be categorized into three major areas:

(1) Allocation of raw material to processing plants: examples in this area would include the distribution of wheat to flour mills, coal to power plants, produce to canneries, and livestock to processing plants.

(2) Allocation of warehouses to plants in a multi-plant system: examples would include the allocation of the distribution of ketchup, appliances, fertilizer, wood products, etc.

(3) Allocation of final customers to either plants or warehouses: there are any number of examples of applications in this area including flour products, canned goods, oil products, soft drinks, beer and so on.

Data Collection Considerations

A number of factors must be considered in developing the data for a transportation problem model.

First, demand and capacity must be uniform over the time span covered by the model. This means that if capacity and demand are represented by annual figures the model can give satisfactory results only if there is no significant seasonality in the demand patterns. If seasonality is a significant factor it may be necessary to have a number of transportation models, each covering a specific part of the seasonal cycle.

Second, the units used in the model must be made consistent. This means that the unit in which the product is measured must be chosen so that it can be made consistent with the freight rates, capacity, and demands. This sounds simpler than it really is and sometimes the choice of units for the unknown X's can be the most important decison in the whole transportation modelling exercise. A good example of this was the application of the transportation method to the distribution of coal. In this case the appropriate unit was found to be the heat content of the coal, because coal faces produce different grades of coal with differing heat contents and demand for coal is in terms of this heat content. Thus, freight rates had to be converted from cost per ton to cost per unit of heat content.

The development of cost information can be relatively complex since the model requires economic costs, not necessarily costs developed using accounting conventions. The basic principle that should be applied is to use only those costs which are out-of-pocket expenditures, and whose magnitude is affected by the proposed distribution decision. This might necessitate a fairly detailed cost study in order to develop the required information. For example, non-linear cost functions may have to be represented by piece-wise linear ones. The determination of capacity at supply points is straightforward once the correct decision on the units of X has been made. The estimation of demands by demand point can be more difficult and is certainly facilitated by the existence of a working forecasting system.

Interpreting the Results

Once the model has been correctly formulated and the various steps of the transportation method carried out, the fundamental answer to the transportation problem has been obtained. This answer indicates the optimal distribution pattern for the system and specifies the operating levels of plants of supply points if total capacity exceeds total demand.

Using this solution the adequacy of the current distribution system can be evaluated. Before doing this, however, it is important to check the model for resonableness, especially with respect to the linearity assumption. We have assumed that transportation costs are linear over certain ranges and the solution values of the X's have not taken us outside this range of linearity. If they have, the correct costs covering the resulting range must be substituted and the problem re-solved. It must also be kept in mind that the model minimizes a specific set of costs only, i.e., those included in the model. The currently operating distribution system may be taking other costs into account and, therefore, cannot be directly compared to the solution to the transportation model. However, if correctly interpreted, the fundamental answer can provide a good picture of the optimal distribution pattern.

Of course, the fundamental answer to the basic transportation model should only serve as the starting point for further investigation into the many possible alternatives that can be considered. To do this the model can be used as a simulation tool to explore the effect of alternatives such as:

- Changes in the capacity at the sources
- Changes in transportation costs due to a different carrier, a new rate schedule, a different ordering policy, etc.
- Changes in demand patterns due to new marketing plans, etc.

Such simulation work becomes much easier to carry out if the initial problem is solved using a computer, since new runs with different input data are easily made. In comparing a variety of alternative possibilities there may be a number of other cost factors that are relevant but not reflected in the model. Therefore, in choosing between alternatives, the cost analysis should always be expanded to include all affected costs before any final decisions are made.

Reporting and Implementation

The reporting system required for any given application of this method must be custom-made to fit the requirements of the particular situation. However, certain basic principles have general application. The primary reporting system is quite straightforward. It provides the person responsible for distribution with the optimal distribution patterns as well as the operating levels of supply points.

A secondary reporting system should be designed to monitor the system through the time span of the model to see how closely the desired distribution pattern is being followed. This system should also be designed to collect up-dated information on costs, capacity and demand so that the model can be quickly up-dated for the next time span.

Finally, the decision maker would receive, from time to time, a number of special reports providing evaluations of possible alternative methods of operation. These would result from using the model as a simulation tool. If these analyses are carefully planned they can be of assistance to the distribution manager in those situations when the monitoring system indicates that the system is not operating according to plan. For example, simulation runs can determine what action should be taken if demand is up by 10 per cent or what the appropriate response is if a strike reduces capacity at a given plant to zero.

Further Extensions

The following list of situations not yet included in the transportation problem are often encountered in practice and can rarely be ignored:

- Forbidden routes
- Overtime production possibilities
- Transshipment
- Alternative transportation modes available
- Carrier with limited capacity
- Several products
- Several products, with restrictions on product mix.

The first three points in this list can be accommodated within the formulation of the transportation model as outlined. To take account of forbidden routes, a very large distribution cost for that route can be introduced and it will not enter the solution. If overtime production is possible at a supply point, a second source at the same location can be introduced with an appropriately modified production and distribution cost. If transshipment among supply points and among demand points is possible, all that is required is to consider every source as a demand point and every demand point as a source. This effectively means adding a row to the table for every demand point and adding a column for every supply point.

The last four extensions to the basic transportation model can only be accommodated within the tabular transportation method with great difficulty. However, if we go back to the algebraic representation of the problem and consider it as a linear programming problem, these four extensions do not present great difficulties since the appropriate constraints can be quite easily written down. But this destroys the simple form of the transportation problem and the more general simplex method must be utilized to solve the problem.

If the basic transportation method were being solved on a computer to begin with, it would likely utilize a standard linear programming package and extending the model as described above makes very little difference in the various computer runs. A common pattern in distribution studies using the transportation method is to make the first rough cut at a solution using the transportation method. Eventually, in order to facilitate the testing of the various alternatives that management very quickly starts to propose, a computer is brought into action. Then, as the model is refined and made more realistic, the various extensions listed above are introduced and eventually the full power of linear programming can be applied. This developmental process can continue over several years and lead to a comprehensive production distribution model which, in some cases could be considered to be a corporate model for the company.

Note

1. M. Sasieni, A. Jaspan, L. Friedman, *Operations Research, Methods and Problems* (John Wiley & Sons, 1959).

13 An Example of the Transportation Problem Solved by Vogel's Approximation Method

by Henry Malcolm Steiner

I. Introduction

This article presents another example of the classic transportation problem of linear programming, meeting the specific needs of readers who are not familiar with the mathematical symbols normally used in such examples. Another reason is the notable lack of examples of this technique in the literature of Business Logistics. Examples of general linear programming problems are plentiful. Some examples of the transportation problem using the Northwest Corner Rule exist. The author has not found any examples of the transportation problem solved by VAM (Vogel's Approximation Method) in the literature of Business Logistics.

Viewed logistically, the transportation problem involves the situation where a number of sources must supply a number of destinations. Each source (for example, a warehouse) has definite and limited quantities of the goods it must supply per time period. Each destination (a mill, for example) must receive difinite and limited quantities of the product (wheat in sacks) per time period. To move a unit of the product along the route from each source to each destination can only be done at a certain cost. The preceding is known and presumed unchangeable for the period. The decision maker now wants to consider the question: "How many units of the goods should be moved from each source to each destination so that transportation costs will be as low as possible?" Each warehouse can supply

---

EDITOR'S NOTE: From *The Logistics Review*, September-October 1969, pp. 29-39. Reprinted by permission of the publisher, Technical Economics, Inc., and author.

no more than its limit, nor can each mill accept more than it can handle per time period.

A possible solution to the problem can be made up by simply looking at the supply and demand figures, and transportation costs, and guessing the quantity to be moved from a given warehouse to a mill. If these quantities are within the given limits, it results in a feasible solution. The possible solutions may run well into the hundreds or thousands, depending on the number of sources and destinations.

To handle the problem logically, when an obvious solution is not apparent, two principal methods have been evolved by mathematicians: (1) The Northwest Corner Rule; and (2) Vogel's Approximation Method.

VAM offers a number of advantages over the Northwest Corner Rule:

1. It usually leads to an optimal solution more rapidly.
2. It requires less manual labor. Simple problems can be solved quickly with a pencil and paper.
3. The initial trial may be optimal.

II. An Example

A private carrier must deliver wheat in sacks from the warehouses having the weekly supplies as listed in Table 13-1.

Table 13-1

Warehouse	Supply/week
1	10,000
2	12,000
3	15,000
Total	37,000

Delivery must be made to mills which require the quantities in sacks per week as given in Table 13-2.

Table 13-2

Mill	Demand/week
A	8,000
B	9,000
C	10,000
D	8,000
Total	35,000

The transportation and handling costs (cents per sack) from each warehouse to each mill are given in Table 13-3.

Table 13-3

Mill	A	B	C	D
Warehouse				
1	13	14	13	20
2	16	13	20	12
3	19	12	17	15

These data are assembled (adding a nonexistent mill, E, in order to balance quantities) in Table 13-4.

Table 13-4

Mill Warehouse	A	B	C	D	E	Supply (000)
1	13	14	13	20	0	10
2	16	13	20	12	0	12
3	19	12	17	15	0	15
Demand (000)	8	9	10	8	2	37

The zero costs within each cell of Column E of Table 13-4 indicate that it will cost nothing to handle and transport sacks of wheat to a nonexistent mill. Or, 2,000 sacks of wheat per week will remain in the warehouse.

VAM requires that a specific procedure be followed in placing quantities to be shipped from a warehouse to a mill. What cell, and how much to put in it, are determined as follows:

In the matrix, Table 13-5, it is noted that the upper left portion is simply a repeat of the previous table, but with the addition of the quantities of the product. The quantities were derived by means of the trials shown to the right and below the original table. *Trial 1* starts in a column—the first to the right of the column headed "Supply"—and continues in a row—the first below the row entitled "Demand." The numbers in the column of *Trial 1* were obtained by looking at the five transportation costs in the row marked *Warehouse 1,* finding the lowest—in this case 0, locating the next lowest, 13, and subtracting one from the other. The same procedure was followed for the remaining two rows. The numbers opposite the row marked *Trial 1* were obtained in a similar way. The 3 under the column headed A is the difference between 13, the lowest transportation cost in the column, and 16, the next lowest cost.

Table 13-5

Mill / Warehouse	A	B	C	D	E	Supply (000)
1	13	14	8[a] 13	20	2[a] 0	10
2	4[a] 16	13	20	8[a] 12	0	12
3	4[a] 19	9[a] 12	2[a] 17	15	0	15
Demand (000)	8	9	10	8	2	37

Trials	1	2	3	4	5
Warehouse 1	13*	1	—	—	—
Warehouse 2	12	1	1	3	4*
Warehouse 3	12	3	3	5*	2

Trials	A	B	C	D	E
1	3	1	4	3	0
2	3	1	4*	3	—
3	3	1	3	3*	—
4	3	1	3	—	—
5	3	—	3	—	—

Note: The superscript "a" indicates a quantity in thousands of sacks allocated to a box.

The largest number available in *Trial 1,* row or column, was selected and marked with an asterisk. It was 13. This meant that row 1 was selected for the first allocation. Accordingly, the lowest cost in row 1 was determined, being 0. As many sacks as possible, considering the constraints of supply and demand, were placed in the box with the lowest cost (box 1E). Only 2,000 could be managed since that was as much as this mill demanded. But placing 2 in that box (meaning 2,000 sacks) effectively removed Mill E from further consideration. A vertical line was drawn to indicate this.

The same procedure was followed for *Trial 2,* and the 4 (asterisked) of column C was selected as the largest number of the trial. The smallest cost in column C was 13 and, therefore, as much as possible was allocated in that box. It was 8,000 sacks which, with the 2,000 previously assigned to *Warehouse 1,* exhausted its supply. Therefore, a horizontal line was drawn through all of the boxes of *Warehouse 1.* The table now consists of 8 boxes.

In *Trial 3* no less than 4 equal highest numbers appeared—all 3's. In case of a tie of this kind, the row or column is chosen arbitrarily. Column D was chosen.

Trials 4 and 5 were performed similarly.

Now what was accomplished? Eight thousand sacks were to go from *Warehouse 1* to mill C; 2,000 sacks were to remain in *Warehouse 1.* Four thousand sacks were to go from *Warehouse 2* to mill A; 8,000 sacks were to go from *Warehouse 2* to mill D. Four thousand sacks were to go from *Warehouse 3* to mill A; 9,000 sacks from *Warehouse 3* to mill B; and 2,000 sacks were to go from *Warehouse 3* to mill C. All mills were to be completely supplied and none will be sent more than it can use.

Is this the best arrangement that can be made?

III. Testing for Optimality

Whether or not the allocation is optimal, the easiest test is the following:

Table 13-6

	A	B	C	D	E	u
1	−2	+6	.	+9	.	13
2	.	+4	+6	.	−1	14
3	.	.	.	0	−4	17
v	2	−5	0	−2	−13	

Each box where a quantity appeared was marked with a dot. The "u" column and "v" row were constructed next by so choosing the "u" column number and the "v" row number that they added up to the transportation cost indicated in the box where they intersect. Arbitrarily, Box 1C was chosen as a starter. Its transportation cost is 13 cents per sack. If 13 is written at the end of row 1 under the "u" column, then 0 must be placed at the bottom of "column C" in the "v" row. (The numbers could have been any two that add up to 13, and the final result would not have been affected.) It is now possible to complete the "u" column and the "v" row. Box 1E had a transportation cost of 0, and −13 is placed in the "v" row under the column headed "E". Another "u" is marked opposite row 3, which was determined by observing that a dot appears in row 3 under a dot in row 1. 17 is filled in at the end of row 3, because the 0 at the bottom of column C plus 17 add up to the 17 in the box (the transportation cost).

The remaining "v" and "u" numbers associated with the dotted boxes were filled in, completing the "u" column and the "v" row.

The −2 in box 1A was determined by the rule stating that the "u" number opposite row 1 plus the "v" number under column A (13 + 2 = 15) is subtracted from the transportation cost in the box (13 −15 = −2).

The rest of the empty boxes are similarly completed.

If any of the boxes contains a number with a minus sign, the solution is not the best possible. In our case several minuses appear. Therefore, a better, i.e., cheaper, arrangement is possible.

By choosing the box which contained the largest minus number (box 3E), any quantity moved to 3E would reduce the transportation cost by 4 cents per unit. In doing this reallocation, the row and column quantities had to be kept balanced so that the new solution would also be possible.

IV. Obtaining a Better Solution

The question of just how much quantity can be moved to 3E arises. Whatever is done, the rows and columns must be balanced. (This means that we must not exceed the supply and demand quantities associated with each warehouse and each mill, including the fictitious one). This is done by tracing a path starting at box 3E (where we will substract the same amount, thus keeping the column balanced), then going to box 1C (where we will add the same quantity, thus keeping row 1 balanced), then moving down to box 3C (where we will subtract the quantity, thus balancing column C and row 3).

How much must we move? Certainly as much as possible, but no more than the greatest amount that can be subtracted in any one box. (We may never move negative quantities.) The original table tells us that the quantity cannot be more than 2.

Moving 2 into box 3E, making the appropriate adjustments described previously, we derive Table 13-7.

Table 13-7

	A	B	C	D	E	Supply
1			10		e	10
2	4			8		12
3	4	9			2	15
Demand	8	9	10	8	2	

Subtracting 2 from boxes 1E and 3C, has removed both, causing a difficulty.

V. Treating Degeneracy

"Degeneracy" occurs when the number of rows plus the number of columns less one is more than the number of boxes filled in with quantities. For example, in the original solution of Table 13-5, the number of rows plus the number of columns less one was 3 + 5 − 1 = 7, being equal to the number of boxes filled in. In Table 13-7, only six boxes are filled in. If we tried to test for "optimality," we could not do it because we lacked one box (allocation). A small letter "e" is placed in either Box 1E or 3C, which disappeared on the last allocation. In Table 13-7, Box 1E was chosen arbitrarily. The little "e" may be thought of as a tiny quantity that will not affect the solution, placed as a sort of marker to allow us to test for optimality. Box 1E will be treated as though it contains an allocation.

The latest allocation of Table 13-7 will be tested for optimality by the method previously described. Table 13-8 results.

Table 13-8

	A	B	C	D	E	u
1	−6	+2	.	+5	.	13
2	.	+4	+10	.	+3	10
3	.	.	+ 4	0	.	13
v	+6	−1	0	+2	−13	

Table 13-8 shows that the solution can be improved by moving some quantity into box 1A. Tracing a path that starts at 1A and touches only occupied boxes leads us to 1E, 3E, and 3A, before returning to 1A. The smallest quantity in a box that is negative for this particular path is "e". Therefore, treating "e" exactly as though it were a real quantity, it is moved to 1A and disappears from 1E.

After making the reallocation, filling in all the quantities in their latest position, and performing the test for optimality, we derive Table 13-9:

Table 13-9

	A	B	C	D	E	Supply	u
1	e	+8	10	+11	+6	10	13
2	4	+4	+4	8	+3	12	16
3	4	9	−2	0	2	15	19
Demand	8	9	10	8	2	37	
v	0	−7	0	−4	−19		

In Table 13-9, the quantities appear without sign, and the test numbers with a sign. A minus appears, showing that the allocation is not the best solution (appearing in cell 3C). The 0 next to it in cell 3D means that if a quantity were moved to that cell, the total transportation cost would remain unchanged. The smallest quantity must be moved into a minus cell of the path 3C, 1C, 1A, 3A, 3C. The quantity is not "e", but 4, and "e" can be dropped since there are again seven allocations. The allocation appears in Table 13-10.

Table 13-10

	A	B	C	D	E	Supply
1	4		6			10
2	4			8		12
3		9	4		2	15
Demand	8	9	10	8	2	

The optimality test results in Table 13-11.

Table 13-11

	A	B	C	D	E	u
1	.	+6	.	+11	+4	13
2	.	+2	+4	.	+1	16
3	+2	.	.	+ 2	.	17
v	0	−5	0	−4	−17	

The signs of Table 13-11 are positive, meaning that the allocation of Table 13-10 is optimal. The absence of zeros indicates that no other optimal arrangement exists.

VI. Total Cost

The total cost of the best way to ship from warehouses to mills is readily obtained. The quantity given in each occupied box is multiplied by the cost shown in the matrix of Table 13-12.

Two thousand sacks remain in warehouse 3 at 0 transportation and handling cost. The lowest cost is $4,660 per week.

Table 13-12

Box	Quantity (sacks)	Cost/unit ($)	Total Cost ($)
1A	4000	0.13	520
1C	6000	0.13	780
2A	4000	0.16	640
2D	8000	0.12	960
3B	9000	0.12	1080
3C	4000	0.17	680
3E	2000	0.00	0
			4660

VII. Conclusion

We have seen how a problem of allocation among warehouses and mills, more generally, origins and destinations, can be solved by the use of a fairly simple technique. With many more warehouses and mills, the problem would become more tedious than it is, in fact, quite unmanageable in any convenient length of time, requiring the use of an electronic computer.

As long as the relationship between cost per unit and quantity shipped is proportional (2,000 sacks cost twice as much to ship as 1,000), given a specific warehouse and mill, the method can be applied.

References and Comments

Fabrycky, W.I., and P.L. Torgersen, *Operations Economy: Industrial Applications of Operations Research.* Prentice-Hall, Inc., Englewood Cliffs, New Jersey; 1966.

The chapter entitled "Distribution Models of Linear Programming" reviews the field and includes a short explanation of VAM.

Hillier, Frederick S., and G.I. Lieberman, *Introduction to Operations Research.* Holden-Day, San Francisco; 1967.

One chapter contains a detailed explanation of the transportation problem, VAM, degeneracy, and the assumptions.

Reinfeld, Nyles V., and W.R. Vogel, *Mathematical Programming.* Prentice-Hall, Englewood Cliffs, New Jersey; 1958.

The first part of the book contains a description of the distribution method and the modified distribution method of solving the transportation problem. It must be read from the beginning in order to understand the authors' phraseology.

14 A Production-Scheduling Decision Model for Demand Exceeding Normal Manufacturing Capacity

by Raphael Perry

In the course of operating a manufacturing facility it will occasionally occur that over a short-term period the demand for manufactured products exceeds the *normal* manufacturing capacity of the facility. Demand is notoriously subject to unforseen fluctuation, but shop capacity must necessarily be based on average, or expected, demand. For this reason it is inevitable that from time to time the facility will be called upon to produce more product than the facility is organized to manufacture.

Under such conditions one plausible solution is to postpone part of the desired production to some future period in which demand will have decreased or production capacity increased. Indeed, if the current increase in demand is sufficiently large and unexpected, there may be no other choice. In the majority of cases, however, postponement is not a real alternative. Commitments have been made, and production schedules must be met—regardless of other considerations.

The other considerations are most often costs. Over a short-term period it is usually possible to increase production above normal capacity by paying premium costs for labor or machinery or both. Because time is short it is not possible (and it might not be desirable) to hire and train additional workers, but existing workers can be asked to work overtime hours for higher rates of pay. Similarly, in a short-term period it is not possible to purchase and install new machinery, but older, comparatively inefficient machinery is often available. Such equipment, which may previously have been deactivated when more efficient facilities were installed, can be

EDITOR'S NOTE: From *The Western Electric Engineer,* July 1966, pp. 15-21. Reprinted by permission of the publisher, Western Electric Company, Inc., and author.

reactivated temporarily to manufacture products at comparatively high costs. Finally, it may be possible to purchase some portion of the desired production volume from another manufacturer, but here again the purchase price is likely to be higher than the manufacturing cost under normal conditions.

In such a situation it is important that the manager make wise choices among the alternatives available to him. If he is committed to meeting (rather than postponing) the production schedules, he is in effect committed to paying premium costs. But such costs, some of which may be very high, can easily get out of hand to seriously reduce, or even destroy, profits for the period. Thus the manager must be particularly careful to choose that combination of available labor and facilities that minimizes the total production cost.

The choice is not a simple one, though, deceptively, it might at first appear so. For example, one might think that he could hold the total cost to a minimum by scheduling the most efficient facility first, the next most efficient facility second, and so forth, until the total production requirements had been accounted for. If only one kind of product were being manufactured, this plan would indeed be correct; however, this plan is not likely to minimize total production cost in the usual situation in which different kinds of products must be manufactured during the same short-term period.

In this situation the problem can, however, be solved by linear programming. In particular, the problem can be shown to be an example of the well known "transportation problem," for the solution which numerous computer programs have been written. Thus it becomes possible to recast the problem in the form of a standard transportation problem and to solve the recasted problem mechanically on a computer with the aid of a computer program already written to do so.[1] The solution yields a production schedule that promises to meet the demand for the short-term period in question and also hold the (necessarily high) total cost to the minimum possible for the given level of demand.

This technique of solution is perhaps best described in terms of a specific example. To this end a generalized job shop provides a good model.

A Job Shop

Consider, for example, a job shop in which a number of different products are manufactured at a number of different machine centers. Each machine center consists of machines performing the same function; however, the different machines in the center may or may not have the same rates of production and costs of operation. Each product in turn must be processed through some particular combination of machine centers.

For such a shop "normal" production capacity over a short term might be defined as the maximum volume of production (depending in turn upon the particular mixture of products required) that can be scheduled during regular working hours on only the most efficient machines within the different machine centers. In the short-term period any demand in excess of this capacity will have to be scheduled either on comparatively inefficient machines or during overtime hours, or even both. (Outside purchase offers a third alternative; however, since many factors in addition to cost are normally involved in a decision to purchase rather than manufacture, this alternative will not be considered.)

As demand begins to exceed this normal capacity, the excess demand is realized at one or more machine centers, which become overloaded. In particular, the slowest machine center becomes a bottleneck, because the maximum capacity of the shop to produce a given product mix is limited by the slowest machine center for that mix. (When the product mix changes, a different machine center can become the bottleneck; however, during the single short-term period under consideration the product mix normally remains constant.)

To increase the total output of the shop in such a situation, it becomes necessary to increase the capacity of the bottleneck machine center. For this reason, in analyzing the situation one need consider only that center. There, with the aid of linear programming, comparatively high-cost methods of operation can be employed in an optimal manner to meet the unusual demand for the least possible total cost.

It should be noted that elimination of one bottleneck machine center will automatically create another slowest machine center, which, depending upon the new output level of the shop, may or may not constitute a bottleneck. If the new slowest machine center is indeed a new bottleneck, the proposed method of solution should in turn be applied to it. The process will necessarily continue until all the overloaded machine centers have been rescheduled optimally to meet the demand.

The Bottleneck Machine Center

Assume that in the job shop under consideration the bottleneck machine center has been determined and that this center includes three machines. The machines all perform the same function (e.g. drilling holes) but at different speeds. Machine number 1, the newest, has the highest rate of output, and machine number 2, only slightly less efficient, operates at 90 percent of the rate of machine number 1. Machine number 3, on the other hand, is an older piece of equipment that operates at only 69 percent of the rate of machine number 1. For this reason machine number 3 is not used under normal conditions.

Assume further that during a particular four-week period this machine center must process seven different products, P_1 through P_7, in the quantities shown in Fig. 14-1. As also shown in that illustration, the different products require different amounts of processing time per unit, with the combined result that, if all the products were to be processed on machine number 1, a total of 718 production hours would be required *on that machine.* (The less efficient machines numbers 2 and 3 would require proportionately more time to perform the same work.)

PRODUCTS	P_1	P_2	P_3	P_4	P_5	P_6	P_7	TOTAL
NUMBER OF UNITS REQUIRED	50	50	150	20	10	50	84	414 UNITS
PRODUCTION HOURS PER UNIT (ON MACHINE NO. 1)	1	2	1	5	5	2	2	
PRODUCTION HOURS EACH PRODUCT (ON MACHINE NO. 1)	50	100	150	100	50	100	168	718 HOURS

Fig. 14-1. Four-week production requirements at the bottleneck machine center. *If all products are processed on the most efficient machine*, a total of 718 production hours are required.

Clearly, the hours of one-shift regular time available on machine number 1—or even on both machine numbers 1 and 2—during a four-week period are insufficient to satisfy the total demand. It will therefore be necessary to employ second-shift work, overtime hours on Saturdays or Sundays, the comparatively inefficient machine number 3, or some combination of these relatively high-cost methods of operation.

The various possibilities are listed in Fig. 14-2. As shown, each machine can be used in each of the possible work shifts. In the course of the four-week period under consideration each machine can be operated within each work shift for the total number of actual hours shown.

Since the different machines have different rates of production, the relative production hours, defined as equivalent hours of production on machine number 1, are somewhat less in the case of machine numbers 2

		ACTUAL PRODUCTION HOURS AVAILABLE	EFFI-CIENCY	RELATIVE PRODUCTION HOURS AVAILABLE	COST PER OPERATOR	
					PER ACTUAL PRODUCTION HOUR	PER RELATIVE PRODUCTION HOUR
MACHINE NUMBER 1	REGULAR TIME	160	100%	160	1(R)	1(R)
	SECOND SHIFT	160		160	1.1	1.10
	SATURDAYS	32		32	1.5	1.50
	SUNDAYS	32		32	2.0	2.00
MACHINE NUMBER 2	REGULAR TIME	160	90%	144	1.0	1.11
	SECOND SHIFT	160		144	1.1	1.22
	SATURDAYS	32		29	1.5	1.67
	SUNDAYS	32		29	2.0	2.22
MACHINE NUMBER 3	REGULAR TIME	160	69%	110	1.0	1.45
	SECOND SHIFT	160		110	1.1	1.59
	SATURDAYS	32		22	1.5	2.17
	SUNDAYS	32		22	2.0	2.90

Fig. 14-2. Machines and work shifts available at the bottleneck machine center. The cost per operator per relative production hour of the alternatives varies from R to 2.90 R dollars.

and 3 than the actual hours available. For example, in 160 hours of regular time, machine number 2, which operates at 90 percent of the rate of machine number 1, can only produce a quantity of output equivalent to 144 hours of production on machine number 1; thus, as shown in Fig. 14-2, machine number 2 is considered to have only 144 relative production hours available.

Next, the costs of operating the different machines are included in a loaded hourly labor rate of R dollars per operator per hour applicable in regular time.[2] In other shifts, as shown in Fig. 14-2, the loaded rate is higher—to a maximum rate of $2R$ dollars per operator per hour for overtime work on Sundays.

The more relevant cost, however, is the loaded cost per operator per *relative* production hour. This adjusted rate takes into account the different rate of output of the different machines and thereby shows the relative costs of equivalent units of production. For machine numbers 2 and 3 the adjusted rates are higher than for the more efficient machine number 1 used as a standard. For example, since machine number 2 in 160 actual hours produces only 144 relative production hours' worth of output and since the cost of using machine number 2 is R dollars per operator per actual hour, the adjusted rate becomes $(160/144)R = 1.11\ R$ dollars per relative production hours. Similar adjusted rates for the different machines and shifts are shown in the final column of Fig. 14-2.

The cost of processing any product is likely to be a function of the product itself as well as of the method of processing employed. In this case products P_1 through P_5 each require only one operator to handle each unit, but product P_6 requires two, and product P_7 three, operators per unit; thus, it costs proportionately more to process products P_6 and P_7. For example, the cost of one production hour on machine number 1 during regular time becomes $1 \times R = R$ dollars per hour for product P_5, which requires only one operator, but $2 \times R = 2R$ dollars per hour for product P_6, which requires two operators.

To further complicate the situation special factors make it impossible to process product P_4 on machine number 1 or to process product P_7 on machine number 2. Although the special factors are not directly related to cost, they can be translated into cost terms by arbitrarily assigning prohibitively high costs to the impossible situations. In this case costs of 100 R dollars per relative production hour are arbitrarily assigned to the machine number 1-product P_4 and the machine number 2-product P_7 combinations; with such high costs involved the proposed method of solution will automatically avoid scheduling these combinations.

It is now possible to develop a complete tableau of the cost of the scheduling the different products onto the different machines within the different operational shifts. Such a tableau is shown in Fig. 14-3. In this illustration the numbers in gray represent the relative costs of scheduling one relative production hour toward each product on each machine within each shift.[3] For example, it costs 2.44 R dollars per relative production hour to process product P_6 on machine number 2 during second-shift operation but 3.18 R dollars per relative production hour to process the same product on machine number 3 during the same shift. (To avoid excessive redundancy the basic rate R has been omitted from the tableau.)

In addition to costs, the tableau also shows the capacity, b_i, in relative production hours available on each machine in each shift and the demand, d_j, in relative production hours required on each product. Finally, now that all possible means of production are under consideration, the total capacity

$$\left(\sum_{i=1}^{12} b_i = 994 \text{ rel. production hours} \right)$$

exceeds the total demand

$$\left(\sum_{j=1}^{7} d_j = 718 \text{ rel. production hours}\right)$$

by 276 relative production hours. To account for this unused capacity, an eighth column has been created in the tableau, and costs of 0 dollars per relative production hour have been inserted to indicate that in this problem it costs nothing *not* to use available hours on any of the machines in any of the shifts.[4]

The problem can now be stated concisely. It is to determine the number of relative production hours X_{ij} that should be scheduled on the machine-

		P_1	P_2	P_3	P_4	P_5	P_6	P_7	UNUSED CAPACITY	RELATIVE PRODUCTION HOURS AVAILABLE
MACHINE NUMBER 1	REGULAR TIME	1(R)	1.00	1.00	100.	1.00	2.00	3.00	0	b_1 = 160
	SECOND SHIFT	1.10	1.10	1.10	100.	1.10	2.20	3.30	0	b_2 = 160
	SATURDAYS	1.50	1.50	1.50	100.	1.50	3.00	4.50	0	b_3 = 32
	SUNDAYS	2.00	2.00	2.00	100.	2.00	4.00	6.00	0	b_4 = 32
MACHINE NUMBER 2	REGULAR TIME	1.11	1.11	1.11	1.11	1.11	2.22	100.	0	b_5 = 144
	SECOND SHIFT	1.22	1.22	1.22	1.22	1.22	2.44	100.	0	b_6 = 144
	SATURDAYS	1.67	1.67	1.67	1.67	1.67	3.34	100.	0	b_7 = 29
	SUNDAYS	2.22	2.22	2.22	2.22	2.22	4.44	100.	0	b_8 = 29
MACHINE NUMBER 3	REGULAR TIME	1.45	1.45	1.45	1.45	1.45	2.90	4.35	0	b_9 = 110
	SECOND SHIFT	1.59	1.59	1.59	1.59	1.59	3.18	4.77	0	b_{10} = 110
	SATURDAYS	2.17	2.17	2.17	2.17	2.17	4.34	6.51	0	b_{11} = 22
	SUNDAYS	2.90	2.90	2.90	2.90	2.90	5.80	8.70	0	b_{12} = 22
RELATIVE PRODUCTION HOURS REQUIRED		d_1 = 50	d_2 = 100	d_3 = 150	d_4 = 100	d_5 = 50	d_6 = 100	d_7 = 168	$\sum_{i=1}^{12} b_i - \sum_{j=1}^{7} d_j = d_8$; $d_8 = 276$	

Fig. 14-3. The problem at the bottleneck center. In view of the hourly costs shown in gray, how many hours should be scheduled to each product on each machine within each shift?

shift combination represented by the *ith* row (i = 1,2, . . . , 12) in the tableau toward production of the product (or the dummy product represented by the unused capacity column) represented by the *jth* column (j = 1,2, . . . , 8) in the tableau.

The numbers X_{ij} are subject to certain constraints. First, since negative hours have no meaning, it is necessary that

$$x_{ij} \geqslant 0, \text{ for all i and j} \qquad (1)$$

Second, since the number of relative production hours available on each machine-shift combination must be completely allocated among products and unused capacity, it is necessary that

$$\sum_{j=1}^{8} x_{ij} = b_i, \text{ for } i = 1, 2, \ldots, 12. \qquad (2)$$

Third, since the number of relative production hours required by each product must be satisfied, it is necessary that

$$\sum_{i=1}^{12} x_{ij} = d_j, \text{ for } j = 1, 2, \ldots, 8. \qquad (3)$$

Subject to these constraints the numbers X_{ij} must be chosen in such a manner that the total cost is minimized. Thus it is necessary to minimize the function

$$\sum_{i=1}^{12} \sum_{j=1}^{8} c_{ij}x_{ij}$$

where the numbers c_{ij} are the costs per relative production hour shown in the tableau.

Solution

The problem has now been stated exactly in the form of the well known transportation problem As described in the BACKGROUND on page 213, the transportation problem is one of transporting a homogeneous product from multiple suppliers to multiple users for the minimum total cost when the transportation cost per unit of product depends upon both the supplier from whom and the user to whom the unit is shipped. In the problem at hand, of course, no product is being shipped; however, one might legitimately conceive that relative production hours are being "transported" from machine-shift combinations to products for costs that depend upon both the particular machine-shift combinations and the products involved.

In any event, because the problem has been stated in the exact *form* of a transportation problem, the problem can be solved directly on a computer by one of the many computer programs already written to solve the transportation problem. One need only feed in the required input information, all of which has already been presented in the tableau displayed as Fig. 14-3.

The computer solution obtained by this method is presented in a new tableau displayed as Fig. 14-4. In this tableau the numbers at the intersections of the rows and columns are the quantities X_{ij}—the numbers of relative production hours that should be scheduled for the different products on the different machines within the various shifts. As can be readily seen, these assignments schedule all of the available relative production hours either to products or to unused capacity and also meet the production requirements of the different products.

		P_1	P_2	P_3	P_4	P_5	P_6	P_7	UNUSED CAPACITY	RELATIVE PRODUCTION HOURS AVAILABLE
MACHINE NUMBER 1	REGULAR TIME							160		160
	SECOND SHIFT			32		20	100	8		160
	SATURDAYS								32	32
	SUNDAYS								32	32
MACHINE NUMBER 2	REGULAR TIME	14			100	30				144
	SECOND SHIFT	36	100	8						144
	SATURDAYS								29	29
	SUNDAYS								29	29
MACHINE NUMBER 3	REGULAR TIME			110						110
	SECOND SHIFT								110	110
	SATURDAYS								22	22
	SUNDAYS								22	22
RELATIVE PRODUCTION HOURS REQUIRED		50	100	150	100	50	100	168	276	

Fig. 14-4. Minimum cost solution at the bottleneck machine center. The numbers of relative production hours shown should be scheduled to each product on each machine within each shift.

Most important, the proposed production schedule results in the least possible total cost for the entire job. In this case one finds that the total cost is

$$\sum_{i=1}^{12} \sum_{j=1}^{8} c_{ij} x_{ij} = 1{,}278.62\, R \text{ dollars}$$

This cost is higher than the normal cost because the normal manufacturing capacity of the shop has been exceeded; however, this cost includes the minimum possible additional cost necessary to perform the job with the existing production facilities.

One final step remains. Although it was convenient to set up and solve the problem in terms of relative production hours, the solution can be applied only in terms of either actual production hours or units of product. Thus it is necessary to convert the solution matrix given in Fig. 14-4 into one or the other of these usable units. In this case actual production hours can easily be determined from relative production hours by dividing the relative production hours scheduled on each machine by the efficiency of the machine. Similarly, the number of units of product to be produced can be determined in each case by dividing the relative production hours required for each product by the actual production hours required per unit of product to produce the same product on machine number 1. The results of both conversions are shown in Fig. 14-5, which expresses the solution in terms of both actual production hours and units of product.

Extended Applications

The basic method of solution proposed lends itself to more difficult problems in which additional factors may complicate the situation. For example, in the event that initial and final inventories are required, they can be taken into consideration by adding another source of supply and another product requirement, respectively. Similarly, the mathematical model can be expanded to include more than one production period. In this case inventory storage costs must be considered. Again, in another situation the manager may wish to introduce a penalty for not meeting demand on time. He can do so by adding a dummy source that supplies fictitious products at a real cost.

The method of solution is thus quite flexible. It can encompass many situations and take into account special restrictions imposed on the decision maker by internal or external conditions. In all cases, however, the three basic restrictions of the linear-programming formulation (equations 1, 2,

Machine	Time	P_1	P_2	P_3	P_4	P_5	P_6	P_7	UNUSED CAPACITY	ACTUAL PRODUCTION HOURS AVAILABLE
MACHINE NUMBER 1	REGULAR TIME							160 HR. 80 UNITS		160
	SECOND SHIFT			32 HR. 32 UNITS		20 HR 4 UNITS	100 HR. 50 UNITS	8 HR. 4 UNITS		160
	SATURDAYS								32 HOURS	32
	SUNDAYS								32 HOURS	32
MACHINE NUMBER 2	REGULAR TIME	15.6 HR. 14 UNITS			111.1 HR. 20 UNITS	33.3 HR. 6 UNITS				160
	SECOND SHIFT	40 HR. 36 UNITS	111.1 HR. 50 UNITS	8.9 HR. 8 UNITS						160
	SATURDAYS								32 HOURS	32
	SUNDAYS								32 HOURS	32
MACHINE NUMBER 3	REGULAR TIME			160 HR. 110 UNITS						160
	SECOND SHIFT								160 HOURS	160
	SATURDAYS								32 HOURS	32
	SUNDAYS								32 HOURS	32
UNITS OF PRODUCT REQUIRED		50	50	150	20	10	50	84		

Fig. 14-5. The solution translated into both *actual* production hours (shown in black) and units of product (shown in gray) to be assigned to each machine-shift-product combination.

and 3) must be strictly obeyed. Others can be added, but the basic ones must remain.

Finally, the size of the problem that can be solved—the number of products and the number of machine under consideration—is restricted only by the size of the computer used and the capacity of the particular program available for that computer.[5]

Background—The Transportation Problem

One important class of practical problems is concerned with minimizing the cost of transporting goods (or allocating resources) from multiple sources to multiple destinations. The basic problem, the solution of which constitutes one of earliest applications of linear programming, was formulated by Hitchcock[6] and independently discussed by Koopmans;[7] thus, the problem is often referred to as the Hitchcock-Koopmans transportation problem.

In this problem it is assumed that a homogeneous product is to be transported from m sources to n destinations. At the i*th* source $(i = 1,2,\ldots, m)$ b_i units of product are available. Meanwhile, at the j*th* destination $(j = 1,2, \ldots, n)$ d_j units of product are required. With regard to these quantities a complete statement of the problem requires that the total number of units available at the sources equal the total number of units required at the destinations; that is, that

$$\sum_{i=1}^{m} b_i = \sum_{j=1}^{n} d_j$$

If, however, this condition is not true, it can arbitrarily be made so by adding either a dummy source with a fictitious capacity or—as illustrated in the problem in the article—a dummy destination with a fictitious demand. Finally, the cost of transporting the product from the i*th* source to the j*th* destination is c_{ij} dollars per unit of product. (In the case of dummy sources or destinations the associated transportation costs are normally zero).

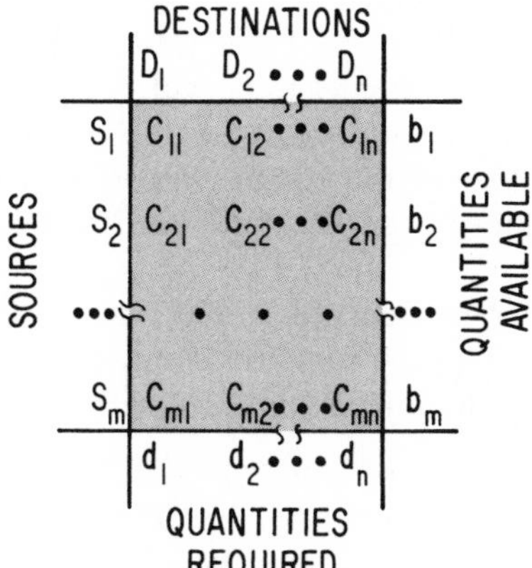

Fig. 14-6. The transportation tableau.

Under these conditions, which are illustrated in the "transportation tableau" shown in Fig. 14-6, the question is: how many units of product should be transported from each source to each destination? The objective is to meet all the requirements for the minimum total transportation cost. More specifically, if x_{ij} represents the quantity of product to be transported from the *ith* source to the *jth* destination, the problem is to determine values of x_{ij} (i = 1,2, . . . , *m*; j = 1,2, . . . , *n*) that minimize the total cost

$$\sum_{i=1}^{m}\sum_{j=1}^{n} c_{ij}x_{ij}$$

subject to the three restrictions

$$x_{ij} \geqslant 0, \text{ for all i and j} \tag{1}$$

$$\sum_{j=1}^{n} x_{ij} = b_i, i = 1, 2, \ldots, m \tag{2}$$

$$\sum_{i=1}^{m} x_{ij} = d_j, j = 1, 2, \ldots, n. \tag{3}$$

Several important theorems pertaining to this problem have been proven. For example, Gass[8] shows: (1) that the problem has a feasible solution; (2) that a feasible solution containing at most $m + n - 1$ positive x_{ij}s exists; (3) that, if the numbers b_i and d_j are nonnegative integers, every basic feasible solution has integral values; and (4) that a finite minimum feasible (least cost) solution always exists.

With this kind of theoretical foundation several people developed techniques for solving the problem. First, Dantzig developed a systematic method of solution[9] which continues to be widely used. This method, which has been termed the "northwest corner rule" by Charnes and Cooper,[10] constitutes a special form of the simplex algorithm. Subsequently, other algorithms were developed—for example, one by Ford and Fulkerson[11] and another by Munkres.[12]

In practice, the different algorithms, all of which involve considerable computation, are normally performed on computers. Very small problems ($m, n \leqslant 6$), however, can be solved manually without excessive labor.

Notes

1. The problem posed could also be solved by the simplex algorithm, which is the more powerful technique applicable to the general linear programming problem. The transportation

problem, however, constitutes a special case of the linear programming problem, and the standard method for solving the transportation problem is much simpler and faster than the simplex algorithm.

2. In the hypothetical case considered, depreciation, maintenance, and operating expenses for all three machines are added together into a common expense, which is then spread out among the operators and collected as a fixed percentage of the basic hourly labor rate. The basic rate plus this percentage loading charge then becomes the loaded labor rate R used in the problem. It should, however, be noted that the method of solution proposed does not depend upon the system of accounting cited; the method is applicable under any accounting system so long as it is possible to ascertain the cost per relative production hour of every machine-work shift-product combination.

3. The cost tableau has been constructed in terms of relative rather than actual production hours so that common units can be used throughout the problem. Actual hours are not suitable units because in this case one hour's production on one machine is not equivalent to one hour's production on another machine. Similarly, the number of units of product processed are not suitable units because the capacity of each machine in each shift is a fixed number of hours; the number of units of product that can be processed within these hours depends upon the particular product mix assigned to that machine. Thus it is expedient to translate the problem into relative production hours, which constitute equivalent units of production, to solve the problem in these common units, and finally to retranslate the answer back into either actual production hours or units of product to be assigned to each machine-shift-product combination.

4. It is entirely conceivable that in other problems costs might be associated with *not* using particular production capacity. In such a case it would merely be necessary to insert the appropriate costs.

5. The capacities of various computer programs available to solve the transportation problem are as follows in terms of the number of rows, m, and the number of columns, n, in the problem:

I.B.M. 7070 computer
Program #12.9001
Capacity: $m \leqslant 50, n \leqslant 500$

I.B.M. 7070 computer
Program #12.9003
Capacity: $m \leqslant 275, n \leqslant 275$

I.B.M. 7090/94 computer
Program #3080 PKTRAN
Capacity: $mn \leqslant 10{,}000$ for 32K machine

I.B.M. 1620 computer
Program #10.1005
Capacity: $10mn + 25m + 20n + 4 \leqslant$ core size $- 4700$

R.C.A. 501 computer
Capacity: $m + n \leqslant 64$

Univac I and II computers
Capacity: $m \leqslant 8, n \leqslant 9000$
or $m \leqslant 18, n \leqslant 6000$
or $m \leqslant 28, n \leqslant 4000$

6. F.L. Hitchcock, "The Distribution of a Product from Several Sources to Numerous Localities", *Journal of Mathematics and Physics,* Vol. XX (1941), pp. 224-230.

7. T.C. Koopmans (ed.), "Activity Analysis of Production and Allocation," *Cowls Commission Monograph 13,* John Wiley and Sons, New York, 1951.

8. S.I. Gass, "The Transportation Problem", *Linear Programming Methods and Applications,* McGraw-Hill Book Company, New York, 1958, pp. 137-156.

9. G.B. Dantzig, Chapter 23—"Application of the Simplex Method to a Transportation Problem", T.G. Koopmans (ed.), *op.cit.*

10. A. Charnes and W.W. Cooper, " The Stepping-Stone Method of Explaining Linear Programming Calculations in Transportation Problems", *Management Science,* Vol. 1, No. 1 (October 1954), pp. 49-69.

11. L.R. Ford, Jr. and D.R. Fulkerson, "Solving the Transportation Problem", *Notes on Linear Programming*— Part XXXII, RM-1736 RAND Corporation, Santa Monica, June 20, 1956.

12. J. Munkres, "Algorithms for the Assignment and Transportation Problem", *Journal of the Society of Industrial and Applied Mathematics,* Vol. V, No. 1 (March 1957), pp. 32-38.

15 Procurement Scheduling: A Transportation Formulation

by Marvin Tummins and R. Frank Page

Management continually encounters problems in which conflicting constraints complicate the decision-making process. For instance, it is desirable to purchase raw materials in periods of low prices, but warehouse space or cash limitations, as well as other factors, interfere with the ability to take advantage of seasonal price movements. Innumerable other illustrations could be given to demonstrate the constraints within which managers must make decisions. Most of these problems have several acceptable solutions. In fact, many of them have an unlimited number of possible solutions. The problem is to select the "best" solution at the time, within the given constraints.

The major purpose of this article is to introduce a solution to the procurement problems facing most retail, governmental, and manufacturing establishments. The article characterizes the benefits to be derived from using the model, illustrates the mechanics of the transportation model as modified, and lays the foundation for further inquiry the foundation for further inquiry and investigation into potentially profitable applications of the various techniques of linear programming.

EDITOR'S NOTE: "Procurement Scheduling: A Transportation Formulation," by R. Frank Page and Marvin Tummins. Reprinted by permission of *Management Services*, September-October.

For the benefit of readers who lack experience with the traditional transportation models of linear programming, the model is explained in detail. However, the novel application of using the transshipment technique and upper as well as lower bounds should prove profitable even to more sophisticated readers.

Mathematical models of the type proposed and explained in this article hold immense promise for widespread use by managers. Models provide opportunities for managers to find definite answers to questions that must be answered, whether by guess, by estimate, or by the use of a technique such as the one suggested here.

Traditional economic lot size or economic order quantity techniques do not effectively handle the number of constraints included in the basic illustrations of this article. The article presents a transportation formulation of a procurement or production scheduling problem incorporating the following constraints:

1. varying periodic unit costs
2. carrying charges
3. storage capacity
4. safety stock (minimum inventory)
5. acquisition restrictions—minimum and maximum quantities
6. maximum periodic inventories.

Advantages of Technique

The formulation should be a worthy addition to the traditional solutions to the economic lot size problem. This formulation provides for timing of acquisitions and indicates optimum periodic inventory levels under the given constraints. The solution procedure requires a transportation format utilizing upper- and lower-bounded cells, transshipment cells, and bounded transshipment cells. Two numerical illustrations are presented, fitted into the transportation format, evaluated, and modified. The evaluation and modification routines are presented in detail.

Illustration 1

For Illustration 1 the problem data may be summarized as follows:

1. Objective—To fulfill demands at the lowest cost.
2. Projected demand in units:

Period	Units (1,000s)
1	22
2	18
3	15
4	21
5	23
6	23
7	22
8	26
9	25
10	40
11	30
	265

3. Required safety stock—10 per cent of projected demand for the next period. (The amount can be adjusted as desired.)

4. Purchase quotations:

a. A 10,000-minimum periodic agreement has been entered into with the supplier. (This restriction can be eliminated or modified if desired.)

b. The maximum available units per period are set at 45,000 units. (This restriction could arise from handling limitations or other similar restrictions and is also subject to adjustment.)

c. Costs vary with a seasonal demand:

Period	Unit Cost
0	$1.00
1	1.06
2	1.04
3	1.03
4	1.09
5	1.14
6	1.11
7	1.05
8	1.14
9	1.10
10	1.16

5. Storage capacity—(This restriction could arise from various conditions such as monetary availability or varying weather conditions requiring internal storage in some periods and permitting external storage in other periods.):

Periods	Upper Limitation On Storage in Units
1 through 3	50,000
4 through 6	80,000
7 through 10	45,000

6. Carrying charges—(Similar to item 5.):

Periods	Carrying Charge Per Period Per Unit
1 through 3	$.05
4 through 6	.02
7 through 10	.05

7. There is a one-period lag between purchase and availability. This delay may be due to delivery time or other factors. The constraint may be eliminated or modified by choosing a period other than one month for the schedule.

8. A maximum inventory level is included. This constraint may be one placed by managerial considerations other than the storage constraint. The maximum ending inventory period, determined as estimated unit sales in the two subsequent periods, follows:

Period	Number of Units
1	33,000
2	36,000
3	44,000
4	46,000
5	45,000
6	48,000
7	51,000
8	65,000
9	70,000
10	20,000*

*Maximum carryover due to minimum purchase requirement of 10,000 and demand of 30,000 in Period 11.

These data are summarized into the transportation format, and a trial schedule is developed, evaluated, modified, and again evaluated until an optimum schedule has been developed.

1) Cell indicating available units for Period B – Cell AB.

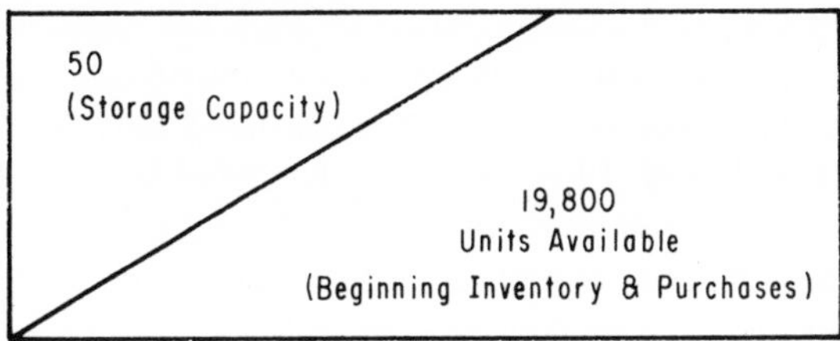

2) Cell indicating ending inventory carried over to Period C – Cell BB

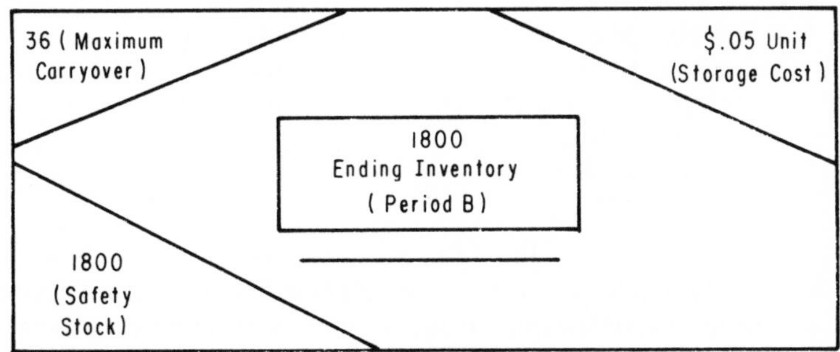

The bar under the ending inventory amount indicates that the minimum inventory level has been reached.

3) Cell indicating purchases to be made in Period O – Cell OP

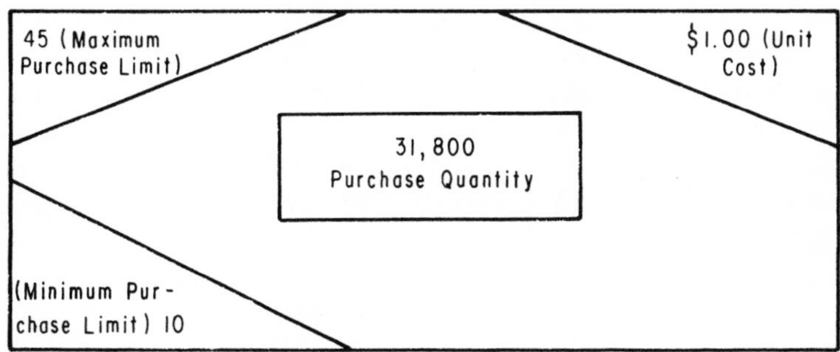

Exhibit 15-1. Sample of cells.

In order to ensure that available supplies at any given time do not exceed storage capacity, the transshipment device is used. This device as used ensures that all periodic acquisitions plus beginning inventories are either used in the period available or transferred into units available for the period immediately following.

The two negative cells in each row (transshipment cells containing rectangles) contain the beginning inventory and purchases for the period. The transshipment cell appearing first in each row contains the beginning inventory; it must not exceed its upper bound and must not fall below its lower bound. The figure in the upper-right-hand corner of this cell is the carrying charge. The two figures on the left-hand side of the cell relate to the upper and lower bounds. The transshipment cells in the purchase column contain three numbers; the upper-right-hand corner contains the unit cost, and the left side contains the upper and lower bounds as set by contract or trade customs.

The third cell (non-negative) is used to ensure that units available in any period do not exceed storage capacity. The cost coefficient of this cell is zero, and the left-hand corner contains the storage capacity constraint.

To facilitate an understanding of the format utilized in deriving the solution, a sample cell of each type is explained in Exhibit 15-1.

The blank cells are inadmissible and are treated as if they contained excessive cost coefficients which will not permit them to come into the solution.

Exhibit 15-2 contains the first solution attempt. The basic feasible solution (all rim requirements met and the number of assignments equaling the number of rim restrictions minus one) was developed by using a trial and error method. To facilitate discussion, periods 1 through 11 have been converted to A through K.

Cell Evaluation Procedures

Evaluation of Cell AP—This cell is at its lower bounds and is evaluated to see whether the number of units purchased should be increased. Cell AP is a transshipment cell, which indicates that in order to add a unit to the evaluation route including this cell a unit must be subtracted in this cell. The evaluation of Cell AP follows (the "R" represents reverse or a negative symbol):

	Subtract one unit
Cell AP	$1.06 R
OA	0
	$1.06 R
	Add one unit
Cell AA	$ .05 R
OP	1.00 R
	$1.05 R

	A	B	C	D	E	F	G	H	I	J	K	Purchases
O	50 31,800											45 10 31,800 1.00
A	33 .05 9,800 2200	50 19,800										45 10 10,000 1.06
B		36 .05 1,800 1800	50 16,500									45 10 14,700 1.04
C			44 .05 1,500 150	50 46,500								43 10 45,000 1.03
D				46 .02 25,500 2100	80 38,300							45 10 12,800 1.09
E					45 .02 15,300 2300	80 25,300						45 10 10,000 1.14
F						48 .02 2,300 2300	80 24,200					45 10 21,900 1.11
G							51 .02 2,200 2200	80 43,500				45 10 41,300 1.05
H								65 .05 17,500 2600	45 27,500			45 10 10,000 1.14
I									70 .05 2,500 2500	45 44,000		45 10 41,500 1.10
J										20 .05 4,000 4000	45 30,000	45 10 26,000 1.16
Sales Demand	22,000	18,000	15,000	21,000	23,000	23,000	22,000	26,000	25,000	40,000	30,000	265,000

Exhibit 15-2. Procurement scheduling matrix—Solution No. 1 (Illustration 1).

The net effect would be to increase the cost by $.01 per unit.

Evaluation of Cell CP—This cell is at the upper bound, so the evaluation should be to see whether fewer units should be purchased in this period. Again, this is a transshipment cell, so in order to subtract a unit from the evaluation route containing this cell a unit should be added to the transshipment cell.

	Add one unit
Cell CP	$1.03 R
DD	.02 R
	$1.05 R
	Subtract one unit
Cell CD	$ 0
DP	1.09 R
	$1.09 R

The net effect would be to increase the cost by $.04 per unit.

Evaluation of Cell FF—This cell is at its lower bound, and the evaluation determines the possibility of increasing the number of units carried over to period G above 2,300.

	Subtract one unit
Cell FF	$ .02 R
DP	1.09 R
EE	.02 R
	$1.13 R
	Add one unit
Cell FP	$1.11 R
DE	0
EF	0
	$1.11 R

The net effect would be to increase the cost by $.02 per unit.

Although all cells are evaluated in a similar manner, the evaluation of Cell JJ will be shown here to illustrate solution modification procedures. This transshipment cell is at its lower bounds, indicating that the evaluation should investigate the desirability of increasing the number of units processed by the evaluation route containing this cell.

	Subtract one unit
Cell JJ	$ .05 R
IP	1.10 R
	$1.15 R
	Add one unit
Cell IJ	$ 0
JP	1.16 R
	$1.16 R

The net effect would be to decrease the cost by $.01 per unit.

The maximum number of units that can be brought into the route is equal to the smallest number of units that will cause a cell in the route to reach an upper or lower bound or lower bound or violate rim requirements. The route for Cell JJ is analyzed in Exhibit 15-3.

Exhibit 15-4 contains the cost summaries for Illustration 1. A uniquely optimal solution to Illustration 1 is shown in Exhibit 15-5.

In Illustration 1 and its solution the maximum inventory level was not an effective constraint. Illustration 2, summarized in Exhibit 15-6 on this page, changes the constraints of Illustration 1 in a manner that makes the maximum inventory constraint effective. An uniquely optimal solution to the modified problem data is presented in Exhibit 15-6. The evaluation of bounded or unused cells is included.

Although the illustrations included in this article concentrate upon one problem facing almost all managers of industrial or governmental operations, the potentials of the model are limited only by the imagination of managers. The mechanics, while tedious to perform, are easy to master, and their application often results in surprising and valuable modifications of operating procedures currently used in many management routines. Profitable applications will increase as knowledge of the procedures becomes more widespread. The following outline suggests several promising applications:

1. Production Planning—Starting with a periodic sales forecast, available plant capacities, and related variable cost factors, it is possible to develop a production schedule that will meet demand at lowest costs.

2. Distribution Analyses—Utilizing forecasted periodic demands of various market areas and outputs of several plants operating at different unit costs, it is possible to develop a production and distribution schedule that will satisfy demands at a minimum cost. This model encourages study of the effects of various changes in demand and production capabilities.

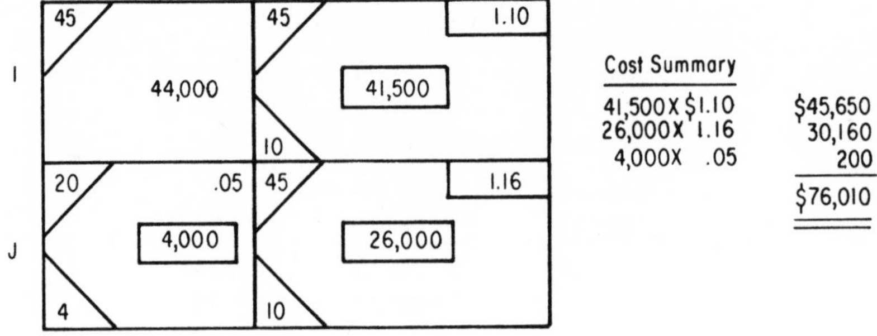

Maximum adjustments for each cell:

Cell JJ (to exceed 4,000) – 20,000 - 4,000 = 16,000 units.
Cell JP (to be less than 26,000 – 26,000 - 10,000 = 16,000 units.
Cell IP (to exceed 41,500) – 45,000 - 41,500 = 3,500 units.
Cell IJ (to exceed 44,000) – 45,000 - 44,000 = 1,000 units.

The greatest number of units which can be moved is 1,000, which will result in a cost reduction of $10 (1,000X $.01), as indicated below:

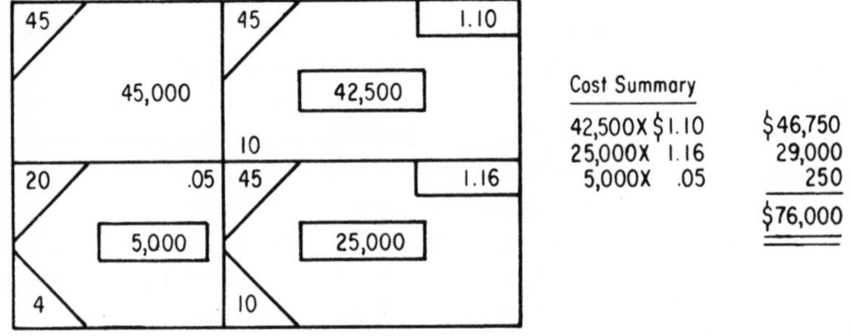

Exhibit 15-3. Evaluation of Cell JJ.

3. *Capital Budgeting*—It is possible to study the effects of output modifications upon multi-plant operations. The effects of equipment modifications also can be analyzed in advance.

4. *Market Research*—The effects of marketing activities upon total profit may be studied. Changes in product lines, changes in product mix, changes in warehouse locations, and other marketing factors may be simulated and studied before instigation of operating plans.

Exhibit 15-4. Cost Summaries for Illustration 1.

Period Label	No.	Purchases (Units)	Unit Cost	Costs	
O	0	31,800	$1.00	$31,800	
A	1	10,000	1.06	10,600	
B	2	14,700	1.04	15,288	
C	3	45,000	1.03	46,350	
D	4	12,800	1.09	13,952	
E	5	10,000	1.14	11,400	
F	6	21,900	1.11	24,309	
G	7	41,300	1.05	43,365	
H	8	10,000	1.14	11,400	
I	9	42,500	1.10	46,750	
J	10	25,000	1.16	29,000	
		Total purchase cost			$284,215

Carrying Costs

	Units	Unit Cost		
Period from 0 to 1	9,800	$.05	$490	
1 to 2	1,800	.05	90	
2 to 3	1,500	.05	75	
3 to 4	25,500	.02	510	
4 to 5	15,300	.02	306	
5 to 6	2,300	.02	46	
6 to 7	2,200	.02	44	
7 to 8	17,500	.05	875	
8 to 9	2,500	.05	125	
9 to 10	5,000	.05	250	
	Total carrying charges			2,811
	Total supply costs			$287,025

	A	B	C	D	E	F	G	H	I	J	K	Purchases
O	50 31,800											45 10 31,800 1.00
A	33 .05 9,800 2200	50 19,500										45 +.01 10,000 1.06
B		36 +.06 .05 1,800 1800 —	50 16,500									45 10 14,700 1.04
C			44 +.02 .05 1,500 1500 —	46,500								45 10 +.04 45,000 1.03
D				46 .02 25,500 2100	80 38,300							45 10 12,800 1.09
E					45 .02 15,300 2300	80 25,300						45 10 +.03 10,000 1.14
F						48 +.02 .02 2,300 2300 —	80 24,200					45 10 21,900 1.11
G							51 +.08 .02 2,200 2200 —	80 43,500				45 10 41,300 1.05
H								65 .05 17,500 2600	45 27,500			45 10 +.04 10,000 1.14
I									70 +.05 .05 2,500 2500 —	45 +.01 45,000		45 10 42,500 1.10
J										20 .05 5,000 4000	45 30,000	45 25,000 1.16
	22	18	15	21	23	23	22	26	25	40	30	265

Exhibit 15-5. Procurement scheduling matrix—Optimum Solution (Illustration 1).

B	C	D	E	F	G	H	I	J	K	Purchases
										45 / 10; [31,800]; 1.00
50; 19,800										45 / 10; +.01; [10,000]; 1.06
36; +.06; .05; [1,800]; 800	50; 16,500									45 / 10; [14,700]; 1.04
	31; +.09; .05; [1,500]; 1500	50; 42,000								45 / 10; [40,500]; 1.00
		21; +.01; .02; [21,000]; 2100	80; 31,000							45 / 10; +.06; [10,000]; 1.09
			33; .02; [21,000]; 1000	80; 31,000						45 / 10; +.09; [10,000]; 1.14
				58; .02; [20,000]; 1100	80; 30,000					45 / 10; +.04; [10,000]; 1.11
					71; .02; [8,000]; 2200	80; 53,000				45 / 10; [45,000]; 1.05
						75; .05; [17,000]; 2600	45; 37,500			45 / 10; [20,500]; 1.14
							75; +.09; .05; [2,500]; 2500	45; +.09; 45,000		45 / 10; [42,500]; 1.10
								25; .05; [5,000]; 4000	45; 35,000	45 / 10; [30,000]; 1.16
18	15	21	10	11	22	36	35	40	35	265

Exhibit 15-6. Procurement scheduling matrix—Optimum Solution (Illustration 2).

16 Job-Assignment Method

by Richard L. Carter and E. Noah Gould

Linear programming is widely used in business and industry to improve decision-making procedures (1,2). (References are given at the end of the article.) The assignment method is a special LP technique for solving problems like choosing the right man for the right job when more than one choice is possible and when each man can perform all of the jobs. The ultimate requirement may be lower overall cost, higher profit, or some other specific goal. Although problems of this type can be solved by trial and error, the assignment method will often provide the easiest and least time-consuming solution.

Assigning Manpower

A typical problem might involve the assignment of four men to four jobs. Each man can do each job, but relative efficiency may vary from one job to another. If the cost per unit output is known for each man's performance of each task, the method will assign the men for minimum cost per unit output. With a slight modification, the same technique will assign men for maximum profit.

EDITOR'S NOTE: Reprinted from *Machine Design,* July 18, 1963.

Selecting a Design Material

The assignment technique can be used in design work to select a material, but only when the selection criteria can be boiled down to a single numerical figure for each material-job combination. The problem must demand material assignments which are mutually exclusive. Usually, this is not the case, and a single material may be used for all of the products. However, choice of materials can be a problem in situations like the following example.

Top management has decided to produce four new models of a television set, and each model is to sell at a different sales price. The designs must, therefore, use different cabinet materials. There are six perfectly good materials which can be used. Each material can be finished to produce an attractive cabinet. However, no material can be used for more than one model. Different production quantities are planned, so method of fabrication will not be the same in each case, leading to a unique cost figure for each material-cabinet combination. The job-assignment method will select the material for each cabinet model to minimize overall cost.

Another kind of material-selection problem can also be handled. Some materials are only available under priority systems, in which priority numbers are assigned to materials and jobs. Suitability of the job-assignment method for this problem depends on having a number of jobs which require essentially the same physical properties in a material. It also depends on having a number of available materials with essentially the same properties but with different priorities.

In more general situations, a solution to the more general simplex problem must be used (3).

Assigning Intangibles

Looking to the future, the assignment technique may be useful in assigning engineers to various kinds of work. This would require the separation of engineering activities into categories which could be given value weights. It would be necessary to establish a unit of output for each category and to assign a cost to each output unit. While engineering has not yet been classified into suitable categories, work sampling has been used in an effort to determine units of output and the cost per unit for engineering personnel.

How the Method Works

Basically, the job-assignment method treats problems as sets of simultaneous linear equations and solves them for the optimum solution. Although the easiest problem is that of pairing an equal number of jobs and men (or the equivalent in other types of problems), a simple alteration is used to apply the procedure when the numbers are not equal. By proper assignment of cost per unit output to each problem type, the method can be used for a number of problems in addition to those mentioned:

- Evaluating alternate methods or improvements to minimize cost or maximize profit.
- Determining which machine to use for which job.
- Determining which man to use on which machine.
- Determining which product to produce in which department.
- Assigning vehicles for materials handling (3).
- Scheduling airplanes for minimum layover cost.
- Determining optimum equipment location in making plant layouts (4).

In each case, the requirements are the same. There must be one figure as the value weight for each source and task combination. The figures must be realistic; application of the assignment method will produce results which are in keeping with the accuracy of the figures used.

USING THE JOB-ASSIGNMENT METHOD

Procedure for Assigning Jobs for Minimum Cost

Suppose that four draftsmen are available for assignment to four drafting jobs. Although all four men can perform the work, their relative efficiencies vary for each job. The goal will be to assign the men to minimize overall drafting cost. On the basis of past performance, the unit-cost data is known.

Although the example involves only four men and four jobs, the same technique can be used where a great many more men and jobs are involved. If the number becomes very large, it is economical to program the problem for a computer.

Step 1: Put cost-per-unit-output information into matrix form A_0. Man M_1 can produce a unit of output on Job J_1 at a cost of eight cents, M_2 at seven cents, M_3 at nine cents, etc.

$$A_0 = \begin{array}{c} \\ J_1 \\ J_2 \\ J_3 \\ J_4 \end{array} \begin{array}{c} \begin{array}{cccc} M_1 & M_2 & M_3 & M_4 \end{array} \\ \begin{bmatrix} 8 & 7 & 9 & 9 \\ 5 & 2 & 7 & 8 \\ 6 & 1 & 4 & 9 \\ 2 & 3 & 2 & 6 \end{bmatrix} \end{array}$$

Step 1a: If the number of men and jobs are not equal, the matrix is made square by adding zeros. For example, if there were two more jobs in the current problem the matrix would be rectangular, with six rows of jobs for the four men. Two more columns of zeros would be added, representing nonexistent men. From this point on, the procedure is identical; the end result will produce no job assignment for either of the "bogey" men. The two most costly jobs will not be assigned. In the case of maximizing profit, the two jobs producing the least profit will not be assigned.

$$A_0 = \begin{array}{c} \\ J_1 \\ J_2 \\ J_3 \\ J_4 \\ J_5 \\ J_6 \end{array} \begin{array}{c} \begin{array}{cccccc} M_1 & M_2 & M_3 & M_4 & M_5 & M_6 \end{array} \\ \begin{bmatrix} 8 & 7 & 9 & 9 & 0 & 0 \\ 5 & 2 & 7 & 8 & 0 & 0 \\ 6 & 1 & 4 & 9 & 0 & 0 \\ 2 & 3 & 2 & 6 & 0 & 0 \\ 4 & 5 & 4 & 7 & 0 & 0 \\ 3 & 5 & 4 & 9 & 0 & 0 \end{bmatrix} \end{array}$$

Step 2: In the first *row* of numbers, find the smallest number in the row, and write it at the right of the row. Repeat for the other rows.

$$A_0 = \begin{bmatrix} 8 & 7 & 9 & 9 \\ 5 & 2 & 7 & 8 \\ 6 & 1 & 4 & 9 \\ 2 & 3 & 2 & 6 \end{bmatrix} \begin{array}{c} 7 \\ 2 \\ 1 \\ 2 \end{array}$$

Step 3: Make a new matrix A_1 from A_0 by subtracting the row minimum (7 for the first row) from each number in the first row of A_0 and writing each of the remainders in matrix A_1 to form the first row.

Repeat for the second, third, and fourth rows, using their minimums. Check A_1; there should be at least one zero in each row.

$$A_1 = \begin{bmatrix} 1 & 0 & 2 & 2 \\ 3 & 0 & 5 & 6 \\ 5 & 0 & 3 & 8 \\ 0 & 1 & 0 & 4 \end{bmatrix}$$

Step 4: Find whether the matrix will give a complete basis for making the optimum assignments of men by first picking out a pattern of zeros in the matrix in such a way that no row or column (in the pattern) contains more than one zero. Identify this pattern by putting a square around each zero selected. (In many cases, as in this one, there is more than one pattern of "squared" zeros. Any one of these patterns is acceptable for this step.) In this particular case, the pattern of zeros is easily found by trial and error. In other cases it cannot be done so easily and the procedure in Steps 4*a* and 4*b* can be used (5).

$$A_1 = \begin{bmatrix} 1 & \boxed{0} & 2 & 2 \\ 3 & 0 & 5 & 6 \\ 5 & 0 & 3 & 8 \\ \boxed{0} & 1 & 0 & 4 \end{bmatrix}$$

Step 4*a*: Starting with the matrix constructed in Step 3 examine each *row* until one is found that has only one zero. Make a square around that zero. If there are any other zeros in the same *column* as the zero just "squared," put X's through them. Repeat until every *row* with just one zero is marked. In the example, the first row is the only one with just one zero.

$$A_1 = \begin{bmatrix} 1 & \boxed{0} & 2 & 2 \\ 3 & \not{0} & 5 & 6 \\ 5 & \not{0} & 3 & 8 \\ 0 & 1 & 0 & 4 \end{bmatrix}$$

Step 4*b*: Now examine *columns* until one is found that has only one unmarked zero. Make a square around it, and put an X through any other zeros in the same *row*. Repeat until all columns have been examined. In the example, the first column is the only one with just one zero in it.

If all zeros had not been already marked, Steps 4*a* and 4*b* would be repeated until all zeros in the matrix had been marked with either a square or an X. In some cases, even this procedure does not result in marking all zeros in the matrix. In such cases, a trial-and-error method must do the job, or a more complicated technique must be used (6).

If the result of Step 4 is a pattern of zeros with exactly one "squared" zero in every row and column, then the matrix is an optimum solution. In this particular case, A_1 is not optimum. If it were optimum, Steps 5 through 10 could be skipped.

$$A_1 = \begin{bmatrix} 1 & \boxed{0} & 2 & 2 \\ 3 & \times\!\!\!\!0 & 5 & 6 \\ 5 & \times\!\!\!\!0 & 3 & 8 \\ \boxed{0} & 1 & \times\!\!\!\!0 & 4 \end{bmatrix}$$

Step 5: In matrix A_1, write the minimum number in each *column* under the column. (A minimum number can be zero as well as any other number.)

$$A_1 = \begin{bmatrix} 1 & 0 & 2 & 2 \\ 3 & 0 & 5 & 6 \\ 5 & 0 & 3 & 8 \\ 0 & 1 & 0 & 4 \end{bmatrix}$$
$$\begin{matrix} 0 & 0 & 0 & 2 \end{matrix}$$

Step 6: Perform the same operations on columns which were performed on rows in Step 3 to form a new matrix A_2. Check matrix A_2. There is at least one zero in every column, which is as it should be.

$$A_2 = \begin{bmatrix} 1 & 0 & 2 & 0 \\ 3 & 0 & 5 & 4 \\ 5 & 0 & 3 & 6 \\ 0 & 1 & 0 & 2 \end{bmatrix}$$

Step 7: Repeat Steps 4, 5 and 6 to determine whether matrix A_2 is an optimum solution. (It is not.)

$$A_2 = \begin{bmatrix} 1 & 0 & 2 & \boxed{0} \\ 3 & \boxed{0} & 5 & 4 \\ 5 & 0 & 3 & 6 \\ \boxed{0} & 1 & 0 & 2 \end{bmatrix}$$

Step 8*a*: In the previous figure put a check mark at the right of each *row* which has no squared zero in it. (In the example, this is Row 3 only.) Put a checkmark under each *column* which has a zero in a checked row.

$$A_2 = \begin{bmatrix} 1 & 0 & 2 & \boxed{0} \\ 3 & \boxed{0} & 5 & 4 \\ 5 & 0 & 3 & 6 \\ \boxed{0} & 1 & 0 & 2 \end{bmatrix} \begin{matrix} \\ \\ \checkmark \\ \\ \end{matrix}$$
$$\qquad\quad \checkmark \text{ (column 2)}$$

Step 8*b:* Make a check mark at the right of each row which has a *squared* zero in a checked column. All rows and columns which can be marked with a check are now marked. If they were not, Steps 8*a* and 8*b* would be repeated until all rows and columns which could be checked were checked.

$$A_2 = \begin{bmatrix} 1 & 0 & 2 & \boxed{0} \\ 3 & \boxed{0} & 5 & 4 \\ 5 & 0 & 3 & 6 \\ \boxed{0} & 1 & 0 & 2 \end{bmatrix} \begin{matrix} \\ \checkmark \\ \checkmark \\ \\ \end{matrix}$$
$$\qquad\quad \checkmark \text{ (column 2)}$$

Step 8*c*: Draw lines through all *un*checked rows and all *checked* columns. The number of lines should be the same as the number of squared zeros.

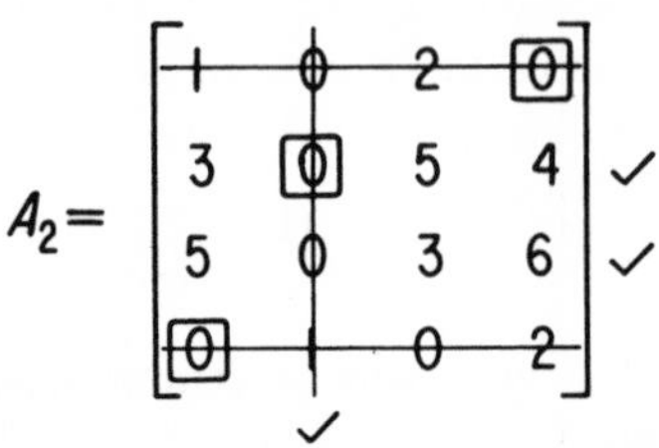

Step 9*a*: Start to from a new matrix A_3. If a number in the previous matrix has only one line through it, copy it into the same position in matrix A_3. Repeat for every number in A_2 which has just one line through it.

Step 9*b*: Find the smallest number in matrix A_2 with no line through it. (In this example the number is 3.)

Step 9*c*: For each number in A_2 with no line through it, subtract 3 (the number of Step 9*b*) from it, and enter the remainder in the same position in A_3.

Step 9*d*: For each number in A_2 which is at the intersection of two lines, add (the number of Step 9*b*) to it, and enter the sum in the same position in A_3.

$$A_3 = \begin{bmatrix} 1 & 3 & 2 & 0 \\ 0 & 0 & 2 & 1 \\ 2 & 0 & 0 & 3 \\ 0 & 4 & 0 & 2 \end{bmatrix}$$

(9*a* through 9*d*)

Step 10: Test matrix A_3 as in Steps 4 and 5. This time, it is an optimum solution. (If it were not optimum, Steps 8, 9, and 10 would be repeated until an optimum solution was reached.)

$$A_3 = \begin{bmatrix} 1 & 3 & 2 & \boxed{0} \\ \boxed{0} & 0 & 2 & 1 \\ 2 & \boxed{0} & 0 & 3 \\ 0 & 4 & \boxed{0} & 2 \end{bmatrix}$$

Step 11: Go back to matrix A_o. The "squared" zeros in A_3 show which numbers to pick out of matrix A_o. Put these numbers into a matrix A_4 by themselves. This new matrix indicates that one optimum solution for the problem is to assign job J_1 to man M_4, job J_2 to man M_1, and so on. The numbers in the matrix show the cost-per-unit-of-output for each assignment indicated. The sum of these numbers, 17 cents, is the minimum total cost. This sum is the same for any of the optimum assignment patterns, if there is more than one.

$$A_4 = \begin{bmatrix} - & - & - & 9 \\ 5 & - & - & - \\ - & 1 & - & - \\ - & - & 2 & - \end{bmatrix}$$

Procedure for Assigning Jobs to Produce Maximum Profit

In the example, cost figures were minimized by use of the assignment technique. For maximizing similar figures, such as profit or saving per man per unit of output, use the following method.

Assume that the numbers in the matrix A_0 are savings to be maximized. Take the largest number in the matrix (9, in this case) and subtract each number in the matrix from it. Place these remainders in a new matrix, A_1. Now go through exactly the same steps as in the minimizing procedure, starting with Step 1, and using minimum numbers where called for. When Step 11 is reached, matrix A_4 represent the maximum figures instead of minimum.

References

1. Charnes, Cooper and Henderson—*An Introduction to Linear Programming, Part II,* John Wiley & Sons Inc., New York, 1953.

2. T.C.Koopmans—*Activity Analysis of Production and Allocation, Cowles Commission Monograph No.* 13, John Wiley & Sons Inc. New York, 1951, Chap. 21.

3. Marice Sasieni, Arthur Yaspan, and Lawrence Friedman—*Operations Research, Methods and Problems,* John Wiley & Sons Inc., New York, 1959, pp. 185-193.

4. C.W. Churchman, R.L. Ackoff, and E.L. Arnoff—*Introduction to Operations Research,* John Wiley & Sons Inc., New York, 1957, pp. 353-363.

5. James M. Moore—"Optimal Locations for Multiple Machines," *Journal of Industrial Engineering,* Sept.-Oct. 1961, Vol. 12, pp. 307-313.

6. Thomas L. Saaty—*Mathematical Methods of Operations Research,* McGraw-Hill Book Co. Inc., 1959, New York, Chap. 6.

17 Dynamic Programming: An Introduction

by Floyd W. Windal

One of the mathematical programming techniques currently receiving attention in the operations research journals is that of dynamic programming. This technique is a valuable planning and problem solving tool, and as such should be of great interest to accountants.

Essentially, dynamic programming is a method whereby a problem can be broken into smaller parts, and each part solved separately and sequentially, with the answer to each preceding part being used in solving the succeeding parts. It enables the problem solver to cut down dramatically on the number of computations which would otherwise have to be made, and to proceed in an orderly, systematic way toward a solution.

Although the term "dynamic" implies decisions made over a period of time, the parts into which the problem is broken need not be actual time periods. The concept of time can be artificially imposed for computational purposes, i.e., the parts of the problem can be treated as if they were time periods.

The purpose of this paper is to introduce the concept of dynamic programming to those not familiar with it. The example used is designed to illustrate the fundamentals of the technique, rather than to closely approximate an actual situation. In this way, extensive mathematical computations are avoided and the basic concepts are easier to see. There are many varied and complicated applications of dynamic programming, but all make use of the same fundamental notions.

EDITOR'S NOTE: From *Management Accounting*, July 1969, pp 47-49. Reprinted by permission of the publisher, National Association of Accountants, and author.

A Cost Minimization Problem

Let us assume we are employed by a manufacturer who is faced with the problem of selecting the least-cost shipping method and route to a specified destination. Each of the different possible routes has a different cost, as shown in Table 17-1.

Table 17-1 Comparative Costs

		Origin					
Destination	**Production town**	**Barge town 1**	**Truck town 1**	**Rail town 1**	**Barge town 2**	**Truck town 2**	**Rail town 2**
Barge town 1	100						
Truck town 1	150						
Rail town 1	200						
Barge town 2		250	150	150			
Truck town 2		200	200	100			
Rail town 2		200	100	100			
Delivery town					100	90	100

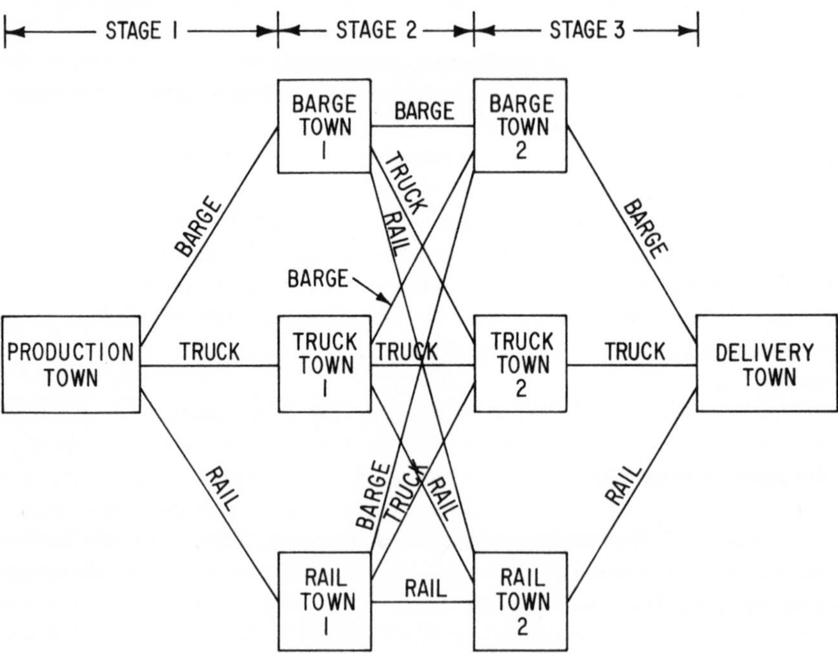

Exhibit 17-1. Shipping modes.

We can use three possible shipping methods: barge, truck or rail. With certain restrictions, as shown in Exhibit 17-1, we can also use a combination of these methods. Once the goods reach one of the number 1 towns, we can choose to continue using the same shipping method, or we can shift to one of the others. The choice we make for this second stage, however, is a binding one in that we must also use the same method for the third stage.

Our dynamic programming approach to solving this problem can either start at the destination and move backward, or start at the origin and move forward. We will arrive at the same answer under each method (Table 17-2).

Table 17-2 Least-Cost Summary

Town	Backward Approach Least cost	Least-cost route from origin
Delivery town (D)	0	Already at destination
Barge town 2 (B2)	100	B2 → D
Truck town 2 (T2)	90	T2 → D
Rail town 2 (R2)	110	R2 → D
Barge town 1 (B1)	290	B1 → T2 → D
Truck town 1 (T1)	210	T1 → R2 → D
Rail town 1 (R1)	190	R1 → T2 → D
Production town (P)	360	P → T1 → R2 → D
Town	**Forward Approach Least cost**	**Least-cost route from origin**
Production town (P)	0	We are at the origin
Barge town (B1)	100	P → B1
Truck town 1 (T1)	150	P → T1
Rail town 1 (R1)	200	P → R1
Barge town 2 (B2)	300	P → T1 → B2
Truck town 2 (T2)	300	{ P → B1 → T2 P → R1 → T2 }
Rail town 2 (R2)	250	P → T1 → R2
Delivery town (D)	360	P → T1 → R2 → D

Backward Approach

Solving the problem first using the backward appraoch, we will systematically examine each town in Exhibit 17-1, starting with the destination and working back toward the origin. At each town, we will ask this question: what is the least-cost route of getting to the destination from this town? The answer to the question is simple when examining Delivery town (D), Barge town 2 (B2), Truck town 2 (T2) and Rail town 2 (R2), because

Delivery town *is* the destination, and for each of the others there is only one possible route and one possible cost:

LEAST-COST ROUTES TO DESTINATION

Town	Cost	Route to D
D	–0–	Already at D
B2	$100	B2 → D
T2	$ 90	T2 → D
R2	$110	R2 → D

When we consider the remainder of the towns, however, we must in each case pick the least-cost route from among several possibilities. In looking at any particular town, we can always split the cost of getting to the destination on one particular route into 2 parts: (1) the cost of getting from the town we are looking at to the next town on the route, and (2) the least cost of getting from the next town on the route to the destination.

For example, let us examine Barge town 1. There are three possible routes out of Barge town 1, and each of these routes has a particular cost. Furthermore, the least cost route to the destination from each of the possible succeeding towns has already been determined from our prior analysis. The computation of the least cost route to the destination from Barge town 1, therefore would be as follows:

BARGE TOWN 1 (B1)

B1 to B2	$250	
Least cost B2 to D	100	$350
B1 to T2	$200	
Least cost T2 D	90	$290*
B1 to R2	$200	
Least cost R2 to D	110	$310

*Least-cost route: B1 → T2 → D = $290

When we are at Barge town 1, the minimum cost of getting our goods to the destination is seen to be $290, and our best route is through Truck town 2. Note that our least cost and optimum route from Truck town 2 to the destination had been determined earlier.

This same kind of computation can be made for Truck town 1, and Rail town 1, as follows:

TRUCK TOWN 1 (T1)		
T1 to B2	$150	
Least cost B2 to D	100	$250
T1 to T2	$200	
Least cost T2 to D	90	$290
T1 to R2	$100	
Least cost R2 to D	110	$210*

*Least-cost route: T1 → R2 → D = $210

RAIL TOWN 1 (R1)		
R1 to B2	$150	
Least cost B2 to D	100	$250
R1 to T2	$100	
Least cost T2 to D	90	$190*
R1 to R2	$100	
Least cost R2 to D	100	$210

*Least-cost route: R1 → T2 → D = $190

Finally, we are able to compute our least-cost route from Production town to the destination, still making full use of least cost information computed earlier for other towns. Note that the cost for any one route is still stated as the sum of only two figures.

PRODUCTION TOWN (P)		
P to B1	$100	
Least cost B1 to D	290	$390
P to T1	$150	
Least cost T1 to D	210	$360*
P to R1	$200	
Least cost R1 to D	190	$390

*Least-cost route: P → T1 → R2 → D = $360

Note that it is only necessary to refer back to the computation for Truck town 1 to get the least-cost route from that town to the destination.

Forward Approach

An equally acceptable solution technique for this type of problem is to start at the origin and move toward the destination. Now, as we examine each town systematically, we will ask the question: what is the least-cost route of getting from the origin to this town?

Again, the answer is simple for our first few towns. For Production town (P), we are *at* the origin, and for each of Barge town 1 (B1), Truck town 1 (T1), and Rail town 1 (R1), there is only one route from the origin and one cost:

LEAST-COST ROUTE FROM ORIGIN

Town	Cost	Route
P	–0–	–0–
B1	$100	P → B1
T1	$150	P → T1
R1	$200	P → R1

From this point on, computations must be made. Once again, we can always split the total cost of any one route into two parts. In getting to any particular town from the origin, the cost always consists of (1) the cost of getting from the immediately preceding town on the route to the town being considered, plus (2) the least cost of getting from the origin to the immediately preceding town. In each case, the second element of the cost will already have been computed in a prior computation.

The cost computations for Barge town 2 are as follows:

BARGE TOWN 2 (B2)

B1 to B2	$250	
Least cost to B1	100	$350
T1 to B2	$150	
Least cost to T1	150	$300*
R1 to B2	$150	
Least cost to R1	200	$350

*Least-cost route: P → T1 → B2 = $300

Note here again that prior computations not only give us the least cost of getting from the origin to each prior town, but also the optimal route that produced that least cost. For instance, after the above computations told us that the least-cost route to Barge town 2 was through Truck town 1, we merely had to look at a prior computation for the best route from the origin to Truck town 1.

The computations for the remaining towns are as follows:

TRUCK TOWN 2 (T2)		
B1 to T2	$200	
Least cost to B1	100	$300*
T1 to T2	$200	
Least cost to T1	150	$350
R1 to T2	$100	
Least cost to R1	200	$300*

*Least-cost routes (Tie):

P → B1 → T2 = $300
P → R1 → T2 = $300

RAIL TOWN 2 (R2)		
B1 to R2	$200	
Least cost to B1	100	$300
T1 to R2	$100	
Last cost to T1	150	$250*
R1 to R2	$100	
Least cost to R1	200	$300

*Least-cost route: P → T1 → R2 = $250

DELIVERY TOWN (D)		
B2 to D	$100	
Least cost to B2	300	$400
T2 to D	$ 90	
Least cost to T2	300	$390
R2 to D	$110	
Least cost to R2	250	$360*

*Least-cost route: P → T1 → R2 → D = $360

Summary

This simple example serves to introduce the fundamental notions of dynamic programming. It illustrates a solution technique which breaks a problem into many parts, solves each part separately and sequentially, and utilizes the solutions to preceding parts in solving succeeding parts. In this way, the number of calculations required is cut down dramatically and an answer is obtained more quickly. Much more complicated, multidimensional problems utilize basically the same technique, although with some variations.

While the basic idea itself is fairly simple, its application to practical situations is more difficult. Ingenuity of the highest order is required to state a problem in dynamic programming form. In some cases, the dimensions of the problem make a dynamic programming solution impractical, even on a computer. Nevertheless, considerable success has already been achieved along these lines. Some of the successful applications to date have been:

1. Computation of the economic amount to order in each of several future periods, given varying costs and demand over the time span.
2. Computation of the most profitable investment of resources in alternative opportunities.
3. Computation of maximum output from production processes of varying efficiencies.
4. Computation of optimum advertising expenditures.
5. Computation of best distribution of sales effort.

Discussion Questions

1. What characteristics should a linear programming problem have in order to be suitable for solution by the transportation method? What are the advantages of using the transportation method instead of the more generalized simplex method?

2. Describe the formulation of a transportation problem using the simplex format. When should the simplex algorithm be used instead of the transportation method for solving a transportation problem?

3. How can one determine that an optimal solution to the transportation problem has been reached? Does the optimal solution to the transportation problem yield any other useful information except the minimum distribution pattern and resulting total cost? Explain fully.

4. What are the most common methods of developing an initial solution to the transportation problem? Discuss the benefits and limitations of each method in terms of ease of use, efficiency of computation, time and effort required to obtain an optimal solution, etc.

5. How does degeneracy arise in the transportation problem? How can the problem of degeneracy be resolved?

6. What procedures can be used to cope with unequal supply and demand conditions in transportation problems? Will the method of handling such conditions have any effect on the final solution? Why?

7. How do transshipment models differ from conventional transportation formulations? For what kinds of applications are transshipment models best suited? Why?

8. What problem conditions are necessary for the assignment algorithm to be suitable for use? For what kinds of applications is the assignment method best suited? Explain fully.

9. How does dynamic programming differ from linear programming? What characteristics should a problem have in order to be suitable for solution by dynamic rather than by linear programming methods?

10. What modifications in the transportation formulation are necessary to permit the transportation method to be used in solving multiperiod or multiphase procurement and production scheduling problems? In such cases is the transportation method really more desirable than the use of the simplex algorithm? Why?

Bibliography

Balinski, M.L. and R.E. Gomory, "A Primal Method for the Assignment of Transportation Problems," *Management Science,* April 1964, pp. 578-593.

Beckwith, Richard E., "The Assignment Problem–A Special Case of Linear Programming," *Journal of Industrial Engineering,* May-June 1967, pp. 167-172.

Chang, Yao and Wesley G. Smith, "A Dynamic Programming Model for Combined Production, Distribution, and Storage," *Journal of Industrial Engineering,* January 1966, pp. 7-13.

Charnes, A. and W.W. Cooper, "The Stepping-Stone Method of Explaining Linear Programming Calculations in Transportation Problems," *Management Science*, October 1954, pp. 49-69.

Cochran, Edward, "Linear Programming—Without the Math," *Industrial Engineering*, November 1970, pp. 14-23.

Dwyer, Paul S., "The Direct Solution of the Transportation Problem with Reduced Matrices," *Management Science*, September 1966, 77-96.

Henderson, Alexander, and Robert Schlaifer, "Mathematical Programming: Better Information for Better Decision Making," *Harvard Business Review*, May-June 1954, 50 pp.

Hocking, Ralph T., "Using a Two-Step Transportation Model," *Journal of Systems Management*, March 1969, pp. 30-33.

Martin, Harold W., "A Quantitative Method of Assigning Functions to Individuals in an Organized Group," *Management International*, No. 1, 1964, pp. 55-67.

O'Brien, George, "Solutions of Assignment Problems," *Management Science: A New Organizational Dimension*, Proceedings, Institute of Labor and Industrial Relations, University of Michigan—Wayne State University, April 28, 1959, E.J. Forsythe and Palmer C. Pilcher, editors, pp. 19-26.

Parsons, James A., "The Assignment Algorithm," *Systems and Procedures Journal*, July-August 1967, pp. 6-7.

Shore, Harvey H., "The Transportation Problem and the Vogel Approximation Method," *Decision Sciences*, July-October 1970, pp. 397-422.

Smith, Spencer B., "Practical Guide to Linear Programming," *Purchasing*, November 9, 1959, pp. 70-76. See also "How to Buy in Fluctuating Markets," *Purchasing*, November 23, 1959, pp. 80-84 by the same author.

Tummins, Marvin, "A Simple Method of Linear Programming," *Management Services,* January-February 1966, pp. 44-50. See also Marvin Tummins and Percy Yeargan, "Mathematical Models and Management," *Managerial Planning*, January-February 1969, pp. 14-20, 23.

Wagener, Ulrich A., "A New Method of Solving the Transportation Problem," *Operations Research Quarterly*, December 1965, pp. 453-469.

PART IV Applications of Mathematical Programming to Marketing, Production, and Financial Problems

Golden and Sanford cite the case of a jewelry company to demonstrate how linear programming can be utilized to develop optimal production schedules for a multiproduct firm subject to market potential, product line capacity, and working capital constraints. The problem solution yields not only a maximum profit production schedule but also useful information concerning the economic value of additional product line capacity and market potential for the various products and territories considered.

Lee and Bird demonstrate how linear programming can be used to determine the optimal allocation of sales effort among various marketing components. Using a simple problem involving the allocation of full-time and part-time sales effort to working hours in a record shop (both regular and overtime are permissible), the authors incorporate multiple goals into the decision problem. The optimal solution satisfies three of the four multiple goals with only the least important remaining unfulfilled. The usefulness of goal programming in media planning, manpower or production scheduling, and financial planning is also indicated.

Engel and Warshaw present two examples which show how advertising dollars can be allocated to various media in order to maximize total advertising effectiveness. Constraints may be imposed to insure that maximum or minimum expenditures for all or only selected media are not exceeded. The success of such approaches is heavily dependent on rating media in terms of their effectiveness in reaching marketing targets.

Tillman and Lee discuss the application of linear programming to the blending of raw materials such as gasoline, dairy feed, or yarn to utilize available resources effectively and minimize total costs. A practical plastics-molding example is used to show how proper amounts of differing grades of raw materials are blended and operating conditions selected so that profits are maximized. The sensitivity of the solution to changes in key variables can also be analyzed.

Sharp illustrates the usefulness of linear programming in developing production schedules for a company with two plants and four products. Forecast demand, product prices, production costs, raw material costs, and production relationships are all incorporated into a computer model to obtain an optimal solution. If desired, both production and distribution costs can be included in the analysis. The production distribution model also yields valuable information about production, marketing, financial, and personnel requirements during a specified study period.

Vitt presents a least-cost scheduling investment program which minimizes the sum of current and capital costs. A key element of the program is a production smoothing model which develops an optimal production plan for each alternative level of plant capacity. For each planning period, alternative plant capacity levels are evaluated, taking into consideration capital investment penalty and production penalty costs at each level. The effects of uncertainty and the time value of money can also be taken into consideration.

Mao illustrates how a linear programming model can be used to determine financing of the seasonal cash needs of a greeting-card business so as to minimize the firm's cost of financing. Several alternative sources of funds are considered, and constraints on lines of credit, commercial paper, installment financing, and the total cash budget are imposed in a realistic manner. The optimal solution contains detailed financing transactions, net interest charges, and the amount of cash charges financed.

Robichek, Ogilvie, and Roach provide a critical review of the theory of capital budgeting. Consideration is given to such project-ranking techniques as payback period, accounting rate of return, net present value, and internal rate of return. Linear programming is suggested as an approach which will provide optimal solutions to certain classes of capital budgeting problems in which net present value or internal rates of return may be maximized subject to constraints on cash investments, earnings per share, amounts which can be invested in any one project, and so forth.

18 A Linear Model for Sales Planning: A Case Study of a Jewelry Firm

by M. Golden and E. Sanford

There is some tendency on the part of many traditional accountants to view the accounting system as "neutral" in its impact on business decision making. They justify this view by noting that the "flow of funds" through the firm may be accounted for in a variety of ways, but the flow represents the same set of facts no matter how the accountant deals with it. The accountant employing the analytical techniques of managerial economics, on the other hand, seeks to unearth the "financial truth" underlying the accounting statements.

Some critical issue that general accounting analysis often overlooks are problems relating to product-line pricing, resource valuation and sales allocation. Since many firms make several related products, the interaction between pricing, resources valuation and sales has important implications in decision making. But business decisions are often made by administrators who, competent as they may be professionally, are not always sensitive to changes in relationship between pricing and sales. These changes, though buried under standard accounting practices, may be significant for resource valuation.

The interdependency of resource allocation and product valuation is demonstrated in this study of a jewelry firm. The focus of the case is directed to the determination of a sales policy which covers an extensive product line sold in numerous sales territories.

EDITOR'S NOTE: From *Cost and Management,* May 1967, pp. 21-26. Reprinted by permission of the publisher, The Society of Industrial Accountants of Canada, and authors.

Background Data

The Sancrest Jewelry Company markets its products through 30 salesmen located in Ontario and Quebec. The bulk of the firm's annual sales, however, is made by only seven salesmen operating in seven separate sales territories. The reason for this is that the other salesmen used Sancrest products only as a supplement to some other distributor's line. The seven leading salesmen followed just the opposite practice, using the products of other manufacturers to augment the Sancrest line. For this reason, the firm sets periodic sales quotas only for these men.

The firm sells nine product lines of merchandise. These are listed in Table 18-1, where each column shows how a dollar in sales in each of the seven territories is distributed among the various product lines as of 1966. For example, the .07 coefficient for the first product, belts, indicates that on the average 7 cents of every dollar of the firm's merchandise sold in territory No. 1 is spent on this item.[1]

Table 18-1—Dollar Value of Sales for 9 Products in 7 Territories (1966)

	Sales Territory						
Product Lines	**No. 1**	**No. 2**	**No. 3**	**No. 4**	**No. 5**	**No. 6**	**No. 7**
1. Belts	.07*	.02	.01	.15	.18	.15	0.00
2. Buckles	.05	0.00	0.00	.10	.10	.07	0.00
3. Package goods	.20	.35	.30	.25	.25	.25	.50
4. Necklaces	.07	.07	.07	.10	.15	.10	.03
5. Earrings	.15	.15	.15	.15	.15	.15	.15
6. Bracelets	.10	.20	.10	.10	.10	.10	.05
7. Gold stone	.18	.10	.17	.10	.05	.05	.12
8. Hematite	.15	.08	.17	.02	.02	.10	.12
9. Job turquoise	.03	.03	.03	.03	0.00	.03	.03
Total	1.00	1.00	1.00	1.00	1.00	1.00	1.00

*Thus, 7 cents worth of belts is sold for every $1 of sales in Territory No. 1. These values represent the A_{ij} coefficients. For example, a_{11} = .07 and indicates the fraction of a dollar in sales that is represented by the first product (belts) sold in territory 1.

The market potential of each sales territory for the planning period is presented in Table 18-2. This is Sancrest's estimate of "potential" demand for its products in 1967 for each of the seven territories at the present level of advertising. These demand forecasts were based upon past sales records and information gathered from trade associations and governmental agencies, as well as independent forecasts made by other consulting firms that specialize in economic analysis of trade areas.

Table 18-2—Market Potential in Each of Seven Selling Areas (1967)

Sales Territory	Market Potential (MP_j)
No. 1	$ 225,000.00
No. 2	135,000.00
No. 3	150,000.00
No. 4	100,000.00
No. 5	210,000.00
No. 6	80,000.00
No. 7	250,000.00
Total	$1,150,000.00

Finally, the cost of a dollar's worth of merchandise required in the production of each product line, together with the corresponding sales commission paid on each dollar of sales, is depicted in Table 18-3.

Table 18-3—Material Costs and Sales Commission for 9 Product Lines (1966)

Product Lines	Cost of $1 in Merchandise	Sales Commission on $1 in Merchandise
1-6 incl.	$.50	$.15
7-9 incl.	.67	.10

A moment's reflection should reveal the nature of the data shown in the three preceeding tables. Referring to the notation developed in the earlier articles, Table 18-1 reflects the value ascribed to each a_{ij} coefficient.[2] As previously indicated, $a_{11} = .07$ denotes that the first salesman (or first territory, since salesman and territory are equivalent) sells on average 7 cents worth of belts for each dollar in sales. Similarly, $a_{53} = .25$ tells us that salesman number 5 sells an average of 25 cents worth of package goods (the third product) in territory number 5 when he makes a dollar in sales.

Table 18-2 illustrates the demand (market) potential in each of the seven territories, that is, the *MPj*'s. Since there are seven sales territories, the *j*'s have been indexed from $j = 1, \ldots, 7$. The company's 1967 demand is forecast at $1,150,000.

Table 18-3 lists the *wij* and *Sij* coefficients which correspond to the cost of merchandise and sales commissions respectively. Thus, products one through six (belts through bracelets) incur merchandise costs of 50 cents and sales commission of 15 cents for every dollar of product sold.

In Table 18-4, the y_i's represent the maximum amount of product line capacity that is available to the firm at the given price and cost structure of the nine product lines. Notice the range of dollar capacity available: $20,000 (second product), to $210,000 (third product). We assume that the firm can acquire sufficient working capital to handle $1,250,000 in sales for the 1967 planning period.[3]

Table 18-4

Lines	Product Line Capacity (y_i) (1966)
1.	$ 70,000.00
2.	20,000.00
3.	210,000.00
4.	70,000.00
5.	150,000.00
6.	100,000.00
7.	150,000.00
8.	150,000.00
9.	30,000.00

Formulating the Linear Model

Let us now piece together the preceeding data and present an integrated view of the linear sales model. The main "fixture" employed in the solution of linear models of this sort is called the "simplex tableau." Essentially, a simplex tableau is just what the term implies: a tabular arrangement of all pertinent information necessary for systematic evaluation of the data relationships. The advantage of using the simplex method is that it is a computational routine which lends itself to such an efficient description of information that once a problem is soundly conceived and correctly formulated, little further judgment is required for its ultimate solution. This is an important advantage because it makes possible the use of high-speed computers to carry out the lengthy and tedious computational details.

The simplex tableau for Sancrest is presented on the following page. Column A shows the nine sales areas. In column B, the seven products *(xj)* and their respective dollar sales-value (a_{ij}) are listed. Column B is simply the data of Table 18-1. Column C defines the dollar value of product-line capacity and represents Table 18-4. Columns D and E (the former duplicating Table 18-3) indicate the net revenue accruing to the firm (r_j) on a unit-product basis, and the territorial market potential (MP_i) respectively.

The data provided by the simplex tableau set the stage for defining the specific equations that comprise the linear model. There are nine equations, one for each separate product line. The equations are found by multiplying each product (x_j's) by its corresponding dollar value (a_{ij}) and summing across each of the seven sales territories. Hence, for the first product line, the structural equation: $.07x_1 + .02x_2 + .01x_3 + .15x_4 + .18x_5 + .15x_6 +$

Table 18-5—Simplex Tableau: Sancrest Jewelry Company*

A	x_j a_{ij}		*B* Products					*C* Capacity
AREA	X_1	X_2	X_3	X_4	X_5	X_6	X_7	y_i
	$							
1	.07	.02	.01	.15	.18	.15	.00	⩽ $ 70,000
2	.05	.00	.00	.10	.10	.07	.00	⩽ 20,000
3	.20	.35	.30	.25	.25	.25	.50	⩽ 210,000
4	.07	.07	.07	.10	.15	.10	.03	⩽ 70,000
5	.15	.15	.15	.15	.15	.15	.15	⩽ 150,000
6	.10	.20	.10	.10	.10	.10	.05	⩽ 100,000
7	.18	.10	.17	.10	.05	.05	.12	⩽ 150,000
8	.15	.08	.17	.02	.02	.20	.12	⩽ 150,000
9	.03	.03	.03	.03	.00	.03	.03	⩽ 30,000
	$							
Revenue	.31	.32	.31	.33	.34	.33	.32	
(rj)	←			*D*			→	
Market Potential	225,000	135,000	150,000	100,000	210,000	250,000		
(MP_j)	←			*E*			→	

$.00x_7 \leqslant 70{,}000$ emerges where the right-hand side value of 70,000 represents total belt capacity. The complete system of linear inequalities (1) represents the quotas for each of the seven products, and the objective form (2) constitutes a sales planning model for the Sancrest Jewelry Company.

The firm's goal is to find the best combination of products which satisfy the production constraints of (1) and provide the largest dollar net revenue for the period (2). Before the simplex algorithm can be considered complete, a change in the formulation of the structural inequalities must be made. What we shall do is add "slack" or "dummy" variables to each inequality stated in expression (1) in such a way as to make them into equations. The mathematical effect of this change is that the somewhat indefinite relationship represented by the inequality sign $\leqslant$ is made more explicit and precise by the value which the slack variable assumes. There is also an economic effect: slack variables indicate the amount of capacity that is going unused. Converting all inequalities representing structural constraints into equations provides model (3).

*The simplex tableau presented above is a modification of the "typical" tableau. Notwithstanding some slight variations, its basic form remains similar to tableaus employed by A.W. Charnes, W. Cooper, and A. Henderson. *Introduction to Linear Programming,* New York: John Wiley and Sons. 1953.

Complete linear model: Sancrest Jewelry Company

$$
\begin{array}{l}
.07x_1 + .02x_2 + .01x_3 + .15x_4 + .18x_5 + .15x_6 \leqslant 70{,}000.00 : \text{BELT CAPACITY} \\
.05x_1 + .10x_4 + .10x_5 + .07x_6 \leqslant 20{,}000.00 : \text{BUCKLE CAPACITY} \\
.20x_1 + .35x_2 + .30x_3 + .25x_4 + .25x_5 + .25x_6 + .50x_7 \leqslant 210{,}000.00 : \text{PACKAGE GOODS} \\
.07x_1 + .07x_2 + .07x_3 + .10x_4 + .15x_5 + .10x_6 + .03x_7 \leqslant 70{,}000.00 : \text{NECKLACES} \\
.15x_1 + .15x_2 + .15x_3 + .15x_4 + .15x_5 + .15x_6 + .15x_7 \leqslant 150{,}000.00 : \text{EARRINGS} \\
.10x_1 + .20x_2 + .10x_3 + .10x_4 + .10x_5 + .10x_6 + .05x_7 \leqslant 100{,}000.00 : \text{BRACELETS} \\
.18x_1 + .10x_2 + .17x_3 + .10x_4 + .05x_5 + .05x_6 + .12x_7 \leqslant 150{,}000.00 : \text{GOLDSTONE} \\
.15x_1 + .08x_2 + .17x_3 + .02x_4 + .02x_5 + .10x_6 + .12x_7 \leqslant 150{,}000.00 : \text{HEMATITE} \\
.03x_1 + .03x_2 + .03x_3 + .03x_4 + .03x_6 + .03x_7 \leqslant 30{,}000.00 : \text{JOB TURQUOISE} \\
x_1 \leqslant 225{,}000.00 : \text{M.P. for TERRITORY \#1} \\
x_2 \leqslant 135{,}000.00 : \text{M.P. for TERRITORY \#2} \\
x_3 \leqslant 150{,}000.00 : \text{M.P. for TERRITORY \#3} \\
x_4 \leqslant 100{,}000.00 : \text{M.P. for TERRITORY \#4} \\
x_5 \leqslant 210{,}000.00 : \text{M.P. for TERRITORY \#5} \\
x_6 \leqslant 80{,}000.00 : \text{M.P. for TERRITORY \#6} \\
x_7 \leqslant 250{,}000.00 : \text{M.P. for TERRITORY \#7} \\
x_1 + x_2 + x_3 + x_4 + x_5 + x_6 + x_7 \leqslant 1{,}250{,}000.00 : \text{W. C. LIMITATION}
\end{array}
\qquad (1)
$$

$$
.31x_1 + .32x_2 + .31x_3 + .33x_4 + .34x_5 + .33x_6 + .32x_7 = \text{R (Max.)} \qquad (2)
$$

Linear model with slack variables: Sancrest Jewelry Company

$$
\begin{array}{ll}
.07x_1 + .02x_2 + .01x_3 + .15x_4 + .18x_5 + .15x_6 + x_8 & = 70{,}000.00 \\
.05x_1 + .10x_4 + .10x_5 + .07x_6 + x_9 & = 20{,}000.00 \\
.20x_1 + .35x_2 + .30x_3 + .25x_4 + .25x_5 + .25x_6 + .50x_7 + x_{10} & = 210{,}000.00 \\
.07x_1 + .07x_2 + .07x_3 + .10x_4 + .15x_5 + .10x_6 + .03x_7 + x_{11} & = 70{,}000.00 \\
.15x_1 + .15x_2 + .15x_3 + .15x_4 + .15x_5 + .15x_6 + .15x_7 + x_{12} & = 150{,}000.00 \\
.10x_1 + .20x_2 + .10x_3 + .10x_4 + .10x_5 + .10x_6 + .05x_7 + x_{13} & = 100{,}000.00 \\
.18x_1 + .10x_2 + .17x_3 + .10x_4 + .05x_5 + .05x_6 + .12x_7 + x_{14} & = 150{,}000.00 \\
.15x_1 + .08x_2 + .17x_3 + .02x_4 + .02x_5 + .10x_6 + .12x_7 + x_{15} & = 150{,}000.00 \\
.03x_1 + .03x_2 + .03x_3 + .03x_4 + .03x_5 + .03x_6 + .03x_7 + x_{16} & = 30{,}000.00 \\
x_1 + x_{17} & = 225{,}000.00 \\
x_2 + x_{18} & = 135{,}000.00 \\
x_3 + x_{19} & = 150{,}000.00 \\
x_4 + x_{20} & = 100{,}000.00 \\
x_5 + x_{21} & = 210{,}000.00 \\
x_6 + x_{22} & = 80{,}000.00 \\
x_1 + x_2 + x_3 + x_4 + x_5 + x_6 + x_7 + x_{23} & = 1{,}250{,}000.00 \\
.31x_1 + .32x_2 + .31x_3 + .33x_4 + .34x_5 + .33x_6 + .32x_7 & = R(\text{Max.})
\end{array}
\qquad (3)
$$

Notice that slack variables are represented by x_j where $j = 8, \ldots, 23$.

The data set forth in (3) were fed into an electronic computer to gain computational efficiency in seeking an optimal solution. The optimal solution consists of those x_j's which maximize the net revenue function (2), and is summarized in Table 18-6.

Table 18-6—Optimal Solution

Quotas (x_j, $j = 1 \ldots 7$)	$ Amount Produced	Slack (x_j, $j = 8 \ldots 23$)	$ Amount Produced
x_1	$ 0	x_8	$ 27,880
x_2	135,000	x_9	0
x_3	150,000	x_{10}	0
x_4	0	x_{11}	16,745
x_5	144,000	x_{12}	55,125
x_6	80,000	x_{13}	14,425
x_7	123,500	x_{14}	84,980
		x_{15}	88,000
		x_{16}	15,435
		x_{17}	225,000
		x_{18}	0
		x_{19}	0
		x_{20}	100,000
		x_{21}	66,000
		x_{22}	0
		x_{23}	615,500

Given the optimal product mix, what is maximum revenue? The answer to this question is found by substituting the computed values of x_2, x_3, x_5, x_6, and x_7 into (2), which yields a maximum net revenue of $204,580.

Notice that the optimal solution excludes sales territories No.'s 1 and 4 and, unless management has some reason for including these sales areas, it would be more profitable to drop them. Selling in territories 1 and 4 will only result in a decline in net revenue.

The final technical aspect of the structural model involves the computation of "implicit" accounting prices.[4] Part of this phase involves the process of allowing the right-hand side of (3) to change in increments and evaluating the effect it has on management objectives. It was pointed out in earlier articles that "implicit" prices can be given a definite economic interpretation. They are what economists call "opportunity" or "economic" costs and are a measure of the value of alternative uses of the firm's fixed inputs and resources. Implicit prices may be used as a basis for assessing the admissible costs of acquiring additional capacity, and hence working capital for temporary or permanent expansion of product lines.

The imputed prices associated with the x_j in the optimal solution are defined as πi; their values are:[5]

$\pi i = 0$, for $i = 1, 4, 5, \ldots, 10, 13$ and 14
$\pi_2 = 1.8$
$\pi_3 = .64$
$\pi_{11} = .096$
$\pi_{12} = .118$
$\pi_{15} = 0.44$

Thus the value to the firm of an additional $1 of buckles (the second product) or package goods (the third product) is $1.80 and 64 cents respectively, while the economic value of any other produce line is zero or virtually so.

The value of an additional $1 of market potential in terrotory No. 2 is 10 cents; in territory No. 3 it is 12 cents; and, in territory No. 6 it is only 4 cents. Additional market potential in the other sales territories will contribute nothing in an economic opportunity cost sense to the firm. These prices should be compared with the estimated advertising and merchandising cost of acquiring additional units of these resources. For example, if additional demand in sales territory No. 3 can be created for less than 12 cents on the dollar, then clearly it will pay for the firm to expand its market potential in this sales territory, until its value to the firm falls or its cost of acquisition increases.

Revenue Curves for Market Potential in Sales Territory No. 5 and for Buckles

Empirically derived net revenue curves for the market potential in sales area No. 5 and for buckle availability are depicted in Figs. 18-2 and 18-3, respectively. The vertical line segment in each drawing represents the amount of that fixed resource currently at the disposal of the firm.

The fact that the net revenue curve for buckles in Fig 18-2 intersects the vertical axist at $165,060.00 means that Sancrest can operate without selling any buckles and still generate $165,060 in revenue by selling its remaining products. In Fig. 18-3 the positive intersection of the net revenue curve with the vertical axis means the firm can earn $200,998.00 in revenue without selling in territory No. 5. Diminishing returns are apparent in the case of both resources though the effect sets in much quicker for market potential in area No. 5. The explanation lies in the high proportion of buckles sold in sales territory No. 5, and the narrow limits on buckle capacity which become a bottleneck to the firm's operations in this territory very rapidly.

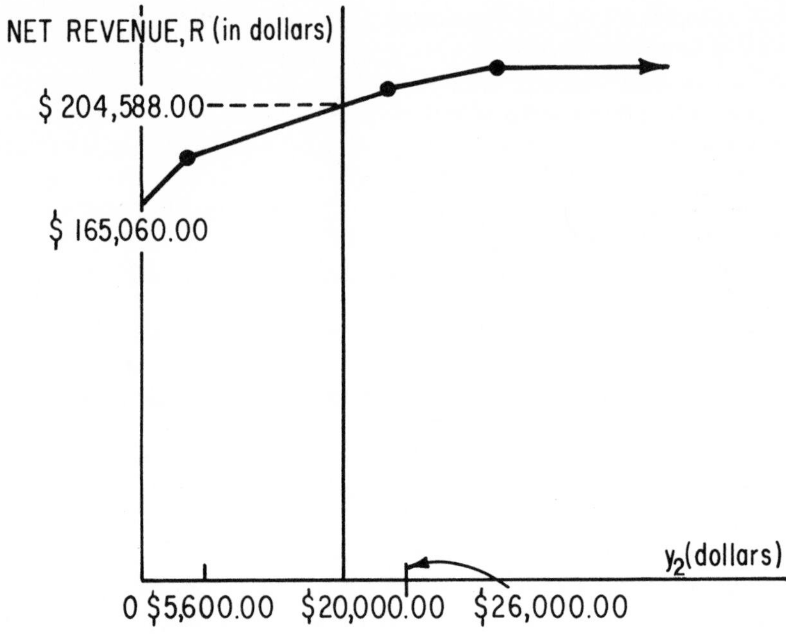

Fig. 18-2. Net revenue as a function of buckle capacity.

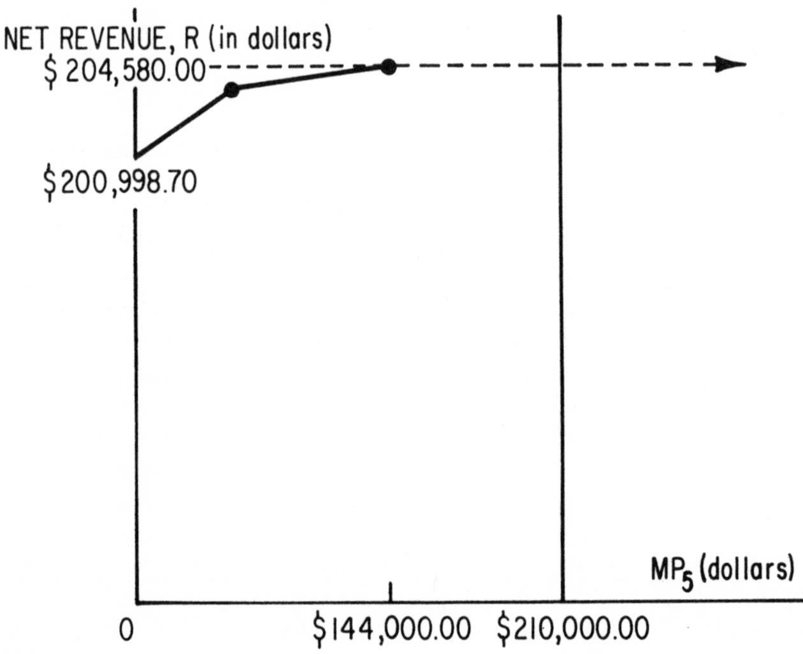

Fig. 18-3. Net revenue as a function of the market potential in Sales Territory No. 5.

It is instructive to follow the changing pattern of the firm's marketing scheme as buckle capacity is gradually increased from zero to $50,000.00. As more and more buckles become available, the firm takes advantage of favorable selling peculiarities within each territory so that the best returns are possible using the available buckle resources. In other words, the selling plan is gradually adapted to the changing resource structure of the firm.

We meet precisely the same situation when the market potential in sales territory No. 5 is gradually increased. As more and more market potential of this relatively profitable territory becomes available, the less profitable territories are successively discarded from the optimal sales plan.

Demand and Supply Curves for Market Potential in Fifth Territory and Buckle Availability

Empirical demand and supply curves for buckles and the dollar volume of market potential in the fifth territory are shown in Figs. 18-4 and 18-5,

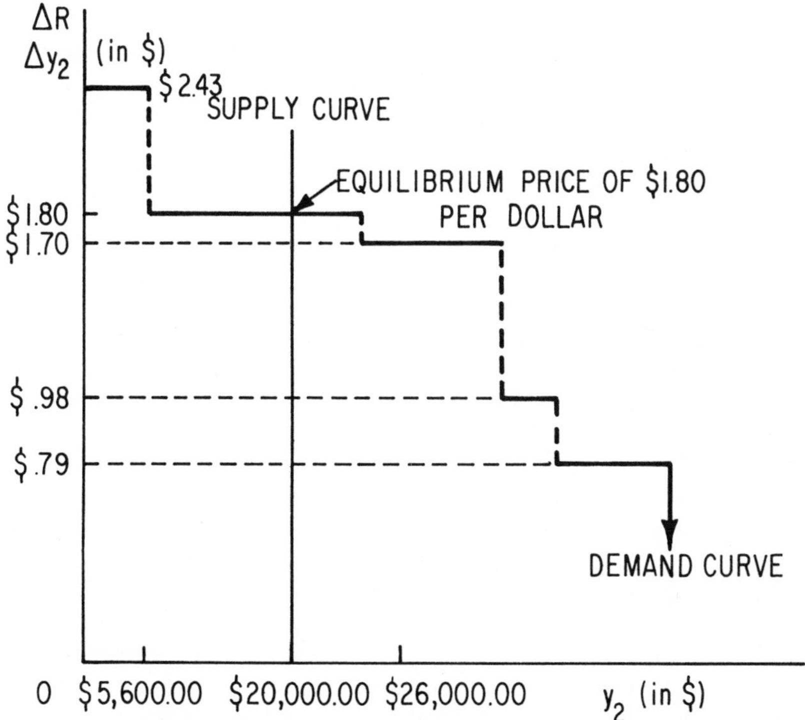

Fig. 18-4. Demand and supply curves for buckles.

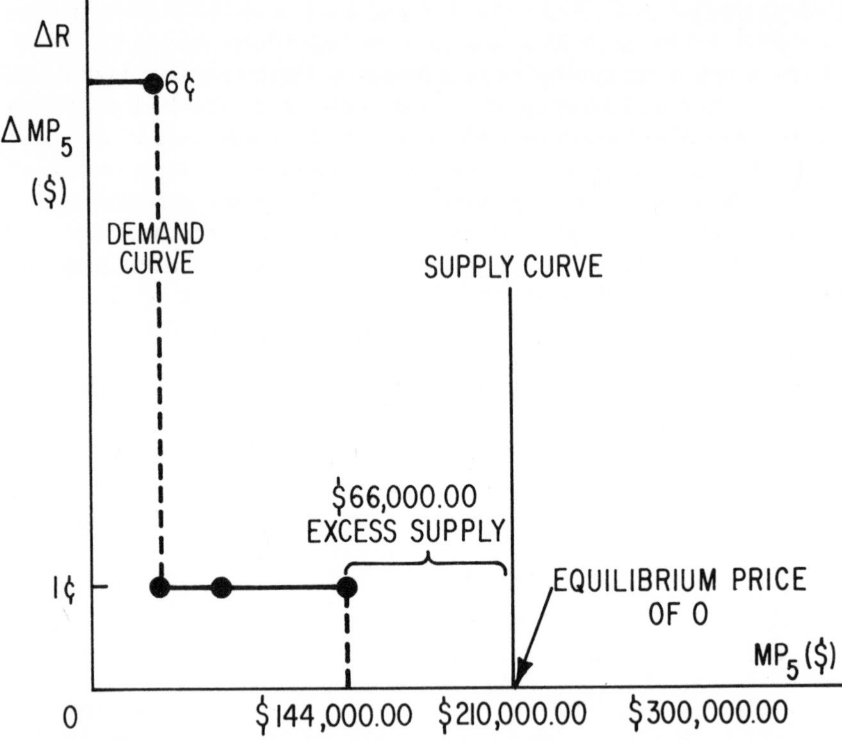

Fig. 18-5. Demand supply curves for market potential in Sales Territory No. 5.

respectively. Each horizontal portion of the stepped-curve corresponds to a straight line segment in the appropriate net revenue curve. The effect of diminishing returns on the shape of the demand curves can be seen quite clearly. In view of the severe buckle limitation (it is only $20,000) and because area No. 5 uses buckles, diminishing returns set in swiftly in the case of the market potential for this sales territory. Thus, the demand curve falls very abruptly.

In the case of the market potential for sales territory No. 5, there is $66,000.00 in excess supply.[6] The value of market potential must fall to zero in order to equate demand and supply.

The demand curve for market potential is essentially an offer curve for the firm's advertising and promotional outlays. For example, if the implicit value of $1 in market potential in area No. 5 is 6 cents and the firm can promote additional potential by merchandising, and advertising at an anticipated cost of 5 cents on the $1., then it is feasible to increase advertising until the cost of additional market potential equals or exceeds 6 cents on the dollar.

Conclusion

This article concludes the investigation of the linear programming model and its "operational significance." As often as not, an inquiry into a particular problem leads unexpectedly to the back door of a host of related issues, the understanding of which reinforces and enriches the investigator's perspective of the original problems. The use of "implicit prices" presents a technique which illustrates this "reinforcing phenomenon" forcefully. The concept of implicit pricing is ground in the economic doctrine of "opportunity cost": the real costs a producer incurs are determined by the alternative uses that are open to his resources. If a superabundance of a particular resource has no alternative uses, its implicit price or value is zero.

Decision makers in business, industry and government realize that sound decisions should reflect opportunity costs rather than accounting or historical cost. We have seen that the determination of opportunity costs is intimately related to a knowledge of optimal opportunities available to the firm. It is hoped that our linear model for sales control and its use of implicit pricing will contribute to a fuller understanding of how opportunity cost pricing can be applied on an intra-firm basis so as to provide a more sound economic footing for business decisions.

Notes

1. These distributions were found to be quite stable over time regardless of the size of the account as long as customers in the same territory (being sold by the same salesman) were compared.

2. Since there is only one salesman in each of the seven sales territories, we can delete the index k which was used to distinguish salesmen in the same territory.

3. This is a situation where nine products are competing for a fixed supply of working capital. If the objective is to maximize profit, it would seem intuitively logical that the product with the greatest profit margin should be installed as the highest "priority" in the use of resources. In fact, this approach is very often accepted in accounting analysis. Deeper consideration soon reveals the fallacious nature of this type of "fuzzy" thinking. It may be that the supply of resources is badly balanced so far as the requirements of the "highest profit" product are concerned, thereby seriously restricting its output potential. Or, its production may exhaust the available supply of an important input factor critically needed for the production of other products. This would result in large quantities of other inputs being virtually wasted (i.e., idle capacity). The picture, then, is one of attempting to base output decisions of individual products on what inputs are available for all products. Individual products are interdependent.

4. These are also termed "shadow prices," "efficiency prices," and "incremental value."

5. Those interested in a lucid description of determining implicit prices by the inverse-matrix method are referred to Walter W. Garvin, *Introduction to Linear Programming*, New York: McGraw-Hill Book Company, Inc., 1960.

6. The $66,000.00 is found by subtracting $144,000.00 (quota for territory No. 5 in Table 18-6) from $210,000.00 (the market potential for territory No. 5, in Table 18-2).

19 A Goal Programming Model for Sales Effort Allocation

by Sang M. Lee and Monroe M. Bird, Jr.

One of the most difficult decision problems in marketing is the determination of the optimum allocation of sales effort among the various market elements. Because of the multiplicity of factors and the complex relationships among these factors, it is often beyond the ability of the sales manager to intuitively identify the optimum allocation alternative. Thus, the ability to understand the capabilities and applications of the various quantitative or operations research techniques should be a prerequisite for the sales manager if he is expected to evaluate thoroughly the alternative allocation opportunities.

The various operations research models previously introduced to marketing have contributed significantly to sales management.[1] For example, linear programming has been widely applied to advertising allocation problems.[2] However, all of the optimization models thus far introduced possess the basic limitation that the objective function of the model must be unidimensional; that is, there can be only one primary goal, such as to maximize profit (utility or effectiveness) or to minimize cost (sacrifice).

The primary difficulty with the linear programming model is not that it fails to represent complex reality. As a matter of fact, empirical studies have shown that a deterministic model can produce quite favorable results even under stochastic conditions.[3] Instead, the primary difficulty with this model is that its application requires cost or profit information which often is impossible to obtain. For example, in solving a sales effort allocation problem, costs associated with changes in employment levels are not easy

EDITOR'S NOTE: FROM *Business Perspectives,* July 1970, pp. 17-21. Reprinted by permission of the publisher, Business Research Bureau, and authors.

to determine if the costs incurred by hiring, laying off, low employee morale, changes in the public image of the firm, etc. are to be considered.

Obviously, the primary units used to express success or failure for a business are monetary in nature. However, most firms also state goals to be accomplished for such nonmonetary items as public service, employment stability, labor relations, etc. Therefore, in a typical decision problem, the sales manager must meet more than one objective. When there are multiple objective criteria, linear programming is not an effective tool for decision analysis. A goal programming model, on the other hand, allows the manager to treat multiple goals in optimization problems.

This article presents the anatomy of the goal programming (GP) technique, and a simplified example of its application to a sales effort allocation problem. This example is designed to demonstrate the advantages of using GP in marketing problems where multiple goals are sought in multiple dimensions. Finally, other potential application areas and some limitations of GP are presented in the conclusion.

The Goal Programming Model

Goal programming is a special type of linear programming. It is capable of handling decision problems which deal with a single goal with multiple subgoals, as well as problems with multiple goals with multiple subgoals.[4] Therefore, an arbitrary conversion of other value measures to a single objective criterion, as required in linear programming, is not necessary.

Often, goals set by management are achievable only at the expense of other goals. Since all these goals cannot be expressed in terms of one objective criterion, there is a need to establish a hierarchy of importance among the various goals. GP treats multiple, conflicting goals according to the importance assigned to them in such a way that the low-order goals are considered only after the higher-order goals are satisfied or have reached the point beyond which no further improvements are possible. Therefore, if management can provide an ordinal ranking of goals in terms of their contributions or importance to the organization and all constraints considered are in linear relationships, GP can solve the problem.

Instead of trying to maximize the objective criterion directly, as does linear programming, GP minimizes the deviations between desired goals and actual results. If all such deviations are minimized to zero, all goals will be achieved. In the simplex method of linear programming, such deviational variables are called "slack variables" and they are used only as dummy variables for the solution algorithm. However, in GP these slack variables, (either positive or negative) not only are real, but the objective function is expressed only by these slack variables. The objective, then, is to minimize these deviational variables according to priorities assigned to them.

The general GP model[5] can be expressed as

$$\text{Minimize } \sum_{i=1}^{m} (d_i^+ + d_i^-)$$

$$\text{subject to} \quad Ax - Id^+ + Id^- = b$$
$$x, d^+, d^- \geqslant 0$$

where m goals are expressed by an m component column vector b (b_1, b_2, . . . , bm), A is an m X n matrix which expresses the relationship between goals and subgoals, x represents variables involved in the subgoals (x_1, x_2, . . . , x_n), d^+ and d^- are m-component vectors for the variable representing deviations from goals, and I is an identity matrix in m dimensions.

Now, each one of the m goals must be analyzed in terms of whether over or underachievement of the goal is satisfactory. If overachievement is acceptable, d_i^+ can be eliminated from the objective function. On the other hand, if underachievement is satisfactory, d_i^- should be left out of the objective function. If the goal must be achieved exactly as defined, both d_i^+ and d_i^- must be in the objective function.

The deviational variables d_i^+ and d_i^- must be ranked according to their priorities, from the most important to the least important. If goals are classified in k ranks, the priority factor P_j (j = 1,2, . . . , k) should be assigned to the deviational variables. The priority factors have the following relationship:

$$P_j >>> nP_{j+1} \ (j = 1, 2, \ldots, k-1),$$

which implies that the multiplication of n, however large it may be, cannot make $P_j + 1$ greater than or equal to P_j.[6]

An Illustration

The manager of the only record shop in a college town is not concerned with market competition. Instead, his major decision problem is the sales effort allocation to achieve the maximum profit. The record shop employs five full-time and four part-time salesmen. The average regular working time is 160 hours a month for the full-time salesman and 80 hours for the part-time salesmen. The average sale of records per hour has been five for the full-time salesmen and two for the part-time salesmen. The average hourly wage rates are \$3.00 for the full-time and \$2.00 for the part-time salesmen.

The average profit from the sale of a record is $1.50. In view of the past sales records and the increased enrollment at the college, the manager feels that the sales goal for September should be 5,500 records. Since the shop is open six days a week, overtime is often required of salesmen. The manager believes that a good employer-employee relationship is an essential factor of business success. Therefore, he decided that a stable employment level with occasional overtime requirement is a better practice than an unstable employment level with no overtime. However, he also feels that overtime of more than 100 hours for the full-time salesmen should be avoided because of the resulting fatigue.

The following constraints can be formulated:

(1) Sales.—The achievement of the sales goal, which is set at 5,500, is based upon the number of working hours of the full-time and part-time salesmen.

$$5x_1 + 2x_2 + d_1^- + d_1^+ = 5{,}500$$

where x_1: total full-time salesman hours in the month
x_2: total part-time salesman hours in the month
d_1^-: underachievement of sales goal as set at 5,500 records
d_1^+: overachievement of sales goal beyond 5,500 records

(2) Sales Force.—The salesman hours are determined by the regular working hours and the number of full-time and part-time salesmen.

$$x_1 + d_2^- - d_2^+ = 800$$

$$x_2 + d_3^- - d_3^+ = 320$$

where d_2^-: negative deviation from the regular full-time salesman hours (800 for the month)
d_2^+: overtime given to full-time salesmen in the month
d_3^-: negative deviation from the regular part-time salesman hours (320) for the month
d_3^+: overtime given to part-time salesmen in the month

(3) Overtime.—The manager tries to avoid giving any overtime beyond 100 hours per month to the full-time salesmen.

$$d_2^+ + d_{21}^- - d_{21}^+ = 100$$

where d_{21}^-: negative deviation of overtime hours given to full-time salesmen *from 100 hours*
d_{21}^+: overtime hours given to full-time salesmen *beyond 100 hours*

In addition to the constraints, variables, and constants described above, the following priority factors are to be defined:

P_1: The first goal of the manager is to achieve the sales goal of 5,500 records in September. Therefore, the highest priority factor, P_1, is assigned to the variable representing the underachievement of sales goal (i.e., d_1).

P_2: The second goal is to limit the overtime of fulltime salesmen to 100 hours. The second highest priority, P_2, is assigned to the variable which represents overtime of full-time salesmen beyond 100 hours (i.e., d_{21}).

P_3: The third goal is to provide job security to salesmen. The manager feels that full utilization of employees is an important factor for a good employer-employee relationship. However, the manager is twice as concerned with the full utilization of full-time salesmen as with the full utilization of part-time salesmen. Hence, $2P_3$ is assigned to the variable representing the under-utilization of full-time salesmen (i.e., d_2^-) and P_3 is assigned to the variable which represents the under-utilization of part-time salesmen (i.e., d_3^-).

P_4: The fourth and last goal is to minimize the sum of overtime for both full-time and part-time salesmen. However, differential weights should be assigned to the minimization of overtime for the full-time and part-time salesmen. Between the full-time and part-time salesmen, the sales efficiency ratio is 5 to 2, while the hourly wage rate is \$4.50 (overtime pay) and \$2.00. The marginal profit per hour of overtime is \$3.00 for the full-time salesmen and \$1.00 for the part-time salesmen. The relative cost of an hour of overtime for the part-time salesmen is three times that of the full-time salesmen. Therefore, $3P_4^+$ is assigned to d_3, whereas P_4 is assigned to d_2^+.

Now, the model can be formulated. The objective is the minimization of deviations from goals with certain assigned priorities. The deviant variable with the highest priority must be minimized to the fullest possible extent. When no further improvement is possible for the highest goal, the other deviational variables are to be minimized according to their assigned priority factors. The model can be expressed as follows:

Minimize

$$P_1 d_1^- + P_2 d_{21}^+ + 2P_3 d_2^- + P_3 d_3^- + P_4 d_2^+ + 3P_4 d_3^+$$

Subject to:

$$\begin{array}{llllllll}
X_1 + X_2 + d_1^- & & - d_1^+ & & & & = & 5{,}500 \\
X_1 & + d_2^- & & - d_2^+ & & & = & 800 \\
X_2 & & + d_3^- & & - d_3^+ & & = & 320 \\
 & & d_{21}^- + d_2^+ & & & - d_{21}^+ & = & 100
\end{array}$$

$$X_1, X_2, d_1^-, d_2^-, d_3^-, d_{21}^-, d_1^+, d_2^+, d_3^+, d_{21}^+ \geqslant 0$$

The solution derived through the simplex method of linear programming is shown in Fig. 19-1. It should be noted that the solution should be initiated from the bottom where the highest priority factor is located. When there is a positive element in the lower priority factor, it cannot be introduced into the program as long as there is negative element in the same column on the row of a higher priority factor.

The sixth iteration presents the optimal solution to the problem. The solution indicates that the first three goals are achieved but the fourth goal could not be attained. This reflects the everyday sales management problems experienced in business when there are several conflicting goals. To achieve the optimal solution, as the sixth iteration indicates, 900 full-time salesman hours and 500 part-time salesman hours should be employed in September. Hence, the overtime hours allocated to full-time salesmen were 100, whereas the overtime hours to part-time salesmen were 180.

Conclusion

Objectives of management vary according to the characteristics, types, and particular conditions of the organization. This implies that there is no single universal goal for business firms. Profit maximization, which is regarded as the sole objective of the firm in the classical economic theory, is accepted as one of the primary goals of management.[7] Yet, in today's dynamic business environment, profit maximization is not always the only objective of management.[8] In fact, business firms quite frequently place higher priorities on noneconomic goals than on profit maximization.[9] Often firms seek profit maximization while simultaneously pursuing other goals.

If we grant that management has multiple goals, then the decision criteria also should be multidimensional. This implies that the linear programming technique has very little value for such problems involving multiple goals. However, the goal programming model can be effectively utilized when the decision problem involves multiple goals in multiple dimensions as demonstrated in this article by the sales effort allocation example.

The record shop illustration demonstrated one example of solving marketing decision problems with GP. Goal programming should also be applicable to a wide range of other managerial problems. Its application to date has been rather scarce primarily because it is a relatively new technique. Thus far, the application of GP has been explored only for the areas of advertising media planning,[10] production scheduling,[11] manpower planning,[12] academic planning,[13] and financial planning.[14]

Although goal programming is an effective decision-making tool for most managerial problems, there are some limitations. The most apparent

C_j					P_1	$2P_3$	P_3			P_4	$3P_4$	P_2
	V	C	X_1	X_2	d_1	d_2	d_3	d_{21}	d_1	d_2	d_3	d_{21}
P_1	d_1^-	5500	5	2	1				−1			
$2P_3$	d_2^-	800	(1)			1				−1		
P_3	d_3^-	320		1			1				−1	
	d_{21}^-	100						1		1		−1
$Z_j - C_j$	P_4	0								−1	−3	
	P_3	1120	2	1						−2	−1	
	P_2	0										−1
	P_1	5500	5	2					−1			
P_1	d_1^-	1500		2	1	−5			−1	5		
	X_1	800	1			1				−1		
P_3	d_3^-	320		1			1				−1	
	d_{21}^-	100						1		(1)		−1
$Z_j - C_j$	P_4	0								−1	−3	
	P_3	320		1		−2					−1	
	P_2	0										−1
	P_1	1500		2		−5			−1	5		
P_1	d_1^-	1000		2	1	−5		−5	−1			(5)
	X_1	900	1			1		1				−1
P_3	d_3^-	320		1			1				−1	
P_4	d_2^+	100						1		1		−1
$Z_j - C_j$	P_4	500						1			−3	−1
	P_3	320		1		−2					−1	
	P_2	0										−1
	P_1	1000		2		−5		−5	−1			5
P_2	d_{21}^+	200		2/5	1/5	−1		−1	−1/5			1
	X_1	1100	1	2/5	1/5				−1/5			
P_3	d_3^-	320		(1)			1				−1	
P_4	d_2^+	300		2/5	1/5	−1			−1/5	1		
$Z_j - C_j$	P_4	1500		2/5	1/5	−1			−1/5		−3	
	P_3	320		1		−2					−1	
	P_2	200		5/2	1/5	−1		−1	−1/5			
	P_1	0			−1							
P_2	d_{21}^+	72			1/5	−1	−2/5	−1	−1/5		(2/5)	1
	X_1	972	1		1/5		−2/5		−1/5		2/5	
	X_2	320		1			1				−1	
P_4	d_2^+	172			1/5	−1	−2/5		−1/5	1	2/5	
$Z_j - C_j$	P_4	860			1/5	−1	−2/5		−1/5		−1 3/5	
	P_3	0				−2	−1					
	P_2	72			1/5	−1	−2/5	−1	−1/5		2/5	
	P_1	0			−1							
	d_3^+	180			1/2	−5/2	−1	−5/2	−1/2		1	5/2
	X_1	900	1			1		1				−1
	X_2	500		1	1/2	−5/2		−5/2	−1/2			−5/2
P_4	d_2^+	100						1		1		−1
$Z_j - C_j$	P_4	1310			3/2	−1 5/2	−3	−1 3/2	−3/2			1 3/2
	P_3	0				−2	−1					
	P_2	0										−1
	P_1	0			−1							

Fig. 19-1. Solution of Goal Programming Problem by Simplex Method.

limitation is that the GP model simply provides the best solution under the given constraints and priority structure. Therefore, if management assigns incorrect priorities to various goals, the model solution will not provide the optimum solution. Another apparent limitation of the GP model is the cost to develop a model for computer solution, and to obtain access to facilities and personnel capable of compiling the program.

Nevertheless, as long as management establishes ordinal importance among goals, the GP model provides management the opportunity to critically review the priority structure in view of the solution derived by the model. Indeed, the most important advantage of the goal programming model is its great flexibility which allows model simulation with numerous variations of constraints and goals.

Notes

1. Philip Kotler, "Operations Research in Marketing," *Harvard Business Review* (January-February 1967), p.30.

2. See Frank M. Bass and Ronald T. Lonsdale, "An Exploration of Linear Programming in Media Selection," *Journal of Marketing Research* (May 1966), pp. 179-188; Douglas B. Brown and Martin R. Warshaw, "Media Selection by Linear Programming," *Journal of Marketing Research* (February 1965), pp. 83-88; Ralph L. Day, "Linear Programming in Media Selection," *Journal of Advertising Research* (June 1962), pp. 40-44; James F. Engle and Martin R. Warshaw, "Allocating Advertising Dollars by Linear Programming," *Journal of Advertising Research* (September 1964), pp. 42-48.

3. B. Dzielinski, D. Baker, and A. Manne, "Simulation Tests of Lot-Size Programming," *Management Science,* 9, 2 (January 1963), pp. 229-253.

4. See A. Charnes and W.W. Cooper, *Management Models and Industrial Applications of Linear Programming* New York: John Wiley & Sons, Inc., 1961); Yuji Ijiri, *Management Goals and Accounting for Control* (Amsterdam: North Holland Publishing Co., 1965).

5. Ijiri, *Management Goals,* pp. 38-50.

6. The relationship between priority factors is not always as rigid as described here. It can be easily modified, if desired, by introducing additional constraints and assigning more priority factors.

7. See Joseph W. McGuire, *Theories of Business Behavior* (Englewood Cliffs, N.J.: Prentice-Hall, Inc., 1964), pp. 46-72.

8. See Richard M. Cyert and James G. March, *A Behavioral Theory of the Firm* (Englewood Cliffs, N.J.: Prentice-Hall, Inc., 1963), pp. 26-43; Max D. Richards and Paul S. Greenlaw, *Management Decision Making* (Homewood, Ill.: Richard D. Irwin, Inc., 1968), pp. 34-35; Peter F. Drucker, *The Practice of Management* (New York: Harper and Brothers, 1954), chap. 7.

9. Robert N. Anthony, "The Trouble with Profit Maximization," *Harvard Business Review* (November-December 1960), pp. 126-134.

10. A. Charnes, *et al.,* "A Goal Programming Model for Media Planning," *Management Science,* 14, 8 (April 1968), pp. 423-430.

11. Veikko Jaaskelainen, "A Goal Programming Model for Aggregate Production Planning," *Swedish Journal of Economics* (forthcoming).

12. A. Charnes *et al.,* "An Extended Goal Programming Model for Manpower Planning," Management Science Research Paper No. 188, Carnegie-Mellon University, June, 1969.

13. Sang M. Lee and Edward R. Clayton, "A Mathematical Programming Model for Academic Planning," a paper presented at the Southern Management Association Meeting, November, 1969.

14. Veikko Jaaskelainen and Sang M. Lee, "A Goal Programming Model for Financial Planning," *Copenhagen Journal of Business and Economics* (forthcoming).

20 Allocating Advertising Dollars by Linear Programming

by James F. Engel and Martin R. Warshaw

Advertisers and advertising agencies alike have recently shown increased interest in the use of mathematical programming to allocate advertising expenditures to media, and the technique of linear programming has received special attention. Indeed, about a year ago full-page ads in the *Wall Street Journal* stated that linear programming had shown one client how to get "$1.67 worth of effective advertising for every dollar in his budget."

Ralph Day [3] led the way in explaining how LP, as we shall call it, might be applied to the allocation of the advertising appropriation. We attempted to implement Day's suggestions, and it became quite clear that the difficult problems in the LP approach pertained to the identification and evaluation of important marketing variables. A great deal of this delineation and quantification was, of necessity, judgmental in nature. Once these definitions and subjective appraisals of marketing variables had been made, however, the mathematical problem was rather straightforward and presented no major difficulties.

It is our purpose to delve more deeply into the problem, beginning where Day and others leave off, by suggesting through simple examples how one might implement the LP approach. Also, the strengths and weaknesses of LP will be stressed to help the thoughtful advertiser judge how this promising tool might be used in his organization. Since the mathematical model of LP and the methods of solution have been well documented in technical terms by Spivey [9], Churchman, Ackoff, and Arnoff [1], Dorf-

---

EDITOR'S NOTE: Reprinted from *Word of Mouth Advertising* by Johan Arndt. © Copyright 1967, by the Advertising Research Foundation.

man, Samuelson, and Solow [4], and others, we shall proceed directly to a simple statement of the mathematical model.

(1) Maximize (or minimize)

$$f = p_1x_1 + p_2x_2 + \ldots + p_nx_n \qquad \text{(objective function)}$$

(2) subject to

$$a_{11}x_1 + a_{12}x_2 + \ldots + a_{1n}x_n \leqslant b_1 \qquad \text{(linear constraints)}$$

$$a_{21}x_1 + a_{22}x_2 + \ldots + a_{2n}x_n \leqslant b_2$$

$$a_{m1}x_1 + a_{m2}x_2 + \ldots + a_{mn}x_n \leqslant b_m$$

(3) and $x_i \geqslant 0$ $(i = 1, \ldots, n)$. (nonnegativity constraint)

Hence LP is uniquely applicable to problems where the purpose is to maximize (or minimize) a given linear function under several constraining conditions represented by linear inequalities.

Equation (1) is called the objective function. The x's represent the variables in the problem while p's express the contribution or value of each x to the objective function. If, for example, the objective function to be maximized is the number of prospects reached by a given media assortment, the x's would be "dollars invested in individual media," and the p's "prospects reached by each medium per dollar invested."

The first constraints are designated by the inequalities (2). The symbol $\leqslant$ means "less than or equal to," and $\geqslant$ means "greater than or equal to." The b's refer to maximum quantities of resources or capacities available, and the a's indicate the extent to which each x uses up or consumes the resource or capacity b. For instance, b_1 may refer to the total advertising budget, which cannot be exceeded by the number of dollars invested in the various media. Factor b_2 may specify the number of insertions allowed in magazine x_2. The flexibility allowed in placing constraining conditions is one of the real strengths of the LP approach. Finally, inequality (3) specifies that all x's in the optimal solution either must assume a value of 0 or some positive number.

Day [3] indicates more specifically the manner in which the general LP model is applied to allocation of advertising dollars:

> In the linear programming media mix model, the objective function shows how particular advertising units contribute to "total advertising effectiveness." The system of inequalities reflects the restrictions imposed on the solution values of the variables by the budget, the characteristics of available media, and other environmental conditions. The nonnegativity requirements prevent infeasible

solutions involving negative values of the variables. Solution of a correctly formulated model will then indicate the particular advertising units to be included in the media schedule and the number of uses of each which will result in the greatest "total advertising effectiveness" obtainable from a given budget (p. 42).

The rest of this article analyzes two examples to show how one moves from the general LP problem to a specific application. The simplest application of LP to media allocation is illustrated in the solution of the McGraw-Edison case [8]. The Pennsylvania Transformer Division of McGraw-Edison manufacturers transformers used by industrial plants, schools, public institutions, commercial construction projects, and hospitals. The plant engineer usually makes the purchase decision, so the objective is to maximize the number of plant engineers reached, given budgetary and other constraints. The company has $25,000 to spend on industrial advertising, and data are available on markets reached by various media. Since ten media are available for analysis, the objective function assumes the following general form:

$$\text{Maximize } f = p_1x_1 + p_2x_2 + \ldots + p_{10}x_{10}$$

where the x's are the number of dollars invested in the various media and the p's represent the number of plant engineers reached in each magazine per advertising dollar invested.

We computed the values of the p's by dividing the total number of plant engineers reached by the six-time bulk page rate in each medium. The data shown in Table 20-1 were gathered:

Table 20-1

	Magazine	Plant Engineers Reached/Cost per Cost per Insertion		Plant Engineers Reached per Dollar
x_1	*Consulting Engineer*	0/475	p_1	0
x_2	*Electrical Construction*	12,000/792	p_2	15.15
x_3	*Electrical World*	24,000/730	p_3	32.87
x_4	*Power*	44,000/890	p_4	49.44
x_5	*Plant Engineering*	52,000/918	p_5	56.65
x_6	*Electrical West*	8,000/456	p_6	17.54
x_7	*Electrified Industry*	44,000/756	p_7	58.20
x_8	*Public Power*	0/700	p_8	0
x_9	*Electric Light and Power*	16,000/680	p_9	23.53
x_{10}	*Transmission and Distribution*	23,000/575	p_{10}	40.00

Thus the objective function becomes:

$$\text{Maximize } f = 0x_1 + 15.15x_2 + 32.87x_3 + 49.44x_4 + 56.65x_5 + 17.54x_6 + 58.20x_7 + 0x_8 + 23.53x_9 + 40.00x_{10}.$$

With only \$25,000 to spend, a budgetary constraint must be established:

$$x_1 + x_2 + \ldots + x_{10} \leqslant \$25{,}000.$$

In addition, constraints must be fixed to prevent more dollars being invested in any one monthly magazine than is necessary to buy 12 insertions. *(Electrical World* is published weekly but insertions have been limited to 12 for purposes of exposition.) Therefore, these constraints are added:

$$\begin{array}{ll} x_1 \leqslant 5{,}700 & x_6 \leqslant 5{,}472 \\ x_2 \leqslant 9{,}504 & x_7 \leqslant 9{,}072 \\ x_3 \leqslant 8{,}760 & x_8 \leqslant 3{,}300 \\ x_4 \leqslant 10{,}680 & x_9 \leqslant 8{,}160 \\ x_5 \leqslant 11{,}016 & x_{10} \leqslant 6{,}900 \end{array}$$

This problem is of the general LP form and can be solved by the Simplex method [9,6], a procedure which moves the objective function from one feasible solution to the next until a solution is reached in which the objective function has the greatest value given the constraining conditions. An IBM 7090 computer was programed for the Simplex method, and an optimal solution indicated that an investment of \$4,912 (roughly 5.5 pages) in *Power* (x_4), \$11,016 (12 pages) in *Plant Engineering* (x_5), and \$9,072 (12 pages) in *Electrified Industry* (x_7) would maximize the number of plant engineers reached for \$25,000.

Obviously, we do not need a computer to solve such a simple problem (which suffers from lack of necessary refinements). It is apparent that some media are better than others for reaching desired objectives, and we need some form of "effectiveness rating," In other words, the media buyer must be certain that he has chosen the media which best match the audience as specified by his objectives. Audience dimensions such as age, income, location should be included in the objective function so that an "optimal" solution maximizes not only the number reached but readers who are likely to be prospects. Let us call this phase of effectiveness rating the "audience profile match."

In addition, media must be analyzed in terms of certain qualitative characteristics, such as the appropriateness of their editorial climate for the product advertised and their proven past ability to provide advertising readership. This second phase of effectiveness rating will be called the "qualitative rating."

Another problem was formulated to illustrate an approach to effectiveness rating. Here the problem is to spend $1,000,000 on advertising of women's electric razors in consumer magazines using full page, four-color, nonbleed advertisements. Twelve media were singled out for analysis: *Cosmopolitan* (x_1), *Mademoiselle* (x_2), *Family Circle* (x_3), *Good Housekeeping* (x_4), *McCall's* (x_5), *Modern Romances* (x_6), *Modern Screen* (x_7), *Motion Picture* (x_8), *True Confessions* (x_9), *Woman's Day* (x_{10}), *Seventeen* (x_{11}), and *Ladies' Home Journal* (x_{12}).

The first step in effectiveness rating is to determine what parts of the market to reach. Suppose that we discovered through multiple correlation analysis that the desired market is composed of women who are: (1) white; (2) 18 to 44; (3) have incomes of $7,000 or more; and (4) live in metropolitan areas. Using the Starch Consumer Magazine Report, we next analyze various media possibilities in terms of these characteristics to arrive at the "audience profile match." In addition, we estimated each magazine's ability to deliver a good potential audience through data on the number of electric shavers bought by readers in the past year. A large percentage of purchases was considered a favorable indication, and these data were useful in the qualitative rating.

If the problem were approached in a manner similar to the McGraw-Edison case, the objective function would be framed in terms of the number of women reached by each magazine divided by the page rate. With the introduction of the effectiveness rating a great many different schemes could be employed. What we did, though, was to devise a rating scale, ranging from 0 to 1.00 to encompass both the profile match and qualitative rating. The total number of women reached by each medium is multiplied by this factor value to arrive at total "effective audience."

Assume that a multiple correlation analysis showed age to be the most important discrimator of prospects. Age would be assigned a weight in the total rating to reflect its relative importance, as would other factors. In the problem at hand we specified what each factor should contribute to the effectiveness rating as follows:

	Maximum Contribution
Age (18–44)	.40
Bought shaver	.30
Income ($7,000 or over)	.15
Metropolitan location	.10
White	.05
Total	1.00

The rating scheme could be modified to reflect any additional values which management assumes to be important. For instance, we could have employed another scale ranging from 0.5 to 1.0 to reflect ratings of the appropriateness of editorial climate. The actual form of the effectiveness rating, then, is entirely dictated by the tasks to be accomplished and the data available.

The profile match is obtained by analyzing each magazine's audience on the various dimensions and then assigning a factor weight. A conversion system, of course, is necessary for this purpose, and in a sophisticated approach one perhaps would derive the conversion scale by expressing the various magazines' characteristics in terms of standard deviations of their distributions. Thus, if the proportion of readership aged 18-44 for the magazines under consideration averaged 50 per cent with a standard deviation of 5 per cent, a specific magazine with 55 per cent of its readership aged 18-44 might be assigned a +1 (one standard deviation above the mean). Another magazine having only 40 per cent of its audience in the 18-44 bracket would be assigned a −2. To eliminate negative weights, −3 standard deviations might be termed a zero with the scale running up to a +6 for a magazine three standard deviations above the mean.

A much simpler conversion scale is used here for expository purposes. Here is the conversion scale for each factor:

Age (18-44) (0 to .4)		**Income ($7,000 or more) (0 to .15)**	
Under 50%	.0	Under 25%	0
50-55	.1	26-30	.03
56-60	.2	31-35	.06
61-65	.3	36-40	.10
66 or over	.4	41 or over	.15
White (0 to .05)		**Metropolitan Area (0 to .1)**	
Under 85%	0	Under 50%	0
85-90	.01	51-55	.03
91-95	.03	56-60	.06
96 or over	.05	61 or over	.10

Previously Bought Shaver (0 to .3)	
Under 4%	0
5-6	.1
7-8	.2
9-10	.3

To illustrate the effectiveness rating procedure, let us take a hypothetical magazine, *Woman's World.* Assume that the audience data shown below are available on market coverage (form Starch Magazine report or the individual medium). Converting the data, these weights would be applied:

	Audience	Weights
Age 18–44	59%	.20
Income $7,000 or over	31	.06
White subscribers	96	.05
Metropolitan coverage	61	.10
Purchased shaver in last 12 months	7	.20
		.61

Suppose this magazine reaches 5,070,492 women. Multiplying this total by a factor of .61 gives an effective audience of 3,093,000 women. Dividing this by the four-color, full-page rate ($29,100) gives "effective readings per dollar spent" of 106. This final figure will appear in the objective function as the coefficient of the variable *(x).*

Using the above procedure for each magazine produced the following objective function:

$$\text{Max } f = 158x_1 + 263x_2 + 106x_3 + 108x_4 + 65x_5 + 176x_6 + 285x_7$$
$$+ 86x_8 + 120x_9 + 51x_{10} + 190x_{11} + 101x_{12} .$$

With the budgetary constraint:

$$x_1 + x_2 + \ldots + x_{12} \leqslant 1{,}000{,}000.$$

And the usual nonnegativity constraint:

$$x_i \geqslant 0 \; (i = 1, \ldots, 12).$$

Also constraints again were established to prevent assigning more than 12 insertions to any of these monthly magazines. Suppose, however, that management had good reason to limit the maximum insertions to less than 12 for media x_2 *and* x_{12} (for example, 7 and 2 insertions respectively.) Thus the constraints are:

$$x_1 \leqslant 58{,}080 \qquad x_4 \leqslant 288{,}000$$
$$x_2 \leqslant 30{,}075 \ (7) \qquad x_5 \leqslant 407{,}400$$
$$x_3 \leqslant 349{,}000 \qquad x_6 \leqslant 52{,}380$$

$x_7 \leqslant 52{,}380 \qquad x_{10} \leqslant 333{,}000$
$x_8 \leqslant 53{,}580 \qquad x_{11} \leqslant 72{,}360$
$x_9 \leqslant 57{,}960 \qquad x_{12} \leqslant 81{,}200$ (2)

Suppose further that the client company has specified certain minimum expenditures in magazines x_2, x_3, x_5 and x_{10}. Therefore:

$x_2 \geqslant 13{,}275$
$x_3 \geqslant 58{,}166$
$x_5 \geqslant 33{,}950$
$x_{10} \geqslant 27{,}750$

Finally, management declared a maximum expenditure of \$280,000 in magazines x_3, x_9, x_{10} and x_{12} and specified the investment of exactly \$85,870 in magazines x_1 and x_8. Thus:

$$x_3 + x_9 + x_{10} + x_{12} \leqslant 280{,}000$$

$$x_1 + x_8 = 85{,}870$$

The above problem is obviously more complex than the McGraw-Edison case, and it is no longer possible to visualize a solution readily. Imagine the difficulties if 50 media were employed with a more complex set of constraints! Also, a variety of subjective restrictions could have been used as alternatives to those shown above. The strength of LP is that for every configuration of subjective constraints, we can readily solve the corresponding problem. Indeed, management might be presented with two or more solutions showing the impact of changes in the subjective constraints upon the optimal solution.

The Simplex method of solution was used on the computer, and an optimal solution to the above problem directed that we make these purchases:

	Medium				
x_1	*Cosmopolitan*	\$ 58,080	x_7	*Modern Screen*	52,380
x_2	*Mademoiselle*	30,075	x_8	*Motion Picture*	27,790
x_3	*Family Circle*	194,290	x_9	*True Confessions*	57,960
x_4	*Good Housekeeping*	288,000	x_{10}	*Woman's Day*	27.750
x_5	*McCall's*	180,484*	x_{11}	*Seventeen*	72,360
x_6	*Modern Romances*	52,380	x_{12}	*Ladies' Home Journal*	0

*Includes reinvested discounts.

After the initial allocation it was necessary to reconsult Standard Rate and Data Service to find the extent of volume discounts which the firm had earned. We discovered that an additional $41,549 was available for expenditure. The Simplex solution indicates, within bounds, where to invest these additional funds. In the problem at hand, it was indicated that the additional dollars should be invested in *McCall's.*

An important point to keep in mind is that quantity discounts could not have been built into the original statement of the problem. The cost function would then have been nonlinear, and LP would no longer have been applicable. Nonlinear programming methods are available, but the solution would become decidedly more complex [5,10].

As suggested earlier, management should not view the Simplex solution as the final phase in the LP approach. It might be quite useful, for example, to engage in a sensitivity analysis by changing the weights used in the effectiveness rating, especially those based on subjective evaluation. If rather large changes can be made in these weights without changing the optimal solution, it is evident that the solution is not dependent on precise evaluations of qualitative characteristics. If, however, the optimal solution changes with slight variations in these weights then it is obvious that the quality of the solution can be little better than the quality of the effectiveness rating procedure.

Let us now state more specifically the steps in a well-conceived LP media allocation procedure:

1. Establishment of specific advertising objectives.
2. Procurement of data on the relative importance of various characteristics of the market to be reached through multiple correlation analysis or other means.
3. Procurement of data on audiences of various candidate media. Often these data are stored in the computer, thus permitting quick access.
4. Application of an effectiveness rating procedure encompassing two phases: audience profile match and qualitative factor rating.
5. Quantification of all constraining conditions, including budgetary limits, limits on media availability, and other environmental factors.
6. Application of an LP computational procedure.
7. Analysis of the resulting media plan to determine its sensitivity to various factors in the effectiveness rating and to changes in constraint conditions.

The LP approach has important strengths and weaknesses which must be recognized by all potential users, and each point will be examined.

Advantages of LP Approach

1. LP forces management to make precise definitions of markets to be

reached. Instead of guesses or hunches, data must be developed which characterize markets along several dimensions. The net result of such analysis cannot help but increase the effectiveness of media allocation.

2. LP requires a quantification of factors which are highly qualitative in nature. Editorial climate is perhaps a highly subjective factor yet management must take this media characteristic and others of a similar nature into account when engaging in media selection.

3. LP creates a definite need for audience profiles of various media. The occasional media audience study no longer will suffice, and instead careful audience profile information must be provided with the regularity of ABC sworn circulation data. LP is certain, therefore, to stimulate the collection of a wealth of previously unavailable facts.

4. LP can be applied to problems involving a variety of media. Although we have discussed only magazines, there is no reason why all possible media cannot be included in the LP approach. If data are available, all media can be considered in the same terms, making it feasible to consider vastly more media at a time than would be possible without the aid of a computer.

5. LP can be used by advertisers and agencies of *any* size. No mumbo jumbo in the methodology limits this approach only to large firms. Furthermore, it is not necessary to confine LP to allocations approaching astronomical sums. Indeed, the allocation of a few thousand dollars can become sufficiently complex to warrant use of the computer, especially when one considers the potential costs of an ineffective allocation.

6. LP allows the blending together of many factors. As Maneloveg [7] points out:

> In the past we have worked at it with stubby pencils and people, many people. However, no matter how much time and how many people, we have had too many factors to contend with. The real advantage of an electronic computer to us then—its principal purpose—is to give us an opportunity to change these relationships, to juggle with them, to work with them while at the same time keeping all of them in the forefront of the operation and to end up with an effort that examines the whole not individual pieces of media the way, incidentally, our customers view the campaign that we're putting together (p.6).

Limitations

1. LP is applicable only if all relationships in the problem are linear or if it is appropriate for management purposes to regard them as so. This is a marketing decision, not a mathematical one. As noted above, the requirement of linearity in cost functions did not permit inclusion of quantity discounts in the initial allocation. Yet the resulting allocation may fail to achieve the maximum discount which might have become available

if dollars were allocated differently. It is difficult to maximize discounts unless constraints require only large purchases of individual media, but, on the other hand, such constraints may unduly limit the solution space to large buys and thereby force an ineffective allocation.

The assumption of linearity becomes more crucial in another respect. Although the cost functions in both examples required purchases of full pages, fractional page purchases appeared in the allocation. The problem arises because the Simplex approach does not guarantee the purchase of only full pages. The cost of a half page, for example, is not half of the page rate, so it may be incorrect to assume that purchases of fractional pages are optimal. In other words, the cost function for various page sizes is actually nonlinear. Then what is the advertiser to do when his answer call for 4.83 pages? Is he safe in rounding this figure to 5.00? He probably would not err greatly if he does, but he still must recognize the danger of arriving at a nonoptimal allocation if he rounds off on a large scale. Furthermore, cost structures may not depart so far from linearity as to preclude meaningful answers. The only feasible way in which to guarantee nonfractional purchases, however, is to use "integer programming," and we are experimenting with this approach.

Finally, it is assumed that successive purchases in a media all contribute the same value to the objective function. It must be recognized that multiple exposure of a given prospect may become increasingly less effective, thus introducing nonlinearity into the response function. This problem may be crucial, but we cannot avoid it without resorting to more complex nonlinear programming methods.

2. Solutions were arrived at without consideration of audience duplication and accumulation. Because of audience overlap, purchase of two or more magazines should result in a total audience that is less than the sum of the individual audiences. Although the Agostini [1] constant may permit estimates of nonduplicated audiences, his approach requires data that are not available on a consistent scale, especially if one is comparing a magazine and a television show. Furthermore, whereas duplication and accumulation of *prospects* are the only truly relevant considerations, existing data are confined entirely to total audiences. Thus at present the LP approach cannot solve effectively the duplication and accumulation problems.

3. Comparable data are not always available for various media in terms of audience dimensions. More and better media data are required before LP can achieve its potential.

4. Finally, resulting solutions give a very misleading illusion of definiteness. Solutions are only as good as the data and assumptions upon which they are built. Weaknesses in data or in analysis of the problem will be compounded, so good judgement is vital.

CONCLUSION

The approach to LP and media allocation described here obviously needs considerable refinement. And it should be abundantly clear that the major problems arise in identifying and quantifying the important marketing variables—not in application of the LP computational procedure. LP is not a magical device that relegates responsibility for management decisions to computers and their programmers. Indeed, the successful use of LP involves three essentials: (1) defining market targets; (2) rating media in terms of their effectiveness in reaching these targets; (3) developing and quantifying monetary and nonmonetary constraints which limit feasible solutions. Thus judgment reponsibilities of the media executive are *sharpened,* not eliminated. The only thing eliminated is laborious clerical work.

Let us conclude by observing that LP is not a breakthrough and that it involves very little more than systematizing steps which have long been followed by successful advertisers. The real gain comes in the time saved and the ability to handle complex problems with greater ease and to deal quickly with alternative subjective evaluations of constraints and weighting factors. We hope the glamor which quantitative methods now hold does not cause advertisers to overlook the inescapable difficulty of identifying and evaluating the important marketing variables. If this problem is fully recognized, then LP is not likely to be blighted in its infancy, as was motivation research, by exaggerated and commercially-motivated claims of a few zealous spokesmen.

References

1. Agostini, J.M., "How to Estimate Unduplicated Audiences," *Journal of Advertising Research,* 13 (March 1961), pp. 11-14.

2. Churchman, C. West, Ackoff, Russell, L. and Arnoff, Leonard E., *Introduction to Operations Research* (New York: Wiley, 1957).

3. Day, Ralph L. "Linear Programming in Media Selection," *Journal of Advertising Research,* 2 (June 1962), pp. 40-44.

4. Dorfman, Robert, Samuelson, Paul A., and Solow, Robert M., *Linear Programming and Economic Analysis* (New York: McGraw-Hill, 1958).

5. Dorn, W.S., "Non-Linear Programming—A Survey," *Management Science,* 9 (January 1963), pp. 171-208.

6. Garvin, W.W., *An Introduction to Linear Programming* (New York: McGraw-Hill, 1960).

7. Maneloveg, Herbert, *Linear Programming,* paper presented at the Eastern Annual Convention (New York: American Association of Advertising Agencies, November 1962).

8. McGraw-Edison Company, *ICH 6m67* (Boston: Intercollegiate Case Clearing House, 1961).

9. Spivey, W. Allen, *Linear Programming: An Introduction* (New York: Macmillan, 1963).

10. Wolfe, Philip, "The Simplex Method for Quadratic Programming," *Econometrica,* 27 (July 1959), pp. 382-398.

21 On-Line Blending for Production Profit

by F. A. Tillman and E. S. Lee

Blending and production control is a dual problem to which linear programming applies in these two ways: proportioning of raw materials subject to quality restrictions (blending gasoline for specified octane rating for example), and proportioning quantities of products that are competing for these raw materials, so that production profit is maximized (gasolines of different octane ratings), Ref. 1 and 2.

In applying linear programming to this dual problem the production aspect may be set up to include distillation, extraction, and reaction since such operations are common in the process industry. Because these operations are usually nonlinear, a set of typical operating points is chosen to linearize them for linear programming. The solution can be made arbitrarily close to the optimum by iteration with different sets of operating points, Ref. 3, 4, and 5.

The Blending and Production Problem

The problem of blending raw materials and determing how to control production of mixed products is extremely complex yet arises constantly on line. Among the decisions that must be made are:

- In what quantities and proportions should a limited supply of raw materials be put in the blend?

- At what setting of the operating range should the plant be operated in view of the effect on capacity, and the material loss or gain from the process?
- How can the overall profit from both raw material blending and production be maximized while meeting product specifications?

The first step in developing a linear programming model that may be applied in such a situation is to determine which are the important variables that must be considered . Usually these variables depend on what parameters can be controlled and what their effect is on profit.

The process considered in this example incorporates recycle and the changes in qualities and quantities of the raw meterial due to processing. The model that is constructed might easily be expanded to include production processes such as chemical reaction and separation.

Three grades of plastic raw material R_1, R_2, and and R_3 are to be blended and molded into a finished product that must possess at least 220 units of quality 1, Q_1, and not more than 40 units of quality 2, Q_2. Q_1 is a desirable quality such as the ability to withstand heat; Q_2 is an undesirable quality such as an unpleasant odor. There is a market of $0.40 per lb for all of the product that can be produced. Table 21-1 presents the cost and quality of the three raw materials.

Table 21-1 List of Raw Materials with Their Respective Qualities and Cost. The Materials are being Blended by a Linear Programming Method.

	R_1	R_2	R_3
Quality 1, unit per lb	220	200	245
Quality 2, unit per lb	48	58	38
Cost, dollars per lb	0.31	0.28	0.35

The three raw materials are blended, then processed into the finished product, Fig. 21-1. The settings S_1, S_2, and S_3 have been chosen arbitrarily as representative of the several possible settings within the operating range of the processing unit. Depending on the setting used, processing may increase or decrease the qualities and quantities of the raw materials. The operating cost per pound also depends upon the setting used. Since there is only one piece of processing equipment available, and since changing the setting is time-consuming and impractical, the assumption is that all raw materials must be processed under the same operating condition—setting.

The problem is to select the proper amounts of the different grades of raw materials that are to be blended and to select the operating condition so that the profit is maximized.

The processing costs and changes in quality and quantity of the original raw materials under the three typical settings are presented in Table 21-2.

Table 21-2 Comparison of Process Settings that were Chosen for the Sample Problem Run.

	S_1	S_2	S_3
Changes in Quality 1, unit per lb	0	0	0
Changes in Quality 2, unit per lb	−18	−13	−7
Loss due to processing, lb per lb feed	0.1	0.1	0.1
Cost dollars per lb	0.132	0.121	0.110
Recycle (S_2 base)	1.1	1.0	0.92

If the solution results in a split between two settings so that part of the material is processed under one operating condition and part under another, the problem is rerun under additional settings until all the material is processed under a single operating condition.

Because of different recycle rates or processing times for different settings, the capacity of the unit differs from setting to setting. This change in capacity is indicated in the last row of Table 21-2. If setting S_2 is used the unit has a capacity of 100 lb per hr. At setting S_1 it is 100/1.1 lb per hr and at S_3 100/0.92 lb per hr.

The objective function expresses the combination of selling price, material cost, and processing cost that will optimize profit:

$$z = 0.40p - 0.31R_1 - 0.28R_2 - 0.35R_3 - 0.132S_1 - 0.121S_2 - 0.110S_3 \quad (1)$$

where all terms are in dollars per hour.

Constraints involving quality of materials, process settings, and final product are:

$$Q_1 = 220R_1 + 200R_2 + 245R_3 \quad (2)$$

$$Q_2 = 48R_1 + 58R_2 + 38R_3 \quad (3)$$

$$220p \leqslant 0.9Q_1 + 0.0S_1 + 0.0S_2 + 0.0S_3 \quad (4)$$

$$40p \geqslant 0.9Q_2 - 18S_1 - 13S_2 - 7S_3 \quad (5)$$

where the terms are in lb-units per hr. The coefficients 0.9 in equations 4 and 5 compensate for loss in raw material during processing. Equations 2 and 3 deal with raw materials quality, while equations 4 and 5 deal with finished product quality.

Material balance in the blending unit, between blending and processing, and in the processing unit are expressed :

$$R = R_1 + R_2 + R_3 \quad (6)$$

$$0.9R = S_1 + S_2 + S_3 \tag{7}$$

$$p = S_1 + S_2 + S_3 \tag{8}$$

where R is the total raw material used in lb per hr.

The final constraint prevents the amount of material produced from exceeding the capacity of the processing unit:

$$100 \geqslant 1.1S_1 + 1.0S_2 + 0.92S_3 \tag{9}$$

where the terms are in lb per hr.

The problem is to find the values of p, S's and R's such that z in Equation 1 will be maximized. Table 21-3 presents the first step in applying the

Table 21-3 Preliminary Matrix Constructed from the Objective Function and Constraints Listed in the Text.

	R_1	R_2	R_3	R	Q_1	Q_2	S_1	S_2	S_3	p	z
Equation 1–Profit	−0.31	−0.28	−0.35				−0.132	−0.121	−0.110	0.40	
Equation 2–Quality 1	220	200	245		−1						0
Equation 3–Quality 2	48	58	38			−2					0
Equation 4–Q change 1					0.9		0.0	0.0	0.0	−220	D_1
Equation 5–Q change 2						0.9	−18	−13	−7	− 40	D_2
Equation 6–Material balance	1	1	1	−1							0
Equation 7–Raw material loss				−0.9			1	1	1		0
Equation 9–Capacity							1.1	1	0.92	−100	D_3
Equation 8–Total product							1	1	1	−1	0

simplex algorithm. Dummy variables have not been included in the constraints that are inequalities. The procedure is similar to the systematic search for an optimum solution in the two-variable case of Fig. 21-1, but is much more complicated. The computed results are:

Maximum profit, z = \$31.04 per hr
Material R_1 = 108.69565 lb per hr
Material R_2 = 0
Material R_3 = 12.07729 lb per hr
$S_1 = S_2 = 0$
$p = S_3$ = 108.69565 lb per hr

The above problem can be generalized by introducing additional products that are produced under different operating settings. A larger number

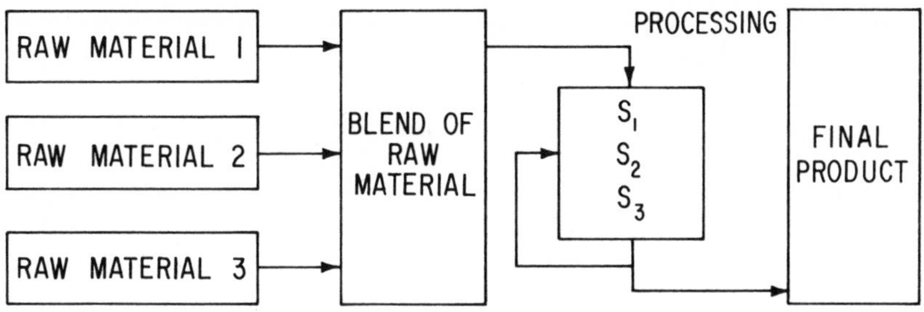

Fig. 21-1. Block diagram of process in which three raw materials are being blended at three different process settings to seek an optimum production profit subject to a set of constraints described in the text.

of settings may be arbitrarily chosen, and there need not be the restriction that the runs be iterated until all products are operated at the same setting. The solution may be conducted (or programmed) to optimize both product mix and the several raw materials blends from a financial viewpoint.

Further generalization may be achieved by applying separation operations such as extraction or distillation and to many chemical reactions.

Limitations on the use of linear programming are that it may be applied to materials balance, product mix, or processing yields, but not to highly nonlinear aspects of reaction or separation processes. Techniques for treating nonlinear situations by linear approximations through evolutionary operations concepts are discussed in Ref. 7 and 8.

The method just described can be applied on-line by placing sensing elements on the raw material sources, production processes, and quality or quantity specification data. As the computer senses that a particular mode of operation, for example, is not producing a product to meet the current specification, immediate action can be taken. It may be that the quality of a raw material, under constant observation, has changed. This condition will affect the corresponding simplex search matrix in computer memory, and may cause programming reruns to reestablish an acceptable profit function.

Linear programming is a powerful analytical tool that control engineers would do well to borrow from the industrial engineering or operations research curricula where it usually appears.

References

1. G. Hadley, *Linear Programming,* Addison-Wesley Publishing Co., Reading, Mass., 1962.

2. A. Charnes, W.W. Cooper, and B. Mellon, "Blending Aviation Gasolines," *Econometrica,* 20, 135, 1952.

3. C.R. Nichols, "Linear Programming Model for Refinery Simulation," *Oil and Gas Journal,* 57, 101, 1959.

4. A. Manne, "Scheduling of Petroleum Refinery Operations," *Harvard Economic Studies,* Vol. 48, Harvard University Press, Cambridge, Mass., 1956.

5. "A Linear Programming Model of the U.S. Petroleum Refining Industry," RM-1757, The RAND Corp., July 1956.

6. J.R. Frazer, *Applied Linear Programming,* Prentice-Hall, Inc., Englewood Cliffs, N.J.

7. "Optimum Design and Operation of Chemical Processes," *Industrial Engineering Chemistry,* 55, 30, August 1963.

8. G.E.P. Box and K.B. Wilson, "On the Experimental Attainment of Optimum Conditions," *J. Royal Statistical Society, Series B,* 13, 1, 1951.

22 Introduction to Linear Programming for Production

by J. Frank Sharp

Enormously complicated industrial situations can be optimized with the computer, using the technique of linear programming. But because of the complexity, linear programming is rarely successful unless key people from each of the related functional areas are involved in setting out the problem.

One of these key people is very often the industrial engineer. Even if you are not mathematically oriented, it pays to understand the principles of LP so that you at least understand what the mathematicians are trying to do to your plant.

In the future, it is expected that LP models will be used even more extensively, not only for the tactical decisions of production and distribution, but also for the strategic decisions of marketing, long-range planning, diversification, and acquisition. As a first step toward understanding LP, consider a simplified LP production model formulated for a hypothetical company.

This company has two plants producing a total of four products according to the flow diagrams in Fig. 22-1. In each plant, the raw material (ARM and BRM) is first processed into an intermediate product. The intermediate product is further processed and then goes either into the production of edible oils (ALIP and BLIP) or feed (AFIP and BFIP). Plant A can produce two oil products (AL1 and AL2) and two feed products (AF1 and AF2). Plant B can produce the same two oil products (BL1 and BL2), but only the first feed product (BF1).

EDITOR'S NOTE: From *The Journal of Industrial Engineering*, December 1970, pp. 10-16. Reprinted by permission of the publisher, American Institute of Industrial Engineers, and author.

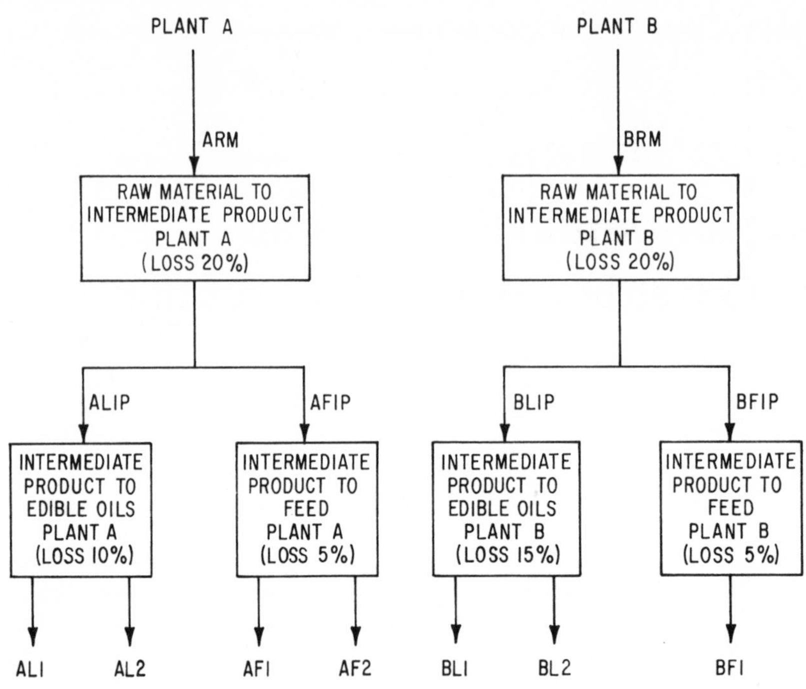

Fig. 22-1. Flow diagram shows the production constraints on the raw material, intermediate material, and finished products.

The loss values in Fig. 22-1 indicate the production yield at various points in the production process. At plant A, 100 pounds of raw material (ARM) is necessary to produce 80 pounds of intermediate product (ALIP or AFIP), while 100 pounds of intermediate product (ALIP) is necessary to produce 90 pounds of oil product, etc.

Additional information needed for the analysis is given in Tables 22-1 through 22-4. This includes capacity restrictions on the amount of raw material that each plant can process, the amount of intermediate product that can be processed, the amount of each product that can be produced, the forecasted demand and price for each product, the processing costs for each production process, and the raw material costs.

Given the prices, production costs, raw material costs, and production relationships, the unit contribution to profits of each product at each plant

Table 22-1 Processing Capacities (100 pounds/period)

Plant A		Plant B		Description
KARM	4000	KBRM	3000	Raw material processing capacity.
KALIP	2500	KBLIP	1700	Processing capacity of intermediate product going to edible oils.
KAFIP	1250	KBFIP	1100	Processing capacity of intermediate product going to feeds.
KAL1	1500	KBL1	1000	Processing capacity for edible oil product 1.
KAL2	1500	KBL2	1000	Processing capacity for edible oil product 2.
KAF1	750	KBF1	1000	Processing capacity for feed product 1.
KAF2	750	–		Processing capacity for feed product 2.

Table 22-2 Forecasted Demands (100 pounds/period) and Prices ($/100 pounds)

Demand		Price	Product
DML1	2000	$12	Edible oil product 1
DML2	2000	$15	Edible oil product 2
DMF1	1200	$ 8	Feed product 1
DMF2	500	$ 7	Feed product 2

Table 22-3 Processing Costs for Each Production Process ($/100 pounds)

Process	Plant A	Plant B
L1	$1.10	$1.20
L2	1.20	1.30
F1	0.90	0.80
F2	0.70	X
LIP	1.00	1.00
FIP	0.95	0.60
RM	0.50	0.60

Table 22-4 Raw Material Costs ($/100 pounds)

Plant A	$2.50
Plant B	2.60

can be determined. For instance, AF1's contribution per 100 pounds of final product would be:

$12.00 (Price)
– 1.10 (Final stage production costs)
– 1.00
(0.9) (Intermediate stage production costs)
– 0.50
(0.8)(0.9) (First-stage production costs)
– 2.50
(0.8)(0.9) (Raw material costs)
= $5.662

All of the calculated unit contributions are given in Table 22-5.

Table 22-5 Contribution for Each Product ($/100 pounds)

Product	Plant A	Plant B
L1	$5.662	$4.918
L2	8.552	7.818
F1	2.153	2.358
F2	1.353	X

Production Facts Put in LP Form

The first step towards optimizing this plant's production is to arrange all the known factors, or constraints, in the form of a matrix, Fig. 22-2. The matrix is like a set of simultaneous equations, except that some of the equations are actually inequalities. There are an infinite number of solutions to the expressions in the matrix. The aim is to find the solution that will optimize a stated function, such as profit.

In the matrix of Fig. 22-2, the names of products and intermediate products are given across the top. These are the variables of the equations and inequalities that make up the matrix. Whenever one of these appears in an equation or inequality its coefficient is written directly below it.

The first production constraint for each plant (Lines MAIL and MAIF) represents the material balance between the amount of edible oil products produced and the amount of intermediate products required. Similarly, the second production constraint for each plant represents the material balance between the amount of feed products produced and the amount of

	AL1	AL2	AF1	AF2	ALIP	AFIP	ARM	BL1	BL2	BF1	BLIP	BFIP	BRM		
REV	12.00	15.00	8.00	7.00				12.00	15.00	8.00					
CØST	1.10	1.20	0.90	0.70	1.00	0.95	3.00	1.20	1.30	0.80	1.00	0.60	3.20		
CØNTR	5.622	8.522	2.153	1.353				4.918	7.818	2.358					
MAIL	1.	1.			-0.9									=	0.
MAIF			1.	1.		-0.95								=	0.
MARI					1.	1.	-0.8							=	0.
RALF					1.	-2.								≤	0.
KAL1	1.													≤	1500.
KAL2		1.												≤	1500.
KAF1			1.											≤	750.
KAF2				1.										≤	750.
KALIP					1.									≤	2500.
KAFIP						1.								≤	1250.
KARM							1.							≤	4000.
MBIL								1.	1.		-0.85			=	0.
MBIF										1.		-0.95		=	0.
MBRI											1.	1.	-0.8	=	0.
RBLF											1.	-3.		≤	0.
KBL1								1.						≤	1000.
KBL2									1.					≤	1000.
KBF1										1.				≤	1000.
KBLIP											1.			≤	1700.
KBFIP												1.		≤	1100.
KBRM													1.	≤	3000.
DL1	1.							1.						≤	2000.
DL2		1.							1.					≤	2000.
DF1			1.							1.				≤	1200.
DF2				1.										≤	500.
	AL1,	AL2,	AF1,	AF2,	ALIP,	AFIP,	ARM,	BL1,	BL2,	BF1,	BLIP,	BFIP,	BRM,	≥	0.

Fig. 22-2. The linear programming model is really a set of equations and inequalities that expresses the production conditions of the plant.

intermediate products needed. The data for these constraints comes from Fig. 22-1. For instance:

$$\text{AL1} + \text{AL2} = 0.9\ \text{ALIP}$$

due to the 10 percent production loss in this process. This is equivalent to the first production constraint

$$\text{AL1} + \text{AL2} - 0.9\ \text{ALIP} = 0$$

The third production constraint for each plant (line MARI) represents the material balance between the amount of intermediate product produced and the amount of raw material required. For instance, from Fig. 22-1,

$$\text{ALIP} + \text{AFIP} = 0.8\ \text{ARM}$$

This constraint indicates that the amount of intermediate product produced at plant A is 0.8 of the raw material processed, due to the 20 percent production loss in this process. In the matrix, all of the variables are moved to the left-hand side of the equality and placed in their respective columns. Also from Fig. 22-1,

$$\text{ALIP} \leqslant {}^2\!/_3(0.8)\ \text{ARM}$$

because of the limitation on the relative production of ALIP. But:

$$0.8\ \text{ARM} = \text{ALIP} + \text{AFIP}$$

Combining these two expressions produces the inequality:

$$\text{ALIP} - 2\text{AFIP} \leqslant 0$$

which is the fourth production constraint for plant A. (Line RALF).

In addition, there are production constraints that give the maximum production rate for each process. These are based on the data in Table 22-1. For instance, AL1 $\leqslant$ 1500, represents the processing capacity for edible oil product one during the period (Line KALI).

The first three rows of the matrix are merely a listing of revenue, cost, and contribution functions for each product. The next 11 rows represent production constraints at plant A, the next ten rows represent production constraints at plant B, while the next four rows represent the forecasted demand for each of the four products. The last row merely states the requirement that no variable can take on negative values.

The CONTR function is the one actually to be optimized. This expression gives the expected total contribution of all the products as listed in Table 22-5–max CONTR = \$5.622AL1 + 8.522AL2 + 2.153AF1 + 1.353AF2 + 4.918BL1 + 7.818BL2 + 2.358BF1. The REV function gives the corresponding total revenue while the COST function gives the corresponding total costs. The coefficients for the REV function are the prices in Table 22-2. The coefficients for the COST function are the processing costs from Table 22-3 and the raw material costs from Table 22-4. The value of REV function minus the value of the COST function equals the value of the CONTR function.

There is one demand constraint for each of the four products. It is assumed that for each product the firm can sell as much as it can produce, up to the forecasted demand. For this example, production capacity is insufficient to satisfy all demands. The constraint for edible oil product one is

AL1 + BL1 $\leqslant$ 2000. (Line DL1)

The forecasted demands are from Table 22-2.

Even if production capacity was sufficient to meet all demands, the same sort of constraints could be used. Then all profitable demands would be satisfied.

Now Find the Solution

Even this simplified example would require several days of hand calculations in order to obtain an optimal solution. However an optimal solution can be obtained in much less time, at much less expense, with much less chance for error, using any one of several canned LP computer codes. This particular example was solved on an IBM Model 360/50 using IBM's MPS/360. The computer time (CPU) was less than 15 seconds for the 15 iterations necessary to obtain an optimal solution.

This example has 28 rows and 13 columns (not counting slack columns). A real-world problem might have several hundred rows and over a thousand columns. Instead of a few seconds, the computer time needed might be an hour or more. (This time can often be reduced considerably by using some of the special options available in the more sophisticated computer codes. For instance, if the first run has been completed and a few modifications made, the computer can start the second run with the previous optimal solution instead of starting from scratch.)

The computer input data is shown in Fig. 22-3 (as output by the computer code). The objective function is coded as OBJ instead of

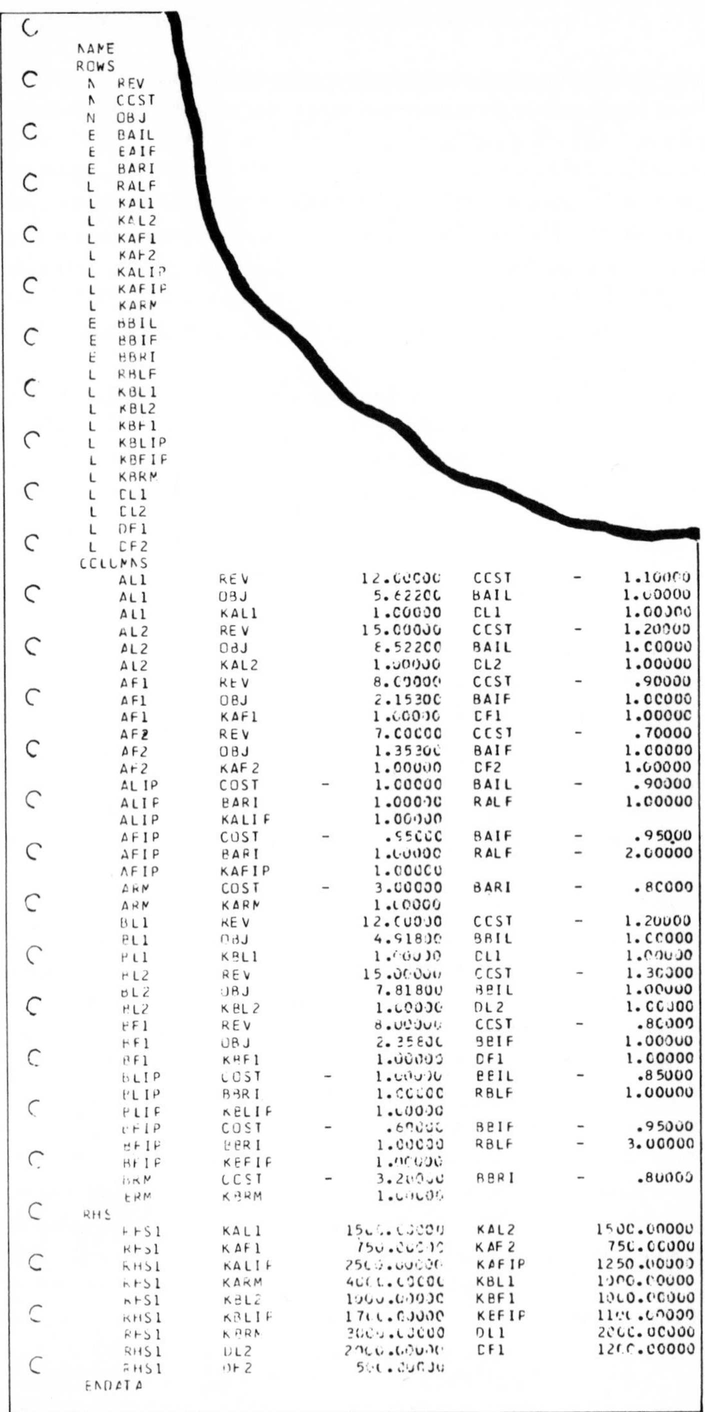

```
NAME
ROWS
 N  REV
 N  CCST
 N  OBJ
 E  BAIL
 E  BAIF
 E  BARI
 L  RALF
 L  KAL1
 L  KAL2
 L  KAF1
 L  KAF2
 L  KALIP
 L  KAFIP
 L  KARM
 E  BBIL
 E  BBIF
 E  BBRI
 L  RBLF
 L  KBL1
 L  KBL2
 L  KBF1
 L  KBLIP
 L  KBFIF
 L  KBRM
 L  CL1
 L  CL2
 L  DF1
 L  CF2
COLUMNS
    AL1      REV          12.00000   CCST    -   1.10000
    AL1      OBJ           5.62200   BAIL        1.00000
    AL1      KAL1          1.00000   CL1         1.00000
    AL2      REV          15.00000   CCST    -   1.20000
    AL2      OBJ           8.52200   BAIL        1.00000
    AL2      KAL2          1.00000   CL2         1.00000
    AF1      REV           8.00000   CCST    -    .90000
    AF1      OBJ           2.15300   BAIF        1.00000
    AF1      KAF1          1.00000   CF1         1.00000
    AF2      REV           7.00000   CCST    -    .70000
    AF2      OBJ           1.35300   BAIF        1.00000
    AF2      KAF2          1.00000   CF2         1.00000
    ALIP     COST    -     1.00000   BAIL    -    .90000
    ALIF     BARI          1.00000   RALF        1.00000
    ALIP     KALIF         1.00000
    AFIP     COST    -      .95000   BAIF    -    .95000
    AFIP     BARI          1.00000   RALF    -   2.00000
    AFIP     KAFIP         1.00000
    ARM      COST    -     3.00000   BARI    -    .80000
    ARM      KARM          1.00000
    BL1      REV          12.00000   CCST    -   1.20000
    BL1      OBJ           4.91800   BBIL        1.00000
    BL1      KBL1          1.00000   CL1         1.00000
    BL2      REV          15.00000   CCST    -   1.30000
    BL2      OBJ           7.81800   BBIL        1.00000
    BL2      KBL2          1.00000   DL2         1.00000
    BF1      REV           8.00000   CCST    -    .80000
    BF1      OBJ           2.35800   BBIF        1.00000
    BF1      KBF1          1.00000   DF1         1.00000
    BLIP     COST    -     1.00000   BBIL    -    .85000
    BLIP     BBRI          1.00000   RBLF        1.00000
    BLIF     KBLIF         1.00000
    BFIP     COST    -      .60000   BBIF    -    .95000
    BFIP     BBRI          1.00000   RBLF    -   3.00000
    BFIF     KBFIF         1.00000
    BRM      CCST    -     3.20000   BBRI    -    .80000
    BRM      KBRM          1.00000
RHS
    RHS1     KAL1       1500.00000   KAL2     1500.00000
    RHS1     KAF1        750.00000   KAF2      750.00000
    RHS1     KALIF      2500.00000   KAFIP    1250.00000
    RHS1     KARM       4000.00000   KBL1     1000.00000
    RHS1     KBL2       1000.00000   KBF1     1000.00000
    RHS1     KBLIF      1700.00000   KBFIF    1100.00000
    RHS1     KBRM       3000.00000   DL1      2000.00000
    RHS1     DL2        2000.00000   CF1      1200.00000
    RHS1     DF2         500.00000
ENDATA
```

Fig. 22-3. Names of all rows and columns and the values of the coefficients that make up the matrix are first input to the computer.

CONTR. A portion of the computer output is shown in Figs. 22-4, 22-5, and 22-6. Figure 22-4 gives the optimal value of the objective function as $27,068.

Figure 22-5 lists the optimal value of the left-hand side of each function and constraint under ACTIVITY. This plus the optimal SLACK ACTIVITY is equal to the RHS value for each constraint. Note that all are under UPPER LIMIT in this example. All of these values in rows 4 through 28 are in 100's of pounds per period. Also given in Fig. 22-5 is the optimal value of the DUAL ACTIVITY (sometimes called shadow price or imputed value). The DUAL ACTIVITY gives the changes in the objective function if the RHS for that constraint is decreased by one unit. The negative of this value gives the change in the objective function if the RHS for that constraint is increased by one unit. The units are dollars per 100 pounds.

Figure 22-6 gives the optimal activity level for each variable (under ACTIVITY). The units are 100's of pounds per period.

Distribution Costs Add Complexity

Some idea of the complexity of real-life problems can now be realized by considering the fact that product costs to the customer depend on transportation as well as production costs. It would be perfectly possible to take the production levels found by the above LP model and find the shipment schedule that would minimize transportation costs. However, the result would only be suboptimum. To find the overall optimum, the LP model must be modified to include both production and transportation.

Instead of one activity representing the production of each product at each plant, there would be one activity representing each customer with a demand for that product. For instance, if there are three customers for the first oil product, then instead of one variable for plant A (AL1) and one variable for plant B (BL1) there would be three variables for each plant (AL11, AL12, AL13, BL11, BL12, and BL13). The coefficients of AL11, AL12, and AL13, in the objective function would differ from the previous coefficient of AL1 only by the corresponding unit transportation cost. (This will vary, depending on who pays for transportation.) Instead of one demand constraint for this product, there would now be one for each customer. For instance, the demand constraint representing the first customer for the first oil product would be

$$AL11 + BL11 \leqslant DML11.$$

Some of the possible outputs of an LP production-distribution model are the expected values of:

Maximum contribution
Total cost and revenue breakdown

SECTION 1 - ROWS

NUMBER	...ROW..	AT	...ACTIVITY...	SLACK ACTIVITY	..LOWER LIMIT.	..UPPER LIMIT.	.DUAL ACTIVITY
1	REV	BS	59328.33333	59328.33333-	NONE	NONE	.
2	COST	BS	32261.00000-	32261.00000	NONE	NONE	.
3	OBJ	BS	27067.86000	27067.86000-	NONE	NONE	1.00000
4	BAIL	EQ	.	.	.	.	5.62200-
5	BAIF	EQ	.	.	.	.	1.35300-
6	BARI	EQ	.	.	.	.	3.80165-
7	BALF	UL	.	.	NONE	.	1.25815-
8	KAL1	BS	420.00000	1080.00000	NONE	1500.00000	.
A 9	KAL2	UL	1500.00000	.	NONE	1500.00000	.
10	KAF1	BS	535.00000	215.00000	NONE	750.00000	.
11	KAF2	BS	478.33333	271.66667	NONE	750.00000	.
12	KALIP	BS	2133.33333	366.66667	NONE	2500.00000	.
13	KAFIP	BS	1066.66667	183.33333	NONE	1250.00000	.
14	KARM	UL	4000.00000	.	NONE	4000.00000	3.04132-
15	BBIL	EQ	.	.	.	.	4.91800-
16	BBIF	EQ	.	.	.	.	1.55800-
17	BBRI	EQ	.	.	.	.	1.48010-
18	BBLF	BS	400.00000-	400.00000	NONE	.	.
19	KBL1	BS	945.00000	55.00000	NONE	1000.00000	.
20	KBL2	BS	500.00000	500.00000	NONE	1000.00000	.
21	KBF1	BS	665.00000	335.00000	NONE	1000.00000	.
22	KBLIP	UL	1700.00000	.	NONE	1700.00000	2.70020-
23	KBFIP	BS	700.00000	400.00000	NONE	1100.00000	.
24	KBRM	UL	3000.00000	.	NONE	3000.00000	1.18408-
25	DL1	BS	1365.00000	635.00000	NONE	2000.00000	.
26	DL2	UL	2000.00000	.	NONE	2000.00000	2.90000-
27	DF1	UL	1200.00000	.	NONE	1200.00000	.80000-
28	DF2	BS	478.33333	21.66667	NONE	500.00000	.

Fig. 22-4. Listed under ACTIVITY are the optimum values for each row. DUAL ACTIVITY shows the sensitivity of the objective function to each constraint.

SECTION 2 - COLUMNS

NUMBER	.COLUMN.	AT	...ACTIVITY...	..INPUT COST..
29	AL1	BS	420.00000	5.62200
30	AL2	BS	1500.00000	8.52200
31	AF1	BS	535.00000	2.15300
32	AF2	BS	478.33333	1.35300
33	ALIP	BS	2133.33333	.
34	AFIP	BS	1066.66667	.
35	ARM	BS	4000.00000	.
36	BL1	BS	945.00000	4.91800
37	BL2	BS	500.00000	7.81800
38	BF1	BS	665.00000	2.35800
39	BLIP	BS	1700.00000	.
40	BFIP	BS	700.00000	.
41	BRM	BS	3[illegible].00000	.

Fig. 22-5. ACTIVITY listing shows the optimum activity level for each variable.

Production levels for each product
Raw materials requirement
Shipments schedule
Process usage
Unfilled demands
Shadow prices for each process
Shadow prices for additional demands.

For this example, these items can be found in the basic computer output shown in Figs. 22-4 and 22-5, but for a large model the output can be voluminous. Also much of the output, such as row and activity names, will be in coded form and will be unintelligible until decoded. The computer output will usually give values to several decimal places. It is usually ridiculous to assume such accuracy, and values should be rounded off.

In addition, certain members of management may be interested in only a small part of the output. For this purpose it is usually necessary to prepare a management report or reports. A FORTRAN program can be written so that the reports will be automatically generated, given the output of the LP computer code as input.

Figure 22-6 is a possible management report for the LP model of Fig. 22-2. A shipment schedule is not given since distribution was not considered in this model. Due to rounding off, there may be slight variations from the original computer output.

Some of the practical problems involved in the formulation and implementation of a product-distribution model are:

Production. What level of detail should be used in modeling the plants? What processes should be included? Should products be grouped according to process?

A. Maximum Contribution ($/Period)

$59,326. Revenue
–32,261. Costs
$27,065. Maximum Contribution

B. Sales Volume (100 pounds/period) and Revenue ($/period) Report

Product	Expected Sales	Unit Price	Revenue	Forecasted Demand	Unfulfilled Demand	Shadow Price
L1	1365	$12.00	$16,380	2000	635	0.00
L2	2000	15.00	30,000	2000	0	2.90
F1	1200	8.00	9,600	1200	0	0.80
F2	478	7.00	3,346	500	22	0.00
			$59,326			

C. Processing Usage (100 pounds/period) and Cost ($/period) Report

Process	Expected Usage	Capacity	Unit Processing Cost	Processing Cost	Excess Capacity	Shadow Price
AL1	420	1500	$1.10	$ 462.	1080	0
AL2	1500	1500	1.20	1,800.	0	0
AF1	535	750	.90	481.	215	0
AF2	478	750	.70	335.	272	0
ALIP	2133	2500	1.00	2,133.	366	0
AFIP	1067	1250	.95	1,014.	183	0
ARM	4000	4000	.50	2,000.	0	3.04
				$ 8,225.		
BL1	945	1000	1.20	1,134.	55	0
BL2	500	1000	1.30	650.	500	0
BF1	665	1000	.80	532.	335	0
BLIP	1700	1700	1.00	1,700.	0	2.70
BFIP	700	1100	.60	420.	400	0
BRM	3000	3000	.60	1,800.	0	1.18
				$ 6,236.		
				$14,461.		

D. Raw Material Requirements (100 pounds/period) and Cost ($/period) Report

Plant	Requirements	Unit Cost	Raw Material Cost
A	4000	2.50	$10,000
B	3000	2.60	7,800
			$17,800

Fig. 22-6. A typical management report.

E. Production Report (100's pounds/period)

Product	Plant A	Plant B	Total
L1	420.	945.	1365.
L2	1500.	500.	2000.
F1	535.	665.	1200.
F2	478.	X	478.

Fig. 22-6. (cont'd.)

Distribution. Should customers be lumped together into regions? What are appropriate regions?

Accounting. Are production costs broken down according to any rational system? How can the appropriate costs be obtained? How should the raw material be costed? How should by-products be costed?

Marketing. How can reasonable demand forecasts be obtained? Should products be grouped according to function, type of customer, etc.? What processes should be used?

Market Research. Are changes in the product line foreseen?

Finance. What are the costs of changes in production facilities? Are new facilities proposed?

Data Processing Systems. Is the necessary input data available in a readily available form? What systems work will be required?

Computer Facilities. What in-house facilities are available? What outside facilities are available?

Personnel. What personnel are available? What is their experience? What are the contacts and availability of help in the above functional areas? Is the proposed completion data reasonable?

A linear programming model can be useful in aiding both tactical and strategic decison making. However, because it is a model and the output is only an approximation, it should be used only as a guide. Knowledge of both the possible uses and limitations of the model is also necessary. One of the greatest benefits of formulating and implementing a model is often the insight gained into the operations of the firm.

Make the model as compact as possible. Try to group products according to similar processing requirements or similar marketing charactersistics, also try to group customers. Avoid unimportant constraints. This is extremely important if the model is ever going to be implemented.

Formulating a model requires a long-term commitment of resources. Estimates must be realistic. Personnel in several functional areas should be assigned, if only part-time. Even after the model is completed, personnel will be necessary for updating, regular runs, and strategic analyses.

References

(1) Alexander, Thomas, "Computers Can't Solve Everything," *Fortune,* LXXX, Number 5, October 1969.

(2) CEIR *Conference on Mathematical Model Building in Economics and Industry,* Hafner, 1968.

(3) Greene, James H., *Production Control: Systems and Decision,* Richard D. Irwin, Inc., Homewood, Illinois, 1965.

(4) Hadley, George, *Linear Programming,* Addison-Wesley Publishing Company, Reading, Massachusetts, 1962.

(5) Hess, Sidney, "Operations Research in the Chemical and Pharmaceutical Industries," (R.T. Eddison and D.B. Hertz editors). *Progress in Operations Research,* John Wiley and Sons, Inc. New York, 1964.

(6) Hertz, David, *New Power for Management Computer Systems and Management Science,* McGraw-Hill Book Company, New York, 1967.

(7) Sears, G.W., "Petroleum," R. T. Eddison and D.B. Hertz (editors), *Progress in Operations Research,* John Wiley and Sons, Inc., New York, 1964.

(8) Withington, Frederic, *The Real Computer: Its Influence, Uses, and Effects,* McGraw-Hill Book Company, New York, 1969.

23 Plant Sizing for a Seasonal Product Demand Using a Linear Programming Model

by Lawrence D. Vitt

INTRODUCTION

This paper presents a method for determining least-cost scheduling-investment programs for a firm with a seasonal product demand. The basic problems to be analyzed are the sizing and the timing of the firm's capital investments for plant and equipment. In investment appraisals, one of the most difficult problems is to determine the profitability of each alternative investment. The capital investment problem for a firm with a pronounced seasonal demand pattern lends itself to this type of analysis because the firm may substitute extra shift production, overtime production, or seasonal anticipation inventories for plant capacity. Thus, in developing its annual production plan a firm may substitute current production inputs, such as overtime production and seasonal inventory stocks, for capital inputs in the form of buildings and production equipment.

An Investment Analysis Model will be developed which analyzes the substitution process for the capital and the current inputs. For each planning period, the firm's planning horizon, an optimum scheduling-investment program will be developed which minimizes the sum of the current and capital costs. A linear programming model of the firm's production smoothing problem is an important element in the Investment Analysis Model and is used to develop an optimum annual production plan for each alternative level of plant capacity. An optimum annual production

EDITOR'S NOTE: From *The Engineering Economist*, Fall 1968, pp. 25-40. Reprinted by permission of the publisher, the Engineering Economy Division of the American Society for Engineering Education, and author.

plan is defined as a production plan which minimizes the sum of the current production input costs. The cost of the optimum annual production plan will, of course, be affected by the available plant capacity. Thus, for each planning period, alternative levels of plant capacity are evaluated, and the annual capital investment penalty costs and the annual production penalty costs of each capacity level are computed by the Investment Analysis Model.

The operation of the model will be illustrated using the costs, demand data, and capacity data that were developed for a medium-sized manufacturing firm. During the four-year test period, 1961-1964, the firm experienced a significant increase in the demand for its product and was thus a good subject for plant-sizing research.

RELATED RESEARCH IN CAPACITY PLANNING

Many alternative combinations of productive capacity and current operating costs can be used in order to produce a given output. The relationship between current production decisions and capital investment decisions has not been thoroughly analyzed by most economic theorists. A notable exception is Vernon L. Smith [8] who has analyzed the relationship between the theory of investment and the theory of production of the firm.

Using a stock-flow theory of cost and production, Smith analyzed the theoretical nature of the interdependence between short-run current production decisions and long-run investment planning. A production function of the form:

$$y = f(x_1, x_2)$$

was used to analyze the relationship between the current and the capital inputs. This example of the production function has one current output, y, one current input, x_l, and one capital input of "size," x_2. If w_l is the price of the current input, and if w_2 is the price of the capital input, then the total current cost can be expressed as:

$$C = w_1x_1 + w_2x_2$$

The Investment Analysis Model used a production function of this type to analyze the cost of alternative scheduling-investment programs.

A production function for the process of gas transmission was developed by Hollis B. Chenery [2]. In this formulation of the production function, the capital inputs are the compressor capacity and the pipeline capacity. Chenery showed that there is a relationship between capacity and output that is a function of the economies of scale, the discount rate, the planning period, and the rate of increase in demand.

Saletin and Caselli [7] developed a mathematical model for determining the optimum design capacity of a chemical plant. The design of a chemical process presents some interesting problems because there are economies of scale in the initial capital investment and it may be necessary to build another plant in order to satisfy increasing demand requirements. Capital investment costs must be balanced against operating costs and future sales revenues. Similar problems for the determination of the optimum reserve generating capacity for an electric utility firm were analyzed by Arnoff and Chambers [1].

The Relationship Between Capital And Current Inputs for a Seasonal Product Demand

The relationship between the plant capacity and the annual production plan for a firm with a seasonal product demand can be observed by an analysis of three alternative annual production plans: (1) a level production plan, (2) a production plan which follows sales, and (3) the optimum production plan. Plants (1) and (2) represent "extreme" production plans, and each would be expected to incur high production penalty costs.

The level production plan would be one which maintained a constant monthly production rate throughout the year. The major features of this plan are a stable work force, excessive seasonal inventory stocks, and a low investment in plant and equipment. The capacity level would be at an absolute minimum because the annual production requirements are separated into twelve equal monthly increments. However, the seasonal anticipation inventory stocks associated with this plan would be very large, and the firm would incur large inventory carrying costs. A discrepancy between the production level and sales in any month would result in a corresponding increase or decrease in the inventory level.

The major features of the production plan which followed sales are low seasonal inventories, a fluctuating work force, and a large investment in plant and equipment. Seasonal anticipation inventory stocks would not be required because each month's production level would be identical with the sales level for that month. The plant capacity would have to be large enough to satisfy the maximum monthly sales demand during the peak season.

Another alternative is the optimum production plan which would minimize the total cost of the current production inputs, and would satisfy any limitations or constraints which the firm may place on the production smoothing problem. The firm may limit the amount of any current or capital input which can be used during the planning period. For example, there may be a limit on the amount of funds which would be available during the period to finance anticipation inventory stocks or long-term capital investments. An optimum production plan for the planning period must be developed within the scope of these constraints. The plant capacity required for the optimum production plan would normally be a capacity level somewhere between those required for the two "extreme" production plans.

A firm with a minimum investment in plant and equipment would be forced to incur extra production costs, such as inventory carrying costs or overtime penalty costs, in order to satisfy seasonal customer requirements. On the other hand, a firm with excess plant capacity would incur a considerable annual investment cost, but would be able to plan monthly production levels to follow sales and would thus minimize the annual inventory carrying costs. Penalty costs in the form of idle plant capacity and changing production levels have been substituted for the other forms of production penalty costs.

THE PRODUCTION SMOOTHING PROBLEM

The capacity of a firm depends upon the manner in which the capacity is used. The capacity is affected by the intensity with which the equipment is used, the size of the work force, the amount of seasonal inventory stocks, the amount of overtime production, the number of shifts, the amount of subcontracting, and the product mix that is to be produced. The basic elements of the production plan can be combined in many ways in order to meet the monthly product demand. The determination of optimum production plans of this type has been termed, in operations research literature, "the production smoothing problem."

The planning period for the production smoothing problem should be for one full demand cycle, normally one year. The beginning of the planning period should be the end of the previous peak demand period when the demand rate falls below the normal production rate. At this point the firm can develop a new production plan for the next period.

A number of mathematical methods have been developed for solving large-scale production smoothing problems.[1] The simplex method of linear programming was considered to be the most efficient method for solving the large number of production smoothing problems that were developed during this research. The linear programming model was used to determine an optimum annual production plan for each capacity level that was evaluated by the Investment Analysis Model. The research linear programming model was a comprehensive application of the basic Hanssmann-Hess model.

THE LINEAR PROGRAMMING MODEL

The linear programming model of the production smoothing problem sought to minimize the objective function $z = c_1 x_1 \ldots c_r x_r$; where c_j was the cost associated with using one unit of the decision variable x_j. Thus, the production smoothing problem became one of minimizing the total cost of the objective function while satisfying constraints of the form:

$$a_{i1}x_1 + a_{i2}x_2 + \ldots + a_{ir}x_r \; \{\geqslant, =, \leqslant\} \; b_i \quad (i = 1, \ldots, m) \qquad (1)$$

where a_{ij} was the amount of each monthly decision variable x_j which was scheduled in the annual production plan.[2]

Equation (1) was the basic form of the constraints which specified the demand requirements, the operational requirements, and the capacity limitations of the test firm. The total number of monthly decision variables for each annual production plan was $r = 139$, and the total number of constraints for the annual production plan was $m = 164$.

The decision variables x_j for the linear programming model were the monthly production factors which were utilized to satisfy the monthly demand requirements. The monthly demand requirements can be satisfied by using the current month's production, the accumulated seasonal inventory stocks, or both of these factors. These relationships can be expressed as:

$$I_0 + P - I = S \qquad (2)$$

where

I_0 = ending seasonal inventory for the previous month (beginning inventory for the current month)
P = total current month's production
I = ending seasonal inventory for the current month
S = current month's sales requirements

The current month's production (P) for the production smoothing problem was classified in terms of the various types of production which the test firm could use to satisfy its production requirements. The choices available to the test firm were: (1) regular production (first shift), (2) partial overtime (first shift), (3) maximum overtime (first shift), (4) extra shift production, (5) partial overtime (extra shift), and (6) maximum overtime (extra shift). Using these decision variables, the total current month's production (P) can be expressed as:

$$P_r + P_2 + P_3 + P_e + P_4 + P_5 = P \tag{3}$$

where

P_r = regular production for the first shift
P_2 = partial overtime production for the first shift
P_3 = maximum overtime production for the first shift
P_e = regular production for the extra shift
P_4 = partial overtime production for the extra shift
P_5 = maximum overtime production for the extra shift

Equation (2) can now be expressed as:

$$I_0 + P_r + P_2 + P_3 + P_e + P_4 + P_5 - I = S \tag{4}$$

The decision variables in equation (4) were the primary monthly decision variables of the linear programming model. A twelve-month production smoothing program can be developed by "linking" together twelve equations of the type shown in equation (4). The basic "link" is the seasonal inventory—the ending inventory for one month becomes the beginning inventory for the following month.[3]

Two additional decision variables were developed from the primary variables. These decision variables were the amount that the current month's production level had increased or decreased from the previous month. The penalty costs for these decision variables were associated with the costs of changing the work force level. Therefore, these decision variables were developed from changing levels of regular production for the first shift and for the extra shift. Overtime production was not considered when computing changes in the work force level because the use of overtime production increases the effective production capacity with changing the actual size of the work force. Thus,

$$P_r + P_e - P_{ro} - P_{eo} = L^+ \tag{5}$$

$$P_{ro} + P_{eo} - P_r - P_e = L^- \tag{6}$$

where

L^+ = amount that the production level has increased
L^- = amount that the production level has decreased
P_{ro} = regular first shift production for the previous month
P_{eo} = regular extra shift production for the previous month
P_r = regular first shift production for the current month
P_e = regular extra shift production for the current month

After equations (4), (5) and (6) had been used to define the major decision variables, additional constraints were added which limited the amount of production that could be scheduled each month for each alternative level of plant capacity. These constraints took the form shown in Table 23-1.

Table 23-1

Constraint	Function
$P_{ri} \leqslant P_{ri}$ max.	Limit on regular production/month
$P_{2i} \leqslant P_{2i}$ max.	Limit on partial overtime/month
$P_{3i} \leqslant P_{3i}$ max.	Limit on maximum overtime/month
$P_{ei} \leqslant P_{ei}$ max.	Limit on extra shift production/month
$P_{4i} \leqslant P_{4i}$ max.	Limit on partial overtime (ES)/month
$P_{5i} \leqslant P_{5i}$ max.	Limit on maximum overtime (ES)/month

The unit of measurement for each constraint was the value of manufactured goods that could be produced each month using the specified type of productive capacity. These constraints for the linear programming model were revised for each alternative level of capital investment that was evaluated. The adjustments made in the major capacity constraints for four sample capacity levels are shown in Table 23-2.

Table 23-2 Capacity Limits for Four Sample Plant Capacities (000 omitted)

Capacity Rating	P_{ri} Max.	P_{2i} Max.	P_{3i} Max.	P_{ei} Max.	P_{4i} Max.	P_{5i} Max.
60,000	21.0	3.0	3.7	9.4	.6	.9
75,000	33.0	4.6	6.0	14.8	.9	1.5
90,000	47.0	6.6	9.9	21.1	1.3	2.5
105,000	54.0	7.5	11.7	24.3	1.5	2.9

Figure 23-1 presents a portion of the simplex linear programming matrix. This matrix shows the constraint equations used for one month of the production program. Changes in the "right-hand side requirements vector" were made whenever the capacity level was changed and whenever a new planning period was being analyzed. The latter type of change affected only the monthly product demand requirement and the limit on the total seasonal inventory.

	November			December											Requirements		
Variable	I	P_r	P_e	I	P_r	P_2	P_3	P_e	P_4	P_5	L^+	L^-	S_1	S_2			
Cost ($)				1.5	0	11.4	13.0	4.5	15.9	17.5	2.5	3.0	0	0		Amount	Type
	1			−1	1	1	1	1	1	1					=	30,766	Sales
		−1	−1		1			1			−1		1		=	0	Determine L^+
		1	1		−1			−1				−1		1	=	0	Determine L^-
				1											$\leqslant$	42,000	Max. Inventory
					1			1							$\geqslant$	12,000	Min. Prod/Mo.
					1										$\leqslant$	21,000	Max. P_r/Month
						1									$\leqslant$	2,940	Max. P_2/Month
							1								$\leqslant$	3,770	Max. P_3/Month
								1							$\leqslant$	9,450	Max. P_e/Month
									1						$\leqslant$	589	Max. P_4/Month
										1					$\leqslant$	942	Max. P_5/Month
											1				$\leqslant$	6,090	Max. L^+/Month
												1			$\leqslant$	6,090	Max. L^-/Month

Fig. 23-1 Sample Linear Programming Matrix for One Month (1961 Planning Period and a Capacity Rating of 60,000)

COST ELEMENTS FOR THE LINEAR PROGRAMMING MODEL

A common unit of measurement was selected which could be related to production schedules, production capacities, and production costs. The manufacturing cost of the goods produced was the unit of measurement selected. Table 23-3 presents the cost elements for the linear programming model.

Table 23-3 Cost per $100 of Product Produced

Variable		Cost
Regular Production	(P_r)	$ 0.00
Partial Overtime	(P_2)	11.40
Maximum Overtime	(P_3)	13.00
Extra Shift Production	(P_e)	4.50
Partial E.S. Overtime	(P_4)	15.90
Maximum E.S. Overtime	(P_5)	17.50
Hiring	(L^+)	2.50
Layoff	(L^-)	3.00
Inventory	(I)	1.50

The production cost are incremental cost based upon the cost of regular production. The most economical manner of producing the product would be to utilize the first shift productive capacity and not to resort to overtime production. The inventory cost is the cost of holding the accumulated seasonal inventory for one month. The total cost of a twelve-month production smoothing problem is the sum of the monthly production and inventory costs.

CAPITAL INVESTMENT COSTS

An annual capital investment cost was developed for the test firm which reflected the annual cost of each alternative level of plant capacity. The annual investment costs were developed as a percentage of the original cost of the production equipment and the manufacturing building. Perhaps another way of looking at this cost would be to ask: How much would we save if we postponed the plant expansion for another year? Once an investment is made in a capital asset, a computed penalty cost would be incurred each year that the firm owns the asset. If the asset is sold at some future date, the penalty cost would no longer be incurred. The annual cost of capital was the major cost element. The annual costs of maintenance and repairs, taxes, insurance, and depreciation of the asset were the other cost elements.

One of the major problems of this research was to determine the total investment in plant and equipment that would be required for each alternative level of plant capacity. These data were developed from an analysis of historical capacity-investment relationships of the test firm.

THE PLANNING HORIZON

Capital investment programs must be evaluated over a specified time period known as the planning horizon. The planning horizon would be different for each firm and would be influenced by such factors as the growth rate of the firm, the effect of the business cycle on the firm's sales, the size and cost of the capacity expansions, the expected life of the capital goods, and the degree of uncertainty associated with the demand forecasts.

A firm which expects sales to increase steadily from year to year, and which is able to make its capacity expansions in relatively small increments, would be able to plan its production scheduling-investment program using a fairly short planning horizon. This was the case with the test firm, and the specific conditions that were present indicated that a planning horizon of one year would suffice.

If, for example, sales in year 2 are higher than in year 1, we would expect the total cost of the scheduling-investment program to be higher in year 2. We would also expect the capacity requirements to be higher in year 2. In this example, the relevant investment decision in year 1 is whether to increase the plant capacity now or to postpone the investment for one year.

One year later an increment of expansion, at least this large, would have to be made in order to satisfy the higher level of sales. The planning horizon in this example is a one-year planning period.

OPERATION OF THE INVESTMENT ANALYSIS MODEL

The objective of the capacity analysis for the test firm, using the scheduling-investment model, was to determine the optimum level of plant capacity for each planning period. The total cost of each annual scheduling-investment program was composed of two elements: the annual production penalty cost and the annual capital investment penalty cost. Both cost elements depended upon the level of plant capacity that was being evaluated. For each level of plant capacity that was evaluated there was an optimum production plan which minimized the sum of the annual production penalty costs. These production penalty costs were computed using the linear programming model of the firm's production smoothing problem. For each level of plant capacity there was a computed annual capital investment penalty cost. Thus, for each level of plant capacity there was a total annual program cost which consisted of the sum of the current and the capital penalty costs.

The best annual production plan varied with each alternative level of plant capacity that was evaluated. Higher levels of plant capacity produced annual production plans with lower production penalty costs but with higher annual capital investment penalty costs. Therefore, the operating procedure for determining the optimum scheduling-investment program at any point in time consisted of sèlecting several alternative levels of plant capacity and computing the total annual program cost for each level of capacity. The lowest annual program cost identified the optimum scheduling-investment for each planning period.

Each annual production plan was developed for a specific annual sales requirement and for a specific capacity rating. Thus, a new set of scheduling-investment programs was required for each planning period that was analyzed, i.e., for each year of the test period.

The procedure that was used to prepare the cost data for each scheduling-investment program was:

(1) determine an optimum annual production plan using the linear programming model.
(2) compute the annual production penalty costs
(3) compute the annual investment penalty cost
(4) compute the total annual program cost

The optimum annual production plan for each program was developed within the capacity constraints of each level of plant capacity. An infeasible solution for the production smoothing problem was obtained when the total available production capacity for the entire year was not sufficient to satisfy the annual sales requirements.

RESULTS OBTAINED USING THE INVESTMENT ANALYSIS MODEL

The annual investment costs and the annual productions penalty costs that were developed by the Investment Analysis Model are shown in Table 23-4. From these data it is possible to determine the optimum level of plant capacity for each planning period by selecting the program with the lowest total annual cost. These results can assist the firm in planning the sizing and timing of its capital investments for production equipment and buildings.

The relationships between the annual capital and current costs are perhaps more clearly illustrated in Fig. 23-2. The total cost curve is relatively flat over a significant range of capacity ratings. Because uncertainty is a major factor in an investment analysis, the nature of the total cost curve for each planning period will be of considerable importance to the business firm. Capacity levels below those shown in Fig. 23-2 produced infeasible solutions which meant that the firm could not satisfy all of its demand requirements.

The test results for the 1964 planning period are of special interest because this was a period of rapid growth and expansion for the test firm. During this planning period the model would have been of greatest value to the test firm. A major expansion in plant and equipment was required to meet the 1964 demand requirements. Furthermore, the cost levels for both capital and current penalty costs were much higher in 1964; this meant that the potential cost savings from improved scheduling-investment planning would be much higher than they had been for the previous planning periods.

Once the test firm has determined the actual level of plant capacity it will use for the next planning period, the linear programming model can be used to develop a production program for the period. Aggregate levels of monthly production and inventories will be specified by the optimum production plan.

CONCLUDING REMARKS

A business firm using an Investment Analysis Model can engage in more precise planning and decision making than it could without the model. The annual production plan would be developed more carefully and accurately if one of the major planning constraints, the plant capacity, were consid-

Table 23-4 Cost of Alternative Scheduling-Investment Programs for Each Planning Period

Planning Period	Capacity Rating	Annual Investment Cost	Annual Production Penalty Cost	Total Annual Cost
1961	60,000	$47,499	$ 4,055	$ 51,554*
	65,000	49,111	2,825	51,936
	70,000	50,723	2,140	52,863
	75,000	52,335	1,572	53,907
	80,000	53,947	1,562	55,509
1962	65,000	$49,111	$ 7,449	$ 56,560
	70,000	50,723	5,645	56,368
	75,000	52,335	4,007	56,342*
	80,000	53,947	2,885	56,832
	85,000	57,526	2,546	60,072
	95,000	64,684	2,258	66,942
1963	70,000		Infeasible Solution	
	75,000		Infeasible Solution	
	80,000	$53,947	$13,110	$ 67,057*
	85,000	57,526	9,675	67,201
	90,000	61,105	8,086	69,191
	100,000	68,263	6,338	74,601
	115,000	79,000	4,941	83,941
1964	85,000		Infeasible Solution	
	90,000		Infeasible Solution	
	95,000	$64,684	$31,852	$ 96,536
	100,000	68,263	26,586	94,849*
	105,000	71,841	23,344	95,186
	125,000	86,157	19,817	105,974

*The optimum scheduling-investment program for the planning period.

ered as another resource variable. In a dynamic planning situation, as would be the case when the product demand is increasing rapidly, all the resource inputs should be considered in the planning process.

The scheduling-investment programs for the test firm were developed using a one-year planning horizon, but future investment planning for the test firm, or investment planning for other business firms, may require a longer planning horizon. Longer planning horizons will require longer demand forecasts with a greater amount of uncertainty. The Investment Analysis Model can be used to evaluate the effect of uncertainty on

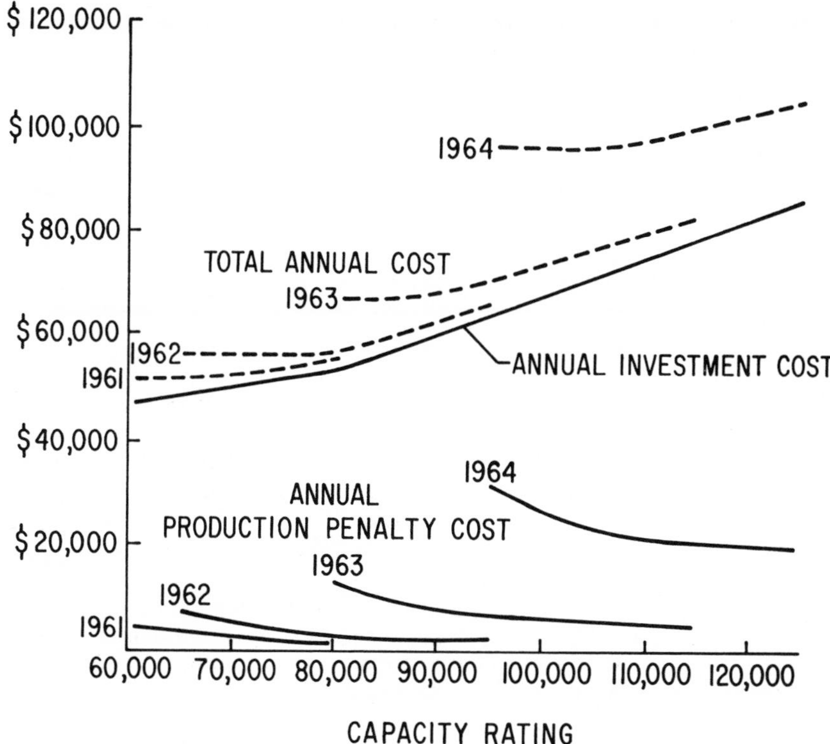

Fig. 23-2. Cost of scheduling-investment programs for alternative levels of plant capacity.

alternative capital investment programs. Longer planning horizons will also require a consideration of the time value of money. Costs or revenues obtained in future time periods may be discounted in order to determine their present value, and the model could be modified to include a discounting procedure for costs or revenues obtained in future time periods.

The annual capital investment costs for the model were based on a computed average increment for capacity expansions. The actual expansions would be in the form of a "step" function, but because the timing of a major investment, such as a building expansion, cannot be precisely determined the use of an average increment appeared to be more appropriate for a planning model.

In research of this type it is important to know how sensitive the results will be to errors made in the development of program cost elements. A sensitivity analysis was conducted, using the research model, to analyze the effect of errors on the total program cost and the plant sizing decisions. The results were relatively insensitive to reasonable errors in estimating the unit-cost elements.[4]

Notes

1. Two well-known methods are the quadratic programming model developed by Holt, Modigliani, Muth, and Simon (see Reference 5) and the simplex linear programming method of Hanssmann and Hess (Reference 4).

2. Linear programming techniques can be used to solve a problem in which the relationships among the decision variables are linear both in the constraints and in the function to be optimized. Linearity can be characterized by multiplicative properties. If a_l is the cost associated with the scheduling of one unit of variable x_l, then the cost of scheduling two units of x_l will be twice that of scheduling only one unit of variable x_l. A comprehensive discussion of linear programming techniques is presented by G. Hadley, *Linear Programming,* Addison-Wesley Publishing Company, Reading, Massachusetts, 1962.

3. A comprehensive presentation of the nature of multistage linear programming problems is provided by George B. Dantzig, "On the Status of Multistage Linear Programming Problems," *Management Science,* October 1959, pp. 53-72.

4. See for example, C.C. Holt, F. Modigliani, J.F. Muth, and H.A. Simon, *Planning Production, Inventories, and Work Force* (Englewood Cliffs, N.J.: Prentice-Hall, Inc., 1960), p. 59. An exploratory analysis of the effects of overestimating cost parameters by 100 percent or underestimating by 50 percent led to decision rules which changed the total cost performance of the model by approximately 11 percent. A more detailed sensitivity analysis of the cost coefficient estimate was performed by C. Van de Panne and P. Bosje, "Sensitivity Analysis of Cost Coefficient Estimates: The Case of Linear Decision Rules for Employment and Production," *Management Science,* October 1962, pp. 82-107.

References

(1) Arnoff, Leonard E., and John C. Chambers, "On the Determination of Optimum Reserve Generating Capacity in an Electric Utility System," *Operations Research,* IV, No. 4, August 1956, pp. 468-480.

(2) Chenery, Hollis B., "Overcapacity and the Acceleration Principle," *Econometrica,* XX, No. 1, January 1952, pp. 1-28.

(3) Coleman, J.R., Jr., S. Smidt, and R. York, "Optimum Plant Design for Seasonal Production," *Management Science,* X, No. 4, July 1964, pp. 778-785.

(4) Hanssmann, Fred, and Sidney W. Hess, "A Linear Programming Approach to Production and Employment Scheduling," *Management Technology,* No. 1, January 1960, pp. 46-51.

(5) Holt, C.C., F. Modigliani, J.P. Muth, and H.A. Simon, *Planning Production, Inventories, and Work Force* (Englewood Cliffs, N.J.: Prentice-Hall, Inc., 1960).

(6) Manne, Alan S., "Capacity Expansion and Probabilistic Growth," *Econometrica,* XXIX, No. 4, October 1961, pp. 632-649.

(7) Saletin, D.I., and A.V. Caselli, "Optimum Design Capacity of New Plants," *Chemical Engineering Progress,* LIX, No. 5, May 1963, pp. 69-75.

(8) Smith, Vernon L., *Investment and Production* (Cambridge, Massachusetts: Harvard University Press, 1961).

24 Application of Linear Programming to Short-Term Financing Decision

by *James C.T. Mao**

I. INTRODUCTION

The technique of linear programming has been studied and used by management scientists for nearly two decades. However, it has only recently been applied to financial decisions, and even this application has been limited to long-term financing and investment decisions. The potential use of the technique for short-term financial decisions was shown for the first time in an article by A. A. Robicheck, D. Teichroew, and J. M. Jones [5] published in 1965. The purpose of this paper is to apply the model developed by these writers (RTJ) to a case study involving the short-term financing decision of a greeting-card business. There are some differences between their model and this one. First, this model is formulated in terms of cumulative variables such as C_i, Q_{ki}, I_{ki}, etc., whereas theirs uses noncumulative variables such as x_i, Y_i z_i, etc. The use of cumulative variables adds to the clarity of exposition. Second, this study discusses imputed values and marginal analysis in a somewhat more extensive way than the RTJ exposition. Since the present financing situation is less complex than that studied by RTJ, we hope that the reader will be able to see more clearly the structure and the workings of the model. The basic

EDITOR'S NOTE: From *The Engineering Economist*, Summer 1968, pp. 221-241. Reprinted by permission of the publisher, the Engineering Economy Division of the American Society for Engineering Education, and author.

*The author is indebted to Mr. B.A. Wallingford for his valuable assistance in the construction of the linear-programming model used in this paper and to Messrs. John Davis and Robert Rene de Cortret for their assistance in executing the model on the computer.

decision, however, remains the same. In essence, the question is how best to finance the seasonal cash needs of a business so as to minimize the firm's cost of financing.

II. THE FANCYCRAFT, INCORPORATED

General Information

Let us consider the short-term financing problem facing the management of the Fancycraft, Inc. Fancycraft is a medium-sized firm engaged in the manufacture of greeting cards and gift wrapping paper. Because of the nature of the greeting-card business, the sales of Fancycraft tend to exhibit pronounced seasonal variations. The company's product line does include certain stable items such as birthday cards, thank-you notes, and wrapping paper which sell fairly uniform rates throughout the year. The bulk of the company's revenue, however, is derived from the sales of items on special occasions such as Christmas, Halloween, Thanksgiving, Easter, and Valentine's Day. The company's sales, therefore, tend to be lowest in the second quarter and highest in the fourth quarter of each year. More specifically, Table 24-1 presents the company's forecast of its monthly sales for the forthcoming year.

Table 24-1 The Sales Forecast of Fancycraft, Inc. for the Next 12 Months

Month	Sales	Month	Sales
January	$183	July	$150
February	183	August	150
March	183	September	150
April	83	October	250
May	83	November	250
June	83	December	250

The manufacture of greeting cards and gift wrapping is a reasonably profitable business. On every dollar of sales, the firm pays fifty cents in production costs divided among the various components as follows: labor, 25 cents; materials, 12.5 cents; cash overhead, 6.25 cents; and depreciation, 6.25 cents. In addition, the firm incurs fixed selling and administrative expenses of $70 per month, and pays taxes and dividends at the rate of 62 percent of its before-tax profits.

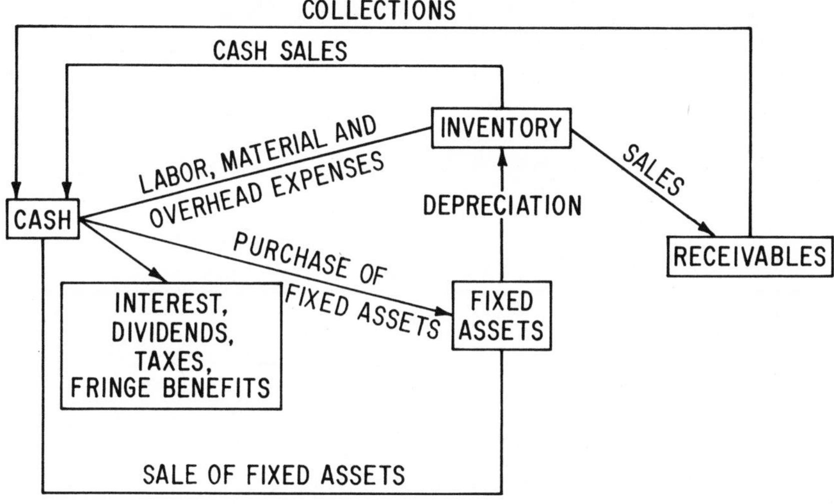

Fig. 24-1. Circular flow of cash.

The Cash Budget

The cash position of a firm is determined by many factors: collection on receivables, cash sales, interest income on securities, payments for materials, labor, and overhead expenses, payments for taxes, dividends, and so on. Cash is converted into inventory which, in turn, becomes accounts receivable, and finally returns in the form of cash. This circular flow is depicted in Fig. 24-1. The arrows indicate the direction of flow. Depending on the relative amounts of cash flowing in and out, the firm experiences a deficit or a surplus. We have assumed that for the year under study, the Fancycraft, Inc., had a cash deficit, which will be financed through short-term sources of funds. Since these sources differ in their cost and flexibility, the particular pattern of cash flow determines which structure of financing will be optimal.

The sales forecast in Table 24-1 provides the basis for deriving the company's cash budget for the next twelve months. (See Table 24-2 and Fig. 24-2.) In deriving this budget, the following assumptions were made regarding payment schedules, terms of sales, rate of capital expenditures, sinking-fund requirements, and so on:

1. Fancycraft, Inc., sells its products on terms of "net 90," meaning that the full amount of a bill is due in 90 days. Thus, sales made in January are collected in April, and those made in February are collected in May.

Table 24-2 The Cash Budget of Fancycraft, Inc. for the Next 12 Months* (in dollars)

Line	Item	Jan.	Feb.	Mar.	Apr.	May	June	July	Aug.	Sept.	Oct.	Nov.	Dec.
	Receipts due to operations:												
1	Accounts receivable	200	200	200	183	183	183	83	83	83	150	150	150
	Disbursements due to operations:												
2	Payments for purchases of materials	23	23	23	10	10	10	18	18	18	31	31	31
3	Labor and cash overhead	25	25	25	47	47	47	78	78	78	57	57	57
4	Selling and administrative expenses	210			210			210			210		
5	Net cash flow due to operations	(58)	**152	152	(84)	126	126	(223)	(13)	(13)	(148)	62	62
6	Change in minimum operating cash balance	28	0	(54)	54	0	(193)	193	0	(118)	118	0	(30)
	Other cash requirements:												
7	Dividends and taxes	0	0	(25)	0	0	(25)	0	0	(25)	0	0	(25)
8	Sinking fund	(20)	0	0	0	0	0	(20)	0	0	0	0	0
9	Purchase of plates	(100)	0	0	0	0	(100)	0	0	0	0	0	0
10	Total cash requirement for period (before interest payments and receipts)	(150)	152	73	(30)	126	(192)	(50)	(13)	(156)	(30)	62	7
11	Cumulative cash requirement (before interest payments and receipts)	(150)	2	75	45	171	(21)	(71)	(84)	(240)	(270)	(208)	(201)

*Key assumptions:

(a) The company's production in any month is always equal to the forecast sales three months hence.

(b) The company has an initial cash balance of $58 and follows a policy of maintaining its month-end cash balance equal to $30 or the net drain during the following month, whichever is larger.

(c) Sales, made on terms of "net 90," equaled $200 monthly during the final quarter of the preceding year.

**In lines 5 to 11, parenthetical figures denote cash requirements which need to be financed.

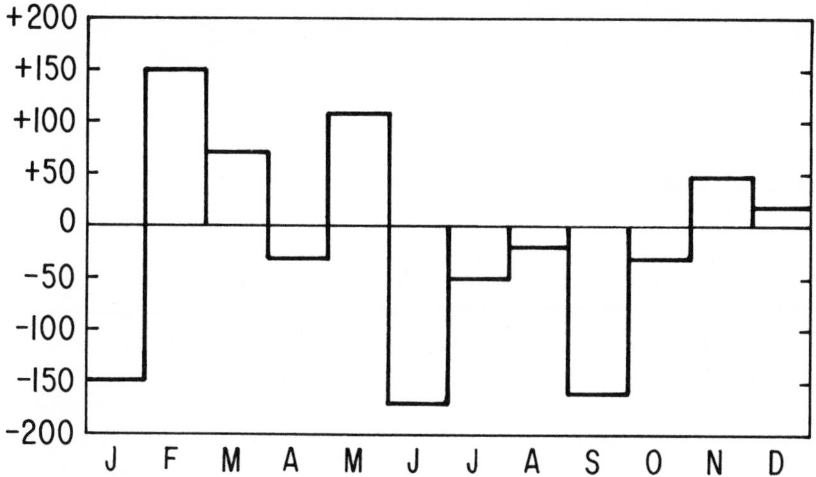

Fig. 24-2. The cash budget of Fancycraft, Inc. (+ indicates inflow and - indicates outflow.)

2. The company's production policy is such that its inventory at the end of a month is always equal to the forecast sales during the next three months.

3. Labor and cash overhead are paid for in cash in the month during which these services are exhausted in the production process, whereas the costs of materials are paid for on terms of "net 90."

4. Selling and administrative expenses are paid for in cash once every 90 days in January, April, July, and October.

5. Dividends and taxes are paid quarterly in March, June, September, and December.

6. The company is annually required to make two sinking-fund payments of $20 each, payable in January and July.

7. The production department has on order two $100 plates, of which one is to be delivered in January and the other in June. The company has the option of paying for these plates on an installment plan calling for monthly payments throughout the year. The exact terms of this alternative will be explained later under the heading of "Sources of Financing."

8. At this moment (December 31), the balance sheet of the company shows the following current assets and liabilities:

Cash	$ 58	Accounts Payable	$ 69
Accounts Receivable	600	Accrued Expenses	210
Inventories	300		

9. The company has a policy of maintaining its month-end cash balance equal to $30 or the net drain during the following month, whichever amount is larger.

10. All borrowing transactions and all interest and principal repayments take place only at the beginning of each month.

11. Finally the company had monthly sales of \$200 during the last quarter of the preceding year.

Source of Funds

To meet the anticipated cash drains, the Fancycraft, Inc., is assumed to have three short-term financing alternatives: (1) line of credit, (2) commercial paper, and (3) installment financing.

Line of Credit—The company can borrow a maximum of \$140 under the line-of-credit arrangement at an annual interest rate of 6 percent per annum. For simplicity of analysis, the amount borrowed at the beginning of any month is assumed to be repayable with interest at the beginning of the following month. Finally, the normal cash balance of the company is regarded to be sufficient for meeting the bank's compensating balance requirement.

Commercial Paper—The company can borrow a maximum of \$120 by issuing 90-day commercial paper bearing an annual interest rate of 5 percent. The interest charges are assumed to be payable monthly rather than at the time of borrowing as is the case in practice. Because of the 90-day maturity, the amount borrowed at the beginning of each month cannot be repaid until the beginning of the third succeeding month. Surplus funds in any month are invested at the beginning of that month in government securities at an interest rate of 4.4 percent per annum.

Installment Financing—The cash budget reveals that the company plans to purchase a \$100 plate in January. The manufacturer of this plate has offered to finance the purchase with a 6-month installment loan up to the price of the plate. If Fancycraft, Inc. decides to borrow z dollars ($z \leqslant \$100$), the loan agreement would call for six monthly payments of $\$z/6(1.0126)$ each, commencing on February 1st. A similar financing arrangement is available to the Fancycraft, Inc. for its second purchase of a plate in June.

Given these three sources of funds, what is the pattern of financing that will minimize the total interest expense during the next 12-month period? This is the short-term financing decision which the management of Fancycraft, Inc. now faces.

III. A LINEAR PROGRAMMING MODEL OF OPTIMAL SHORT-TERM FINANCING

In this section we shall solve the above short-term financing problem by adapting the linear-programming model which Robicheck, Teichroew, and

Jones [5] presented in their article. The presentation will start with the definition of symbols, to be followed by a discussion of the constraints in the problem and of the objective function which the firm wishes to minimize.

Definition of Symbols

x_i = amount of financing through line of credit at the beginning of period i. ($i = 1, 2, \ldots, 12$)

y_i = amount of commercial paper sold at the beginning of period i. ($i = 1, 2, \ldots, 12$)

z_1 = amount of installment financing obtained at the beginning of period *1*.

z_2 = amount of installment financing obtained at the beginning of period *6*.

s_j = slack (or surplus) variable associated with the jth constraint.

C_i = cumulative cash requirement in period i.

Q_{ki} = total outstanding debt (excluding accrued interest) in period i from source k, where $k = 1$ denotes line of credit, $k = 2$ denotes commercial paper, $k = 3$ denotes installment financing in January, and $k = 4$ denotes installment financing in June.

I_{ki} = cumulative interest payments from period *1* to period i on money borrowed from source k, where k ($= 1, 2, 3, 4$) has the same meaning as above.

I_{5i} = cumulative interest receipts from period *1* to period i on surplus funds invested in government securities.

Constraints of the Problem

Constraint on Line of Credit. Under the line-of-credit arrangement, the amount of borrowing at any moment cannot exceed \$140. This statement can be symbolically expressed

$$Q_{1i} \leqslant \$140 \quad (i = 1, 2, \ldots, 12) \tag{1}$$

For convenience of analysis, we shall assume that the company always repays its bank loan at the beginning of the following month. If the funds continue to be needed, then a new loan is taken out immediately after the old one has been paid off. This means that total bank loan outstanding during a given period is exactly equal to the loan actually taken out at the beginning of that period. Hence, constraint (1) can be written alternatively as:

$$x_i + s_i = \$140 \quad (i = 1, 2, \ldots, 12) \tag{2}$$

where each s_i is a slack variable that converts an inequality into an equality. These twelve equations, one for each of the twelve months in the planning period, fully characterizes the maximum limit on bank credit.

Constraint on Commercial Paper. The total amount of commercial paper outstanding during any given month cannot exceed \$120:

$$Q_{2i} \leq \$120 \quad (i = 1, 2, \ldots, 12) \tag{3}$$

Since all commercial paper issued by this company matures in 90 days, the total amount of commercial paper outstanding in period i $(i \geq 3)$ is made up of paper issued in periods $i - 2$, $i - 1$, and i. Hence, constraint (3) can be written alternatively as:

$$y_i + y_{i-1} + y_{i-2} + s_{i+10} = \$120 \quad (i = 3, 4, \ldots, 12) \tag{4}$$

where each s_{i+10} is a slack variable in one of the above equations. Note that $y_1 + y_2 + y_3 \leq 120$ implies that y_1 and y_2 are both less than \$120. Therefore, constraints (4) also limit the total amount of commercial paper in periods 1 and 2 to be less than \$120. These ten equations, one for each of the last ten months in the planning period, fully characterize the maximum limit on the issuance of commercial paper.

Constraint on Installment Financing. Since the installment loan cannot exceed the price of the plate, we limit the amount of each installment financing transaction to \$100:

$$\left.\begin{aligned} z_1 &\leq \$100 \\ z_2 &\leq \$100 \end{aligned}\right\} \tag{5}$$

Or, equivalently:

$$\left.\begin{aligned} z_1 + s_{23} &= \$100 \\ z_2 + s_{24} &= \$100 \end{aligned}\right\} \tag{6}$$

where s_{23} and s_{24} are the slack variables in the above equations. The smaller number of equations in (6) reflect the fact that there are only two occasions during the year for obtaining installment financing.

The Cash Budget Constraint. It will be recalled that the cumulative cash requirement, as presented in line 11 of Table 24-2, was arrived at before taking into account the interest payment on borrowed funds and the interest receipts on surplus funds. When interest payments and receipts are included, the cash budget constraint states that during any month the total outstanding borrowing from all sources must be equal to or greater than the cumulative cash requirement (line 11 of Table 24-2) plus the cumulative interest payments on all types of borrowing minus the cumulative receipts on surplus funds. This constraint can be symbolically expressed:

$$Q_{1i} + Q_{2i} + Q_{3i} + Q_{4i} \geqslant C_i + I_{1i} + I_{2i} + I_{3i} + I_{4i} - I_{5i} \ (i = 1, 2, \ldots, 12) \qquad (7)$$

Or, equivalently:

$$\sum_{k=1}^{4} Q_{ki} - s_{24+i} = C_i + \sum_{k=1}^{4} I_{ki} - I_{5i} \ (i = 1, 2, \ldots, 12) \qquad (8)$$

where s_{24+i} are the surplus variables in the above equations. We proceed next to express this constraint in terms of noncumulative variables such as x_i, y_i, z_i etc.

Recall that total bank loan outstanding during a given period is exactly equal to the loan actually taken out at the beginning of that period. Therefore,

$$Q_{1i} = x_i \quad (i = 1, 2, \ldots, 12) \qquad (9)$$

We know also that because of the fixed maturity of commercial paper, the total amount of commercial paper outstanding during any given period is given by the expression

$$Q_{2i} = \begin{cases} y_1 & \text{for } i = 1 \\ y_1 + y_2 & \text{for } i = 2 \\ y_i + y_{i-1} + y_{i-2} & \text{for } i \geqslant 3 \end{cases} \qquad (10)$$

Finally, since the installment contract requires that the principal be fully amortized in six equal monthly payments, the amount of installment credit outstanding during any month is given by the expression

$$Q_{3i} = \begin{cases} z_1 - \frac{z_1}{6}(i-1) & \text{for } i \leqslant 6 \\ 0 & \text{for } i > 6 \end{cases} \qquad (11)$$

$$Q_{4i} = \begin{cases} z_2 - \frac{z_2}{6}(i-6) & \text{for } i \geqslant 6 \\ 0 & \text{for } i < 6 \end{cases} \qquad (12)$$

where all terms are as defined above.

In deriving the expression for the cumulative interest payments, we shall assume that the firm pays its interest on the first of each month on the debt that was outstanding the previous month. Accordingly, the cumulative interest payments on bank loans in any month i is calculated as follows:

$$I_{1i} = \begin{cases} 0 & \text{for } i = 1 \\ \sum_{j=1}^{i-1} x_j \ (.005) & \text{for } i > 1 \end{cases} \tag{13}$$

where *.005* is the monthly interest rate on bank borrowings.

The formula for the cumulative interest payments on commercial paper takes only a little longer to derive. In general, with the maturity of commercial paper fixed at 90 days, the firm pays interest in any given month on commercial paper issued during the three preceding months. However, since the company had no commercial paper outstanding at the end of previous December, it pays no interest until February. Moreover, the interest payments in February are limited to commercial paper issued in January, and payments in March are limited to commercial paper issued in January and February. These considerations, together with the assumed 5 percent annual interest rate, lead to the following formula for calculating interest payments on commercial paper:

$$I_{2i} = \begin{cases} 0 & \text{for } i = 1 \\ .0042\, y_1 & \text{for } i = 2 \\ .0084\, y_1 + .0042\, y_2 & \text{for } i = 3 \\ .0126 \sum_{j=1}^{i-3} y_j + .0084\, y_{i-2} + .0042\, y_{i-1} & \text{for } i \geqslant 4 \end{cases} \tag{14}$$

Similarly, it can be shown that the interest payments on installment financing are given by the formulas:

$$I_{3i} = \begin{cases} 0 & \text{for } i = 1 \\ (.00243)(i-1)z_1 & \text{for } 1 < i \leqslant 6 \\ (.0146)z_1 & \text{for } i > 6 \end{cases} \tag{15}$$

$$I_{4i} = \begin{cases} 0 & \text{for } i \leqslant 6 \\ (.00243)(i-6)z_2 & \text{for } i > 6 \end{cases} \tag{16}$$

In addition to paying interest on borrowed funds, the company also receives interest on surplus funds which it invests in government securities. Since s_{24+i}, the surplus variable in expression (8) is by definition equal to the surplus funds in period i, .0037 s_{24+i} is the interest receipts in period $i+1$. The cumulative interest receipts from period 1 to period i, I_{5i}, is accordingly given by the formula:

$$I_{5i} = \begin{cases} 0 & \text{for } i = 1 \\ .0037 \sum_{j=1}^{i-1} s_{24+j} & \text{for } i > 1 \end{cases} \tag{17}$$

Now, if expressions (9) to (17) are substituted into the equations in (8), we get, upon simplification, the following set of new equations:

$$\left.\begin{array}{l}
x_1 + y_1 + z_1 - s_{25} = C_1 \\
-.005\,x_1 + x_2 + .9958\,y_1 + y_2 + .8309\,z_1 + .0037\,s_{25} - s_{26} = C_2 \\
-.005\,x_1 - .005x_2 + x_3 + .9916\,y_1 + .9958\,y_2 + y_3 + .6618\,z_1 + .0037\,s_{25} \\
\qquad + .0037\,s_{26} - s_{27} = C_3 \\
-.005 \sum_{j=1}^{i-1} x_j + x_i - \sum_{j=1}^{i-3} (.0126)y_j + .9916\,y_{i-2} + .9958\,y_{i-1} + y_i \\
\qquad + z_1\,[1 - .1691\,(i-1)] + (.0037) \sum_{j=1}^{i-1} s_{24+j} - s_{24+i} \\
\qquad \text{(for } i = 4, 5\text{)} \qquad = C_i \\
-.005 \sum_{j=1}^{i-1} x_j + x_i - \sum_{j=1}^{i-3} (.0126)y_j + .9916\,y_{i-2} + .9958_{i-1} + y_i \\
\qquad + z_1[1 - .15455\,(i-1)] + z_2[1 - .1691\,(i-6)] + .0037 \sum_{j=1}^{i-1} s_{24+j} \\
\qquad - s_{24+i} = C_i \\
\qquad \text{(for } i = 6\text{)} \\
-.005 \sum_{j=1}^{i-1} x_j + x_i - 0.0126 \sum_{j=1}^{i-3} y_j + .9916\,y_{i-2} + .9958\,y_{i-1} + y_i - 0.0146\,z_1 \\
\qquad + [1 - .1691\,(i-6)]z_2 + .0037 \sum_{j=1}^{i-1} s_{24+j} - s_{24+i} = C_i \\
\qquad \text{(for } i = 7, 8, \ldots, 12\text{)}
\end{array}\right\} \tag{18}$$

where the c_i's have values as given in line 11 of Table 24-2. These twelve equations, one for each of the twelve months in the planning period, fully characterize the cash budget constraint.

The Objective Function

The objective of the firm is to finance its short-term fund requirements in such a way as to minimize its net interest cost during the next twelve months. The interest payments on bank loans, commercial paper, and installment financing are measured respectively by $.005 \sum_{i=1}^{12} x_i$, $.0126 \sum_{i=1}^{12} y_i$, and $.0146(z_1 + z_2)$, where *.005* is the monthly interest rate on back loans, *.0126* is the quarterly interest on commercial paper, and *.0146* is the semi-annual rate on installment financing.[1] The total interest receipts on surplus funds invested in government securities is given by the expression $.0037 \sum_{i=1}^{12} s_{24+i}$, where *.0037* is the monthly interest rate on government securities. Accordingly, the objective of the firm is contained in the statement:

$$\text{Minimize } f = .005 \sum_{i=1}^{12} x_i + .0126 \sum_{i=1}^{12} y_i + .0146\,(z_1 + z_2) - \\ - .0037 \sum_{i=1}^{12} s_{24+i} \tag{19}$$

The complete linear-programming problem, therefore, can now be summarized: Find the value of 62 variables:

x_i $(i = 1, 2, \ldots, 12)$
y_i $(i = 1, 2, \ldots, 12)$
z_i $(i = 1, 2)$
s_i $(i = 1, 1, \ldots, 36)$

subject to the maximum borrowing constraints (2), (4) and (6) consisting of 24 equations; the cash budget constraints (18) consisting of 12 equations; the nonnegativity conditions on all the variables; and which at the same time minimize the objective function (19).

IV. THE OPTIMAL SOLUTION AND ITS INTERPRETATION

Using the "revised simplex algorithm," the IBM 7090 computer solved the above linear programming problem in slightly less than two minutes.

The Optimal Solution

Table 24-3 presents the optimal solution with details on the financing transactions, net interest charges, and the amount of cash requirements financed. Thus, in order to meet the cash requirements of $150 in January, the optimal solution calls for borrowing $140 from the bank and $10 in the commercial paper market. In February, since the company has a cash surplus of $151.26 after the payment of interest, the optimal solution calls for the reduction of $140 in bank loan and the acquisition of $11.26 in government securities. The transactions in all subsequent months can be

Table 24-3. The Optimal Pattern of Financing for the Fancycraft, Inc.* (In dollars)

	Bank Credit			Commercial Paper			Installment Financing			Holdings of Government Securities			Net Interest Charges**		
Month	New Borrowing	Repayment of Principal	Amount Outstanding	New Borrowing	Repayment of Principal	Amount Outstanding	New Borrowing	Repayment of Principal	Amount Outstanding	Purchases	Sales	Amount Held	Payments	Receipts	Cash Requirement Financed (F) or Cash Surplus Invested (I)†
Jan.	140.00		140.00	10.00		10.00									150.00 (F)
Feb.		140.00				10.00				11.26		11.26	0.74		152.00 (I)
March						10.00				73.00		84.26			73.00 (I)
April					10.00						39.73	44.53		0.27	30.00 (F)
May										126.16		170.69		0.16	126.00 (I)
June							34.28		34.28		157.09	13.60		0.63	192.00 (F)
July				61.13		61.13		5.71	28.57	5.39		18.98	0.03		50.00 (F)
Aug.						61.13		5.71	22.85		18.98		0.27		13.00 (F)
Sept.	106.78		106.78	55.27		116.40		5.71	17.14				0.34		156.00 (F)
Oct.	140.00	106.78	140.00	64.73	61.13	120.00		5.71	11.42				1.10		30.00 (F)
Nov.	85.00	140.00	85.00			120.00		5.71	5.71				1.28		62.00 (I)
Dec.	140.00	85.00	140.00		55.27	64.73		5.71					1.00		7.00 (I)

*All blank cells indicate a value of zero.

**Computed in accordance with assumptions in the text. The interest payments on December borrowings are not shown in this table, since they are not payable until January 1.

†Cash requirements financed = Σ (new borrowings) − Σ (repayments) − Purchases of government securities + sale of government securities − net interest payments + net interest receipts. This sum, if negative, is designated as cash surplus invested.

similarly interpreted. Summing the net interest payments over the 12-month period, we find that the net interest cost associated with the optimal solution is equal to $4.70.

To see the logic of the optimal solution, let us recall that (1) bank credit costs .005 per month and is repayable in one month, (2) commercial paper costs .0043 per month and is repayable in three months, and (3) installment financing costs .0048 per month (effectively) and is repaid in six monthly installments. Any surplus funds in the business are invested in government securities at a return of only .0037 per month. Given these interest rates and repayment schedules, the following two financing principles appear to be sound. First, the firm should rely on commercial banks for meeting cash needs that last only one month, and should rely on commercial paper and/or installment financing for meeting cash needs that last three months or longer. Second, because of the relatively low return on government securities, the firm should in general sell its holdings of government securities before undertaking any borrowing.

A careful examination of Table 24-3 reveals that these two financing principles are generally adhered to in the optimal solution. For example, since the cash needs of $150 in January are followed by cash surpluses of $152 and $72 in the two subsequent months, the optimal solution calls for borrowing the maximum amount of $140 from the commercial bank, only $10 in the commercial paper market, and nothing at all from installment financing. These transactions are consistent with the first of the two principles mentioned above. In April, the firm has a cash drain of $29.73 (after interest income has been taken into account). Since the firm has $84.26 in government securities, the optimal solution calls for the sale of a sufficient number of government securities both to meet this drain of $29.73 and to reduce outstanding commercial paper by $10.00. These transactions are consistent with the second of the two financing principles.

The optimal solution, however, does contain two exceptions to the second of the two principles mentioned above. Notice that the optimal solution calls for $34.28 of installment financing in June, when the firm has an ending balance of $13.60 in its government securities account. In July, the optimal solution again calls for $61.13 of commercial paper financing, when the firm is in fact increasing its government securities holdings by $5.39. In these two months, why is it profitable for the firm to borrow before it has exhausted its supply of government securities? This question is best answered in the next subsection where we discuss implicit prices and their meaning for marginal analysis.

Finally, notice that the Fancycraft, Inc. has a total outstanding debt of $204.73 at the end of December. Subtracting from this figure the net interest charges of $3.71 already paid, we get $201 (ignoring rounding errors) as the cumulative amount of cash requirements financed as of the end of December.

Imputed Values and Marginal Analysis

In addition to the optimal solution, the revised simplex algorithm also includes in its computer output the imputed values associated with all the variables in the linear-programming problem. These imputed values reveal the amounts by which the firm's net interest cost will be altered as a result of marginal shifts in the values of the variables. Before analyzing the specific imputed values in this problem, however, let us briefly review our understanding of imputed values as they pertain to linear programming problems in general.

Suppose a linear-programming problem has a total of n variables and m constraining equations, where $n > m$. If the problem is not degenerate,[2] then we would expect to find in the optimal solution exactly m variables with nonzero values. These nonzero variables, known as basic variables, must be positive by virtue of the nonnegativity condition. The remaining $n - m$ variables, known as nonbasic variables, must all be exactly equal to zero. It should be emphasized, however, that the distinction between basic and nonbasic variables should not be confused with that between decision and slack variables. Both a decision variable and a slack variable may be either basic or nonbasic in the optimal solution. Variables in the optimal solution, therefore, fall into one of four classifications: basic decision variable, nonbasic decision variable, basic slack variable, and nonbasic slack variable. Moreover, since the optimal solution produces the best attainable value for the objective function, the imputed values of the basic variables must all be zero. A value of zero here means that the results of the linear program cannot be further improved through marginal adjustments in the associated basic variable. Similarly, since the results of the linear program will be adversely affected if any of the nonbasic variables are allowed to become positive, the imputed values associated with nonbasic variables must all be positive. A positive value here measures the increase in cost or decrease in profit resulting from marginal adjustments in the associated nonbasic variable.

The present problem has a total of 62 variables, constrained by 36 equations. Since the problem is not degenerate, the optimal solution contains 36 basic variables of which 20 are decision variables and 16 are slack variables. Since the problem has a total of 26 decision variables, the fact that 20 are basic means that 6 are nonbasic. Table 24-4 presents the optimal values of the entire set of decision variables together with their respective imputed values.

Much can be learned from the analysis of the imputed value presented in Table 24-4. Since the meaning of zero imputed value is straightforward, we shall accordingly concentrate our analysis on those imputed values which are positive. Consider first the imputed values of .0013 associated with $x_2, x_3, \ldots, x_7$. In each of these six months, the Fancycraft, Inc. has

Table 24-4. Decision Variables and Their Values (in dollars)

Variable*	Optimal Value	Imputed Value	Variable	Optimal Value	Imputed Value
x_1	140.00	0	y_2	0	0.0015
x_2	0	0.0013	y_3	0	0.0015
x_3	0	0.0013	y_4	0	0.0015
x_4	0	0.0013	y_5	0	0.0015
x_5	0	0.0013	y_6	0	0.0013
x_6	0	0.0013	y_7	61.13	0
x_7	0	0.0013	y_8	**	0
x_8	0	0.0011	y_9	55.27	0
x_9	106.78	0	y_{10}	64.73	0
x_{10}	140.00	0	y_{11}	0	0.0037
x_{11}	85.00	0	y_{12}	0	0.0076
x_{12}	140.00	0	z_1	0	0.0001
y_1	10.00	0	z_2	32.28	0

*The letters x, y, z stand respectively for bank loan, commercial paper and installment financing. The subscripts 1, 2, . . ., 12 designate the months of the year.

**Very small nonzero value.

sufficient funds to invest in government securities. Therefore, any further increase in bank borrowings during these months would only increase the company's government securities holdings. Since government securities yield only .0037 per month, and bank credit costs .005 per month, a one-dollar increase in bank credit would therefore increase net financing cost by .0013 per month.

But if the marginal values of bank borrowing equal .0013 for February through July, why does this value drop to .0011 during August? To answer this question, we re-solved the original linear-programming problem with the added constraint that x_8 must equal one dollar. Table 24-5 presents the optimal solution to the linear-programming problem with this added constraint. Observe that since the firm has no government securities after July, the cost effect of an increase in bank credit in August is no longer measured directly by the difference between the interest rate on bank credit and the yield on government securities. Notice also that the amount of installment financing in June cannot be reduced below \$34.28, or else there will be insufficient funds to meet the maximum cumulative cash requirement in October. An extra dollar of bank credit in August, therefore, can only be used to reduce the amount of commercial paper in August. In fact, the solution in Table 24-5 calls for the firm to reduce its commercial paper by \$1 in July and September as well as in August. The reduction in commercial paper during July and September is to be offset by the sale of government securities in July and increased bank credit in September. The

Table 24-5. The Optimal Pattern of Financinc with Added Constraint*
(in dollars)

Month	Borrowing from Bank	Sale of Commercial Paper	Installment Financing	Gov't. Securities
January	140.00	10.00	0	0
February	0	0	0	11.26
March	0	0	0	84.26
April	0	0	0	44.53
May	0	0	0	170.69
June	0	0	34.28	13.60
July	0	60.13	0	17.98
August	1.00	0	0	0
September	107.78	55.27	0	0
October	140.00	64.73	0	0
November	85.00	0	0	0
December	140.00	0	0	0

*The added constraint: $x_8 = 1$.

reader can verify for himself that when the repercussions are fully accounted for, an extra dollar of bank borrowing in August will cost the firm $0.0011 more than the original optimal program. The imputed values of the remaining decision variables can be explained in a similar way.

An important reminder, however, is in order before we conclude this discussion of marginal analysis. The imputed values in Table 24-4 are valid figures only if we consider the effects of small changes in the respective variables. Take for instance variable y_7 (sale of commercial paper in July) which has an imputed value of zero. The value of zero says, in effect, that other things being equal *small* deviations in the value of y_7 from its optimal value of $61.13 will have no effect on the firm's net financing cost. It would be wrong, however, to infer from this statement that the firm's net financing cost will remain at the minimum of $4.70 in the face of large changes in the value of y_7. To illustrate this point, let us recall that we had some question earlier about the wisdom of the firm's borrowing the full $61.13 in the commercial paper market when its government securities account showed a balance of $18.98. Would it not be more profitable to finance the needs for July by selling these $18.98 of government securities, thereby reducing the amount to be borrowed in the commercial paper market? To answer this question, we re-solved the orginal linear-programming problem with the added constraint that y_7 must equal $42.15 (=$61.13 minus $18.98). The optimal solution reveals that this new financing program costs the firm $0.0153 more than the orginal optimal solution. The example clearly illustrates the fact that implicit values such as those given in Table 4 may become invalid when large changes in the associated variables are being contemplated.

V. QUALIFICATIONS

This paper has applied the linear-programming model developed by Robichek, Teichroew, and Jones to a case study involving the short-term financing decision of a greeting-card business. A key assumption underlying the linear programming model in this paper was the absence of uncertainty. The Fancycraft, Inc. was assumed to know its sales, collections, manufacturing costs, selling and administrative expenses, dividends, and taxes, and hence was able to forecast with complete certainty its future net cash requirements. Since the cash budget was known with certainty, the firm was able to use linear programming in solving for that pattern of financing which minimized net interest expense.

This assumption of certainty was made for the purpose of simplifying the analysis. Realistically, however, business operations are characterized by change and uncertainty, and many of the terms appearing in the cash budget are not constants, but variables subject to random fluctuations. The financing requirement during any given period is determined jointly by the initial cash balance and by the current cash flow. The initial cash balance, in turn, can be viewed as the cumulative result of past cash flows. Any meaningful forecast of future financing needs, therefore, requires not only the individual probability distributions of cash flows, but also the joint probability distributions of an entire set of cash flows. With the financing requirements not only random, but possibly also correlated over time, the search for the optimal pattern of financing becomes a considerably more difficult task. Several methods have been suggested for incorporating uncertainty into the model. One of these, the simulation approach, will be applied to the short-term financing decision in a forthcoming paper.

Notes

1. Since total interest is equal to the semiannual rate of .0146 multiplied by the initial amount of the debt and since the debt is fully amortized in six months, the effective borrowing cost is approximately 5.84 percent per annum. For the mathematics of installment financing, see Neifeld [3].

2. A linear-programming problem with m constraints is said to be degenerate if it can be satisfied with fewer than m variables with positive values.

References

1. W.W. Garvin, *Introduction to Linear Programming* (New York: McGraw-Hill Book Company, Inc., 1960).

2. G. Hadley, *Linear Programming* (Reading, Mass.: Addison-Wesley, 1962).

3. M.R. Neifeld, *Guide to Installment Computations* (Easton, Penna.: Mack Publishing Company, 1951).

4. A.A. Robichek and S.C. Myers, *Optimal Financing Decisions* (Englewood Cliffs, N.J.: Prentice-Hall, Inc., 1965).

5. A.A. Robichek, D. Teichroew, and J.M. Jones, "Optimal Short-Term Financing Decision," *Management Science*, Volume 12, September 1965.

25 Capital Budgeting: A Pragmatic Approach

by Alexander A. Robichek, Donald G. Ogilvie, and John D.C. Roach

The present state of capital budgeting is characterized by a dichotomy between theory and practice. A number of financial theoreticians have derived and conceptualized sophisticated models that attempt to provide answers to the operating problems of modern financial managers. These theoretical models have made significant contributions to the state of the art, and, within the stated assumptions, their logic has been unimpeachable. However, there has been relatively little spillover from the world of the theoretician to the pragmatic realm of the financial manager.

This article will provide a critical review of the theory of capital budgeting and an attempt to reconcile it with the reality that faces the financial executive. An approach using linear programming is described as a possible practical alternative.

THEORY OF CAPITAL BUDGETING

The unwillingness on the part of financial managers to accept in practice the decision rules proposed by theoreticians can be attributed to several factors:

- The assumptions of the theoretical models are not applicable to the real world. The internal logic of the model may be consistent, but if the model rests on questionable assumptions it will find little or no acceptance among financial managers who are held responsible for their decisions.

EDITOR'S NOTE: From *Financial Executive,* April 1969, pp. 26-38. Reprinted by permission of the publisher, Financial Executives Institute, and authors.

- A reluctance on the part of financial managers to make radical departures from the traditional techniques of capital budgeting. The risk associated with new techniques often inhibits experimentation.
- A general lack of confidence in the ability to quantify such variables as future cash flows and appropriate discount rates.

It should be carefully noted at the outset that the efficacy of a model for capital budgeting can be judged *only in relation to the firm's objectives and goals.* If the objective that is given top priority by management is to "maximize next year's earnings per share," it may be foolhardy indeed to adopt a capital budgeting technique that attempts to "maximize the net present value of a stream of future cash flows." Because of the inherent differences between accounting income and incremental cash flows it would be only by coincidence that an "optimal" decision would result. The responsibility rests heavily on the shoulders of top management to define clearly and specifically what the objectives of the capital budgeting system should be; without such a definition there can be no measure of its effectiveness, and one model appears just as acceptable as the next.

SELECTING THE FIRM'S OBJECTIVE

The need for a clearly stated objective is easy to identify but difficult to define in an operationally meaningful way. In designing a sound capital budgeting system, top management must find answers to the following questions:

- What "objective" should the system maximize?
- Which factors in the capital budgeting decision contribute to this objective?
- What relationships exist between the decisional factors and the objective?

Many answers have been suggested to these questions, and they are often in conflict with one another. To complicate further the situation, many firms have multiple objectives which are difficult, if not impossible, to place in a well-structured hierarchy with appropriate weights attached to each. The management of a corporation, charged with setting goals and objectives, must evaluate and weigh the often conflicting claims of employees, customers, and stockholders; each of these groups will have a different hierarchy of objectives for the corporation.

Without wishing to enter this normative controversy, let us accept the premise that the objective of the corporation in making capital investment decisions is to attempt to maximize the value of the firm to its current shareholders.[1] The problem then becomes one of defining *value* and the factors that affect it.

A great deal of valuable theoretical work has been done in an attempt to determine the "value" of a firm.[2] In theory the value of the firm has come to be defined as the present value of all expected future dividends, discounted at the "appropriate" cost of capital rate.

It is important to note that the dichotomy between theory and practice begins at this very basic level. In the ethereal realm of perfect markets, perfect foresight, and no taxes, few would disagree with the statement that the market price of the firm should be equal to the discounted present value of the future dividends. Regrettably, we do not live in a world of perfect capital markets, and expected future dividends are difficult to predict. Furthermore, despite a number of research efforts, the determination of the firm's appropriate cost of capital remains a much debated issue.

Because of the great uncertainty associated with forecasting streams of dividends to perpetuity, and the generally limited horizons of many investors, a number of financial managers have become increasingly concerned with the "earnings capacity" of the firm, since the firm's ability to pay future dividends rests on its capacity to generate future earnings. Also, financial analysts are more confident in their predictions of earnings in the near future than they are of forecasting an infinite stream of cash dividends. All of these factors have led investment analysts to continue to use formulas that relate the value of the firm to its expected ability to generate earnings.[3]

Still others have developed approaches relating the value of the firm to a wide variety of variables (such as growth rates in earnings, variability, debt ratios, etc.).[4] The results of all this work have made most theoreticians and virtually all financial managers painfully aware that the firm's market price is a function of many variables. The real confusion arises because nobody knows exactly which variables affect market price, much less what the relative importance of each should be at any point in time.

INVESTMENT EVALUATION CRITERIA

On the one hand, it seems appropriate to base capital budgeting decisions on criteria that relate directly to the objective of the firm, i.e., the maximization of the value of the firm to its current shareholders. On the other hand, it is apparent that *the* objective of the firm is a rather elusive concept. Still, decisions in the area of capital budgeting must be made. These decisions are frequently made on the basis of crude rules-of-thumb or intuitive-feel that may or may not have any direct relevance to an objective. In addition, a number of rather sophisticated techniques for capital budgeting analysis have recently been introduced, such as discounted cash flow (DCF), internal rate of return (IRR), and present value (PV), and have gained gradual acceptance among the modern financial managers. Few would question the value of these contributions to our understanding of financial management; a great deal of progress has been made. The point that needs to be recognized is that many of these modern techniques may not be compatible with the overall objectives of the firm and may lead to inappropriate decisions. A theoretical model that maximizes the value of the firm under a given set of theoretical assumptions will not necessarily perform well when it is applied to the real world. Even though there is no agreement, even in theory, as to which factors affect value, the modern financial manager still needs a capital budgeting system that will allow him to consider the various factors that, *in his opinion*, have strategic importance.

A large number of methods for evaluating investment proposals are commonly used. A brief, critical examination of the principal methods is given below.

"Necessary" Projects

Many large corporations still use "necessity" or "urgency" to justify capital investments that appear to defy financial analysis. The real difficulty associated with this type of an approach is that it is entirely subjective and relies on the persuasiveness of the individual proposing the project. Unless the contribution from this type of project is considered to be of such magnitude so as to make an analytical evaluation unnecessary, it is impossible for the financial executive to relate the contribution from the project to the primary corporate objectives.

Payback Period

One of the most commonly used evaluation techniques is the length of time required for the initial capital investment to be recovered from the incremental cash flow of the project. The deficiencies associated with this method are well known: payback ignores the pattern of cash flows over time, neglects the time-value of money, and attaches no value to the cash-generating ability of a project after its payback period. Payback places unwarranted importance on liquidity and neglect the overall profitability of the project. Some financial managers argue that the method contains a built-in hedge against risk in that it limits the amount of time the firm's capital is exposed to loss. This argument is only true to the extent that risk is strictly a function of time and that all projects, whether of long or short duration, have the same risk exposure during their payback period.

The modern financial executive will find the payback value of little use in attempting to relate directly his financial decisions to the corporate objectives. It would be only by coincidence if the application of the payback criterion were to lead to the maximization of earnings, dividends, or return on investment of the firm.

Accounting Rates of Return

A technique that is often used to evaluate the profitability of an investment is the accounting rate of return. The rate of return on the original investment is calculated by dividing either the first-year income or the average annual income by the initial investment (or the average investment). This technique relies on accounting or book profits rather than on incremental cash flows. While the present accounting techniques are well-suited for the preparation of meaningful financial statements, they tend to focus on figures that are not necessarily meaningful in terms of the incremental analysis that is relevant for an effective capital budgeting system.

This technique, like the payback period, fails to recognize the pattern of cash flows and the time-value of money. In this sense, it may result in undesirable or incorrect decisions. However, the technique does focus upon a factor of great importance to the financial executive: the ability of the project to generate accounting income. The short-run earnings capacity of a project, or more importantly its lack of earnings, may be given substantial weight by the market. Many financial executives would be extremely reluctant to accept a project that would have a significant adverse impact on reported income in the short-run, unless this fact could be offset by incomes from other accepted projects.

Net Present Value (NPV)

The concepts of incremental cash flow analysis and the time-value of money gave rise to the technique of net present value. This method reflects the difference between the present value of a stream of future cash inflows and the present value of all cash outflows, all discounted at the "appropriate" discount rate. Obviously, the real difficulty is to define this discount rate.

Most of the theoretical models define the appropriate discount rate as the firm's "cost of capital." Regrettably, this cost of capital is easier to derive in theory than in practice. Under the theoretical assumptions of the model the firm can, and should, increase its value by accepting any project with a positive net present value per dollar of investment.

This method of evaluating proposed investments is concerned only with maximizing their "net present value," based on cash projections and estimates of cost of capital made by management. In theory, adding projects that have a positive net present value should lead to an increase in the value of the firm. But both management and the market may be concerned with other criteria that affect value, such as earnings, and the net present value techniques may yield suboptimal decisions.

Internal Rate of Return (IRR)

The internal rate of return of a project is that rate which equates the present value of the net cash inflows to the original investment. This technique allows a simple ranking of projects by their profitability and avoids the difficulty of setting and justifying a discount rate.

Financial theory has demonstrated that all proposed investment projects that have a rate of return greater than the firm's cost of capital should be accepted. Under capital rationing, the projects should be ranked according to their rates of return and accepted in that sequence until the capital constraint becomes binding.

As simple as this technique may appear, it is characterized by a number of weaknesses that, unless they are recognized and compensated for, may result in a suboptimal decision. First, a number of authors have demonstrated that certain projects may have multiple rates of return, and the solution will be ambiguous.[5] Secondly, when comparing mutually exclusive projects with various economic lives, the internal rate of return technique may yield selection rules different from the net present value method. None of these deficiencies are insurmountable in practice, but they require careful analysis before they can be resolved.

CAPITAL BUDGETING PRACTICES

The results of a recent survey showed an increasing acceptance by the large manufacturing firms of techniques using concepts of discounted cash flow.[6] The percentage of firms using either IRR, NPV, or both increased from only 9 per cent in 1955 to 47 per cent in 1965. However, some 65 per cent of the firms still used the payback period as an evaluation technique in 1965, and 62 per cent accepted some projects on the basis of "necessity."

The theoretical models of capital budgeting "demonstrate" the advantages of accepting *all* projects with a positive NPV or an IRR greater than the cost of capital. Yet the study indicated that 80 per cent of the companies imposed some overall capital constraints. This capital rationing was largely self-imposed by the firms rather than by external forces. Since capital rationing practices are imposed by some of the most profitable corporations, this evidence would indicate that financial executives may impose capital rationing to reflect factors other than the "cost of capital."

The 163 respondents in the survey were asked to rank their financial objectives in order of importance. By a large margin the firms ranked "maximization of earnings per share" as their primary objective. But frequently the decision rule indicated by a discounted cash flow analysis may be in direct conflict with this particular objective. A short example may serve to illustrate this point.

Assume a firm has two unrelated projects in which it can invest; the capital rationing constraint makes it possible to accept only one of the projects. Project A will generate relatively higher cash flows, but because of the depreciation and the amortization associated with it, the accounting earnings during the first years of its life will be quite small. The IRR on Project A is 20 per cent. By way of contrast, Project B has an IRR of only 15 per cent, but its first-year contribution to accounting income would be significantly greater than Project A's. The question facing the financial manager of this firm is how to evaluate each of these factors. Should he blindly follow the rules of the theoretical model and accept Project A, or should he introduce the "next year's earnings" objective into the picture? If he should consider earnings, how much IRR would he be willing to sacrifice for an additional $0.25 earnings per share? One per cent? Two per cent? Maybe he should accept Project B instead. After all, those additional first-year earnings may help the firm achieve its budget objectives. For that matter, it may also be in the best interest of the stockholders as well, because it is well known that the market often reacts to reported growth (or decline) in earnings.

The difficulty of the decision-making process is further compounded as the number of projects and the size of the capital budget is increased. Imagine the complexity of selecting the "optimum set" of projects from 150 alternatives.

NEED FOR NEW PROCEDURE

The preceding discussion illustrates the dilemma financial managers often face in attempting to decide among alternative investment proposals. The lack of confidence in the pure theoretical approach is blatantly apparent when a manager is confronted with a situation where the acceptance of the "theoretically optimal" solution has a significant adverse effect on other operational goals such as current earnings or return on investment. It is obvious that a more pragmatic approach is required to benefit the operational financial manager. Yet, the recently developed and recommended discounted cash flow concepts should not be abandoned because they give the manager information as to the "long-run" effect on objectives. What is needed is a procedure that combines the best features of both theory and practice to give the manager a workable and feasible approach. Furthermore, this procedure must be flexible so that it can be modified and adapted to meet the specific needs of any individual company.

For a method to be practicable, it must allow the operational manager to state a range of objectives or factors that he considers important for his company. These relevant factors should be integrally included, not excluded, from the procedure used in deciding among various investment alternatives. As implied above, these considerations could, and probably should, differ from one company to another. Some factors that are most often deemed pertinent are as follows:

Level of Current Earnings per Share

Many managers feel that one of their most compelling goals is to prevent earnings per share from dropping from one year to the next. Others feel that a certain level of earnings per share is desirable or acceptable; this level is usually greater than the preceding year's earnings, although it could conceivably be lower. Depending on the degree of corporate commitment to this goal, the level of earnings per share can have an extremely strong effect on the capital budgeting decision.

In recent years more and more companies have publicly expressed their corporate objectives in such terms as, "Our goal is to increase earnings per share by 10 per cent per year." If the management is really committed to this goal, and if the market's valuation of the common stock is considerably influenced by this expectation, then rigid adherence to an objective such as "maximize the net present value of future cash flows" is questionable indeed.

Level and Rate of Growth of Dividends per Share

An important objective of many companies is to maintain or increase dividends per share. If the attainment of these dividend goals is deemed an important determinant in the valuation of the shares of this company, then the ability to pay current dividends must certainly be considered in the capital budgeting decision of this firm.

Rate of Return on Stockholder Investment (ROI)

A number of companies consider the rate of return on stockholder capital to be a key variable. Investments are accepted or rejected depending on whether they will decrease or increase ROI. While ROI appears to have an influence on the market value of the shares, strict adherence to this objective may lead a company to reject proposals that may in fact enhance the value of the company through increased earnings per share.

Research and Development Expenditures

The continued importance of advanced technology in many industries has made it necessary for some firms to spend considerable amounts of capital for research and development. Although the objective of such expenditures is either to enhance future earning power or to protect current earnings, it is extremely difficult to measure the value of these benefits. This inability to estimate either the amount or timing of probable future benefits makes quantitative analysis difficult. The practical method most often used in determining how much of the budget is to be allocated to R&D is usually something like x per cent of sales, or y per cent of this year's budget.

Necessary Expenditures

Similar to R&D, companies sometimes feel they must spend \$$x$ for investments they consider "necessary." This would include such items as new furniture for the offices, employee recreational facilities, and contributions to charities or foundations. Although the management may fully expect to recoup its investment through such benefits as increased employee morale and improved community relations, it is virtually impossible to calculate the net present value or the rate of return for such projects. However, management needs to be fully aware of the opportunity cost they incur when they forego profitable investment proposals to accept the necessary projects.

A SUGGESTED APPROACH

The utilization of a theoretically optimal investment criterion, such as (1) accept any investment proposal which has a net present value greater than zero, or (2) accept those projects with the highest rate of return until the cutoff rate is reached, does not directly consider such practical constraints as those enumerated above. Furthermore, a pragmatic approach such as "accept those projects that appear desirable" is equally unpalatable. One possible method of treating both theoretical and practical considerations is to examine all possible combinations of investment alternatives to determine the effect of each combination on all of the corporate objectives. Although this method will certainly work, the computational task becomes huge when a large number of projects is considered. Thus, a more efficient and operational method is required.

A possible approach to this problem is to use the technique of linear programming to determine the optimal set of investment proposals. The objective of the approach would be to maximize the IRR or the NPV of those investment alternatives under consideration subject to a set of constraints. The constraints, in addition to the supply of capital available, would be those factors, such as earnings per share, ROI, dividends per share, R&D expenditures, etc., which management feels should be considered as operational or practical objectives of the firm.

It should be pointed out that ours is not the first attempt to apply linear programming techniques to the capital budgeting decision. In a doctoral dissertation published in 1963, H. Martin Weingartner attempted to utilize linear programming and integer programming in analyzing certain traditional problems of capital budgeting; namely, investment planning under capital rationing and under imperfect capital markets.

Other authors, such as Van Horne and Charnes, have also attempted to apply linear programming to capital budgeting problems. More recently, in a parallel study less broad in scope, Lerner and Rappaport describe an approach using linear programming and the net present value of projects. All of these authors have been influential in their attempt to introduce linear programming to the realm of capital budgeting decisions.

Capital Budgeting as a Linear Programming Problem

Linear programming (LP) is a mathematical technique that provides optimal solutions to certain classes of problems. The problem must meet the following requirements: (1) the objective to be maximized must be stated in mathematical form; (2) the maximization of the objective must be subject to constraints or limits on certain resources or variables in the problem; (3) all relationships must be linear in character; and (4) there must be more than one way of solving the problem.[7]

In a typical practical capital budgeting situation, the objective may be to maximize IRR or NPV, subject to constraints on the amount of cash available for investment, required earnings per share, limitations for particular projects, etc.

Perhaps the best way to illustrate how LP can be applied in practice is to present a simple case example. The example is intended merely to illustrate the methodology and is not necessarily representative of a real life situation.

CASE ILLUSTRATION

The Company, its Current Status, and its Objectives

The relevant information for this hypothetical company is shown in Exhibit 25-1. The company is relatively small, with after-tax earnings of $500,000 for the year just ended. Since there are 100,000 shares outstanding the earnings per share were $5.00. Management estimates earnings for the current year before any new investments to be $470,000 or $4.70 per share. Total cash currently available is $1.2 million and estimated cash flow for the current year from existing projects without any new investment is $1.13 million.

Exhibit 25-1B summarizes the factors that the management feels reflect the company's operational goals. Desirous of a 6 per cent growth in EPS, next year's goal is earnings of at least $5.30 per share, or $530,000 total. Management feels a 40 per cent divident payout ratio is appropriate. Therefore a dividend of $2.00 per share ($200,000) is expected to be paid soon based on last year's earnings. Management estimates that $300,000 should be expended for R&D projects, and $60,000 is required for certain other necessary projects. Since the total capital available is $1.2 million, the amount available for new projects is $640,000. A minimum cash flow of $1.3 million is considered desirable for the current year.

Investment Opportunities

With this company background information in mind, we can now analyze the investment opportunities open for consideration. Exhibit 25-2 summarizes five possible investment alternatives. The data for these projects are presented so that both the accounting income and the cash flow for each year are evident. The calculations in Exhibit 25-2 assume that the revenues and expenses estimated for determining the marginal accounting income are identical to the marginal revenues and marginal expenses necessary for calculating the cash flows. Under traditional accounting practices, this equality is not always maintained. Also for the sake of simplicity, straight-line depreciation is assumed for all projects for both tax and reporting purposes.

Exhibit 25-1. Company Information

A. *Current Data*		
Actual Earnings After Taxes Last Year		$ 500,000
Number of Shares Outstanding		100,000
Earnings per Share		$ 5.00
Cash Available for Investments and Dividends		$1,200,000
Estimated Earnings for Current Year Without New Investment		$ 470,000
Estimated Cash Flow for Current Year Without New Investment		$1,130,000
B. *Goals and Requirements for Current Year*		
Earnings per Share—Minimum (6% increase)		$ 5.30
Total Earnings Required		$ 530,000
Less: Estimated Earnings Without New Investment		470,000
Incremental Earnings Required From New Investment		60,000
Cash Flow Required—Minimum		$1,300,000
Less Estimated Cash Flow Without New Investment		1,130,000
Incremental Cash Flow Required From New Investments		$ 170,000
Minimum R&D Expenditures		$ 300,000
Minimum "Necessary" Expenditures		$ 60,000
Minimum Dividends on Last Year's Earnings (40% of Earnings)		$ 200,000
Cash Available for New Investments		$1,200,000
Less: R&D Expenditures	$300,000	
Necessary Expenditures	60,000	
Dividends	200,000	560,000
Net Cash Available for New Investments		$ 640,000

Exhibit 25-3 shows the initial investment required, the first year's accounting income, the first year's cash flow, and the computed internal rate of return for each of the five projects. In calculating the rate of return, the investment cost was assumed to have been incurred on the first day of the first year, and all of the revenues and expenses were assumed to occur at the end of the respective periods.

Application of the LP Procedure

For this particular example, the assumption will be made that management wishes to maximize the average IRR subject to the the various constraints noted above. The formulation of the problem is as follows:

Exhibit 25-2. Investment Opportunities (All Figures in $1000's)

Period (1)	Investment (2)	Revenues (3)	Expenses (4)	Depreciation (5)	Operating Income (6) = (3) – (4 + 5)	Taxes (50%) (7 = .5(6)	Accounting Income (8) = (6) – (7)	Cash Flow (9) = (3) – (4) – (7)
					Project A			
1	100	140	85	25	30	15	15	40
2		175	100	25	50	25	25	50
3		175	100	25	50	25	25	50
4		175	100	25	50	25	25	50
					Project B			
1	300	100	80	60	(40)	(20)	(20)	40
2		400	200	60	140	70	70	130
3		1100	600	60	440	220	220	280
4		900	400	60	440	220	220	280
5		1500	800	60	640	320	320	380
					Project C			
1	200	300	140	100	60	30	30	130
2		200	80	100	20	10	10	110
					Project D			
1	300	230	105	75	50	25	25	100
2		300	125	75	100	50	50	125
3		350	145	75	130	65	65	140
4		400	165	75	160	80	80	155
					Project E			
1	200	200	110	40	50	25	25	65
2		200	110	40	50	25	25	65
3		220	120	40	60	30	30	70
4		240	130	40	70	35	35	75
5		270	140	40	90	45	45	85

Exhibit 25-3. Summary of Investment Opportunities

	Project				
	A	B	C	D	E
Initial Investment ($1000's)	100	300	200	300	200
First Year's Accounting Income ($1000's)	15	–20	30	25	25
First Year's Cash Flow ($1000's)	40	40	130	100	65
Internal Rate of Return	30.4%	45.6%	13.5%	24.2%	22.2%

Maximize:

$$Z = .304\ X_1 + .456\ X_2 + .135\ X_3 + .242\ X_4 + .222\ X_5,$$

where the X_j's represent the amount of funds (in thousands of dollars) committed to project j and the coefficients preceding each X_j stand for the project IRR's shown in Exhibit 25-3. Average IRR is obtained by dividing Z by 640, the total funds available.

Subject to:

1. Budget Constraint.

$$X_1 + X_2 + X_3 + X_3 + X_5 \leqslant 640.$$

The amount allocated to all projects cannot exceed $640,000, the total amount available.

2. Project Constraints.

$$0 \leqslant X_1 \leqslant 100.$$
$$0 \leqslant X_2 \leqslant 300.$$
$$0 \leqslant X_3 \leqslant 200.$$
$$0 \leqslant X_4 \leqslant 300.$$
$$0 \leqslant X_5 \leqslant 200.$$

The commitment of funds to any one project cannot exceed the project's maximum required funds or be negative.

3. Earnings Constraint.

$$\frac{15}{100} X_1 - \frac{20}{300} X_2 + \frac{30}{200} X_3 + \frac{25}{300} X_4 + \frac{25}{200} X_5 \leqslant 60.$$

The first year's earnings contributions from the accepted new project must be at least $60,000.

4. Cash Flow Constraint.

$$\frac{40}{100} X_1 + \frac{40}{300} X_2 + \frac{130}{200} X_3 + \frac{100}{300} X_4 + \frac{65}{200} X_5 \leqslant 170.$$

The first year's cash flow from the new projects must be at least $170,000.

The results of this capital budgeting model are given in Exhibit 25-4.[8] As indicated in these results, the optimal solution is to accept all of Projects A and E, place $55,500 into Project B and $284,500 in Project D. No funds are committed to Project C. If this optimal allocation is made, the average IRR will be 26.4 per cent. This is the highest obtainable average IRR given the management constraints on the allocation process. (It should be noted that our formulation permitted acceptance of fractional projects. Should such fractional projects not be feasible, a technique called integer programming may have to be substituted for LP.)

Exhibit 25-4. Results of the Linear Programming Model

X_1 = Project A = 100.0
X_2 = Project B = 55.5
X_3 = Project C = 0
X_4 = Project D = 284.5
X_5 = Project E = 200.0
Z = Objective = 168.97

$$\text{Average IRR} = \frac{Z}{640} = \frac{168.97}{640} = 26.4\%$$

If the management of this company is convinced that no addtional capital can be raised, and if they are unwilling to reduce any of their requirements for earnings, dividends, R&D, or necessary expenditures, then the usefulness of the LP model is exhausted. The optimal allocation has been determined. However, we seriously doubt that any management is so totally recalcitrant that they will not even question these requirements. This is where the additional information made available by LP becomes invaluable.

DUAL VARIABLES

In addition to the data shown in Exhibit 25-4, the LP solution provides values for the so-called dual variables. These values are not reproduced here, but they provide the basis for testing the sensitivity of the solution to the changes in the various management-imposed restraints. For example, we can determine that the addition of $1,000 to cash available for new projects would increase Z by .360; that is, the IRR on the marginal $1,000 would be 36.0 per cent. With this type of evidence confronting management, a decision may well be made either to raise additional capital from outside sources or to reduce the originally planned level of expenditures for R&D, necessary projects or dividends.

Even more striking is the value of the dual variable for the earnings constraint,—1.42. This means that if management were to reduce their earnings requirement by $1,000 (from $60,000 to $59,000) the value of Z would increase by 1.42 and the average IRR would rise from 26.40 per cent to 26.73 per cent.[9] This increase is accomplished by switching $6,667 from Project D to Project B. In other words, the reduction in earnings requirements permits a shift of funds from a project with a relatively low IRR but an attractive first-year earnings to a project that offers a very high rate of return, but reports an accounting loss in the first year. Although ours is not the job to judge the validity or reasonableness of this earnings requirement, the LP solution points out the dramatic and severe opportunity cost associated with this policy.

On the other hand, analysis of the LP solution indicates that the mininum cash requirement presents no problems and that for practical purposes the minimum cash constraint has no effect on the allocation procedure.

This analysis in depth of the LP solution illustrates the value that can be obtained from utilizing a linear programming procedure to solve capital budgeting problems. It forces management to question the real worth of their various "practical" goals of constraints. Furthermore, it gives them a number, the value of the dual variable, against which they can compare, analyze, and question their own set of objectives.

CONCLUSION

The state of the art of capital budgeting has come a long way in the last 15 years. Corporate management has grown increasingly aware of the overwhelming importance of financial decisions on the future growth and profitability of the firm. A great deal of valuable theoretical work has been done in identifying and evaluating the critical variables in the firm's investment and financing decision, and some of this work has been adopted on a practical basis.

However, we are a long way from having the theory provide the answers to all the questions of the modern financial manager. The contemporary financial executive is painfully aware of the multiplicity of corporate goals and objectives which he must keep in a delicate balance. The model proposed in this article is designed to help bridge the gap between theory and practice. We do not propose it as the ultimate solution to these difficult problems, but we do believe it is a step in the right direction.

Notes

[1]The rationale underlying the selection of this particular objective is discussed at length by Solomon, chap. 1.

[2]See, for example, Modigliani and Miller, Gordon, and Robichek and Myers, chap. 6.

[3]The practical investment literature abounds with examples.

[4]For examples, refer to Benishay, Gordon, etc.

[5]See Lorie and Savage.

[6]The results were compiled from a questionnaire containing responses from 163 manufacturing firms in the *Fortune 500* as reported by Robichek and McDonald.

[7]For a more detailed discussion of linear programming the interested reader is referred to any of a number of excellent books on the subject.

[8]The solution was derived by using the facilities of the Stanford Graduate School of Business time-sharing computer system.

[9]$(168.97 + 1.42) \div 640 = 26.73\%$.

Bibliography

1. Benishay, Haskell, "Variability in Earnings-Price Ratios of Corporate Equities," *American Economic Review*, LI, March 1961, pp. 81-94.

2. Charnes, A.A., Cooper, W.W., and Miller, M.H., "Application of Linear Programming to Financial Budgeting and the Costing of Funds," *Journal of Business*, January 1959.

3. Gordon, M.J., *The Investment, Financing and Valuation of the Corporation*, R.D. Irwin, Homewood, Illinois, 1962.

4. Lerner, E., and Rappaport, A., "Limit DCF in Capital Budgeting," *Harvard Business Review*, September-October 1968, pp. 133-139.

5. Lorie, J., and Savage, L.J., "Three Problems in Capital Rationing," *Journal of Business*, October 1955.

6. Modigliani, F. and M. Miller, "Dividend Policy, Growth, and the Valuation of Shares," *Journal of Business 34*, October 1961, pp. 411-432.

7. Robichek, A.A. and McDonald, J.G., *Financial Management in Transition*, Long Range Planning Service Report No. 268, Stanford Research Institute, Menlo Park, California, January 1966.

8. Robichek, A.A., and Myers, S.C., *Optimal Financing Decisions*, Prentice-Hall, Englewood Cliffs, N.J., 1965.

9. Solomon, Ezra, *The Theory of Financial Management*, New York: Columbia University Press, 1963.

10. Van Horne, James, "Capital Budgeting Decisions Involving Combinations of Risky Investments," *Management Science*, XIII, October 1966, B84-92.

11. Weingartner, Martin H., *Mathematical Programming and the Analysis of Capital Budgeting*, Englewood Cliffs, N.J.: Prentice-Hall, Inc., 1963.

Discussion Questions

1. In the Sancrest Jewelry Company Case:

a. Product X_5 has the largest unit profit. Should it be given priority in resource allocation? Would your answer be the same if the unit profit was increased from $0.34 to $0.40? Why?

b. Why should an additional $1.00 of buckles be worth $1.80 to the firm? An additional $1.00 of market potential in territory number 3 be worth 12 cents? What implications does this have for management planning of production, marketing, and financial programs?

c. Which constraints (e.g., production capacity, market potential, working capital limit) are most binding on the problem solution? Least binding? Why? Explain fully.

2. The record shop goal programming model incorporates multiple goals in the following priorities: (1) Sales Goal, (2) an overtime limitation on full-time salesmen, (3) full utilization of employees, and (4) minimum overtime for both full-time and part-time salesmen.

a. How does goal programming differ from conventional linear programming formulations?

b. Why was it impossible to attain the fourth goal? To what extent would other goals have to be sacrificed in order to fully attain the fourth goal?

c. If the sales goal was increased to 6,000 records, what effect would this be likely to have on the final solution?

3. The use of linear programming to allocate advertising media is illustrated by use of the McGraw-Edison Case.

a. Assume the size of the advertising budget was increased to $50,000. What effect would this have on the final problem solution?

b. Advertising analysts estimate that the plant engineers' per dollar figures could be in error by as much as ±15%. Is this likely to have any impact on the validity of the optimal linear programming solution? Why?

c. Should the analyst accept the linear programming solution as the best possible media allocation and proceed to implement it at once? Why or why not?

d. What problems are likely to be encountered in expanding the linear programming approach to more complicated advertising media problems? How can these problems be overcome?

4. The plastics blending problem involves blending raw material into a variable production process in such a manner that profits are maximized while meeting product specifications.

a. Are there any circumstances under which the linear approximations of nonlinear blending or process control applications might be misleading in attempting to optimize such processes? If so, what are these? Explain fully.

b. Which of the three raw materials, R_1, R_2, or R_3, and the two process settings, S_1 or S_2 are most binding on the problem solution?

c. What problems are likely to be encountered in using such models for on-line blending in a closed loop system? How can these be overcome?

5. In the multiproduct, two-plant (A and B) production scheduling illustration:

a. What effect would a 50-cent increase in raw material cost at Plant A have on the optimal solution?

b. If the processing capacity for edible oil units was increased from 1,500 to 1,600 units, what impact would this have on the optimal solution?

c. Forecast demand for edible production 1 is increased to 2,200 units. How will this affect the optimal solution?

d. What modification in the simplex tableau must be made in order to include transportation costs as well as production costs? What additional information is provided by the expanding matrix?

e. Suppose that management decides that production costs at Plant A must be minimized at all costs. What effect is this decision likely to have on the optimal solution for the total company?

6. In the R&D Resource Allocation problem:

a. What effect are errors in estimating project revenues and outlays likely to have on a mathematical programming solution? Will the choice of a discount rate for discounting cash flows have any measurable effect on the problem solution? Why?

b. What is the significance of the difference between the linear solution and the integer solution to the problem? Under what circumstances would the integer solution be preferred, since it is more complex, cumbersome, and costly to derive?

c. What benefits and problems would likely occur if the linear programming analysis was extended to include multiple periods and resource flexibility (i.e., possible shifting from project to project within a given period)? Explain fully.

7. How does the seasonal product demand model differ from conventional linear programming formulations? What effect will an increase in production penalty costs have on the optimal solution? An increase in investment penalty costs? Will an increase in the planning horizon really improve production scheduling and investment planning? Why? Explain fully.

8. In the Fancycraft Greeting Card problem involving short-term financing planning, what effect will each of the following changes likely have on the optimal solution:

a. An increase in the cost of commercial paper? An increase in the cost of installment financing? An increase in the interest rate earned on funds invested in government securities?

b. Increasing the line of credit maximum to $150? Decreasing the constraint on commercial paper to $100?

c. In what circumstances is it profitable for the firm to borrow before it exhausts its supply of government securities? Why?

d. What conclusions can be drawn from he imputed values for bank loan, commercial paper, and installment financing by months? What are the implications for financial planning by the firm?

9. In the article entitled "A Pragmatic Approach to Capital Budgeting," a number of objections to present investment evaluation methods are spelled out.

a. What are the major limitations of current evaluation methods and how can linear programming help to overcome such limitations?

b. Is it likely that integer programming would provide a better problem solution than linear programming? Explain fully.

c. What effect would an increase in the earnings constraint from $60 to $100 (000's) and in the cash flow constraint from $170 to $200 (000's) be likely to have on the optimal solution?

10. How sensitive is the optimal solution in the paper procurement problem to changes in demand? In reel cost? In mill capacity? From the problem statement, does it appear that integer rather than linear programming should be used? Explain fully.

Bibliography

Baumol, William J., and Charles H. Sevin, "Marketing Costs and Mathematical Programming," *Harvard Business Review*, September-October 1957, pp. 52-60.

Bass, Frank M., and Ronald T. Lonsdale, "An Exploration of Linear Programming in Media Selection," *Journal of Marketing Research*, May 1966, pp. 179-188.

Beckmann, Martin J., "A Technical Note: Alternative Approaches to the Production Programming Problem," *Engineering Economist*, Spring 1968, pp. 173-187.

Beckwith, Richard E., "The Assignment Problem—A Special Case of Linear Programming," *Journal of Industrial Engineering*, May-June 1957, pp. 167-172.

Beged-Dov, Aharon G., "Solving a Paper Procurement Problem by Linear Programming," *Western Electric Engineer*, October 1965, pp. 2-10.

Bennion, Edward G., "Econometrics for Management," *Harvard Business Review*, March-April 1961, pp. 100-112.

Bertoletti, M.E., "Planning Continuous Production by Linear Programming," *Management Technology*, January 1960, pp. 75-80.

Boas, A.H., "Optimizing Via Linear and Dynamic Programming," *Chemical Engineering*, April 1963, pp. 85-88.

Brigham, G., "A Classroom Example of Linear Programming," *Operations Research*, Vol. 7, No. 4, July-August 1959.

Burton, Richard M. and H. Peter Holzer, "To Buy or Make," *Management Services*, July-August 1968, pp. 26-31.

Chapiro, Jorge, M.E. Bertoletti, and Horacio R. Rieznik, "Optimization of Investment—A Solution by Linear Programming," *Management Technology*, January 1960, pp. 64-74.

Charnes A., and W.W. Cooper, "Management Models and Industrial Applications of Linear Programming," *Management Science*, 1957, pp. 38-91. See also "Breakeven Budgeting and Programming to Goals," *Journal of Accounting Research*, Spring 1963.

Charnes, A., and W.W. Cooper, "The Stepping-Stone Method of Explaining Linear Programming Calculations in Transportation Problems," *Management Science*, October 1954, pp. 49-69.

Charnes, A., W.W. Cooper, and R.O. Ferguson, "Optimal Estimation of Executive Compensation by Linear Programming," *Management Science*, Vol. 1, No. 2, 1955.

Charnes, A., W.W. Cooper, and B. Mellon, "Blending Aviation Gasolines—A Study in Programming Interdependent Activities in an Integrated Oil Company," *Econometrica*, 1952. See also, "Optimality and Degeneracy in Linear Programming," by A. Charnes in the same volume.

Charnes, A., W.W. Cooper, and M.H. Miller, "Application of Linear Programming to Financial Budgeting and the Costing of Funds," *Journal of Business*, January 1959, pp. 20-46.

Dantzig, George, "Linear Programming: Examples and Concepts," *Managerial Economics*, Edwin Mansfield, editor, W.W. Norton Co., 1966, pp. 165-174. See also "Thoughts on Linear Programming and Automation," *Management Science*, January 1957, pp. 131-139, and "On the Status of Multi-Stage Linear Programming Problems," *Management Science*, October 1959, pp. 53-72.

Day, Ralph L., "Linear Programming in Media Selection," *Journal of Advertising Research*, June 1962, pp. 40-44.

Demski, Joel S., "An Accounting System Structured on a Linear Programming Model," *Accounting Review*, October 1967, pp. 701-712. See also "Some Considerations in Sensitizing an Optimization Model," *Journal of Industrial Engineering*, September 1968, pp. 463-467.

Deutsch, Donald, "Linear Programming Finds Semiconductor Production Quantities," *Industrial Engineering*, February 1969, pp. 14-21.

Diegel, Adolf, "A Linear Approach to the Dynamic Inventory Problem," *Management Science*, March 1966, pp. 530-540.

Dorfman, Robert, "Mathematical, or 'Linear' Programming: A Nonmathematical Exposition," *American Economic Review*, December 1953, pp. 797-825.

Driebeek, Norman J., "An Introduction to Linear Programming," *Ideas for Management*, 1966, pp. 139-145.

Dwyer, Paul S., "The Direct Solution of the Transportation Problem with Reduced Matrices," *Management Science*, September 1966, pp. 77-96.

Eisemann, Kurt, and William M. Young, "Study of a Textile Mill with the Aid of Linear Programming," *Management Technology*, January 1960, pp. 52-63.

Engel, James F., and Martin R. Warshaw, "Allocating Advertising Dollars by Linear Programming," *Journal of Advertising Research*, September 1964, pp. 42-48.

Erickson, Virgil, "An Application of Linear Programming to the Assignment of Materials Handling Equipment," *Journal of Industrial Engineering*, December 1957, pp. 386-388.

Farag, Shawki M., "A Planning Model for the Divisionalized Enterprise," *Accounting Review*, April 1968, pp. 312-320.

Ferrara, W.L., "Breakeven for Individual Products, Plants, and Sales Territories," *Management Services*, July-August 1964, pp. 38-46.

Fetter, Robert B., "A Linear Program Model for Long Run Capacity Planning," *Management Science*, July 1961, pp. 372-378.

Fisher, Walter D., and Leonard W. Shruben, "Linear Programming Applied to Feed Mixing Under Different Price Conditions," *Journal of Farm Economics*, November 1953, pp. 471-483.

Garvin, W.W., H.W. Crandall, J.B. John, and R.A. Spellman, "Applications of Linear Programming in the Oil Industry," *Management Science*, July 1957, pp. 407-430. See also A.R. Catchpole, "The Application of Linear Programming to Integrated Supply Problems in the Oil Industry," *Operational Research Quarterly*, Vol. 13, No. 2, 1962.

Gensch, Dennis H., "Computer Models in Advertising Media Selection," *Journal of Marketing Research*, November 1968, pp. 414-424.

Godfrey, James T., W. Allen Spivey, and George B. Stillwagon, "Production and Market Planning with Parametric Programming," *Industrial Management Review*, Fall 1968, pp. 61-75.

Golden, M. and E. Sanford, "A Linear Programming Model for Sales Planning: A Case Study of a Jewelry Firm," Parts 1, 2, and 3, *Cost and Management*, March, April, May 1967.

Gomory, R.E., "The Trim Problem," *IBM Systems Journal*, September 1962, pp. 77-82. See also P.C. Gilmore and R.E. Gomory, "Linear Programming Approach to the Cutting Stock Problem," *Operations Research*, November 1963, pp. 863-888.

Hanson, G.E., *Linear Programming Sensitivity Analysis*, General Electric Technical Information Series, R63CD12, 1964, 32 pp.

Hanssmann, Fred, and Sidney W. Hess, "A Linear Programming Approach to Production and Employment Scheduling," *Management Technology*, January 1960, pp. 46-51.

Hartley, Ronald V., "Some Extensions of Sensitivity Analysis," *Accounting Review*, April 1970, pp. 223-234. See also "Linear Programming: Some Implications for Management Accounting," *Management Accounting*, November 1969, pp. 48-51 by the same author.

Henderson, Alexander, and Robert Schlaifer, "Mathematical Programming: Better Information for Better Decision Making," *Harvard Business Review*, May-June 1954, 50 pp.

Henry, Bruce B., and Curtis H. Jones, "Linear Programming for Production Allocation," *Journal of Industrial Engineering*, July 1967, pp. 403-412.

Hofflander, A.E., and Milton Drandell, "A Linear Programming Model of Profitability, Capacity, and Regulation in Insurance Management," *Journal of Risk and Insurance*, March 1969, pp. 41-54.

IBM Corporation, An Introduction to Linear Programming, E20-8171-0, Data Processing Application, 1964, 64 pp.

Ijiri, Yuji, F.K. Levy, and R.C. Lyon, "A Linear Programming Model for Budgeting and Financial Planning," *Journal of Accounting Research*, Autumn 1963, pp. 198-212.

Koeningsberg, Earnest, "Some Industrial Applications of LP," *Operations Research Quarterly*, June 1961, pp. 105-114.

Lee, A.S., and J.S. Aronofsky, "Linear Programming Model for Scheduling Crude Oil Production," *Journal of Petroleum Technology*, July 1958, pp. 51-54. See also J.S. Aronofsky, "Linear Programming: Problem Solving Tool for Petroleum Industry Management," *Journal of Petroleum Technology*, July 1962, pp. 729-736.

Lee, Sang M., and Monroe M. Bird, "A Goal Programming Model for Sales Effort Allocation," *Business Perspectives*, 1970, pp. 17-21; and S.M. Lee, et.al., "Goal Programming: Management's Math Model," *Industrial Engineering*, February 1971, pp. 30-35.

Lockett, A.G., and A.E. Gear, "Linear Programming to Aid Resource Allocation in R&D," *Journal of Management Studies*, May 1970, pp. 172-182.

Mao, James C.T., "Application of Linear Programming to Short-Term Financing Decision," *Engineering Economist*, Summer 1968, pp. 221-241.

Martin, Harold W., "A Quantitative Method of Assigning Functions to Individuals in an Organized Group," *Management International*, 1965, pp. 55-65.

Masse, P., and R. Gibrant, "Application of Linear Programming to Investments in the Electric Power Industry," *Management Science*, January 1957, pp. 149-166.

"MATRIX METHODS: Solving Systems of Equations with Matrix Techniques," *Systems and Procedures Journal*, January-February 1968, pp. 8-9; March-April 1968, pp. 8-9.

Metzger, R.W., and R. Schwarzbek, "A Linear Programming Application to Cupola Changing," *Journal of Industrial Engineering*, March-April 1961, 16 pp.

Mulligan, James E., "Basic Optimization Techniques—A Brief Survey," *Journal of Industrial Engineering*, May-June 1965, pp. 192-197.

Nichols, C.R., "How to Formulate a L-P Model for Refinery Simulation," *Oil and Gas Journal*, February 1959, pp. 101-106.

O'Brien, George, "Solutions of Assignment Problems," *Management Science: A New Organizational Dimension Proceedings*, April 28, 1959, E.J. Forsythe and Palmer C. Pilcher, editors. Institute of Labor and Industrial Relations, University of Michigan—Wayne State University, pp. 19-26.

Onsi, Mohammed, "Linear Programming: An Accounting Information Model," *Management Accounting*, December 1966, pp. 46-52.

Otto, Gus H., "The Use of Linear Programming in Corporate Budget Development," a paper presented at the Southwestern Management Science Association meeting, April 4, 1969, at Houston, Texas, 16 pp.

Parsons, James A., "Matrix Methods: Branching and Bounding," *Journal of Systems Management*, May 1969, pp. 11-13. See also "The Assignment Algorithm," *Systems and Procedures Journal*, July-August 1967, pp. 6-7.

Paltz, Alan L., "Linear Programming Applied to Manpower Management," *Industrial Management Review*, Winter 1970, pp. 31-38.

Perry, Raphael, "Production Scheduling for Minimum Cost," *Automation*, May 1967, pp. 98-102. See also "A Production-Scheduling Decision Model," *Western Electric Engineer*, July 1966.

Rapaport, Leo A., and William P. Drews, "Mathematical Approach to Long Range Planning," *Harvard Business Review*, 1962, pp. 75-87.

Rehmus, Frederick P., and Harvey M. Wagner, "Applying Linear Programming to Your Pay Structure," *Business Horizons*, Winter 1963, pp. 89-98.

Robichek, A.A., D. Teichroew, and J.M. Jones, "Optimal Short Term Financing Decision," *Management Science*, Vol. 12, No. 1, September 1965, pp. 1-36.

Rosen, Robert W., "Least Cost vs. Opportunity Cost in Make or Buy Decisions," *Financial Executive*, January 1966, pp. 40-43.

Sharp, J.F., "Linear Programming Optimizes Use of Common Labor," *Industrial Engineering*, January 1971, pp. 16-19.

Shetty, C.M., "Sensitivity Analysis in Linear Programming," *Journal of Industrial Engineering*, September-October 1959, pp. 379-386.

Smith, S.B., "Planning Transistor Production by Linear Programming," *Operations Research*, January-February 1965.

Sochin, E.L., "Linear Programming for Merchandising Decisions," *Journal of Retailing*, Winter 1964-65, pp. 37-41, 58-59.

Sweeney, Robert B., "Business Use of Linear Programming," *Management Accounting*, September 1965, pp. 39-45.

Symonds, G.H., *Linear Programming: The Solution of Refinery Problems*, Esso Standard Oil Company, N.Y., 1955, 74 pp.

Thelwell, Raphael R., "An Evaluation of Linear Programming and Multiple Regression for Estimating Manpower Requirements," *Journal of Industrial Engineering*, March 1967, pp. 227-236.

Tillman, F.A., and E.S. Lee, "On-Line Blending for Production Profit," *Control Engineering*, October 1968, pp. 111-115.

Trainor, Richard J., "Mathematical Programming," *Interdisciplinary Studies in Business Behavior*, Joseph W. McGuire, editor, Southwestern Publishing Company, 1962, pp. 117-131.

Tummins, Marvin, "A Simple Method of Linear Programming," *Management Services*, January-February 1966, pp. 44-50.

Van De Panne, C., "Linear Programming for Production Planning," *Journal of Industrial Economics*, November 1965, pp. 259-280.

Van Horne, James, "A Linear-Programming Approach to Evaluating Restrictions Under a Bond Indenture or Loan Agreement," *Journal of Quantitative and Financial Analysis*, June 1966, pp. 68-83.

Vitt, Lawrence D., "Plant Sizing for a Seasonal Product Demand Using a Linear Programming Model," *Engineering Economist*, Fall 1968, pp. 25-40.

Wagner, Harvey M., "The Simplex Method for Beginners," *Operations Research*, Volume 6, 1958, 7 pp.

Waugh, Frederick V., and Glenn L. Burrows, "A Short Cut to Linear Programming," *Econometrica*, January 1955, pp. 18-29.

White, C.R., "Applying Linear Programming Models to Production and Inventory Control," *Production and Inventory Management*, 4th Quarter 1968, pp. 56-65.